The Selected Letters of Florence Nightingale

"*I have done my duty*"

Florence Nightingale. This water-colour sketch ~~~~~~~~ ave been done from
a photograph taken shortly after her ~~~~~~~~~~~~~~~ The lines of hardship
and illness apparent in the ~~~~~~~~~~~~~~~~~~~~~~~~~ ned

"*I have done my duty*"

Florence Nightingale in the Crimean War 1854–56

edited by Sue M. Goldie

Manchester University Press

Published by
Manchester University Press
Oxford Road, Manchester MI3 9PL

British Library cataloguing in publication data
Nightingale, Florence
 'I have done my duty': Florence Nightingale and the Crimean War, 1854–56.
 1. Crimean War, 1853–1856–Medical Care.
 2. Crimean War, 1853–1856–Personal narratives, British
 1. Title   11. Goldie, Sue.
 947'073   UH258 1853/6

ISBN 0 7190 1960 5 *hardback*

Typeset in Great Britain
by Alan Sutton Publishing Ltd., Gloucester
Printed and bound in Great Britain
by Billings & Sons Limited, Worcester.

Contents

Illustrations

Abbreviations

Abbreviations in the letters

Accts	Accounts
Adj*t*. Gen*l*.	Adjutant General
B'clava	Balaclava
Br.	Brigadier
Card., Card*l*.	Cardinal
C.B.	Companion of the Bath
cd.	could
Cl.	Class
Col.	Colonel
Comm*g*.	Commanding
Commn.	Commission
compd.	compound
Constan*te*.	Constantinople
Dec.	December
De.,Dep*y*., D*y*.	Deputy
Dep*t*.	Department
Dep*y*.	Deputy
Dic*y*.	Dictionary
dr.	dear
D*y*.	Deputy
Eccl.	Ecclesiastical
Feb., Feb*y*.	February
Gds.	Guards
Gen., Gen*l*.	General
Gen*l*. Hosp*l*.	General Hospital
G.O.	General Orders
Gov*t*.	Government
gt.	great
H.M., H.M*y*.	Her Majesty

H. of C., Ho. of C.	House of Commons
High*rs*.	Highlanders
H*o*.	House
Hosp., Hosp*l*.	Hospital
Insp*r*.	Inspector
Insp. Gen*l*. of Hosp*ls*.	Inspector General of Hospitals
Jan., Jan*y*.	January
K.C.B.	Knight Commander of the Bath
Ld.	Lord
Lt.	Lieutenant.
L.T.C.	Land Transport Corps
Ly.	Lady
Med., Med*l*.	Medical
Mem*a*.	Memoranda
Mem*m*.	Memorandum
Mil*y*.	Military
M.O.	Medical Officer
morn., morn*g*.	morning
Morn. Chron.	*Morning Chronicle*
obed*t*.	obedient
Parl., Parl*t*.	Parliament
pol*l*. ec*y*.	political economy
P.M.O.	Principal Medical Officer
P.O.	Post Office
Purv*r*.	Purveyor
Purv*r*. Gen*l*.	Puveyor General
qy.	query
R.C.	Roman Catholic
Reg*t*.	Regiment
Rev., Rev*d*.	Reverend
Sec*y*.	Secretary
Serj*t*.	Serjeant
serv*t*.	servant
sh*d*.	should
So.	Society
S.S.	Staff Surgeon
Sup*t*.	Superintendent
Surg*n*.	Surgeon
wd.	would
wh.	which
W.O.	War Office
Xian	Christian
Xmas	Christmas
yr.	your, yours

Abbreviations

Manuscript collections

B.L.	British Library
G.L.R.O.	Greater London Record Office
P.R.O.	Public Record Office
R.A.M.C.	Royal Army Medical Corps
Wellcome	Wellcome Institute for the History of Medicine.

Calendar of the Letters of Florence Nightingale

	Section	Fiche No.	Frame No.	Reference No.
Cal.	B	4	A2-G14	1–378

Acknowledgements

I wish to thank the following for permission to publish the letters of Florence Nightingale included in this selection: Messrs Radcliffes & Co., solicitors for the Trustees of the Henry Bonham-Carter Will Trust, who control the copyright in the letters of Florence Nightingale deposited in the British Library under the terms of the Trust; the Keeper of Manuscripts of the British Library; Sir Ralph Verney, Bt, for the many family letters in the Claydon collection; the Earl of Harewood for the two letters to Lady Canning lodged in the Leeds District Archives, and also to Mr W. J. Connor, District Archivist with the West Yorkshire Archive Service; the Chief Nursing Officer, St Thomas's Hospital, for permission to include the letters of Sir John McNeill, which are lodged with the St Thomas's Hospital nursing papers in the archives of the Greater London Record Office; the Trustees of the Wellcome Institute for the History of Medicine for the letters to Colonel Lefroy, and the use of their holdings of copies of letters; Sir John Bowman, Bt, for permission to include the letter to Sir William Bowman; the Rev. Mother Superior, Convent of Our Lady of Mercy, Bermondsey, for the letters to Rev. Mother Grace Moore of Bermondsey; Miss Monica Lawson for permission to quote George Lawson's letters, *George Lawson, Surgeon in the Crimea*, ed. Victor Bonham Carter, Constable & Co., London. Transcripts of Crown copyright records in the Public Record Office appear by permission of the Controller of Her Majesty's Stationery Office.

I am particularly grateful to Colonel R. Eyeions, Curator of the R.A.M.C. Historical Museum, Aldershot, for his kindness and hospitality while I was working on the magnificent collection of the papers of Sir John Hall, as well as for permission to include some of this material. My grateful thanks also to Colonel R. B. Merton, Secretary of the Royal Hussar Museum, Winchester, permitting me to see and quote from the diary of Serjeant Major G. Loy Smith of the 11th Hussars, with its fascinating account of conditions in the Crimea; and also to Hilary Jenkins, of the History Department, University College, Dublin, and the Rev. Maurice Carey, Dean

Acknowledgements

of Cork, who were able to help elucidate some mysterious allusions in the letters; and to Dr John Shepherd, F.R.C.S., for information on the staff of the civil hospitals at Renkioi and Smyrna, and many others interesting matters.

Above all I must express my deepest gratitude to Ms Brenda Sutton of the Wellcome Institute for the History of Medicine, who has been so generous with her time and trouble for so long in pursuit of Nightingale hares. And finally I must thank my husband for his endless patient help in reading, checking and advising on the preparation of the manuscript.

Sue Goldie
Dublin

Introduction

On 9th October 1854, in a despatch describing the "glorious" victory of the Alma, William Howard Russell first alerted readers of *The Times* to the fact that all was not well with the medical arrangements in the army. His brief sentences might well have passed unnoticed in the general euphoria surrounding a great victory; but on the 13th and 14th further reports from Constantinople described the condition of the sick and wounded in such dramatic and harrowing terms that comfortable middle-class liberal opinion in England was roused to a frenzy of indignation.

The immediate response was overwhelming. Philanthropic ladies and gentlemen rushed to offer their services on behalf of the poor wounded soldiers. Among the many was Florence Nightingale.

At this time Miss Nightingale had been established as Superintendent of the Hospital for Invalid Gentlewomen in Harley Street for eighteen months. But in August she had warned her committee that she might wish to withdraw should she get the opportunity to conduct a training establishment for nurses; Harley Street was unsuitable for such a purpose, and she was in fact already negotiating with the authorities of King's College Hospital.

The despatches in *The Times* suggested a more immediate arena for the exercise of her vocation, and when she was invited by Lady Maria Forrester to take charge of a small private party of nurses she hardly hesitated.

On 14th October she wrote to her old friend Elizabeth Herbert as a member of the Committee of Harley Street, asking whether the committee would release her immediately to go to Scutari and whether Mr Herbert, then Secretary at War, would support the party with introductions to the authorities as Constantinople. Without such support they would never have been admitted to the hospitals at Scutari, for the medical authorities, almost to a man, were denying the need for any assistance.

But Sidney Herbert himself had a different plan. At the beginning of the war he had toyed with the idea of introducing female nurses to the military hospitals but had dropped the scheme in the face of military and medical

1

hostility, and the difficulty of finding suitable women to undertake such work. Now, on 15th October, he wrote to Miss Nightingale asking her to go out to Scutari at the head of a large *official* band of nurses sponsored by the government. This preliminary exchange, together with Sidney Herbert's official Instructions as Secretary at War, and his letter to the papers explaining Miss Nightingale's mission and the basis upon which the nurses had been and would in the future be recruited, have been included in this selection of Florence Nightingale's Crimean letters, for they provided a fruitful source of controversy at the time, and were the direct cause of many of her subsequent troubles in the East.

One of the most remarkable things about Florence Nightingale's Crimean correspondence is its sheer magnitude. From the day she arrived, when she dashed off an eager note to her family, a steady stream of letters poured from her pen, providing a complete and detailed picture of her life and thought, of the triumphs and failures, the doubts and frustrations that beset her during the next twenty months. Over three hundred written between 4th November 1854, when she arrived at Scutari, and the end of July 1856, when she left the East, have survived. They form a unique body, set apart in content and style from the more than thirteen thousand written during her active life which have been traced and listed in the *Calendar of the Letters of Florence Nightingale*. Of these three hundred some hundred have been included in this selection.

In themselves Florence Nightingale's letters encompass the entire panorama of the Crimean *débâcle*. It is a scene of limited perspective, viewed from a particular and individualistic standpoint. Nevertheless the whole picture and all the characters are to be found brutally exposed in the spotlight of Miss Nightingale's penetrating judgement.

The letters fall broadly into three categories: first the long, detailed reports, official and unofficial, to Sidney Herbert and his successors at the War Office. In these Miss Nightingale identified and analysed the causes of the Crimean disaster, attributed blame, and proposed immediate measures for the practical reform of the entire hospital administration. Side by side with this body of correspondence are letters written to the recruiting ladies in London and to her assistants in distant hospitals on nursing matters; letters to friends and colleagues showing her implementing measures for the well-being of the soldiers – establishing and furnishing coffee huts and reading rooms, providing educational and recreational facilities, arranging for the remission of money home, providing for the care of the wives and children of the troops. The picture is completed and illumined by the letters to her family, in which she gave free rein to her innermost feelings. The vividly dramatic and highly emotional content of many of these letters is highlighted by the level-headed practicality of the official and semi-official correspondence.

In making the selection I have striven to reflect as faithfully as possible the overall picture provided by the correspondence. But within this framework certain themes have been followed through in some depth.

Most of the immensely long letters written to Sidney Herbert during the first six months have been included, for they show the development of Florence Nightingale's ideas in response to the exigencies of the ever changing situation, as well as providing a devastating picture of conditions at Scutari and a searing indictment of the officials responsible for the disaster.

Another theme followed in detail is Florence Nightingale's battle with the Medical Department for the recognition of the nursing establishment. This developed into a bitter personal confrontation with the head of the department in the Crimea, Dr John Hall. Inextricably entwined with this episode was the religious problem involving the Irish nuns, which likewise became personalised in a battle of wills with their Superior, the Rev. Mother Francis Bridgeman. These two, Dr Hall and Mother Bridgeman, formed an unlikely alliance, their common aim being to dislodge Miss Nightingale.

A large proportion of the correspondence relating to these two subjects has been included, as well as such supplementary letters and excerpts from letters of the other protagonists as are necessary to the understanding of the unfolding story. These conflicts have recently become the centre of renewed controversy as historians have reappraised several aspects of the Crimean disaster in the light of newly available documents.

The role of Sidney Herbert. When Sidney Herbert decided to ask Florence Nightingale to undertake the nursing at Scutari, he had known her intimately for seven years. They had met in Rome in the winter of 1846 when the Herberts were on honeymoon. During the next few years Miss Nightingale frequently visited at Wilton. The Herberts strongly approved of her visit to Kaiserswerth in search of training and experience. Elizabeth Herbert, as a member of the Committee of Harley Street, supported her appointment as Superintendent in 1853.

Sidney Herbert was a born reformer. He had already shown himself interested in improving conditions in the hospitals, and as Secretary at War he had promoted measures to improve the welfare of the troops. At the beginning of the war, when he had canvassed the idea of introducing female nurses to the military hospitals, the time was not ripe. When it did come, Florence Nightingale was the obvious choice. They were united by community of thought and interest.

Florence Nightingale's letters to Herbert are well known. They have been widely used and extensively quoted by her biographers. Her graphic account of conditions in the hospitals, her chilling assessment of the doctors and officials around her, her contempt for the nurses, as well as the hysterical denunciations of Herbert himself for betraying her, have all been noticed repeatedly. Yet her first biographer, Cook, had warned of a danger. "It would be possible to make isolated extracts which would suggest that the writer was a censorious and uncharitable scold, but such a selection would convey a misleading impression."[1] But the temptation to quote her colourful invective is irresistible and many writers have fallen into the trap. A reading of the letters in their entirety may help restore the balance.

When considering the tone of these letters it should be remembered that at the time Florence Nightingale was working in the wards for twelve to fifteen hours a day in the most harrowing conditions, while at the same time engaged in a Laocoönian struggle with officials to try and reduce the vast chaos of the hospitals to some sort of order and regularity. Her reaction was not surprising. From being at first humane and helpful, the medical men became callous and inhuman, indifferent to suffering, selfish and obstructive; the nurses were drunken and undisciplined, the officials of the purveying and commissary departments incapable and corrupt. When informed of the imminent arrival of a further forty-five females under Mary Stanley, in direct contravention of Sidney Herbert's express undertaking published in the papers, Florence Nightingale felt betrayed, and said so with all the passion of her impulsive nature. She refused to receive her old friend, or the nurses under her, officially, and thereby laid up an endless store of future trouble for herself.

The fact that she felt able to unburden herself in so unrestrained a manner says much for the strength of the understanding between herself and Herbert, and the fact that he accepted her abuse with unfailing kindness and courtesy, never wavering in his support, even more.

The fury expressed in those bitter letters lasted a fortnight. By the beginning of January Miss Nightingale put aside the minor irritations associated with the nurses and braced herself to face the catastrophe which was threatening to overwhelm the army in the hospitals. She formulated a series of practical reforms designed to alleviate the situation. The War Office under Sidney Herbert was already taking steps to improve the performance of the purveying and commissariat departments; an attempt was made to raise an improved orderly corps; some of the oldest and most inefficient officers were replaced by younger, more energetic men. The system began to operate more smoothly, but the improvements were, in Miss Nightingale's eyes, purely superficial. What was needed, and what she now determined to work for, was radical reform of the whole machinery of hospital and sanitary administration within the army.

Unfortunately Mr Herbert, who had borne her up so steadfastly, went out of office in February 1855. Nevertheless she continued to write to him on hospital and nursing matters for several more months, during which time he represented the interests of the nursing establishment to the new incumbents at the War Office, Lord Panmure and Benjamin Hawes.

Florence Nightingale as reformer. If Sidney Herbert was a born reformer, so too was Florence Nightingale. Confident that she understood his intentions, he had given her the opportunity she needed to prove herself in the restricted arena of nursing. Now, impelled by circumstances, she went far further than either had envisaged. She herself became the focus of and agent for promoting wide-ranging reform of the hospital administration.

As soon as she arrived at Scutari the divisions within the Medical Department and its supporting services became evident. Those young and energetic men, who found their efforts to cope with the situation developing in the hospitals frustrated by the inertia of their superiors combined with the rigidity of outworn systems, turned in ever increasing numbers to the one person who had the will, the means and the power to by-pass the bureaucratic entanglement. Such men, exemplified by Dr McGrigor at Scutari, and later Dr George Taylor at Balaclava, enthusiastically accepted and used the nurses, ordered their supplies through Miss Nightingale, and began to use her as their mouthpiece to urge essential reforms on the authorities. She rapidly came to be regarded as a worker of miracles and to be credited with very much more than she was in fact responsible for. "I have an unbounded admiration of Miss Nightingale's qualifications but I see dozens of things placed to her credit which I know she had nothing to do with," asserted one medical officer in evidence before the Roebuck Committee.[2]

In fact Miss Nightingale was prepared to work with any who sought the same ends as herself and willingly put forward unpopular ideas in her own name if she approved the end. She was sensitive to the difficulty faced by those men who risked their own career or even livelihood if they fell foul of their senior officers. But she deeply despised those who would not relax one jot of the regulations to save life, for fear of the consequences. She expressed her attitude to Herbert: "The real humiliation, the real hardship of this place . . . is that we have to do with men . . . who will neither make use of others, nor can be made use of."[3]

The Army Medical Department. The official Instructions defining Florence Nightingale's position in relation to the medical authorities were, in the light of the situation prevailing in October 1854, perfectly clear: she was to place herself in communication with the Chief Army Medical Officer *at Scutari,* that is, Dr Menzies, under whose orders and direction she was to carry on the duties of her appointment. She herself recognised the need for the subordination of the nursing department to the medical; and she was to continue to maintain consistently that she never acted except in the strictest subordination to the doctors' orders — though others had different views on this.

But as the situation developed it became clear that the original instructions did not adequately cater for the developing situation or define the War Office's intentions sufficiently clearly. Miss Nightingale's position in relation to the Head of the Medical Department in the East, Dr John Hall, was not touched on; nor, as he was later to complain, was he *officially* informed of the government's intention to introduce female nurses to the military hospitals; he was not even sent a copy of Miss Nightingale's Instructions.

This, combined with her vigorous denunciations of the organisational deficiencies in the hospitals, made his resentment unsurprising.

During the first month, by careful deference to the wishes and requirements of those few medical officers at Scutari who were willing to use the nurses, Florence Nightingale succeeded in winning a measure of acceptance for them. As the crisis deepened they became indispensable. There were, however, many veterans of the Peninsular War who continued to exclude them from the wards.

In January 1855 the situation was complicated when the Commander in Chief, Lord Raglan, requested that nurses be sent up to the Crimea to assist in the General Hospital at Balaclava. Such a situation had never been contemplated either by Sidney Herbert or by Florence Nightingale herself. She opposed the scheme at the time, and although eight of Mary Stanley's party went more or less independently, Miss Nightingale continued to protest against it for several months, until in April she decided to go up to the Crimea herself.

By that time the situation had altered radically. The hospitals on the Bosphorus were better organised and better supplied, and with the coming of spring the mortality in the wards was rapidly diminishing. Meanwhile Florence Nightingale had, at her own request, been relieved of responsibility for the nursing in the recently opened hospitals at Koulali, and her jurisdiction limited to Scutari, which was all she had felt capable of managing during the period of greatest mortality in January and February. But by March, with the easing of the pressure at Scutari, she wished to reassert her authority over the whole military nursing establishment in the East to ensure the adoption of her system, in line with the clear intention expressed in her original Instructions.

In the Crimea she was again welcomed by those who had at last some hope of being able to carry out essential reforms, and acquire the supplies necessary for the efficient performance of their professional duties. But her presence was bitterly resented by Dr Hall and the conservative doctors.

Open hostilities were postponed for a while when Miss Nightingale fell ill, and Dr Hall hoped that she might be forced by ill health to retire. When it was apparent that she was not to be so easily got rid of, he set about making her position in the Crimea untenable. To this end he accepted the offer of the Rev. Mother Bridgeman to bring her nuns to the General Hospital in October 1855, and encouraged Miss Wear to flout Miss Nightingale's authority.

Battle was joined, and developed into a bitter personal confrontation between Dr Hall and Miss Nightingale. The problem was exacerbated by the appearance a couple of months later of the Deputy Surveyor's "Confidential Report" criticising the nursing in the Crimea. The issue was only resolved, and Miss Nightingale's position secured, by the publication of the General Order in March 1856 by which her jurisdiction over the

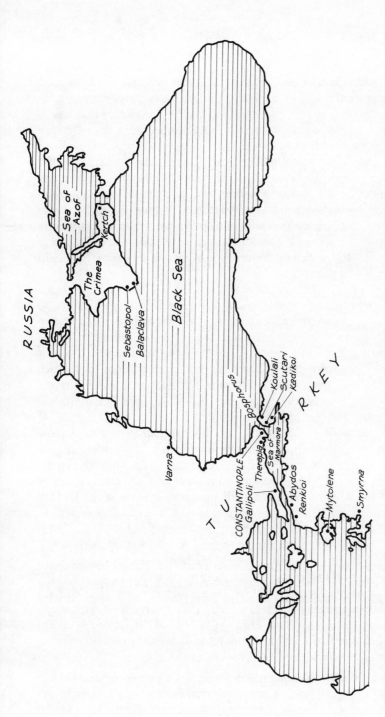

British hospitals in the East during the Crimean War. *Varna, Gallipoli, Abydos*: general hospitals with no female nurses; *Smyrna, Renkioi*: civil hospitals set up in 1855 to relieve Scutari, had staffs of female nurses independent of F.N.; *Therapia* naval hospital also had independent female nurses. The remaining hospitals came under F.N.'s jurisdiction during the periods indicated. *Scutari*: General, November 1854–July 1856; Barrack (her headquarters), November 1854–July 1856; Stables (overflow hospital during emergency); Haidar Pasha, for 400 officers, considered as part of the Scutari complex, was situated at Kadikoi, several miles to the south, and never came under F.N. *Koulali*, General and Barrack, came under F.N. only from the end of January 1855 to 1st March, when she resigned control. *Balaclava*: General, January–September 1855, April–June 1856; Castle, April 1855–June 1856; St George's Monastery, October 1855–1856, but F.N.'s authority was not recognised by Miss Weare; Land Transport Corps hospitals, March–June 1856

entire army nursing establishment in the East was confirmed. Sir John Hall, as he had somewhat anomalously been created, was officially censured for his conduct by the Secretary for War.

This vindication of Florence Nightingale was not achieved without considerable opposition within the War Office, as the correspondence in file WO 43/963 in the Public Record Office shows. But her victory had less to do with the strength of her social and political connections than Dr Hall supposed: Florence Nightingale won the day because her ideas were in tune with the time. She represented the party of reform. The government had come to power pledged to better the performance of its predecessors; the War Office under Lord Panmure was therefore committed to continue and improve on the work begun by Sidney Herbert. Panmure and Benjamin Hawes accepted the advice of Colonel Lefroy, who regarded a strong centralised nursing department as not merely desirable but essential if it was to survive at all. And Florence Nightingale was seen as the only person capable of establishing it.

Sir John Hall lost not because he was traduced by Florence Nightingale but because he represented those forces of conservative inertia which had so miserably failed to rise to the challenge of the situation of 1854. He and men of like mind, many of whom were veterans of Wellington's Peninsular campaigns, were quite unable to appreciate "that the health and comfort of the troops are judged now by a very different standard from that which prevailed on former occasions."[4] He was not simply a victim of the "nipping parsimony" so vividly described by Kinglake,[5] which had brought about the disaster, but one of its arch proponents.

Florence Nightingale is credited by Hall's sympathisers with having destroyed him from overweening ambition compounded by malice. But her judgement, given in a moment of dispassionate calm, is perhaps the fairest verdict on him, and not without compassion: "An able and efficient officer in many ways and who . . . has been justly provoked in many ways. Dr Hall is indefatigable in *detailed* work, and wants only a governing system to work under. But he is wholly incapable of originating one."[6]

There was no place for him in the reformed Army Medical Department which Florence Nightingale and Sidney Herbert were to devote their energies to organising in the years after the war.

The female nursing. During the first weeks after her arrival at Scutari, Florence Nightingale was continually in the wards undertaking the nursing of the most onerous cases herself until she could have the measure of the nurses under her command. Sidney Goldolphin Osborne, who arrived a few days after the nurses, witnessed her at work in the wards:

> Her nerve is wonderful; I have been with her at very severe operations; she was more than equal to the trial. She had an utter disregard of contagion; I have known her spend hours over men dying of cholera or fever. The more awful to every sense a particular case, especially if it was that of a dying man, her slight form would be seen

bending over him, administering to his ease in every way in her power, and seldom quitting his side till death released him.[7]

Such accounts formed the basis of the Nightingale legend. Miss Nightingale herself seldom mentioned this aspect of her work; there is surprisingly little of clinical detail in her letters. But the few which do deal with such matters demonstrate her intense interest in the practicalities and technicalities of nursing, particularly surgical nursing. This is well illustrated in the "surgical letter" to Dr Bowman.[8]

The pressure on her at this time was enormous. Besides her nursing she was performing all the duties of "Barrack Mistress" – organising cooking, washing and the distribution of stores while pursuing a running battle with the officials of the Purveyor's Department. To add to these difficulties there was trouble within the nursing department.

Her experience at Harley Street had not taught Florence Nightingale how to manage subordinates happily, and in this time of pressure she added greatly to her own problems by her neglect of the sensibilities of those under her command. All she said of the ignorance, indiscipline and drunkenness of many of them may have been true, but she made no attempt to win their support. She failed to see the propriety of trying to explain her difficulties to them. Instead she demanded blind obedience of women unaccustomed to discipline. The nurses of St John's House wrote miserable letters home to their superiors, regretting coming and complaining of the contempt and unkindness with which they were treated. When Miss Jones, the Superintendent of St John's House, suggested that such women needed encouragement, Miss Nightingale replied with arrogance that she had no time to attend to such trivial matters, and she expected others to be too busy so to indulge themselves.

But Miss Jones's remonstrance must have made an impression, for a few weeks later one of the newcomers was able to report her pleasure at finding her friends so well and happy. A very much pleasanter atmosphere seems to have developed among the nurses, though there were still incidents of drunkenness and impropriety. Later letters show Florence Nightingale deeply concerned with the welfare of individual nurses, and she became much more tolerant and understanding of their lapses.

Her views on nursing and its organisation naturally developed considerably during her period in the East. She had, some time before the war, worked out a detailed scheme of organisation and training. This she modified in the light of experience. In particular she came to regard the welfare of the nurses as of the first importance. A long letter to Lady Canning written in September 1855 foreshadowed much of the system she was to establish in her Training School at St Thomas's Hospital.

She has been accused of plagiarising the ideas and systems of others; but in the field of nursing, as in the wider area of sanitary reform, she would have considered such borrowings entirely justified. Hers was a mind "observing and adapting itself to wants and events",[9] and, equally, adapting the ideas and systems of others to her own requirements.

While Florence Nightingale was unusual in having decided to devote her life to nursing, she was by no means unique. Philanthropic ladies were founding and joining sisterhoods to provide nursing for the sick poor; two such institutions, the Devonport Sisters of Mercy and St John's House, provided superintendents and nurses to serve in the East. St John's House had instituted a rudimentary hospital "training" of a fortnight, while the Roman Catholic nursing orders provided a systematic training for the nursing nuns which Miss Nightingale herself had sought earlier in her life in Dublin and Paris. A few impoverished but daring ladies had even, by the middle of the century, taken up posts as Matrons in large hospitals. Florence Nightingale chose to establish her Training School at St Thomas's precisely because the Matron was *already* undertaking the reform of the nursing, before the war.

Florence Nightingale is generally credited with being the founder of modern nursing, but this is not strictly the case, even in Great Britain. In this, as in the wider sphere of medical and military reform, she exemplified a broader movement, an ideal, which came to fruition in her career, and to which she gave impetus by her life and work. In more tangible form the foundation of the Nightingale Training School for Nurses at St Thomas's Hospital with the proceeds of the Fund donated by a grateful nation in recognition of her services formed a permanent memorial to her achievements as Chief of the Nursing Department in the Crimea.

The collections. Most of the collections from which this selection has been taken have been long known and used extensively in the various biographies: Sir Edward Cook, *The Life of Florence Nightingale*, London, 1914; Rosalind Nash, *Life of Florence Nightingale*, London, 1921; I. B. O'Malley, *Florence Nightingale, 1820–1856*, London, 1931; Cecil Woodham-Smith, *Florence Nightingale, 1820–1910*, London, 1950; Sir Zachary Cope, *Miss Florence Nightingale and the Doctors*, London, 1958, to name but a few. The foundation of all Nightingale research must be the vast manuscript collection comprising letters, notes, diaries and other documents in the British Library, amounting to nearly two hundred volumes. The earliest part of this collection formed the basis of Sir Edward Cook's official biography, published in 1914. Since then there have been several notable additions, such as the material donated by the family of Florence Nightingale's cousin, Harry Bonham Carter, who was Secretary of the Nightingale Fund for over fifty years. By far the largest number of letters in the selection have come from this collection.

Another major source is the great collection of family correspondence held by the Verneys of Claydon. Florence's sister, Parthenope, married Sir Harry Verney in 1858, and Florence came to regard his family as her own.

Almost all the letters of her childhood and youth, as well as those written to her family during the Crimean period, are in this collection, as well as notes to her Aunt, Mrs Mai Smith, on the day-to-day administration of the hospitals from autumn 1855 to July 1856; drafts of official letters; and record copies, made by Miss Nightingale herself, and by her family.

A third important London collection is that amassed by St Thomas's Hospital which is at present housed in the Greater London Record Office. Most of these letters are concerned with the foundation and administration of the Nightingale Training School, which was opened in 1860, and so are outside the scope of this selection, but recently two significant small holdings have been added: letters to and from the authorities of St John's House, which provided parties of nurses to serve under Florence Nightingale in the East; and the original letters to Sir John McNeill, with whom Miss Nightingale corresponded over many years from the time she met him in the Crimea in 1855.

The Public Record Office holds a file of Florence Nightingale's official correspondence with the War Office, including some interesting supplementary material shedding light on the difficulties of her position in relation to the medical and military authorities, and the sectarian dissensions which caused such trouble within the nursing department.

Also in London is a large collection of Nightingale material in the Wellcome Institute for the History of Medicine, which encompasses not only a number of original letters but also hundreds of copies of holdings from around the world accumulated during preparation of the *Calendar of Letters of Florence Nightingale* (compiled by S. Goldie and W. J. Bishop) which was commissioned by the International Council of Nurses and supported by the Wellcome Trust, 1983.

Editorial apologia. The major collections of Nightingale letters have long been known and repeatedly worked over by biographers and historians since Edward Cook wrote his official biography immediately after her death. But a biography is inherently a subjective assessment. The writer selects and interprets according to his or her preconceptions and prejudices. The subject may become obscured in the mists of interpretation.

I, too, have my own ideas about Florence Nightingale, and realise that in the very act of selecting I am making a statement about her. But in reproducing these letters, each in its entirety, I have attempted to let Miss Nightingale present herself in all the complexity of her subtle nature, without the interposition of an editorial smokescreen.

To this end I have sought to retain as far as possible the full flavour of each individual letter. This is not simply a matter of accurate transcription. Every letter, written in her own distinctive hand, vividly reflects the circumstances in which it was written, communicating the mood of the moment, her feelings towards the recipient, her reaction to the events and characters under review. The drama and impact lie in the immediacy of her response to events in which she was an active participant. Her very handwriting reflected the savage indignation she felt as she recorded the waste of life and fulminated against the system which perpetuated the situation. At the height of her fury her pen stabbed at the paper with long tearing dashes, her normally neat, rather prim handwriting sprawling across the page. Her spelling, impeccable in times of calm, faltered picturesquely as she sought a suitably opprobious "synonime" to describe a wretched official who was frustrating her work.

Were all irregularities and inconsistencies tidied up and edited out of such material a generally false impression of calm and balance might tend to be imparted. At the same time there is much that makes reading these letters needlessly difficult. I have, therefore, generally followed a few simple rules in dealing with Miss Nightingale's capricious punctuation and idiosyncratic spelling.

Punctuation. Where she used a dash, long or short, in place of or in conjunction with a full stop, a simple stop has been substituted. But within sentences the original punctuation, no matter how bizarre, has been retained – except for the impossibility of reproducing in print some of the more ferocious stabs. In the same way I have preserved the underlinings, so characteristic of Victorian correspondence, and which in Florence Nightingale's writing are so important in imparting the correct cadence to her sentences. These have been indicated in the usual way.

Spellings and abbreviations. Florence Nightingale's original spelling and abbreviations have likewise been retained, except where the latter are likely to be unintelligible, in which case the missing letters have been inserted in brackets. In other cases the abbreviations are either in common usage today or are so obvious as to present no difficulty.

As for the spelling of exotic place names, these were not standardised at the time and were dependent on the writer's ability to grasp and transmit the Turkish sound. Apart from Florence Nightingale's five or six versions of Scutari and Koulali, at least another five or six were current at the time – some almost unrecognisable. In the most up-to-date atlases Scutari is rendered Uskudar. All such names have been reproduced as in the original.

Variant forms. In a number of instances, particularly in the case of letters to government officials, several versions exist – drafts, copies, some in Miss Nightingale's own hand, some in that of a copyist – and the final finished product. In such cases the preferred version for inclusion in this selection is the one that was actually sent ("sent" version) provided it has been positively identified – not always an easy matter. The correspondence with Sir John McNeill and Colonel Lefroy provide two such instances. In the case of the letters to Sir John McNeill, of which only excerpts appear in the epilogue of this volume, typed copies as well as some copies in Miss Nightingale's own hand are housed in the British Library, and these were used by Cook. But a volume of letters also in Florence Nightingale's own hand, which appear to have been mounted by Sir John McNeill or by a member of his family, and which may therefore be presumed to be the "sent" versions received by himself, has only recently been added to the St Thomas's Hospital collection housed in the Greater London Record Office. These are the ones used here. Another similar case is provided by the letters to Colonel Lefroy. The "sent" versions have been acquired by the Wellcome Institute, while the British Library has drafts or copies and perhaps one or two originals. In both these cases there are differences between the variant forms which are most interesting. They suggest that some of Florence Nightingale's apparently most spontaneous effusions were in fact carefully worked for maximum dramatic effect. This is not to say that she was not sincere in what she wrote, rather that she was a consummate literary craftswoman, and that she wrote with a purpose.

Where copies have been included, whether in Florence Nightingale's own hand, or made by contemporaries, or of later date, the fact has been indicated at the head of the letter concerned.

In a few instances an alien hand has clearly been at work "bowd-lerising" Miss Nightingale's work – for the edification of family and friends among whom the letters were circulated. In such cases I have reproduced the original text – when it can be deciphered.

Order. The letters have been arranged in chronological order exept in a few instances where I have thought it better to follow some episode or theme before reverting to strict date order: the correspondence between Florence Nightingale and the authorities of St John's House in December 1854 is one such instance; the exchange with Sir John Hall over the "starvation" of the nuns in spring 1856 is another. In both these cases, and one or two others, letters to Florence Nightingale have been included as being necessary to the understanding of her position and to the coherent development of the story.

Link passages. The commentary linking the letters has been kept as short as is compatible with providing the necessary background. In the case of the correspondence surrounding the struggle with Dr Hall, first over the appointment of the Irish nuns (chapter 5), the Purveyor's Confidential Report (chapter 6) and finally the battle over requisitions *v.* rations (chapter 7), official documents have been quoted at some length in order to explain why Florence Nightingale took the position she did, and what her contemporaries thought of it.

Notes. The notes include references to sources cited. In addition they fill out details of events and personalities mentioned in the letters, and indicate any wider significance of such events and personalities in Miss Nightingale's future life.

Location of letters. The location of each letter is given at its foot, together with its reference in the *Calendar of the Letters of Florence Nightingale.*

Introduction

Three further volumes of *The Selected Letters of Florence Nightingale* are planned, dealing with her early years, her work for public health in the army and in India, and the development of nursing during her active life.

Notes

1 Cook, I, p. 218.
2 Cook, I, p. 214.
3 F. N. to Sidney Herbert, 18th March 1855 (p. 105).
4 C. E. Trevelyan, 13th February 1854 (Stanmore, I, p. 276 note).
5 Kinglake, VII, pp. 29–30.
6 F. N. to Col. Lefroy, 28th January 1856 (p. 204).
7 Sidney Godolphin Osborne, *Scutari and its Hospitals*, ch. IV.
8 Page 36.
9 F. N. to Sidney Herbert, 6th January 1856 (p. 184).

1

A great and national work

"The finest army that ever left these shores," proclaimed the *Times* correspondent gaily as he reviewed the thirty thousand men who marched through Portsmouth to embark for the seat of war in the East at the end of March 1854. But it was all a sham, a magnificent parade of toy soldiers, most of whom had never fired a gun in anger, and whose military experience was confined to intricate manoeuvres on the parade ground. The senior officers had either never seen active service, or had last been engaged as very junior officers in Wellington's Peninsular campaigns. The Commander in Chief, Lord Raglan,[1] was himself just such a man. A few of the middle-ranking officers had had some appropriate experience in colonial wars, mainly in India; but these professional soldiers were despised and their experience was discounted by the aristocrats at Horse Guards.

The causes of the war they were going off to fight were mysterious, and the objectives shadowy. Few could understand why they were being asked to protect the crumbling Ottoman Empire against a Christian country; it was a rotten cause.[2] But behind the army the politicians perceived that the balance of power in Europe, which had ensured peace for the forty years since the defeat of Napoleon at Waterloo, was again being threatened by the rise of a new great power, Russia, in the East. The British in particular, who regarded the Mediterranean as their own especial sphere of interest, were alarmed by the growing threat posed by the development of Russian sea power based on the great naval dockyard of Sebastopol in the Crimea. Nor were these fears groundless. The Czar, who already had some right to protect the Christians of the Danubian provinces of the decaying Turkish empire, used a riot in Jerusalem over the control of the holy places as a pretext for the invasion of Moldavia and Wallachia. The Cabinet on the whole remained anxious to preserve peace, but were sufficiently alarmed to order the Royal Navy to Besika Bay, off the Dardanelles.

The slide towards war gathered momentum when at the end of October 1853 the Sultan declared war on Russia. Then, on 30th November, the Russians destroyed the entire Turkish fleet at the "massacre" of Sinope, and at last British public opinion turned in favour of war, roused by the outraged thundering of *The Times*. The fleet was ordered into the Black Sea in a final unsuccessful attempt to intimidate the Russians into withdrawal. But still the Cabinet under Lord Aberdeen held back from a land war. It was not until 27th March 1854 that Aberdeen bowed to the inevitable and, in alliance with France, declared war on Russia.

The hopelessly inadequate planning and organisation of the expedition became apparent as soon as the troops arrived at Constantinople. They landed at Gallipoli and Scutari, where they found themselves in competition for quarters and services with the French, who had already appropriated the best of everything. The French seemed to be far better organised, a fact which Florence Nightingale was to notice in her letters to Sidney Herbert the following January.[3]

On 9th June it was decided to transfer both armies to Varna, a small port on the Bulgarian shore of the Black Sea, from where the border fortress of Silistria, besieged by the Russians, could be relieved. But the Russians, as unprepared for an engagement as the allies, raised the siege and retired, pursued by the Turks, who defeated them at Giurgevo. They abandoned Moldavia and Wallachia.

The British and French armies, numbering about sixty thousand men, encamped in the country around Varna to await events and further orders. Back in London *The Times* demanded the destruction of the Russian Eastern Fleet and its base at Sebastopol. Somewhat reluctantly Aberdeen, who felt that with the withdrawal of the Russian forces the purpose of the war had been achieved, gave in to public opinion, and on 28th June the Duke of Newcastle, Secretary for War, instructed Lord Raglan to attack Sebastopol. Raglan, uneasily aware of the implications of his lack of transport, and the deficiency of his intelligence regarding the strength and disposition of the Russian forces in the Crimea, was not happy.

But the army was suffering severely from the unhealthiness of Varna. As the summer progressed the heat became unbearable for the unsuitably clothed troops. Diarrhoea and dysentery became universal; by the end of July a full-scale cholera epidemic was raging.[4]

As early as February, when he was ordered to prepare for the impending expedition, Dr Andrew Smith, Director General of the Army Medical Department, had sent three doctors to the proposed seat of war to discover what they could about the climate, sanitary conditions and prevailing diseases, and on the basis of their discouraging findings he made certain recommendations to Horse Guards. Virtually all his advice was ignored, and now the army began to pay the price.[5] The general hospital at Varna, an old and decrepit Turkish barracks, became a pest hole out of which it was believed no one ever emerged alive.

So, despite misgivings, Lord Raglan decided that an expedition to Sebastopol would have the advantage of improving both the health and the morale of his army. The force sailed from Varna on 7th September, and six days later, on the 13th, the troops began to land on the barren beach of Calamita Bay, about thirty-five miles to the north of Sebastopol. On the 19th the army marched south towards Sebastopol, abandoning almost all its baggage, including the men's kits and tents, together with most of the Commissariat stores, for lack of transport.

On 20th September the exhausted men, who had had little to eat or drink since the landing five days earlier, engaged the enemy on the banks of the river Alma. In the ensuing battle the British bore the brunt of the fighting, and their losses were heavy. But for the men who survived unscathed it was a glorious victory, and their morale received a much needed boost, as Serjeant Major Loy Smith of the 11th Hussars recorded:

Just before dark, double rations were issued, of biscuit, fresh meat and rum, which we stood much in need of. As we sat round our bivouac fire waiting for the pots to boil, and talking over the incidents of the day, never I should say were men happier – one said, I wonder if we shall get a medal for this battle, I said, what will the people of England say when they hear of it . . .[6]

But the cholera which had plagued the army since Varna continued to take its toll through the night to offset any exultation at the victory.

The next morning one [a corporal who had died during the night] was conveyed rolled up in his blanket, a little distance from the bivouac and buried – seeing one man interred who had died of pestilence was more depressing than seeing all the hundreds that surrounded us, that had fallen in fair fight – one was the work of man, the other a visitation of the Almighty.[7]

The mismanagement which bedevilled the entire campaign now became apparent. William Howard Russell's despatch from the battlefield, published in *The Times* on 9th October, more than a fortnight after the event, shocked complacent liberal opinion with a disconcerting paradox:

Our victory has been glorious . . . but there has been a great want of proper medical attention; the wounded were left, some for two nights, the whole for one, on the field. From the battle they have been bundled on board ship by 600 and 700, without any proper means for removing the wounded from the field . . . The number of lives which have been sacrificed by the want of proper arrangements and neglect must be considerable.[8]

Nor was the neglect confined to the battlefield. Three days later a further philippic drew attention to the horrifying state of the hospital at Scutari:

It is with feelings of surprise and anger that the public will learn that no sufficient preparations have been made for the proper care of the wounded. Not only are there not sufficient surgeons – that, it might be urged, was unavoidable; not only are there no dressers and nurses – that might be a defect of the system for which no one is to blame; but what will be said when it is known that there is not even linen to make bandages for the wounded? The greatest commiseration prevails for the sufferings of the unhappy inmates of Scutari, and every family is giving sheets and old garments to supply their wants. But why could not this clearly foreseen want have been supplied? Can it be said that the Battle of the Alma has been an event to take the world by surprise? Has not the expedition to the Crimea been the talk of the last four months? And when the Turks gave up to our use the vast barracks to form a hospital and depot, was it not on the ground that the loss of the English troops was sure to be considerable when engaged in so dangerous an enterprise? And yet, after the troops have been six months in the country, there is no preparation for the commonest surgical operations! Not only are men kept, in some cases, for a week without the hand of a medical man coming near their wounds; not only are they left to expire in agony, unheeded and shaken off, though catching desperately at the surgeon whenever he makes his rounds through the fetid ship; but now, when they are placed in the spacious building, where we were led to believe that every thing was ready which could ease their pain or facilitate their recovery, it is found that the commonest appliances of a workhouse sick-ward are wanting, and that the men must die through the medical staff of the British army having forgotten that old rags are necessary for the dressing of wounds.[9]

And on the next day, the 13th, a further furious instalment appeared:

It is impossible for any one to see the melancholy sights of the last few days without feelings of surprise and indignation at the deficiencies of our medical system. The manner in which the sick and wounded are treated is worthy only of the savages of Dahomey . . . The worn-out pensioners who were brought as an ambulance corps are totally useless, and not only are surgeons not to be had, but there are no dressers or nurses to carry out the surgeon's directions, and to attend on the sick during the intervals between his visits. Here the French are greatly our superiors. Their arrangements are extremely good, their surgeons more numerous, and they have also the help of the Sisters of Charity who have accompanied the expedition in incredible numbers. These devoted women are excellent nurses.[10]

It was useless for the Secretary at War to protest that lint had been sent out by the ton; for the Director General of the Army Medical Department to insist that he had provided all that was needed in the way of men and stores – and he was able to prove that such was indeed the case in the many inquiries which were later set up; or for Dr Hall, Inspector General of Hospitals, to prove that he had ordered supplies from Varna and Scutari. The fact remained that such supplies were not where they were most needed, and the protestations of the various officials responsible only served to emphasise the completeness of the breakdown of the administrative functions of the army in the East.

The response to Russell's despatches was immediate and overwhelming. Numbers of philanthropic ladies and gentlemen offered to go out to Scutari to help care for the sick and wounded in various capacities. So it was in no way surprising that Miss Florence Nightingale, already looking for a fresh outlet for her restless energies after reorganising the Harley Street Institution for Sick Governesses,[11] should have decided impulsively and spontaneously, on reading *The Times*, that the military hospital at Scutari might well provide a suitable field for her endeavours. Nor was it surprising, in view of her experience, together with her medical and social connections, that she should at the same time have been approached by others, such as Lady Maria Forester,[12] to lead a party of nurses. So when she wrote to Elizabeth Herbert[13] on 14th October it was purely as a private person answering the challenge offered by the *Times*'s correspondent that she solicited her friend's infuence to release her from her contract with the Harley Street Institution. Moreover, it was equally natural that she should enlist the help and influence of her friend's husband, the Secretary at War, who was also well known to her for the past seven years, to exert his influence on behalf of this private venture, which quite certainly would never have been allowed past the hospital doors without official support. There is no evidence in this letter of the long-term contriving on the part of Florence Nightingale in pursuit of personal ambition which has recently been suggested, nor anything strange in the fact that it was written to Mrs Herbert rather than to her husband.[15]

To Mrs Herbert   1 Upper Harley St
                                                                   14th October 1854

My dearest

I went to Belgrave Sq. this morng., for the chance of catching you, or Mr Herbert even, had he been in town.

A small private expedition of nurses has been organized for Scutari & I have been asked to command it. I take myself out & one Nurse. Lady Maria Forester has given £200 to take out three others. We feed & lodge ourselves there, & are to be no expence whatever to the country. Lord Clarendon[16] has been asked by Lord Palmerston[17] to write to Lord Stratford[18] for us, & has consented. Dr Andrew Smith of the Army Medical Board, whom I have seen, authorizes us, & gives us letters to the Chief Medical Officer at Scutari.[19] I do not mean to say that I believe the Times accounts, but I do believe that we may be of use to the wounded wretches.

Now to business

(1)   Unless my Ladies' Committee feel that this is a thing which appeals to the sympathies of all, & urge me, rather than barely consent, I cannot honourably break my engagement here. And I will write to you as one of my mistresses.

(2)   What does Mr Herbert say to the scheme itself? Does he think it will be objected to by the authorities? Would he give us any advice or letters of recommendation? And are there any stores for the Hospital he would advise us to take out? Dr Smith says that nothing is needed.

I enclose a letter from Σ.[20] do you think it any use to apply to Miss Burdett Coutts?[21]

We start on Tuesday, IF we go, to catch the Marseilles boat of the 21st for Constantinople, where I leave my nurses, thinking the Medical Staff at

Scutari will be more frightened than amused at being bombarded by a parcel of women, & cross over to Scutari with someone from the Embassy to present my credentials from Dr Smith, & put ourselves at the disposal of the Drs.

(3)   Would you or some one of my Committee write to Lady Stratford to say "this is not a lady but a real Hospital Nurse", of me. "And she has had experience."

My uncle went down this morning to ask my father & mother's consent. Would there be any use in my applying to the Duke of Newcastle for his authority?

Believe me, dearest
in haste
ever yours

Perhaps it is better to keep it quite a private thing & not apply to Govt. qua Govt.

B.L. Add. Ms. 43396, f. 11 (*Cal.* B, 4, A3, 2)

Another letter written to Miss Nightingale's dictation on the same day, probably to Mrs Bracebridge, further suggests the impulsive spontaneity of her actions at this time. In it she argues with strong common sense in favour of going out at the head of a small private party, as being more likely to win the approval of the medical authorities at Scutari. The advantages, especially in personal prestige, of going as the head of a large official group did not appear yet to have occurred to her, nor at this stage was she insisting on sole control. On the contrary, she clearly recognised the possibility that there might be other independent parties. The insistence on sole authority was to develop only after she received Sidney Herbert's quite different proposal, and was first put by *him* as essential for the maintenance of discipline among such a large body as he proposed.

Probably to Mrs Bracebridge. Letter headed "From F's dictation", i.e. not in F.N.'s own hand.

[15th October 1854]

My dear Friend

We are as much accredited as we ever can be i.e. we have an order from the head of the Army Medical Board Dr. Andrew Smith, to the Chief Medical Officer, at the Hospital at Scutari to admit us to that Hospital, & we have a letter from Lord Clarendon to Lord Stratford – but our fate lies entirely in the hands of Dr. Smith. He is exceedingly irritated at the accounts in the Times. If we go quietly & privately, his influence is all for us, but if we went with a great body of nurses to take possession of the Hospital he would decidedly oppose us. His own proposition was, that a few should go out at once, & that another detachment should follow in 10 days, if found desirable. Amputations, cases of hemorrage or gangrene, are well or dead in 3 weeks. His first expression was, "You are too late. If Sebastopol began on the 6th, it will be already 3 weeks before you get there as it is not supposed that the fighting will continue much after the fall of Sebastopol. One of his objections was, the troops may be moved from Scutari & you cannot follow the army about like Sisters of Charity.

Secondly, I did not think of going to give myself a position, but for the sake of common humanity. If I wait 3 weeks, I do not see that I gain anything, & the miserable creatures are dying all the while.

Thirdly – they cannot find anybody else, & if I don't go the whole thing falls to the ground. Money, I am sure will not fail. There is a Kaiserswerth establishment at Constantinople, who have been written to to prepare rooms for us, I know all the sisters, & am sure they will greatly smooth our way – I have written to the Sydney Herberts who are both at Wilton – Lady Maria Forester (this is the lady whom I called Mrs. Forester) would go with us or, which is what I advise, follow with the next detachment of nurses. To me it would be infinitely easier to pioneer the way with 3 or 4 women than to march in, (even supposing it possible) with a great batch of undisciplined women not knowing what places to assign them, in so new a position as a military hospital.

Mrs. Clarke has volunteered to go with me – & I shall take either her or one of the Nurses from this place.

I will not ask you to recommend my undertaking to my Mother, because I know that you have not thought favourably of my going out on Tuesday, but I will ask you to explain what it is without unfavourable comment because I hope if I see you and her tomorrow, to do away with your objections.

Miss Nightingale added a covering note in her own handwriting for the benefit of her mother and sister:

> 1 Upper Harley Street
> 15th October 1854

In the hope that I shall see my dearest Mother & Sister tomorrow, & that they will give me their blessing on our undertaking, I shall leave it to Mrs. Bracebridge to explain what that undertaking is.

Claydon; copy, Wellcome (*Cal.* B. 4. A3, 1).

If this last letter was indeed to Mrs Bracebridge, as the accompanying note in Florence's own hand suggests, then it is clear that the Bracebridges knew of her plans well in advance of the suggestion made by Sidney

Herbert in his letter of the 15th that they might be willing to accompany her.

According to the popular legend, Florence Nightingale's letter to Mrs Herbert crossed with letters from Sidney Herbert and his wife urging her to undertake just such a mission. In his essay on "Miss Nightingale at Scutari," in *Forence Nightingale:Reputation and Power,* Professor F. B. Smith finds such a coincidence too much to swallow, and considers that "The unusual briskness of Herbert's letter and its remarkable confidence that Miss Nightingale would accept such an extraordinary commission for the War Office and place herself instantly at its disposal allow us to infer that Herbert's letter was the formal product of a prior understanding."[22] Several passages in the letter, however, suggest quite the opposite. For instance, the reference to Lady Maria Forester's proposal to Dr Andrew Smith makes it clear that Herbert did not know at the time of writing that Florence Nightingale herself was in any way connected with it. Nor does the letter seem to display any "remarkable confidence" in Miss Nightingale's acceptance of the proposal; rather it is a carefully moving appeal to her. Furthermore the timing of the events makes it unlikely, if not impossible, that Herbert's request could have been the result of Miss Nightingale's coaching through his wife. Russell's despatches alerting the readers of *The Times* to the condition of the sick and wounded appeared between 9th and 13th October; Florence Nightingale's letter to Elizabeth Herbert was written on the 14th, Sidney Herbert's letter from Bournemouth on the 15th. Both Stanmore and Cook [23] – the latter Florence Nightingale's official biographer and a great admirer – assumed that the idea of sending nurses to the hospital at Scutari originated with Herbert, whose interest in promoting the welfare of the troops was already long established. Finally, the evidence of the Duke of Newcastle, Secretary for War, given before the Roebuck Committee in March 1855, would seem conclusive:

The question of the employment of nurses in the hospital had been mooted at a very early stage, (before, in fact, the army left this country) and the general opinion of military men was adverse to their employment ... but when we found the great complaints that were made ... we felt it to be our duty to take such steps as we could to remedy such a state of things, and we reverted, amongst other things, to the proposal of nurses. The difficulty was to find any lady who was competent to undertake so great a task as the organisation of such a body; and I confess I despaired, having seen one or two, of making the attempt, until Mr. Sidney Herbert, then Secretary-at-War, being personally acquainted with Miss Nightingale, with whom I had also the honour of being acquainted, suggested that it might be possible to induce her to undertake so great a task, though we felt great delicacy in proposing it. We found, however, at once, that she was willing, and we felt that anything which she undertook would be successful.[24]

The proposal made by the Secretary at War on 15th October was in fact very different from that put forward by Florence Nightingale the previous day.

*Copy of letter from Sidney Herbert to Florence Nightingale in the hand of
Caroline Beresford*

Bournemouth
15th October 1854

Dear Miss Nightingale

You will have seen in the papers that there is a gt. deficiency of nurses at
the Hospital at Scutari. The other alleged deficiencies namely, of medical
men, lint, sheets etc., must, if they have really ever existed, have been
remedied e're this; as the number of medical officers with the Army
amounted to one to every 95 men in the whole force, being nearly double
what we have ever had before, & 30 more Surgeons went out there 3 weeks
ago, & must by this time therefore be at Constantinople – a further supply
went on Monday & a fresh batch will sail next week. As to medical stores
they have been sent out in profusion, lint by the *ton* weight, 15,000 prs. of
sheets, medicines, wine, arrowroot in the same proportion, & the only way
of accounting for the deficiency at Scutari, if it exists, is that the mass of
stores went to Varna, & was not sent back when the Army left for the
Crimea, but four days wd. have remedied that. In the meanwhile, fresh
stores are arriving.

But the deficiency of female nurses is undoubted, none but male nurses
having ever been admitted to Military Hospitals. It wd. be impossible to
carry about a large staff of female nurses with an army in the field. But at
Scutari, having now a fixed Hospital, no military reason exists against the
introduction, & I am confident they might be introduced with great benefit,
for Hospital orderlies must be very rough hands, & most of them, on such
an occasion as this, very inexperienced ones. I receive numbers of offers
from ladies to go out – but they are ladies who have no conception of what
an Hospital is, nor of the nature of its duties, & they would, when the time
came, either recoil from the work, or be entirely useless, & consequently,
what is worse, be entirely in the way, nor would those Ladies probably ever
understand the necessity, especially in a Military Hospital, of strict obedience to rule etc.

Lady Maria Forrester (Lord Roden's daughter) has made some proposal
to Dr. Smith, the head of the Army Medical Department, either to go with,
or to send out trained nurses. I apprehend she means from Fitzroy Sqr.
Johns St. or some such establishment. The Revd. Mr. Hume, once chaplain
to the General Hospital at Birmingham, (& better known as Author of the
scheme for transferring the City Churches to the suburbs) has offered to go
out himself as Chaplain with 2 daughters & 12 nurses. He was in the army 7
years & has been used to Hospitals & I like the tone of his letter very much.
I think from both of these offers practical effect may be drawn.

But the difficulty of finding nurses, who are at all versed in their business
is probably best [25] known to Mr. Hume. Lady Maria Forrester probably has
not tested the willingness of the trained nurses to go, & is incapable of

23

directing or ruling them. There is but one person in England that I know of, who would be capable of organizing & superintending such a scheme & I have been several times on the point of asking you hypothetically if, supposing the attempt were made, you wd. undertake to direct it. The selection of the rank & file of nurses will be very difficult, no one knows that, better than yourself. The difficulty of finding women equal to a task after all full of horror, & requiring besides knowledge & goodwill, great energy, & great courage will be great. The task of ruling them & introducing system among them, great; & not the least, will be the difficulty of making the whole work smoothly with the medical & military authorities out there. This it is, which makes it so important, that the experiment should be carried out by one with administrative capacity & experience. A number of sentimental, enthusiastic ladies, turned loose into the Hospital at Scutari would probably, after a few days be mises à la porte, by those whose business they would interrupt, & whose authority they would dispute. My question simply is, would you listen to the request to go out & supervise the whole thing? You would of course, have plenary authority over all the nurses, & I think I could secure you the fullest assistance & cooperation from the medical Staff, & you would also have an unlimited power of drawing on the Govt. for whatever you think requisite for the success of your Mission. On this part of the subject, the details are too many for a letter, & I reserve it for our meeting, for whatever decision you take I know you will give me every assistance & advice. I do not say one word to press you. You are the only person who can judge for yourself, which, of conflicting or incompatible duties is the first or the highest; but I must not conceal from you that I think, upon yr. decision, will depend, the ultimate success or failure of the plan. Your own personal qualities, your knowledge, & your power of administration, & among greater things, your rank & position in society, give you advantages in such a work, which no other person possesses.

If this succeeds, an enormous amount of good will be done, now, & to persons deserving everything at our hands, & a prejudice will have been broken through, & a precedent established, wh. will multiply the good to all time. I hardly like to be sanguine as to your answer. If it were, yes, I am certain the Bracebridges would go with you & give you all the comfort you wd. require, & wh. her society & sympathy only could give you. I have written very long, for the subject is very near my heart. Liz is writing to Mrs. Bracebridge telling her what I am doing. I go back to Town tomorrow morning. Shall I come to you between 3 & 5? will you let me have a line to the War Office to let me know. There is one point which I have hardly a right to touch upon, but I know you will pardon me. If you were inclined to undertake this great work would Mr. & Mrs. Nightingale consent? This work would be so national & the request made to you proceeding from the Govt., who represent the Nation, comes at such a moment, that I do not despair of their consent. Deriving your authority from the Govt. your position would ensure the respect & consideration of everyone, especially in a service where official rank carries so much weight. This would secure you any attention or comfort on your way out there, together with a complete submission to your orders. I know these things are a matter of indifference to you, except so far as they may further the great objects you would have in view, but they are of importance in themselves, & of every importance to those who have a right to take an interest in your personal position & comfort.

I know you will come to a right & wise decision. God grant it may be one in accordance with my hopes. Believe me, dear Miss Nightingale

ever yours

Claydon; copy, Wellcome.

In a brief covering note of the same day Elizabeth Herbert joined her husband in urging Florence to go.

Mrs Herbert to Florence Nightingale

Bournemouth
15th October 1854

Dearest Florence

Sidney wishes to know at what hour he can see you tomorrow? Will you send a note to the War Office to say? He is going to write to you himself to explain his wishes, & so I can only say God guide you right in your decision. I do feel that if you refuse, you will have lost the most noble opportunity of doing the greatest possible amount of good, & just *the* sort of good which *you* alone can do. We have plenty of hands offered but no Head, & the folly of some women is perfectly inconceivable. There will be no difficulty in getting a substitute in Harley St. Every one feels the immense importance of the other work so strongly that not a word will be said or even thought of a broken engagement of such a minor kind. It is a great & national work to which you are called & it is God's work besides. I will say no more

ever yours

Claydon; copy, Wellcome.

While it is unlikely that the private letter of the 15th was the result of prior collaboration between Sidney Herbert and Florence Nightingale, the formal Instructions issued by the Secretary at War to the Lady Superintendent were undoubtedly a joint production. In the future these Instructions were to be the cause of a great deal of trouble and misunderstanding from what has been called loose drafting. But they need to be seen as a practical set of working rules drawn up to meet the immediate perceived circumstances, rather than as providing the formal structure for military nursing. Thus Miss Nightingale's authority was limited to Scutari because Scutari was the only base hospital in existence at the time; such limitation was almost certainly not meant by Sidney Herbert, any more than by Florence Nightingale herself, to exclude her specifically from any future hospitals. In the same way, it was not at the time considered appropriate to send females to the regimental hospitals at the front, so her status in the Crimea was not mentioned; she herself was to deny the suitability of sending nurses to the Crimea until the end of January 1855, which was not the same thing as renouncing control over them when their presence was commanded; or being deliberately and officially excluded, as was to be claimed in some quarters later on. For the time being an attempt was made to define the relationship between nurses and Superintendent, and between the Superintendent and the medical authorities, with some precision.

Finally came the provision which was to cause almost more trouble than any other. This was the attempt to avoid the danger, clearly foreseen by both Miss Nightingale and Herbert, of sectarian troubles among the nurses.

Sidney Herbert's official Instructions to Florence Nightingale

War Office
20th October 1854

155656/3
Madam,

Having consented at the pressing instance of the Government to accept the Office of Superintendent of the female nursing establishment in the English General Military Hospitals in Turkey, you will on your arrival there place yourself at once in communication with the Chief Army Medical Officer of the Hospital at Scutari under whose orders and direction you will carry on the duties of your appointment.

Everything relating to the distribution of the nurses, the hours of their attendance, their allotment to the particular duties, is placed in your hands, subject of course to the sanction and approval of the Chief Medical Officer; but the selection of the nurses in the first instance is placed solely under your controul or under that of persons to be agreed upon between yourself and the Director General of the Army and Ordnance Medical Department, and the persons so selected will receive certificates from the Director General or the principal Medical Officer of one of the General Hospitals without which certificate no one will be permitted to enter the Hospital in order to attend the sick.

In like manner the power of discharge on account of illness, or of dismissal for misconduct, inaptitude, or other cause, is vested entirely in yourself, but in case of such discharge or dismissal the cost of the return passage of such person home will, if you think it advisable and if they proceed at once or so soon as their health enables them, be defrayed by the Government.

Directions will be given by the Mail of this day to engage one or two houses in a situation as convenient as can be found for attendance at the Hospital, Scutari, or to provide accommodation in the Barracks if thought more adviseable, and instructions will be given to Lord Stratford de Redcliffe to afford you every facility and assistance on landing at Constantinople as also to Dr. Menzies, the chief Medical Officer of the Hospital at Scutari, who will give you all the aid in his power and every support in the execution of your arduous duties.

The cost of the passage both out and home of yourself and the Nurses who may accompany you or who may follow you will be defrayed by the Government as also the cost of House rent, subsistence, etc. etc. and I leave to your discretion the rate of pay which you may think it adviseable to give to the different persons acting under your authority. In the meanwhile Sir J. Kirkland, the Army Agent, has received orders to honor your drafts to the amount of one thousand pounds for the necessary expense of outfit, travelling expenses etc. etc. of which sum you will render an account to the Purveyor of the Forces at Scutari.

You will for your current expenses, payment of wages etc. apply to the Purveyor through the Chief Medical Officer in charge of the Hospital who will provide you with the necessary funds. I feel confident that with a view to the fulfilment of the arduous task you have undertaken you will impress upon those acting under your orders the necessity of the strictest attention to the regulations of the Hospital and the preservation of that subordination which is indispensable in every Military Establishment, and I rely on your discretion and vigilance carefully to guard against any attempt being made among those under your authority selected as they are with a view to fitness and without any reference to religious creed to make use of their position in the Hospitals to tamper with or disturb the religious opinions of the patients of any denomination whatever and at once to check any such tendency and to take if necessary severe measures to prevent its repetition.

I have the honour to be
Madam,
Your Obedient Servant

B.L. Add. Ms. 43393 f. 1; P.R.O. WO 43/963, f. 251. There are slight variations between the two copies of the Instructions listed here, mainly in the matter of punctuation. The version reproduced is the one in the British Library, Florence Nightingale's own copy, with the addition of a few commas.

These Instructions were in a sense supplemented by a letter Sidney Herbert wrote to the editor of the *Morning Chronicle* on 21st October and which was published on the 24th. In it he acknowledged the generous flood of offers of help which was pouring in to the government from the sentimental and philanthropic. But he pointed out that it required a certain kind of woman, with very special experience and skills, to fill such a novel and exacting position as that of nurse in a military hospital. In the course of the letter he made the assertion which led Miss Nightingale to heap coals of fire on his head in December when the second party arrived under Mary Stanley: he stated clearly and categorically that no further nurses were to be sent out except on the specific requisition of Miss Nightingale.

In view of the perspicacity displayed in this letter in foreseeing the very difficulties which were to beset the whole enterprise, it is all the more surprising that Sidney Herbert should have despatched the second party only a fortnight later as he did; and the less surprising that Florence Nightingale should have reacted as vehemently as she did.

Sidney Herbert to the Editor, Morning Chronicle

War Office
21st October [1845]

. . . The Government have felt that it would be impossible to throw open a military hospital, or indeed any hospital, to the indiscriminate nursing of any persons whose benevolence or wish for employment might induce them to offer themselves, without evidence of their experience or fitness to perform the arduous duties they undertake.

The duties of a hospital nurse, if they are to be properly performed, require great skill as well as strength and courage, especially where the cases are surgical cases, and the majority of them are from gun-shot wounds. Persons who have no experience or skill in such matters would be of no use whatever, and in moments of great pressure, such as must, of necessity, at intervals occur in a military hospital, any person who is not of use is an impediment.

Many ladies, whose generous enthusiasm prompts them to offer their services as nurses, are little aware of the hardships they would have to encounter, and the horrors they would have to witness, which would try the firmest nerves. Were all accepted who offer, I fear we should have not only many inefficient nurses, but many hysterical patients, themselves requiring treatment instead of assisting others.

Nor, even if capable in other respects, would they always be ready to yield that implicit obedience to orders so necessary to the subordination of a military hospital.

In self defence, the surgeons, before long, might find themselves compelled to exclude all the female nurses, good and bad, with a view to rid themselves of the troublesome and inefficient.

The Government have come to the conclusion that the best mode of obviating these dangers and inconveniences would be to appoint some one person on whose energy, experience, and discretion they can rely, who should be the one authority to select, to superintend, and direct, in the British General Hospitals in Turkey, a staff of female nurses, herself acting under the immediate orders of the medical authorities.

Miss Nightingale, who has, I believe, greater practical experience of administration and treatment than any other lady in this country, has, with a self-devotion for which I have no words to express my gratitude, undertaken this noble but arduous work.

She will act in the strictest subordination to the chief medical officer of the hospital; and the nurses who accompany, or who follow her, will in the same manner be placed completely under her authority, nor will anyone be admitted as a hospital nurse except she have a certificate signed by the Director General of the Army Medical Department upon Miss Nightingale's recommendation, or that of some person deputed by her. I trust that all confusion will be avoided by this arrangement ...

No additional nurses will be sent out to her until she shall have written home from Scutari, and reported how far her labours have been successful, and what number and description of persons, if any, she requires in addition.

Should more be required, a register of their names will be kept, and applications may be made to Miss Stanley ... or the Hon. Mrs. Herbert ... or to St. John's Hospital, Queen's-square, Westminster ...

But, in the meanwhile, no one can be sent out until we hear from Miss Nightingale that they are required; nor would any one going out there be admitted to the hospital unless provided with the certificate I have already described.

All I have said as to the necessity of order and authority as regards the attendance on the sick and wounded, so far as their physical wants are concerned, applies with still more force to the provision for their spiritual wants.

It would be impossible to run any risk of the military hospitals being made the arena of hostile efforts directed by rival creeds one against the other ...

Morning Chronicle, 24th October 1854, p. 4, col. a.

Notes

1 Lord Fitzroy James Henry Somerset (1788–1855), first Baron Raglan, served as Wellington's military secretary from 1810 to 1852; on Wellington's death he was appointed Master General of the Ordnance. In spite of having been deskbound for forty years, when the army was being prepared for war against Russia in 1854, he was deemed the most suitable candidate to command it. For the history of his disastrous Crimean campaign see Christopher Hibbert, *The Destruction of Lord Raglan,* London, 1961.

2 Hibbert, p. 9.

3 Hibbert, p. 18; F.N. to Sidney Herbert, 19th February 1855, B.L. Add. Ms. 43393, f. 164.

4 Hibbert, pp. 27–32.

5   Dr (Sir) Andrew Smith (1797–1872), Director General of the Army Medical Department 1853–58. F.N. always held Dr Smith to have been one of the main authors of the Crimean disaster, but in this she was scarcely just. He did all in his power to inform himself of the conditions prevailing in the area of operations, and made what preparations he could in the face of the "nipping parsimony" of the Treasury. He described his course of action, as well as his "doubts and indescribable anxieties," in the preface of the *Medical and Surgical History of the British Army which served in Turkey and the Crimea during the War against Russia in the Years 1854–55–56*, 2 vols, London, 1858. *Parliamentary Papers*, 1857–58, 38, in 2 pts. See also P. R. Kirby, *Sir Andrew Smith*, Cape Town and Amsterdam, 1965.

6   Diary of Serjeant Major G. Loy Smith of the 11th Hussars, Royal Hussar Museum, Winchester, pp. 38–9.

7   *Ibid.*

8   *Times* 9th October 1854, p. 6, col. e.

9   *Times* 12th October 1854, p. 8, col. a.

10   *Times* 13th October 1854, p. 8, col. a.

11   On 26th July 1854 F.N. told her mother that she had had a proposal from King's College Hospital to enter into treaty with her to undertake the superintendence of a training school for nurses. (Nightingale papers, Claydon).

12   Lady Maria Forester, or Forrester (d. 1894), widow of the Hon. Charles Weld Forester, was a lady of strong evangelical views and devoted to good works. She wrote to Parthe, "I was so anxious something should be done, that I would have gone myself, only I knew that I should not have been the slightest use." (Cook, I, p. 148.)

13   Elizabeth, daughter of General Charles Ashe à Court, married Sidney Herbert in August 1846.

14   Sidney Herbert (1810–61) entered Parliament as member for South Wiltshire in 1832. He held several government offices under Peel before joining the Cabinet as Secretary at War for the first time in 1845. While visiting Rome in autumn 1846 he and his bride met F.N., who was accompanying the Bracebridges. The deep and lasting friendship that developed between F.N. and both Herberts was to have a significant influence on her life. After her return home she frequently visited Wilton, and supported Mrs Herbert through at least one confinement. (F.N. to Mme Mohl, 7th February 1851, B.L. Add. Ms. 43397, f. 303.) Himself a born reformer, Sidney Herbert was very much in sympathy with F.N.'s aspirations, and shared her interest in hospital administration and nursing. She used their influence to persuade her unwilling family to permit her to spend three months at the Institution of Deaconesses at Kaiserswerth in 1851. Later, in 1853, Mrs Herbert supported F.N.'s candidacy for the post of Superintendent of the Institution for Sick Gentlewomen, Harley Street, and it was in this capacity that F.N. wrote to her friend in October 1854 when she was considering giving up that position.

15   F. B. Smith, *Florence Nightingale: Reputation and Power*, London and Canberra, 1982.

16   George William Frederick Villiers, fourth Earl of Clarendon (1800–70), Foreign Secretary 1853–58.

17   Henry John Temple, third Viscount Palmerston (1784–1865), Home Secretary 1852–1855; Prime Minister 1855–58 and 1859–65. The Nightingales were personal friends of the Palmerstons and on several occasions F.N. mentions

having dined with them. After the war Lord Palmerston supported F.N. in her campaign for army sanitary reform, though she frequently felt he could have done more.

18   Stratford Canning, first Viscount Stratford de Redcliffe (1786–1880), was ambassador to Turkey 1841–52 and 1852–58.

19   Dr Duncan Menzies (1803–75).

20   Sigma was the nickname bestowed by the Nightingales upon Mrs Selina Bracebridge (*née* Mills, d. 1874), wife of Charles Holt Bracebridge of Atherstone, who was for many years one of F.N.'s closest friends and confidantes. Mrs B. and her husband supported F.N. in her battle to free herself from her family and encouraged her to pursue her vocation.

21   Angela Georgina, Baroness Burdett-Coutts (1814–1906), well known Victorian philanthropist.

22   Smith, *Reputation and Power*, p. 26.

23   Stanmore, *Lord Herbert of Lea*, I, p. 337; Cook, I, p. 149.

24   *Third Report from the Select Committee on the Army before Sebastopol, 1855, Parliamentary Papers, 1854–55, 34*, p. 132.

25   The original of this letter has not been traced, but in both the copy made by Caroline Beresford, which is the version used here, and in the one which appeared in the *Morning Chronicle*, 30th October 1854, p. 3, col. f, the wording of this sentence is: "But the difficulty of finding nurses, who are at all versed in their business is probably *best* known to Mr. Hume" (my italics). This rendering would make more sense than that used by Cook (I, p. 152), where the word "not" has been substituted for "best." For, as Professor Smith has pointed out, it is unreasonable to suppose that the Rev. Mr Hume, with his years of experience of the army and in hospitals, would *not* be aware of the difficulty of finding nurses versed in their business. (*Reputation and Power*, p. 26.).

2

Scutari: "this gigantic desolation"

Frantic preparations were made to collect a party of suitable nurses. In the Public Record Office is a large box containing hundreds of applications from all sorts and conditions of women, from kitchen maids, through all grades of household servants, to monthly nurses and hospital matrons.[1] Very few indeed had had any experience or training to fit them for the work. Such applicants as appeared in any way suitable were summoned for interview by Mrs Herbert, Mrs Bracebridge and Mary Stanley at the Herberts' house in Belgrave Square. The various nursing institutions and public hospitals of the capital were scoured in the attempt to find experienced and reliable women. But by 21st October, the day of departure, only thirty-eight had been found, including ten nuns who had already left at the behest of the Roman Catholic Bishop of Southwark, Dr Thomas Grant. They were ordered to wait for Miss Nightingale in Paris.

After a brief stay in Paris under the protection of the ambassador, the party travelled on to Marseilles, where they boarded the *Vectis,* "a splendid steamer belonging to the P. & O. Coy."[2]

The passage was stormy and most of the party were ill, including Miss Nightingale, always a suffering sailor. But as they sailed up the Bosphorus she ventured on deck to observe the scene, and recalled her last visit to the East in 1849, when she had visited Egypt and Greece with the Bracebridges, who once more accompanied her.

In spite of her recent sickness she managed a hurried letter home before being swallowed up in the hell that awaited her as the victims of the battle of the Alma were swelled by those wounded during the battle of Balaclava, including the survivors of the charge of the Light Brigade, who were waiting to be disembarked even as she wrote her note:

To her family   Constantinople
4th November 1854
on board the Vectis

Dearest people

32

Anchored off the Seraglio Point – waiting for our fate from Skoutari, whether we can disembark *our* Seraglio direct into the Military Hosp*l.* which is what with such a heterogeneous mass ripe for disorganization we should prefer.

At 6 o'clock yesterday morning I staggered upon deck to look at the plains of Troy, the tomb of Achilles, the mouths of the Scamander, the little harbour of Tenedos, between which & the Mainshore Vectis with stewards' cabins & galley torn away, blustering, creaking, shrieking, storming, rushed on her way. It was in a dense mist that the ghosts of the Trojans answered my cordial hail, through which nevertheless the old Gods still peered down from the hill of Ida upon their old plain. My enthusiasm for the heroes was undiminished by wind & wave. We made the castles of Europe and Asia by 11 (Dardanelles) but alas! we made Constantinople this morning at 9 in a thick & heavy rain, thro' which St. Sophia, Suleiman, the Seven Towers, the Walls & the golden Horn looked like a bad Daguerreotype washed out – & Sta. Sophia was drowned in tears.

We have not yet heard what the Embassy or the Mil*y.* Hosp*l.* have done for us, nor received our orders.

Bad news from Balaklava – tho' not so bad as we heard on first anchoring. You will hear the awful wreck of our poor cavalry in the masked battery, 400 wounded arriving *at this moment* for us to nurse – the bad conduct of the Turkish commanders – cowardice in one – the other shot. Our two ships damaged, Arethusa & Albion. But Lord Raglan says he shall take Sebastopol. We have just built another Hospital at the Dardanelles.[3] It is quite true that a sortie of 8000 Russians was repulsed by 1500 of ours. One man killed 14 Russians with his own hand.

Do you want to know about our crew? Wilson has turned out a swindler. She came drunk, to the London Br. Station on Monday morng. was turned away by the Station Master then went to you (the rest you know) joined us at Marseille, travelling 1st class all the way, has proclaimed her intention publicly that *she* did not come out for the paltry 10/- a week, but to nurse noblemen, & means to desert the first opportunity. She has made acquaintance with all the surgeons & is a regular bad one. We are only waiting to get on shore to settle what is to be done with her.

Just starting for Scutari. We are to be housed in the Hospital this very afternoon. Everybody very kind. The first wounded I believe to be placed under our care. They are landing them now.

Claydon; copy, Wellcome (*Cal.* B. 4, A4, 4).

There is some evidence that on her first arrival Florence Nightingale was agreeably surprised by the condition of the hospitals at Scutari, having expected far worse from the lurid descriptions in *The Times*. Dr Menzies wrote to Dr Hall on 8th December that "Miss Nightingale . . . stated on her arrival here that, after all she had heard, she was surprised at the regularity and comfort which appeared in every one of our wards."[4] And he was to repeat this testimony in his evidence before the Roebuck Committee. But this was the man who had written indignantly to Dr Hall on 26th October:

I beg to state that every preparation that kindness and humanity could suggest was in readiness to alleviate the sufferings of both sick and wounded ... and it is extremely mortifying that a public journal of so respectable a character as *The Times* should advance statements so utterly false. There was no want of either linen or bandages, but an ample supply of both ... As for there being "no preparations for the commonest surgical operations," this statement is false in every particular ... There never was such a tissue of falsehood fabricated![5]

Other visitors were appalled. The Rev. Sidney Godolphin Osborne, a friend of Herbert's with a considerable experience of hospitals, was assured by Menzies when he arrived two days after Miss Nightingale that "they had every thing – nothing was wanted." But, he found;

... these vast hospitals were absolutely without the commonest provision for the exigencies they had to meet; but that there was in and about the whole sphere of action an utter want of that accord amongst the Authorities in each Department, which alone could secure any really vigorous effort to meet the demands, which the carrying on of the war was sure to make upon them. It is quite true, that as ship after ship brought down their respective cargoes of wounded and sick, the Medical and other Officers, with Miss Nightingale and her corps of nurses, did work from morning till night and through the night, in trying to meet the pressure upon their scanty resources; but the whole thing was a mere matter of excited, almost frenzied energy, for where so much that was necessary was absent, it followed that all that zeal and labour could effect, was by various temporary expedients, to do that, which when done was wholly inadequate to what was really required.[6]

Of course, the Rev. Sidney Godolphin Osborne was connected with *The Times* and might therefore be suspected of having a vested interest in supporting his colleague. But the ambassador also failed to persuade the medical authories at Scutari to avail themselves of his help. He met with the same response. Nothing was lacking; nothing was wanted.[7] The melancholy truth was that there were no disinterested, objective observers on the scene. As Mary Stanley was to write to Parthenope, "It is a *horrid* place – no one trusts another – no one speaks well of another ... I am so shocked with the falseness of people. They abuse you behind your back & flatter you to your face."[8]

Whatever the truth about the conditions at Scutari, they can hardly have been ideal, or even moderately comfortable, for the unfortunate nurses crammed into a small tower of the vast Barrack Hospital. Nevertheless, in her letter to Dr Bowman,[9] of King's College Hospital, Miss Nightingale wrote with exhilaration as she rose to the challenge:

Barrack hospital and cemetery at Scutari

To Dr William Bowman
"I came out Ma'am, prepared to submit to every thing – to be put upon in every way – but there are some things, Ma'am, one can't submit to – There is caps, Ma'am, that suits one face, and some that suits anothers, and if I'd known, Ma'am, about the caps, great as was my desire to come out to nurse at Scutari, I wouldn't have come, Ma'am." Speech of Mrs. Lawfield,[10] Nov. 5th

Barrack Hospital, Scutari,
Asiatic Side
14th November 1854

Dear Sir,

Time must be at a discount with the man who can adjust the balance of such an important question as the above – and I, for one, have none, as you will easily suppose when I tell you that on Thursday last we had 1715 sick and wounded in this Hospital, (among whom 120 Cholera Patients), and 650 severely wounded in the other building, called the General Hospital, of which we also have charge – when a message came to me to prepare for 570 wounded on our side of the Hosp*l*. who were arriving from the dreadful affair of the 5th of Nov*ber*. at Balaclava, where some 1763 wounded, & 442 killed, besides 96 Officers wounded & 38 killed. I always expected to end my days as Hospital Matron, but I never expected to be Barrack Mistress. We had but half an hour's notice before they began landing the wounded. Between one and nine o'clock, we had the mattresses stuffed, sewn up, and laid down, alas! only upon matting on the floors, the men washed and put to bed, & all their wounds dressed – I wish I had time or I would write you a letter dear to a surgeon's heart, I am as good as a "Medical Times".

But oh! you gentlemen of England, who sit at home in all the well-earned satisfaction of your successful cases, can have little idea from reading the newspapers, of the horror & misery (in a military Hosp*l*.) of operating upon these dying and exhausted men – a London Hosp*l*. is a garden of flowers to it – we have had such a sea in the Bosphorus, and the Turks, the very men for whom we are fighting, carry our wounded so cruelly, that they arrive in a state of agony – one amputated stump died two hours after we received him – one compound fracture just as we were getting him into bed, in all 24 cases on the day of landing – the dysentery cases have died at the rate of one in two – then the day of operations which follows – I have no doubt that Providence is quite right and that the Kingdom of Hell is the best beginning for the Kingdom of Heaven, but that this is the Kingdom of Hell no one can doubt. We are very lucky in our Medical Heads – two of them are brutes, and four of them are angels – for this is a work which makes *either* angels or devils of men, and of women too. As for the Assistants, they are all cubs, and will, while a man is breathing his last breath under the knife, lament the 'arrogance of being called up from their dinners by such a fresh influx of wounded'. But wicked cubs grow up into good old bears, tho' I don't know how – for certain it is, the old bears are good. We have now four miles of beds – and not eighteen inches apart. We have our quarters in one Tower of the Barrack – and all this fresh influx has been laid down between us and the Main Guard in two corridors with a line of beds down each side, just room for one man to step between, and four wards.

Yet, in the midst of this appalling horror (we are steeped up to our necks in blood) – there is good. And I can truly say, like St. Peter, 'it is good for us to be here' tho' I doubt whether, if St. Peter had been here, he would have said so. As I went my night-rounds among the newly wounded that first night, there was not one murmur, not one groan, the strictest discipline, the most absolute silence & quiet prevailed, only the step of the sentry and I heard one man say, I was dreaming of my friends at home, & another said And I was thinking of them. These poor fellows bear pain and mutilation with unshrinking heroism, and die or are cut up without a complaint. Not so the Officers, but we have nothing to do with the Officers. The wounded are now lying up to our very door, and we are landing 540 men from the "Andes" – I take rank in the army as Brigadier-General, because 40 British females, whom I have with me, are more difficult to manage than 4000 men. Let no lady come out here who is not used to fatigue & privation – for the Devonport Sisters,[11] who ought to know what selfdenial is, do nothing but complain. Occasionally the roof is torn off our quarters, or the windows blown in – and we are flooded and under water for the night. We have all the Sick Cookery now to do, and have got in four men for the purpose, for the prophet Mahomet does not allow us a female. And we are now able to supply these poor fellows with something besides Gov*t*. rations. The climate is very good for the healing of wounds.

I wish you would rcall me to Dr. Bence Jones's[12] remembrance, when you see him, and tell him that I have had but too much occasion to remember him in the constant use of his dreadful presents. Now comes the time of haemorrhage and Hospital Gangrene, and every ten minutes an orderly runs, and we have to go and cram lint into the wound till a Surgeon can be sent for, and stop the bleeding as well as we can. In all our Corridors I think we have not an average of three limbs per man – and there are two ships more "loading" at the Crimea with wounded, this is our phraseology. Then come the operations and a melancholy, not an encouraging list is this. They are all performed in the wards – no time to move them. One poor fellow, exhausted with haemorrhage, has his leg amputated as a last hope and dies ten minutes after the surgeons have left him. Almost before the breath has left his body, it is sewn up in its blanket and carried away – buried the same day. We have no room for corpses in the wards. The Surgeons pass on to the next, an excision of the shoulder-joint – beautifully performed and going on well – ball lodged just in the head of the joint, and fracture starred all round. The next poor fellow has two stumps for arms – and the next has lost an arm and leg. As for the balls, they go in where they like, and do as much harm as they can in passing. That is the only rule they have. The next case has one eye put out, and paralysis of the iris of the other. He can neither see nor understand. But all who can walk come into us for Tobacco, but I tell them that we have not a bit to put into our own mouths. Not a sponge, nor a rag of linen, not anything have I left. Everything is gone to make slings and stump pillows and shirts. These poor fellows have not had a clean shirt nor been washed for two months before they came here, and the state in which they arrive from the transport is literally *crawling*. I hope in a few days we shall establish a little cleanliness. But we have not a basin nor a towel nor a bit of soap nor a broom – I have ordered 300 scrubbing brushes. But one half the Barrack is so sadly out of repair that it is impossible to use a drop of water on the stone floors, which are all laid upon rotten wood, and would give our men fever in no time. The next case is a poor felow where the ball went in at the side of the head, put out one eye, made a hole in his tongue and came out in the neck. The wound was doing very nicely when he was seized with agonizing pain and died suddenly, without convulsion or paralysis. At the P[ost] M[ortem], an abscess in the anterior part of the head was found as big as my fist – yet the man kept his reasoning faculties till the last. And nature had thrown out a false coat all round it.

I am getting a screen now for the Amputations, for when one poor fellow, who is to be amputated tomorrow, sees his comrade today die under the knife it makes impression – and diminishes his chance. But, anyway, among these exhausted frames the mortality of the operations is frightful. We have Erysipelas Fever and Gangrene. And the Russian wounded are the worst. We are getting on nicely though in many ways. They were so glad to see us. The Senior Chaplain[13] is a sensible man, which is a remarkable providence. I have not been out of the hospital wards yet. But the most beautiful view in the world lies outside. If you ever see Mr. Whitfield, the House Apothecary of St. Thomas's, will you tell him that the nurse he sent me, Mrs. Roberts,[14] is worth her weight in gold. There was another engagement on the 8th, and more wounded, who are coming down to us. The text which heads my letter was expounded thus – Mrs. Lawfield was recommended to return home and set her cap, vulgarly speaking, at some one elsewhere than here, but on begging for mercy, was allowed to make another trial. Mrs. Drake[15] is a treasure – the four others are not fit to take care of themselves nor of others in a Military Hosp*l*. This is my first impression. But it may modify, If I can convince them of the absolute necessity of discipline and propriety in a drunken Garrison.

Continued on inside flap of envelope.

Believe me, dear Sir, yours very truly and gratefully,

This is only the beginning of things. We are still expecting the assault.

Sir John Bowman, Bt. (*Cal*. B. 4. A5, 6). Copy, in Parthe's hand, Claydon. The copy is much shorter than the original Bowman letter, omitting all the clinical descriptions of the wounds, reflecting the family feeling that Miss Nightingale's interest in such things was disgusting. Copies of several letters have been bowdlerised in this way for circulation to friends, and in some cases the original letters have been heavily defaced.

On 25th November Florence Nightingale wrote two letters to Sidney Herbert. The first, official, letter merely reported the safe arrival and reception of the party, ten of whom she had placed in the General Hospital, where there were about nine hundred patients; and twenty-eight in the Barrack Hospital, which, at that time, contained about 2,300.[16]

The second, private, letter gave a very different picture. Miss Nightingale went straight to the heart of the matter, and in her criticism of the lack of any central authority to control or accept responsibility for the various departments concerned with the provisioning and servicing of the hospitals foreshadowed the many long, detailed, impassioned letters to Herbert in which she demanded wholesale reform of the administrative machine.

To Sidney Herbert

British Sisters Quarters
Barrack Hospital, Scutari
25th November 1854

Private

Dear Mr. Herbert

(1) It appears that, in these Hospitals, the Purveyor considers washing both of linen & of the men a minor "detail" – & during the three weeks we have been here, though our remonstrances have been treated with perfect civility, yet no washing whatever has been performed for the men either of body-linen or of bed-linen except by ourselves & a few wives of the Wounded, – & a story of a Contractor, with which we have been amused, turns out to be a myth. The dirty shirts were collected yesterday for the first time, & on Monday *it is said*, that they are to be washed, – we are organizing a little Washing Establishment of our own — for the bandages etc.[17] When we came here, there was neither bason, towel nor soap in the Wards, nor any means of personal cleanliness for the Wounded except for the following. Thirty were bathed every night by Dr. MacGrigor's orders in slipper-baths, but this does not do more than include a washing once in eighty days for 2300 men.

The consequences of all this are Fever, Cholera, Gangrene, Lice, Bugs, Fleas – & may be Erisypelas – from the using of one sponge among many wounds.[18]

And even this slipper-bathing does not apply to the General Hospital.

(2)   The fault here is, *not* with the Medical Officers, but in the separation of the department which affords every necessary supply, except medicines, to them – & in the insufficient supply of minor officers in the Purveying Department under Mr. Wreford, the Purv*r*. Gen*l*. – as well as in the inevitable delay in obtaining supplies, occasioned by the existence of one single Interpreter only, who is generally seen booted.

(3)   Your name is also continually used as a bug-bear, – they make a deity of cheapness, – & the Secretary at War stands as synonymous here with Jupiter Tonans, whose shafts end only in "brutum fulmen." The cheese-paring system, which sounds unmusical in British ears, is here identified with you by the Officers who carry it out. It is in vain to tell the Purveyors that they will get no "kudos" by this at home. See Note A.

(4)   The requirements are, unity of action & personal responsibility.

It is a sad joke here that a large reward has been offered for any one who is personally responsible, barring the Commandant.

(5)   Another cause is, the imperfection of distinct orders in England as to *packing*. The unfortunate "Prince"[19] who was lost at Balaclava had on board a quantity of medical comforts for us which were so packed under shot & shell as that it was found impossible to disembark them here & they went on to Balaklava & were lost at the same time as your Commiss*r*. Dr. Spence

(6)   In consequence of the Duke of Newcastle's letter to Mr. Cumming,[20] the latter has not taken the command here, & in consequence of Dr. Spence being lost on board the "Prince," the Commission of Enquiry has not yet begun its labours[21] – Mr. Maxwell[22] visits us *en amateur*.

(7)   Two or three hundred Stump pillows, ditto Arm Slings, ditto *Paddings for Splints* – besides other Medical Appliances are being weekly manufactured & given out by us – & no provision appeared to have been made for these things before.

All the above is written in obedience to your PRIVATE instructions. Do not let me appear as a Gov*t*. spy here which would destroy all my usefulness & believe me, in greatest haste,

yours every truly

P.S. Lord Napier & the visitors generally remark that the Hospital is improved since we came.

Note A
The habits & the honor of the Purveying Depart*mt*. as inferior officers, fix their attention upon the correctness of their book-keeping as the primary object of life.

Note B
Mr. Osborne & Mr. Macdonald have been profuse of offers. We have accepted wine, shirts, flannel, calico, sago, etc, etc. delay being as fatal to us as denial in our requisitions.

ENTRE NOUS, will you let me state that Lady Stratford, with the utmost kindness & benevolent intentions, is, in consequence of want of practical habits of business, nothing but good & bustling, & a time-waster & impediment. As the Commission is not yet doing anything, the Ambassador should send us a *man* who, with prompt efficiency, can also defend us from the difficulties & delays of mediating between conflicting orders in the various departments – to which I ascribe most of the signal failures, such as those in washing etc., which have occurred.

P.S. Mrs. Herbert gave me a fright by telling Mrs. Bracebridge that your private letter to me had been published. That letter was shown to no one but my own people & it appears to me impossible that it can have found its way into any other hands.[23]
P.P.S. We are greatly in want of Hair Mattresses or even Flock, as cheaper. There are but 44 Hair mattresses in store. Our very bad cases suffer terribly from bed-sores on the Paillasse, which is all we have – while the French Hospital is furnished throughout with mattresses having an elastic couche of Hair between two of Flock & a Paillasse underneath.

B.L. Add. Ms. 43393, f. 13 (*Cal.* B. 4. A7, 10).

On 5th December she again wrote to Herbert to complain of the difficulty in getting essential work done.

To Sidney Herbert

Barrack Hospital, Scutari
5th December 1854

Dear Mr. Herbert

I enclose copies of two letters, viz. one from me to the Ambassador, & his reply.

To make the matter clear, I should state that the workmen for repairing the dilapidated wards were put on by Lady Stratford's order viz. to Mr. Gordon, the Chief Officer of Engineers – at which time she had long conferences with the Commandant & the Purveyor Gen*l*. note-book in hand – that she distinctly stated to me & others that she was the authorized intermediary between the Ambassador & the authorities of the Hospitals – & that she offered herself as my correspondent in that capacity. Four or five days subsequently, Lord Stratford himself accompanied her here.

The enclosed copies explain what followed – viz. the employing 125 workmen, their strike, & my putting on 200 workmen – (I may add that we are daily expecting 6 or 700 wounded at least in an already overcrowded Hospital & that Lord Raglan has written to say that we may expect sick from the cold. The dilapidated & now *un*inhabitable wards are capable of holding 800 patients).

By Lord Stratford's letter to me & in an interview between him & Mr. Gordon, Lord S. virtually denies knowledge of Lady S.'s proceedings.

My own feeling is that the Ambassador would not have done, what he is the only person who has any power to do, & what is a matter of primary importance as regards 800 wounded.

What I have done has been done with the concurrence of Dr. McGrigor,[24] Senior Medical Officer of the Barrack Hosp*l*., & (as I subsequently found) to the great satisfaction of Mr. Gordon, who expected to be blamed for that which he could not help.

As far as I can reason upon this, it appears to me certain that nothing would have been done if I had not acted in this way.

Mr. Bracebridge will tell you about the Jetty Landing Place & the Washing Est[ablishment] which was exactly the same story as the interiorly re-building of these wards (one fourth of the whole Hosp*l*.)

Believe me ever yours

B.L. Add. Ms. 43393, f. 19 (*Cal.* B. 4. A8, 13).

As if she had not enough trouble with these fundamental problems, Miss Nightingale was forced to recognise the fact that the women under her command were not all behaving with the devotion she expected. Some of the St John's House nurses in particular were becoming restive under the draconian discipline she imposed. They wrote home disconsolately complaining of the poor food and the tyrannical behaviour of Mrs Clarke, Miss Nightingale's housekeeper. For her part, Miss Nightingale had little sympathy with their unhappiness and complained to their superiors at home of their frivolous behaviour and lack of skill.

To Miss Gipps
Barrack Hospital
Scutari
5th December 1854

Dear Miss Gipps

I have no time but to make the shortest communication, as you may suppose when I tell you that I have not yet written to my own people.

I have now had one month's experience of the St. John's Sisters.

Mrs. Drake is invaluable, kind, careful, modest.

Mrs. Lawfield, since the "blow-up" about the caps of which Mr. Bowman may have told you, has been quite a different person & she is now, though not skilful (she does not know a facture when she sees it) one of the most valuable nurses I have from her great propriety of conduct & kindness. Her very expression of countenance is altered & improved.

With regard to the other four, I fear that nothing can be made of them here – tho' I have no doubt that, as private nurses in England, they may be very good. Their manners are so flibberty-gibbet,[25] (though, with the exception of Mrs. Higgins, I suspect no greater impropriety) that they do not command the respect imperatively necessary where forty women are turned loose among three thousand men. They do not keep the rules which I have made to ensure female decorum, but run scampering over the wards by themselves at night, feeding the men without medical orders. Their dressings of wounds are careless & slovenly – & they will not take a hint, except from me. I have consequently employed them less in nursing, & more in making Stump Pillows etc. for the men than I should otherwise have done, with the view of protecting them. And they said, which is very true, that they did not come out for needlework. They have consequently done little or nothing. I fear they must be recalled which I should very much prefer should arise thus, because you want them, rather than because I don't.

Yours ever

I hope you are better.

G.L.R.O. HI/ST/NC.3/SU 14.

This letter was passed on to Miss Jones, the Lady Superintendent of St John's House, who, considering it in conjunction with the unhappy letters from her nurses, felt called on to remonstrate with Miss Nightingale:

> I cannot pass over your letter without expressing regret, that in a matter of such grave import to the nurses as a complaint of their conduct to the authorities of the Institution to which they belong, expressions should have been used which would seem to betoken a want of consideration towards women who volunteered to aid in carrying out, under your control & guidance a good, though difficult – & arduous work on an, hitherto, untried field of labour . . .
>
> I am at a loss to know what amount of significance you wish me to attach to the term "flibberty gibbet." I think you will recollect that your most express instruction to these nurses, and which you asked me to impress upon them, was that they *were to obey no one but you, nor to take ordes from any one else.* Perhaps they have interpreted this too literally.
>
> To the complaint of want of skill to pronounce decidedly upon a fracture etc. etc. I can but reply that the Council of this Institution have only contemplated training women who should observe, & carefully carry out, as *nurses,* the directions of the Physician or Surgeon, as the case may be; and do not engage to send out any possessed of skill as actual surgeons.
>
> You will not imagine, dear Miss Nightingale, from anything in this letter, any want of appreciation on my part of your own arduous labors, or of the difficulties you have to encounter in so arranging that those under you and working with you shall orderly and effectually carry out your wishes & intentions, for I am quite sure you will readily understand my feeling that whilst it is my duty, as the appointed head of these nurses, to suffer no fault or wrong behaviour to pass unrebuked. I am equally bound to care for their well being during the performance of any duty to which they may be sent.[26]

Miss Nightingale was not at the time prepared to accept this rebuke with grace. Her reply to the Council of St John's House, written on 11th January 1855, shows umbrage.

To the Council of St John's House

Barrack Hospital
Scutari
11th January 1854

Gentlemen

I have the honor to acknowledge the receipt of a letter from Miss Jones, Lady Sup*t*., of the 22nd ult. & I have also had a letter from Mr. Bowman of the 26th ult.

From these letters it appears that the St. John's Nurses have expressed themselves as aggrieved by a rule restricting them from "speaking to patients" by "want of sympathy from others" & "want of due consideration towards themselves". It seems also to be thought that I passed some severe censure upon their want of "surgical" skill.

In reply I have only to say that it was by the information alone which I received from the Nurses (for I felt it necessary to ask their explanation) that I could understand what the above weighty expressions could refer to – which seem derived from a very serious examination of the hasty & inaccurate letters of those not much accustomed to detail facts or to explain their feelings in writing.

The rule against reading to patients in a Military Hospital without the Chaplain's leave (observed alike by everyone) is the only approximation to the supposed interdiction of speaking. As to "sympathy" & "consideration", they can only explain that "Mrs. Clarke" did not "speak to them *respectfully* & they were not accustomed to it." Mrs. Clarke, as I believe though somewhat brusque, sets them an example of incessant labor & anxiety to fulfil her duties. But their main complaints were against Mrs. Lawfield, one of their own body, and jealousies of Mrs. Drake.

Had they given me an opportunity of setting matters right, I might have convinced them of the impropriety of lightly taking offence. The enormous pressure of the sick cases on us, the supplying them with proper food, & the supply of the wards with utensils, clothing etc. form a task of so very heavy a nature that I am wholly unable to enquire with trifles which I know nothing of, & which were not intimated to me at all, though constantly passing the common room for at least sixteen hours out of the twenty four.

In conclusion, I trust that it may not be deemed offensive to say that the frivolous & really unfounded charges of these letters, which have obtained such grave consideration at your hands, confirms me in the idea that the St John's Nurses are not well fitted for the work of this Hospital, – nor have they improved by experience.

I have therefore given to four of them your letters of recall, since receiving their explanations, & shall only await a convenient opportunity for their return.

I had hoped to have found some serious devotion to the cause we are engaged in – but have no other complaint to make. I am obliged by the letter of recall having been sent which I can now make use of & am Gentlemen,

Your obdt. Servt.

P.S. I cannot too strongly draw your attention to the difference between a Military & a London Hospital – to the consequent necessity of different rules & to the probability of the Nurses in question doing extremely well in private nursing at home – but not among the officers here.

G.L.R.O. HI/ST/NC.3/SU 18. (*Cal* omitted).

In spite of the sharpness of the rejoinder Miss Nightingale must have taken Miss Jones's letter to heart, for Elizabeth Drake subsequently reported that she was very kind to her, while others wrote that they were well fed.[27]

In the meantime Florence at last found the time to unburden herself to her family. While she used her correspondence with Sidney Herbert as a safety valve, finding relief in furious and bitter ranting about the many evils she perceived about her, she rarely displayed any self-doubt. In the letters home, very much shorter, she often revealed quite another side of her character, often depressed and full of heart-searching. But she was borne up through these moments by her absolute conviction that she was going God's will.

To her family

[Scutari, 5th December 1854]

Dearest people

Could you but see me, you would not wonder that I have no time to write – when my heart yearns to do so. Could any one but know the difficulties and heart sinkings of *command,* the constant temptation to throw it up, they would not write to me, as good Mr. Garnier does, praying for grace that I may bear the praise lavished upon me. I who have never had time to look at a Paper since I came. Praise, good God. He knows what a situation He has put upon me. For His sake I bear it willingly, but not for the sake of Praise. The cup which my Father hath given me shall I not drink it? But how few can sympathize with such a position! Most of all was I surprised at dr. Aunt Mai's sanguine and gleeful view of it. But do not suppose that I shrink. Without us, nothing would have been done here – & I am satisfied. All this is, of course, private

I subjoin a list of small wants*

Pray *date* your letters.

Ever yours

I should like to hear about Harley St.

---

* There are several lists of small wants among the Claydon papers, but it is not clear which this refers to.

Claydon; copy, Wellcome (*Cal.* B. 4. A8, 14).

The women were just beginning to settle into a useful routine and to be recognised by the medical authorities when news came that a second party of nurses and nuns had been recruited and was about to be despatched. Exhausted with overwork and all the harassment of perpetual opposition as she must have been, it is not surprising that Miss Nightingale was appalled.

To Sidney Herbert

Barrack Hospital
Scutari
PRIVATE   10th December 1854

Dear Mr. Herbert
   With regard to receiving & employing a greater number of Sisters & Nurses in these Hospitals, I went immediately, (on reading Mrs. Herbert's letter of the 23rd, addressed to Mr. Bracebridge,) to consult Mr. Menzies, the principal Medical Officer, under whose orders I am.
   He considers that as large a number are now employed in these Hospitals as can be usefully appropriated, & as can be made consistent with morality & discipline. And the discipline of forty women, collected together for the first time, is no trifling matter – under these new & strange circumstances.
   He considers that, if we were swamped with a number increased to sixty or seventy, good order would become impossible. And in all these views I so fully concur that I should resign my situation as impossible, were such circumstances forced upon me.
   For our quarters are already inadequate to preserving in health our number. More quarters cannot be assigned us. The sick are laid up to our door, – we had even to give up a portion of those quarters which had been assigned us (at the General Hospital) to the Wounded.
   With regard to taking a house at Scutari, the medical officers considered it as simply impossible. Regularity could not be preserved, where the Sisters & Nurses were living from under our own eye – the difficulties of transport are what no one in England would believe, & the going to & fro between the two Hospitals is becoming daily less easy. That I should not accept a responsibility, which I could not fulfil, is equally the opinion of the Medical Officers & mine.
   If, in the course of the winter, we have out ten or twenty more, & send back some of those we have, the Medical Officers are of opinion that that number will be sufficient, i.e. forty efficient ones being picked out eventually for the two Hospitals – averaging 3000 sick.
   Lastly, I have found from this last month's experience that, had we come out with twenty instead of forty, we should not only have been less

hampered with difficulties, but the work itself would have been actually better & more efficiently done. About ten of us have done *the whole work*. The others have only run between our feet & hindered us – & the difficulty of assigning to them something to do without superintendence has been enormous. It is the difference between the old plough with the greatest amount of power & the greatest loss in its application – & the Gee-ho plough with reins – accomplishing twice the work with half the power & much more efficiently.

We were so alarmed at the general terms in which Mrs. Herbert described the nurses as instantly to be sent off – that we held council & decided on writing the enclosed to the Ambassador as the only means of protecting them & ourselves. In other words, we could neither house nor keep them.

English people look upon Scutari as a place with inns & hackney-coaches & houses to let furnished. It required yesterday (to land 25 casks of sugar) four oxen & three men for six hours – plus two passes, two requisitions, Mr. Bracebridge's two interferences, & one apology from a Quarter Master for seizing the Araba, received with a smile & a kind word, because he did his duty. For every Araba is required on Military-store or Commissariat duty. There are no pack-horses & no asses, except those used by the peasantry to attend the market 1¼ miles off. An Araba consists of loose poles & planks extended between two axle-trees, placed on four small wheels, & drawn by a yoke of weak oxen.

There is not a Turkish house which is not in a fragmentary state – roof & windows pervious in all directions – there is not a room in our quarters which does not let in the rain in showers, whenever the weather is bad. We can only buy food through the Commissary & are sometimes without wood or charcoal.

For want of a carpenter & a man to put up a stove, in the absence of all hands (the workmen available being all employed in repairing the Sick Wards, the matter of first importance) we have been unable during the last week to effect the move of some of our nurses into the Gen*l*. Hosp*l*., or even to get in a few poor soldiers' wives into our little Lying-in Hospital,[28] which the pressure of the misery of these poor women had compelled us to begin.

All this will tend to explain the impossibility of having more women, & especially ladies, out here at present.

Mr. Bracebridge has put down some mem*a*. as they occurred to him.

What we may be considered to have effected is:

(1)   the kitchen for extra-diets, now in full action, for this Hospital – with regular extra diet tables sent in by the Ward-Surgeons.

(2)   A great deal more cleaning of Wards – mops, brooms, scrubbing brushes, & combs, given out by ourselves, where not forced from the Purveyor.

(3)   2000 shirts, cotton & flannel, given out, & washing organised – & already carried on for a week.

(4)   Lying-in Hospital begun.

(5)   widows & soldiers' wives relieved & attended to.

(6)   a great amount of daily dressings & attention to compound fractures by the most competent of us.

(7)   the supervision & stirring-up of the whole machinery generally, with the full concurrence of the chief medical authorities – & the practical proof which our presence has given that Gov*t*. were determined to know all they could & do all they could.

(8)   the repairing of wards for 800 wounded which would otherwise have been left uninhabitable. And this I regard as the most important.

The Government could not do otherwise than send a number of Female Assistants worthy of it, viz. 30 or 40. Of these, at most 16 are efficient. The personal qualities of five or six have effected (under God's blessing) the results already obtained.

I am willing to bear the evil of governing (& preventing from doing mischief) the non-efficient *or scheming* majority, which is my great difficulty & most wearing-out labor – because I acknowledge the moral effect produced, which could not have been produced by smaller numbers. But I am not willing to encounter the crowding greater numbers to exhaust our powers & make us useless & incapable by wasting our time & nervous energy in governing that which cannot be governed.

Lastly, at the moment we came out, the "Times" commissioner & his fund were prepared immediately to go into opposition – as they have actually done at Balaclava, where the "Times" supplies have been refused – as well as admission to Mr. Stafford [29] – whereas here, instead of opposition, we have had support. Nothing has been given here except through us & we have had abundant supplies more than we asked, from Mr. Macdonald & Mr. Osborne – who have held daily consultations with us. Mr. Stafford, who was on the point of going into extreme opposition, has shewn nothing but kindness & zeal.

The great fault here lies in our geography – in our being on this side of the water. Four days in the week we cannot communicate with Constant*e*., except by the other harbour, 1¼ mile off, of Scutari proper, to which the road is almost impassable.

I add the Pièces Justicatives.

The grand administrative evil emanates from home – in the existence of a number of departments here, each with its centrifugal & independent action, un-counteracted by any centripetal attraction viz. a central authority capable of supervising & compelling combined effort for each object at each particular time.

Excuse confusion
In great haste
ever yours

P.S. The remedy which was proposed in making Mr. Cumming Inspector General was distinctly neutralised, 1*st* by his own caution in not assuming a power not legally his & waiting for Ld. Raglan's orders 2*nd* by the D. of Newcastle's letter assigning him the post of Head Commissioner, which arrived at the same time as Ld. Raglan's reply. The result has been that Mr. Cumming has not acted as Inspr. Genl. & that the Commissioners were three weeks before they began to sit – having replaced poor Dr. Spence by the selection of an efficient Medical Officer here.

Mr. Cumming's habit of mind & delicacy towards Mr. Menzies led him to be very chary in giving advice till the arrival of your letter, since which he has given it AS advice.

B.L. Add. Ms. 43393, f. 22 (*Cal.* B. 4. A9, 15).

Her letter was too late. A heterogeneous assortment of ladies, nurses and nuns had already sailed under the leadership of Mary Stanley. The party arrived on 15th December, and Miss Nightingale refused to receive it.

A great deal of controversy has since surrounded Florence Nightingale's reception, or rather refusal, of this party, and certainly it was a tactical blunder on her part, leading to untold difficulties in both the short and the long term which on occasion threatened to destroy her mission, and which, had she been more conciliating, might have been avoided.

On the other hand her attitude was not altogether unreasonable: the original party was showing signs of disaffection and indiscipline. And they were horribly cramped. Mother Bridgeman, the Superior of the Kinsale nuns who accompanied Mary Stanley, who was to become one of Miss Nightingale's severest critics, was appalled by the conditions in which she found the Bermondsey and Norwood nuns of the first party.[30] Nor was it easy, as Miss Nightingale pointed out, to take a house away from the hospital. If the nurses were living out, they were less amenable to discipline, and could be of less use generally.

Interestingly enough, a few passages in the correspondence between Mrs Stanley, Mary Stanley and Parthe suggest that the Stanleys were aware of the possibility of trouble between the two women. On 24th November Mary had written to Parthe, "I know you will be glad I am going – & glad I am not to stay." That she was going at all had been a last-minute decision. Her mother wrote on 27th November:

You will be startled but pleased to hear that *probably* after all Mary is going out with the Nurses on Saturday – ! Every stone has been turned in vain to get some one & this morning the nail was clinched by a letter from Mrs. Bracebridge that whatever was done a *good head* must be sent out to keep the nurses together on their way, so the Herberts urged the thing so *very strongly* that Mary has consented to take them out & deliver them into Florence's hands. They ask for 10 or 20 & hence 40 are going – much against my judgment but it may enable them to send the useless ones home.

Mary has all the qualifications for *this* job – good traveller & voyager – head & all as you know – she *has not* for the Hospital work & would not think of attempting but *this* she feels she can do – amalgamating & bringing them together & now the doors may be closed against all further applications.

And on the 6th December:

Mary in the natural course of things, would stay a fortnight or so just to look about her. She stipulated she was not to come back without having seen Constantinople.[31]

Florence Nightingale was undeniably jealous of her position. Had she taken in the nurses and made shift to accommodate them, Mary Stanley would have gone straight home. As it was she felt obliged, much against her will, to stay until they were satisfactorily established.

Nor, although he had by some oversight consigned the nurses to Dr Cumming rather than to Miss Nightingale – a fact which she was repeatedly to advert to – did Sidney Herbert mean anything other than that she should have the superintendency of the entire party. Mrs Stanley again bears this out: "S.H. addressed the nuns ... and told them to obey F.N. Mrs. H. reminded him of Mary who he then mentioned as Miss N.'s representative till she cd. direct them."[32]

To Sidney Herbert

Private

Barrack Hospital, Scutari
15th December 1854

Dear Mr. Herbert

When I came out here as your Sup[erintenden]t it was with the distinct understanding (expressed both in your own hand-writing & in the printed announcement which you put in the Morng. Chron.[33] which is here in every one's hands) that nurses were to be sent out at my requisition only, which was to be made only with the approbation of the Medical Officers here.

You came to me in your distress, & told me that you were unable for the moment to find any other person for the office, & that, if I failed you, the scheme would fail. I sacrificed my own judgment, & went out with forty females, well knowing that half that number would be both more efficient & less trouble – & that the difficulty of inducing forty untrained women, in so extraordinary a position as this, (turned loose among 3000 men) to observe any order or even any of the directions of the Medical Men, would be Herculean. Experience has justified my foreboding. But I have toiled my way into the confidence of the Medical Men. I have, by incessant vigilance, day & night, introduced something like system into the disorderly operations of these women. And the plan may be said to have succeeded in some measure, *as it stands*. But the Medical Officers, (under whose orders my written instructions & my own judgment equally concur in placing me) have, while expressing themselves satisfied with things as they are, repeatedly given their opinion that more women cannot be usefully employed nor properly governed. And in this opinion I entirely agree.

To have women scampering about the wards of a Military Hosp*l*. all day long, which they would do, did an increased number relax their discipline &

increase their leisure, would be as improper as absurd.

At this point of affairs arrives, at *no one's* requisition, a fresh batch of women, raising our number to eighty-four.

You have sacrificed the cause, so near my heart. You have sacrificed me, a matter of small importance now. You have sacrificed your own written word to a popular cry.

I will not say anything of the cruel injustice to me. The Medical Men are disgusted, & decline absolutely to employ more, or to make any change in existing arrangements – as far as they are concerned.

Under these circumstances, the only thing I can do is to discharge twelve of those I have, to fill their places with the new ones – to crowd in twelve more into quarters already over-crowded for health (as there is not a square inch of room to be spared in these Hospitals) & to take a house in Scutari for the remaining twenty-two – whom it will be impossible to employ in these Hospitals, & who must wait till you can employ them at Therapia or elsewhere – or till you recall them. Of course these unoccupied women will "go to the devil" to use the expression which was used to me when, in conjunction with my Medical Advisers, I decided on these expedients. The quartering them *here* is a physical impossibility – the employing them a moral impossibility.

You must feel that I ought to resign, where conditions are imposed upon me which render the object for which I am employed unattainable – & I only remain at my post till I have provided in some measure for these poor wanderers.

You will have to consider where the 22 are to be employed – at Malta, Therapia or elsewhere – or whether they are to return to England – & you will appoint a Superintendent in my place, till which time I will continue to discharge its duties as well as I can.

Believe me, dear Mr. Herbert, ever yours very truly

P.S. Had I had the enormous folly to write, at the end of eleven days' experience, to require more women – would it not seem that you, as a statesman, should have said, "Wait, till you can see your way better." But I made no such request.

The proportion of R. Catholics, which is already making an outcry, you have increased to 25 in 84. Mr. Menzies has declared that he will have two only at the Gen*l*. Hosp*l*.[34] – & I cannot place them here in a greater proportion than I have done, without exciting the suspicion of the Medical Men & others.

Written 15*th* December
Posted 18*th*   "

I must again refer to the deficiency of knives & forks here, the men tear their food like animals. The Medical Officers request me to state that boxes of Sheffield cutlery, say

1000 knives & forks
1000 spoons
should be sent out immediately – as there are none in store. I will meanwhile
do what I can in Constantinople to stop the gap.

B.L. Add. Ms. 43393, f. 34 (*Cal. B. 4. A9, 16*).

Although she had offered her resignation, as she was in honour bound to
after her letter of 10th December, it is very doubtful whether she ever
seriously considered such an action. However, she continued to tease
Herbert with the threat.

She was unable to withdraw her restless mind from the challenge of the
problems that beset her, and continued to bombard him with complaints
about the deficiencies in the Purveying Department, which indeed appeared
to have broken down completely.

To Sidney Herbert

Barrack Hospital, Scutari
21st December 1854

Dear Mr. Herbert
The brain is wanting at home in the combination of authorities between
the purchasing & shipping & sending off & landing not only here. The
"Army & Navy" is just reported with nothing but Hospital Clothing &
Bedding on board not an utensil of any kind. The head or the will is wanting
in the Admiral here.[35] Twelve days ago, in obedience to requisition from
Balaklava, stores of Arrow-root, Sago etc. were shipped on board the
"Medway" for Balaklava, where everything is deficient, with the promise
that the "Medway" was to sail next day. The "Medway" is still here & her
hold is filled with things *above* the Medical Stores. The hospital at
Balaklava is still in want.

This morning I foraged in the Purveyor's store – a cruise I make almost
daily, as the only way of getting things. No mops, – no plates, no wooden
trays (the Engineer is having these made) – no slippers, no shoe brushes, no
blacking, no knives & forks, no spoons, no scissors (for cutting the men's
hair which is literally alive, nor for the Hospital Serjeants) – no basins, no
towelling – no Chloride of Lime.

Will you send us
1000 mops (sticks can be made here)
3000 tin plates (these we *are* having made here, but they are so
  expensive that 3000 from England would not be misplaced)
500 tin dishes, deep, to hold soup or meat
2000 yds towelling (very coarse) – canvass or huckaback so that
  each ward may have its round towels marked with its name.
200 prs common large scissors – two sizes – for the purposes

above mentioned.

50 Quart bottles of Sir Wm. Burnett's Disinfecting Chloride of
Lime

The other articles mentioned above as not now in store can be had at Constantinople.

After consulting with the Medical Officers, I mean to send to Marseilles for another thousand yds towelling.

The new wards just opened by our exertions & Mr. Gordon's activity received 500 men on the 19th from the ships "Ripon" & "Golden Fleece".

They were received in the wards by Dr. McGrigor & myself & were generally in the last state of exhaustion. Orderlies were wanting – utensils were wanting – even water was wanting. The first point is the difficulty of any Medical Officer getting any man from the military Authorities for any service.

I supplied all the utensils, including knives & forks, spoons, cans, etc. etc. etc., towels etc., clearing our Quarters of these, & was also able to send on the instant Arrow Root in huge milk-pails (with two bottles of Port Wine in each) for five hundred men. The Doctors expressed themselves obliged – & the report that night was four only dead, & this morning one more. Tea & bread could not have been issued to the men till a late hour of the evening. Boiling time was over.

You may refer to what Mr. Bracebridge said of Dr. MacGrigor having founded this Hospital. We have increased proofs ever since of his capacity, energy, powers of combination & management of detail. There is reason to fear that these very qualities & the compelling rapid action in his whole department is causing intrigue against him.[36]

As he was the origin, so he is the main spring of the whole thing. We had rather lose all the heads of departments together than him (these words said advisedly)

Mr. Cumming is with us daily. The Commission is working slowly, we hope effectually.

Mr. Osborne is gone home.

My case is even stronger than before about the matter of the 46 Therapians. The two gentlemen [37] have been here yesterday, thrown all responsibility upon me, today have brought Mary Stanley, with whom I am going to begin business – I am therefore clearly to bear all the blame. I shall not the less continue to act as my discretion dictates for the good of the service *alone*. All that I said in my last letter to you I say still more strongly. Please to read it & consider that I withdraw nothing.

Believe me, dear Mr. Herbert, in great haste

ever yours

B.L. Add. Ms. 43393, f. 41 (*Cal.* B. 4. A10, 17)

The arrival with Miss Stanley's party of fifteen more nuns under the Rev. Mother Frances Bridgeman of Kinsale [38] further complicated an already difficult situation. Both Miss Nightingale and Mr Herbert had been alive to the possibility of religious difficulties and had done what they could to obviate the danger by the final provision in Miss Nightingale's formal Instructions.

The Rev. Mother Bermondsey and her nuns had received explicit orders from their bishop, Dr Grant, to place themselves under the direction of Miss Nightingale, and she never experienced the slightest difficulty or unpleasantness in her dealings with them. Mother Bermondsey, indeed, became one of her most valued helpers and their friendship continued until the reverend Mother's death. The case of the Kinsale nuns was from the outset different.[39] Their employment had been negotiated by Dr Manning, and while they were ordered to recognise the authority of Miss Nightingale in hospital matters their Superior, Mother Bridgeman, was ordered specifically to retain her autonomy in all other matters.

Had Florence Nightingale received these nuns more graciously it is just possible that she would have avoided much future friction, for Mother Bridgeman always acknowledged that she and her party had been consigned to the superintendency of Florence Nightingale in the first place, and were therefore bound to acknowledge her authority in hospital matters. But she considered herself released from this obligation when Miss Nightingale refused to accept her.

On the other hand her party came out under fundamentally different conditions of service from the first, though it is certain that Herbert never meant it to be so. Friction may well have been inevitable.

In the first place Mother Bridgeman remained under the direction of her superiors in Ireland and had constantly to refer back to them for decisions even in such matters as the disposition of nuns in the hospitals. She was ordered to keep her party together under herself, which meant that an over-large body of Roman Catholic nuns would have had to be employed in one hospital, in direct contravention of government intentions as expressed to Miss Nightingale in her Instructions. This situation was confirmed by Father Ronan, the nuns' Spiritual Adviser (another source of embarrassment to the government, which had expressly forbidden such an appointment in the negotiations with Manning). In a peremptory letter to Miss Nightingale Father Ronan ordered "That the fifteen Sisters of Mercy last arrived be placed under Mother Bridgeman, for she is their duly appointed Superior and cannot transfer her authority to any other."[40]

Furthermore, in spite of government and Florence Nightingale's insistence that all nurses were selected only from the point of view of fitness as nurses, Mother Bridgeman was insistent that the Irish Sisters came out to the military hospitals as nursing Sisters of Mercy; that they would continue to minister to the spiritual as well as to the bodily necessities of the Catholics; that she would ever openly maintain this freedom and right to instruct Catholics and would not continue in the British hospitals if prevented from so doing.[41]

As it was, Miss Nightingale was prepared to accommodate five of the nuns in the General Hospital, and hoped to disperse others to various positions. This, of course, Mother Bridgeman would not agree to. Five, including herself, did go to the General Hospital under Miss Nightingale for some months. But when the hospitals at Koulali were opened at the end of January, Mother Bridgeman took over the nursing of the General Hospital under the nominal superintendence of Miss Amy Hutton, one of Miss Stanley's Protestant ladies. Here the Irish nuns became very popular with the medical authorities for their disciplined behaviour and skilful nursing, thus belying some of Florence Nightingale's misgivings. But the seeds were sown of much future discord.

To Sidney Herbert

Barrack Hospital, Scutari
Xmas Day 1854

Dear Mr. Herbert

You have not stood by me, but I have stood by you. In this new situation, I have taken your written instructions as my guide, &, carrying them out with the best discretion which God has given me, I have endeavoured to establish – in circumstances, however perplexing & anomalous, a consistent action. Had I not done this, we should have been turned out of the Hospitals in a month, & the War Office would have borne the blame of swamping the experiment.

You shall judge for yourself such a tempest has been brewed in this little pint-pot as you could have no idea of. But I, like the ass, have put on the lion's skin, & when once I have done that, (poor me, who never affronted any one before), I can bray so loud that I shall be heard, I am afraid, as far as England.

However this is no place for lions & as for asses, we have enough.

The ἤθος [ethos, essence] of my instructions appears to me to be this.

(1) Establish no separate action from the medical men but be their lieutenant & purveyor to carry out their intentions.

(2) Control among your charge all these different sects & views so as to prevent these Hospitals from becoming a "polemical arena" – I quote your own words.

The first proposition for the utilizing of the Therapians which Miss Stanley makes is that ten of these Protestants should be appropriated as Clerical females by the Chaplains, ten of the nuns by the priests, *not as nurses* but as female ecclesiastics. With this of course I have nothing to do. It being directly at variance with my instructions, I cannot of course appropriate the Govt. money to such a purpose, Mr. Cumming's answer you will propably have by this post.

The second proposition which the Superior of the new Nuns (who is obviously come out with a *religious* view – (not to serve the sick, but to

55

found a convent, completely mistaking the purpose of our mission) makes is that the *whole* of the 15 nuns should come in *or none* – they cannot separate & they cannot separate from *her* – Why? Because it would be *"uncanonical."* As, by this word, she has brought herself against the barrier of the War Office Instructions, & as, for the good of the service, I consider two Superiors disadvantageous (our former Sup*t*. being the one whom I prefer)[42] & as, to house fifteen more nuns is impossible, I have taken the course to be mentioned hereafter.

The third element in the question is (which bears upon the *first* part of my Instructions) that the Medical Men fix positively the No. of females for the two Hospitals at fifty as a *maximum*, in which judgment I entirely concur for reasons which I shall explain hereafter.

Episode 1. The publication of the letter of one of the Sellon Sisters in the Times of the 8th Dec., her examination & mine by the Commission, which proves her letter to be partly exaggerated, partly untrue, & my determination that she should resign.[43]

Upon these premises, my course is like a proposition in Euclid. And, till I am superseded, I shall carry it out at any expense to me of odium, tho' no human being can stand for two months what I am doing now.

The Candia, the finest vessel in the service, being to sail before night on the 23rd, the day I had all those interviews, – in four hours I sent off ten of my old party, 5 nuns,[44] 2 Sellons, including the offender, & 3 nurses. For each one of these I had to stand a *blackguarding* (there is no other word in the English language to express it). Of the one from Father Michael Cuffe for the five nuns, I enclose a Mem*m*. He told me that I was like *Herod* sending the Blessed Virgin across the desert. We shall hear more of this.

(And, I assure you that, in the midst of my own overwhelming troubles, my heart bleeds for you that you, the centre of the parliamentary row, should have to attend to these miseries, – tho' you have betrayed me)

My reasons for selecting *these* nuns to go back (out of the whole number) I have writtren to Dr. Manning.

I then wrote to the Superior of the new lot to offer to fill the places with five of the new party, to work under the old superior whom we brought out with us & who is invaluable, stating that we could neither house fifteen, nor could I have two superiors – in so small a number. My belief is that we shall hear no more about what is "uncanonical." But that they will worm their way in & intrigue with the Priests afterwards – (But I must put in my proviso, viz. that the Bermondsey nuns, who came out with us, are the truest Xtians I ever met with – invaluable in their work – devoted, heart & head, to serve God & mankind – not to intrigue for their Church).

I cannot tell what will be the issue of all these questions. To send back the fifteen new nuns will be awful. To take them impossible. But, if they will not separate? — — — —

I am now going to incorporate what I can of the Sisters & Nurses – in which I must in conscience, exercise my right of selection.

I am no nearer distributing any of the party elsewhere – Balaklava has virtually fallen through. Merchant Seamen's Hospital has declined altogether. So have the Medical Men for the Convalescent Hospitals.

Here is where we are.

The Sellons are, as may be expected, furious at the dismissal of their confederate, & charge me with tyranny, who acted only under the advice, though perfectly in unison as to judgment, with the Commission. For such letters cannot be passed unnoticed. The Superior has been invited to read over the evidence & declined.

Pray confirm Father Michael Cuffe in his position here! It is the only agreeable incident I have had!

I believe it may be proved as a logical proposition that it is impossible for me to ride through all these difficulties. My Caique is upset – but I am sticking on the bottom still. But there will be a storm will brush me off – None the less shall I do what I believe to be your first will & that of Common Sense.

B.L. Add. Ms. 43393, f. 45 (*Cal.* B. 4. A11, 19).

To Sidney Herbert

Xmas Day [1854]

Dear Mr. Herbert

Three things I wish to say, after thanking you very much for your Purveying letter.

1*st* Messrs Wreford, Ward & late Reade, veterans of the Spanish War, come or came to me for a moment's solace trembling under responsibility & afraid of informality. On the last occasion, Wreford said, when I read him part of your letter to me of the 4*th* "This is the first time I have had it *in writing* that I was not to spare expence. I never knew that I might not be thrown overboard."

2*nd* The state of the troops who return here, particuarly those (about 500) who were admitted on the 19*th*, is frost-bitten, demi-nude, starved, ragged. If the troops, who work in the trenches, are not supplied with warm clothing, Napoleon's Russian Campaign will be repeated here. It is *said* that 40,000 sets of winter clothing were lost on board the "Prince". But the 18*th* is now gone up, as I am told, without warm clothing. Your dates will best tell you by what mistake the naked state of the frost bitten wretches who came in here between Dec. 19*th* & 23*rd*, originated.

3*rd* Mr. Maxwell conducted the examination of that unfortunate Sellon (at which I was present) with the utmost forbearance & courtesy. My own feeling was, – had he pressed her, to what shame & confusion of face might he not have put her? Yet the whole Sellon lot are accusing him of vile forensic habits.

We are so busy that I cannot write a letter for the Queen to see till next

The camp of the First Division, looking north towards the camp of the Second Division, the Heights of Inkerman in the distance

post. I am in the Hospitals all day & writing all night – besides all this business of the Therapians on my hands.

The things we want are

(1) Socks 1000 prs (I get them also by the hundred from Const*e*.)

(2) Flannel 10,000 yds or Flannel shirts, if you prefer it.

(3) Slippers 2000 prs. Warm shoes I would suggest for the troops. But that is not my affair as Deputy Inspector of Hospitals

(4) Drawers & Mits the Drs. suggest – you will judge

(5) Soap ad libitum – the soap here is bad

(6) Knives & forks & spoons. 3000 more besides what we asked for

(7) Cocoa Nut Matting with the long pile such as is used for mats to clean feet in Workhouses is most necessary here, where our *Sick* Corridors become by feet of Orderlies like muddy roads.

(8) Air Cushions 100 – fifty round with hole in middle — for bed sores.

But the Queen ought to give something which the man will feel as a daily extra comfort which he would not have had without her. Would some woollen material do to cut up into comforters for the neck when the man begins to get out of bed? This I think would answer the above purpose.

Or a brush & comb for each man? Or a Razor for each man?

As to the Eau de Cologne, a little gin & water would do better.

As the Queen is sending out soap, a most acceptable present, a zinc or tin basin (say 2000) & towelling, towelling, towelling would be appropriate. I am having our coarse canvass sheets cut up into round towels. The men were touched to the heart by the Queen's message. "It is a very feeling letter," they said. "She thinks of us" with tears. "Each man of us ought to have a copy which we will keep till our dying day" etc. etc. etc. I will tell many more things by next post.

12 o'clock

I have just written my ultimatum to the new R.C. Superioress. She has offered herself & five others here as a pis aller until she can receive orders from her Superiors whether to come in here with the fifteen, or in case of my refusal, withdraw altogether. I have replied, (you will remember you did so in the case of Miss Sellon) that I can receive no other Superior, that I consider them as Nurses as regards myself. As Nuns they have every protection in the Rev*d*. Mother already here & the priests.

We have not the slightest doubt that this woman not only intends to turn our house out of windows but to trample upon & disperse the ruins, when out. (They are also to have a Chaplain of their own).

Oh!! My War Office!

Mem*m*. to Purveyor's stores by "Army & Navy" – correction of last note.

She *had* 2074 lbs. Tea, Sago, Arrow Root, Soap, Tow etc. besides Bedding & Hospital clothing – which last the Deputy Purveyor stated to be all her lading. But negatively his statement was true, viz. that she did not bring out any utensil of any kind.

As to Medical Department, Mr. Menzies is ill & doing his business with less ease. Mr. Cumming is occupied with the Commission – tho', when interfering occasionally, always interfering efficiently. Mr. Cruikshanks, now Superior Officer at Barrack Hospital, come ten days since, overlooks only.

Of Dr. McGrigor, the Founder of this Hospital, as Mr. Bracebridge mentioned, I have been requested (not by McG. himself) & feel bound to make the following statement.

Dr. McGrigor began this Hospital & was the head of it when we came, 4*th* November. Dr. McIlree was then placed Junior to him in one third of it. Mr. Cruikshanks was subsequently placed Senior to him. Lastly is come Dr. Tice (from Gen*l*. Hosp*l*.) to take half of what McGrigor has left. And now it is reported that McGrigor is to be sent to inspect Smyrna, (probably a job). In this increased state of numbers, it is therefore proposed to take away the practical originator of this Hosp*l*. & he who gives it its momentum. You will say, why not interfere? My reply is, I should do harm by meddling.

I shall carry out the washing, & purveying instructions given in your last letter & am ever yours, dear Mr. Herbert

[P.S.] The reports of store & ships' arrival at Constant*e*. made from today by this mail will lead you to know what of the Articles requested has already been sent.

B.L. Add. Ms. 43393, f. 51 (*Cal.* B. 4. A10, 8).

To Sidney Herbert

Barrack Hospital, Scutari
28th December 1854

Dear Mr. Herbert

Your Orders shall be obeyed. I have got the Turkish washing-house, belonging to these Barracks ceded to me, & the Commissariat chopped straw taken out. By the time the washing machines come out, I hope to be ready to furnish every man in Hospital with a clean shirt twice a week. If by that time I am superseded, I trust the Purveyor may be induced to carry it on.

I learn that, while our men come back to us ragged, naked & starved, there is an immense quantity of warm clothing lying at Balaklava, NOT sent up to camp from difficulty of transport. The French convey all our sick for us down to Balaklava, they carried 1100 in one day. I cannot too strongly reiterate what I said before about the necessity of warm clothing being actually in use by our troops. Otherwise we shall have an Army in Hospital.

With regard to our own little minor matter of nurses etc. for minor it is in this ghastly whole, I only wish to say that every well-judging man out here concurs in the Doctors' verdict of fifty women the maximum in these two Hospitals – & I will point to the experience, 3 centuries old, of the French which allots to their General Mily. Hosp*l*. at Pera (1200 patients) only sixteen Soeurs – tho' they have a depot of Soeurs ad libitum at Galata. Bear in mind too that theirs are trained & vowed females, mine untrained & undisciplined. I will say no more on the subject. The fifteen New Nuns (in conjunction with Mary Stanley) are leading me the devil of a life, trying to get in "vi et armis", & will upset the coach, there is little doubt of that.

Farewell – I wait your orders
ever yours

I will write Purveying business more fully by next post.

B.L. Add. Ms. 43393, f. 57 (*Cal*. B. 4. A11, 20)

Towards the end of December the crisis in the hospitals was taking on a new dimension as the wretched victims of the Crimean winter began flooding the Scutari hospitals by the boatload. To Florence Nightingale the problems posed by the nurses paled into insignificance beside those of how to provide for this new situation in the face of the total breakdown of the Purveying Department.

To Sidney Herbert

Barrack Hospital, Scutari
4th January 1855

Dear Mr. Herbert

I enclose copies of three curious historical documents, Mémoires pour servir to the history of the largest hospital in the world. There are in this Hospital 2500 men & odd – in the Gen*l*. Hosp*l*. 1122 men – in the Sultan's Serail were today lodged 250 more – chiefly Convalescents from hence, but also from the "Queen of the South", just arrived from Balaklava. There were in the Bosphorus yesterday, arriving from Balaklava, 1200 sick. Of these we have landed say 300 (There is in the Hospital matériel for making about 800 men tolerably comfortable) & in the Gen*l*. Hosp*l*. say 500. Bear in mind that these new cases are all dysenteric & low fever.

In this emergency I went to the Purveyor's stores with the enclosed questions – which have been reiterated nearly every day for the last fortnight – & I received the next day the following note,
"Dear Miss Nightingale

I herewith enclose the requisitions for Stores you gave me to enquire about yesterday. I have marked opposite to each article whether they are in store or not."

This letter was signed by an excellent active 1st C*l*. Staff Surg*n*. Dr. O'Flaherty, at the Gen*l*. Hosp*l*., but who would not like to have it known by that old smoke-dried Dr. Andrew Smith, who is the God of the Officials here, that he had been "interfering."

The next morng. I went to the Purveyor, shewed him the negatives, in which he acquiesced, – asked him, "Are you expecting any of these things from England?" No. "Are you taking means to get any from Stamboul?" No. "Are they to be had at Stamboul?" – If they are, I don't know how to get them. (N.B. *I* have got all these things at Stamboul).

I send you a copy of one of the hundred requisitions which come in to me every day – another today was for 1½ loaves of bread – another for carrots for poultices, which the Purveyor said he could not get – another for a curtain 16 ft. by 12 ft. high, a stove & charcoal.

There is a far greater question to be agitated before the country than that of these eighty-four miserable women – eighty-five including me. This is whether the system or no-system which is found adequate in time of peace but wholly inadequate to meet the exigencies of a time of war is to be left as it is, – *or* patched up temporarily, as you give a beggar halfpence, – *or* made equal to the wants, not diminishing but increasing, of a time of awful pressure. There will be three things to be considered for this last alternative (1) the purveying of Hospitals of this enormous magnitude with all Hospital matériel which includes 1*st* Hospital clothing & bedding 2*nd* Cooking including Extra Diets 3*rd* washing (2) organizing a proper corps of Orderlies (3) rigging out each man when he goes out of Hospital by means of the Quarter Master or his substitute, the Divisional Serjeant of his Regiment, so that he should not carry away as he does now, all his Hospital gear, by which my work of purveying is continually recurring.

Each one of these points would require a pamphlet. Will you let me write my notes & experiences to you, never mind whether I am superseded or not? You need not take the suggestions of poor me, but consult somebody, (*not* an official *hoping for promotion*) who undestands the question.

With regard to the minor question of the women, the Army Medical Board has sent out the dressers to supersede the nurses – the W. Office does not care whether its one remedy neutralizes the other, but tries both to humour the country. Had I *received* the eighty-four, there is no question that the Medical Men would have made it an excuse to turn the whole out in a week. And Cumming, for which we owe him eternal thanks, really did his best to favor the females when he fixed their No. at fifty.

The Therapians, after expressly setting me aside (vide official letter from Meyer) by addressing themselves to Cumming & not to me, & getting a Receipt from him, are throwing the whole responsibility upon me of refusing them & settling them (or not settling them) elsewhere & Mr. Percy has sneaked home like a commander who has set so many Robinson Crusoes on a desert island & said, "Now you will shift very well for yourselves."

The Roman Catholic question remains unsettled. *Brickbat,* the Rev*d.* Mother of Kinsale, refusing to let five of her nuns come here without her to be under our Rev*d*. Mother thereby shewing that she has some second view besides nursing – & I refusing to let our little Society become a hotbed of R. C. intriguettes – Of course we shall have a R. C. storm – But *our* Rev*d*. Mother, heart & hand with us, is doing her best to stop it.

Eno' of this subject, of which, amid these realities of life & death, I am thoro'ly sick, & you too.

I am desired to mention by the Medical Men that the vacancy made last night by poor old Ward's death of Cholera (he was a Purveyor, & his widow died tonight, also of Cholera) we nursed them both – might very properly be filled by a very active young man of the name of *Rogers* who was, at the beginning of this Hospital, sole Purveyor to it – & is now here.

I am afraid to get back *today* to my immense first question how this Hosp*l*. is to be purveyed – how, instead of living from hand to mouth, – we pouring in stores which are to be renewed again every 4 or 5 weeks, the men having left with all the stores on their backs – we ought to know (1) exactly how many beds there are in Hospital, purveyed ready for use (2) how many vacant, (3) how many patients to come in, – each ward ought to have its own complement of shirts, socks, bedding, utensils etc. etc. etc. – the new sick succeeding to the old sick's things – instead of keeping a Caravanserai, as we do – how the kitchen ought to be inspected – the washing d*o*. clean shirts twice a week – instead of my cooking all the Extra Diets, getting all the vegetables thought necessary for scurvy – in fact I am a kind of General Dealer – in socks, shirts, knives & forks, wooden spoons, tin baths, tables & forms, cabbage & carrots, operating tables, towels & soap, *small tooth combs,* Precipitate for destroying lice, scissors, bedpans & stump pillows.

There is a new Medical Head [45] today, a new Commandant [46] expected next week, & a new Admiral, [47] we hope, on Saturday. And to help us out of all this scrape you send us – a Dragoman for the Command*t*. who I hope will turn him over to me to be my Purveyor in vegetables & lemon juice, the two desiderata of the Doctors at this moment.

I will send you a picture of my Caravanserai, into which beasts come in & out. Indeed the vermin might, if they had but "unity of purpose", carry off the four miles of beds on their backs, & march with them into the War Office, Horse Guards. This last catastrophe is occasioned by the sick from the ships bringing in their dirty blankets with them, instead of leaving all at the gate, & finding the clean Hosp*l*. bed prepared for them.

Dr. Forrest, the new Medical Head, has called, but I shall not probably see him before post time, to know whether he confirms the dictum of Menzies.

Believe me, dear Mr. Herbert, ever yours

B.L. Add. Ms. 43393, f. 60 (*Cal.* B. 4. A12, 23)

Following this letter are four sheets, ff. 71–4, comprising two invoices in

Miss Nightingale's own hand, and two typed copies of invoices, all confirming the sorry state of the Purveyor's store. Items lacking included bolsters, slippers, knives & forks, spoons, shirts, socks, drawers, plates, tin drinking cups, pails for tea. The only things that appeared to be in store were "a few" tea and coffee pots, "some" bedpans, "plenty" of close stools but frames wanting, and plenty of urine pots!

Notes

1   P.R.O. WO 25/264.

2   Letters of Assistant Surgeon D. Greig, 26th October 1854, R.A.M.C. Historical Museum, Aldershot.

3   At Abydos.

4   Menzies to Hall, 8th December. 1854, S. M. Mitra, *The Life and Letters of Sir John Hall, M.D., K.C.B., F.R.C.S.*, London, 1911, p. 338; Dr Spence, Hospitals Commissioner, also wrote to Herbert on 5th November, "Just returned from Scutari, perfectly delighted to find things so well managed." (Stanmore, I, 346.) And C. H. Bracebridge, who was later to cause a great deal of trouble with his exaggerated account in *The Times,* 16th October 1855, at the time wrote to Herbert, 8th November 1854, ". . . The place is clean and airy; few bad smells." (Stanmore, I, p.345.)

5   Stanmore, I, pp. 334–5.

6   Sidney Godolphin Osborne, *Scutari and its Hospitals*, London, 1855.

7   S. Lane Poole, *The Life of . . . Viscount Stratford de Redcliffe,* London, 1888, II, p. 374.

8   Mary Stanley to Parthe Nightingale, 25th January 1855, Nightingale Papers, Claydon.

9   Dr (Sir) William Bowman (1816–92) ophthalmologist; on staff of King's College Hospital. Bowman had been associated in 1844 with the foundation of St John's House Institution for training nurses, from which Florence Nightingale had six nurses. F.N. nominated him to the Council of the Nightingale Fund. (For her relationship with Bowman see Sir Zachary Cope, *Florence Nightingale and the Doctors*, London, 1958.)

10   Mrs Rebecca Lawfield, one of the six St John's House nurses. In spite of this unpromising beginning, Mrs Lawfield became one of F.N.'s most valued assistants and remained in the East to the end.

11   The party included eight Sisters from the Sisterhood of the Holy Cross, set up in 1845, and the Society of the Most Holy Trinity, founded by Miss Priscilla Lydia Sellon in 1848, who together were generally known as Sellonites. The Sisters had gained their nursing experience mainly in the cholera epidemics of 1848, 1849 and 1853. (Anne Summers, "Ladies and nurses in the Crimean War," *History Workshop*, No. 16, pp. 33–5.)

12   Dr Henry Bence Jones (1813–73), M.D., F.R.C.P., frequently called Ben Johnson by F.N. (See Cope, *F.N. and the Doctors.*)

13   The Rev. J. E. Sabin later came under F.N.'s displeasure and incurred the censure of Lord Panmure for his religious intolerance.

14   Mrs Roberts, an experienced nurse from St Thomas's Hospital, nursed F.N.

through her illness in the Crimea, and remained in the East to the end. In her final "Report on Nurses and Ladies returning, June 26/56" F.N. wrote of her, "Having been 23 years 'Sister' in St. Thomas's Hospital, her qualifications as a *Nurse* were, of course, of an infinitely superior character to any others of those with me. She is indeed a Surgical Nurse of the first order – of that race which is now almost extinct, since, in Civil Hospitals, dressers now do almost all that the 'Sisters' used to do . . . Her total superiority to all the vices of a Hospital Nurse – her faithfulness to the work – her disinterested love of duty & vigilant care of her Patients, her power of work, equal to that of *ten* Nurses, have made her one of the most important persons of the expedition." (B.L. Add. Ms. 43402, f. 23.) Mrs Roberts was paid £120 per annum; the other nurses were paid between 10*s*. and 18*s*. a week, i.e. less than £50 per annum.

15   Mrs Elizabeth Drake, one of the St John's House nurses. Although F.N. thought highly of her, she was not at all happy under F.N.'s discipline and wrote home to the Superintendent of St John's to say so. "We could not say that we was happy or comfortable . . . We are not allowed to go in the wards without one of the Lady Nuns. We must not speak one word of comfort to a poor dying man or reed to him. We are prevented from doing what our hearts prompt us to do. We feel we are not so useful as we expected to be. We are kept back . . . We never get a kind word. I do most heartily wish we did not come out without some one with us from home." (4th December 1854, G.L.R.O. HI/ST/NC.3/SU 13.) Mrs Drake died at Balaclava in August 1855.

16   B.L. Add. Ms. 43393, f. 5.

17   F.N.'s evidence before the Hospitals Commission, given on 20th February 1855: "I gave notice to the staff surgeons, that there was such an establishment, if they chose to have their patients' shirts washed. I was told by the non-commissioned officers, that the men had been unwilling to give up their shirts to be washed either by the contractor, or by the soldiers' wives, because . . . they either did not get back any shirt at all, or they got a bad one in place of a good one. I also found, that the washing of the soldiers' wives was quite insufficient. They washed in a tub, generally in cold water; and it is necessary that shirts in hospital should be boiled, because it is impossible to get out, otherwise, the animal matter. This is particularly detrimental, when A. gets B.'s shirt." M. Wreford to A. Smith, 12th February 1855: ". . . I know nothing officially of the subsidiary washing establishment to which you allude, the necessity for which has never been made apparent to me." (*Report upon the State of the Hospitals of the British Army in the Crimea and Scutari,* London, 1855. *Parliamentary Papers,* 1854–55, **33.**)

18   Throughout her life F.N. maintained an ambivalent attitude to infection. She resolutely denied the possibility of the existence of "germs." But her actions were always inconsistent with her articulated theory. In pre-Listerian days she insisted on the importance of absolute cleanliness. In this instance she appeared to be perfectly aware that infection might be transmitted by the use of one dirty sponge among many. Likewise, in the matter of the inadequately washed shirts, she was able to say that unboiled "animal matter" might be "detrimental." Such instances of inconsistency were to be repeated many times during her life. She warmly embraced Lister's antiseptic techniques, and later the aseptic theories.

19   The steamship *Prince* was wrecked in the hurricane which devastated the Crimea on 14th November. Medical comforts were not the only things that went

down with her: winter overcoats and boots for the whole army were also lost.

20 Dr Alexander Cumming (*c.* 1790–1858) one of the three-man commission appointed to enquire into the state of the hospitals (see note 21) had come out to Scutari with F.N. According to custom he should have superseded Menzies, P.M.O. at Scutari, to whom Cumming was senior. But his appointment as commissioner made him independent of the regular organisation. Nevertheless his appointment caused difficulty. Menzies alleged to the Roebuck Committee that "during a portion of this time he was placed in an anomalous position, by the arrival, on 4 November of Dr. Cumming, his superior officer, who had been sent from England as member of the Commission of Enquiry, and to supersede him in his office when the inquiry of that Commission had been brought to a close." (*Fifth Report of Select Committee on the Army before Sebastopol. Parliamentary Papers, 1854–55, 43,* p. 20.)

21 The Commission of Enquiry appointed to report on the state of the hospitals . . . in the Crimea and Scutari, by Instructions dated 23rd October 1854, consisted of Dr Alexander Cumming, Dr Thomas Spence and P. Benson Maxwell, barrister. Dr Spence was lost with the *Prince*. He was replaced as junior commissioner by Dr P. Sinclair Laing.

22 Peter Benson Maxwell (1817–93), barrister, was third member of the Hospitals Commission. He was knighted in 1856.

23 Despite her protestations, F.N.'s worst fears were justified. Sidney Herbert's private letter appealing to her to go out to the hospitals in the East had been published in the *Daily News*, 28th October 1854 and *Morning Chronicle*, 30th October 1854, p. 3, col. f. It was used to stir up the very furore of religious bickering that Herbert and F.N. had both worked to avoid. (Cook, I, pp. 154, 245.)

24 Dr Alexander McGrigor, or McGregor (1810–55) was P.M.O. at the Barrack Hospital under Menzies when F.N. arrived. He seems, almost alone of the medical staff, to have welcomed Miss Nightingale and her nurses, and to have made the fullest use of them. Throughout the winter and spring he laboured to introduce essential reforms, and F.N. had him promoted Deputy Inspector General over the heads of other longer-serving officers, provoking much jealousy. He died in autumn 1855 of cholera. See also Cope, *F.N. and the Doctors*.

25 When Mrs Stanley heard about this letter she wrote gleefully to Parthe, "One thing will make you laugh – wh. is a relief. F. writes as you know advising the recall of the St. John's nurses. In the one to Miss Jones she described the conduct of the sisters or whatever they are by their being Flibberty-gibbet, here there & everywhere – thought I to myself at the time, what will Miss Jones make of that? – accordingly I heard the other day that she had consulted Lady Alderson' who Flibberty-gibbet could be, she had never heard of such a person.' I send this to Mary, saying if Florence had a smile left in her it would call it out." (Nightingale papers, Claydon.)

26 Mary Jones to F.N., 22nd December 1854, G.L.R.O. HI/ST/NC.3/SU 17.

27 Elizabeth Woodward to Miss Jones, 3rd January 1855, G.L.R.O. HI/ST/ NC.3/SU 17.

28 The initiative for the establishment of the little Lying-in Hospital, and for other measures for the care of the soldiers' wives, seems to have come from Mr Bracebridge, who left a lengthy manuscript memorandum describing the conditions of these unfortunate women, and recommending various measures that the government ought to undertake for their welfare. (Bracebridge papers, R.A.M.C. Historical Museum, Aldershot; also incorporated in *Statements exhibiting the Voluntary*

Contributions received by Miss Nightingale for the use of the British War Hospitals in the East, London, 1857.) F.N. herself often seemed to have little patience with them, calling them the Allobroges, after the wild women who accompanied the ancient Gauls to war. But she did enlist the aid of Lady Alicia Blackwood to organise the women to help with washing and mending. Lady Alicia left an account of this work in *A Narrative of Personal Experiences & Impressions . . . on the Bosphorus throughout the Crimean War,* London, 1881. F.N. also included the wives and children in her plans for reform after the war. (*Notes on Matters affecting the Health and Hospital Administration of the British Army. . . ,* London, 1858.)

29   Augustus Stafford (1811–57), M.P. acting as commissioner for the *Times* fund, conducted a private investigation into the state of the hospitals at Scutari and in the Crimea. He drew on this experience to describe what he had seen to the House of Commons on 29th January 1855 during the debate on Roebuck's motion which led to the resignation of Aberdeen's government. His harrowing description of the plight of the sick and wounded confirmed those of other observers, including F.N.'s (Hansard, *Parliamentary Debates,* 3rd series, vol. 136.)

30   "One room for ten R.C. sisters," Bracebridge to Herbert, 8th November 1854. Mother Bridgeman recorded her impressions in her diary, on which Evelyn Bolster has based her account of *The Sisters of Mercy in the Crimean War,* Cork, 1964.

31   These letters from Mary Stanley and her mother to Parthe are among the Nightingale papers, Claydon; copies in the Wellcome Institute for the History of Medicine.

32   C. Stanley to Parthe, 2nd December 1854, Nightingale papers, Claydon.

33   Sidney Herbert to editor, *Morning Chronicle,* 24th October 1854, p. 4, col. a, p. 28 above.

34   Writing to *The Times* on 18th January 1855, "Our own correspondent" from Scutari: "When the batch of sisters and nurses brought out by Miss Stanley arrived here very considerable difficulty was experienced by Miss Nightingale in turning the services of even a portion of them to useful account. Having proved herself a vigorous reformer of hospital misrule, she was at that moment contending against the tacit opposition of nearly all the principal medical officers; her nurses were sparingly resorted to even in the Barrack Hospital, and in the General Hospital, Dr. Menzies' headquarters, she held a very insecure footing." *Times,* 1st February 1855, p. 10, col. b.

35   Lord Raglan to Lord Stratford, 21st November 1854: "As regards Admiral Boxer I am powerless. No human power can make him a man of arrangement. He may be, and I believe is, a good officer afloat, and he is well intentioned; but he has shewn no aptitude for the duties with which he is at present charged." (Lane Poole, *Life of . . . Viscount Stratford de Redcliffe,* p. 382.)

36   F.N.'s fear that McGrigor was the victim of "intrigue" was well founded. Hall evidently complained to Andrew Smith about him, for on 29th October 1854 Smith wrote to Hall, "If McGrigor does not improve let him be sent home. I will find the best man I can to replace him." (Hall Papers, box 11, R.A.M.C. Historical Museum, Aldershot.)

37   Dr John Meyer and the Hon. Josceline Percy, who accompanied Miss Stanley's party. Dr Meyer remained in the East as superintendent of the civil hospital at Smyrna. Percy, who undertook the financial affairs of Miss Stanley's party, returned home within a few weeks.

38 The Rev. Mother Mary Frances Bridgeman, sometimes referred to as "Mrs" Bridgeman, or the Rev. Brickbat, came out with Mary Stanley as the Superior of a party of fifteen nuns collected from convents throughout Ireland, Liverpool and Chelsea. The names and origins of the individual nuns of the party are given by Sir Shane Leslie, "Forgotten passages in the life of Florence Nightingale", *Dublin Review*, October 1917, pp. 179–98.

39 The Roman Catholic point of view in the ensuing troubles has been extensively aired by Evelyn Bolster, *The Sisters of Mercy in the Crimean War*.

40 Bolster, p. 113.

41 Bolster, p. 112.

42 Georgina Moore, Rev. Mother Bermondsey.

43 Apart from the fact that Sister Elizabeth's letter, which she had clearly not intended for publication, was exaggerated and partly untrue, her evidence before the commission made it clear why F.N. was anxious to be rid of her. She asserted that the wards she was assigned to contained the worst cases of diarrhoea, dysentery, fever and diseases of the chest. She was never able to give as much of the restoratives ordered by Dr McGrigor as she wanted. She claimed to have had six years' experience of nursing, especially in the cholera epidemic of 1849 in Plymouth. (*Report upon the State of the Hospitals . . . in the Crimea and Scutari*, 1855, pp. 329–30.) In fact Sister Elizabeth, like the St John's House Sisters, was too independent and resented F.N.'s draconian regime. It was a fault common especially in those women who had had a little "training" and a little experience.

44 The five nuns sent home had come from an orphanage in Norwood. They had had no experience of nursing and ought never to have been sent out, but the bishop, Dr Grant, was anxious that the Roman Catholics should be seen to be useful in that sphere, in an effort to counteract some of the current religious bigotry against them.

45 Dr John Forrest (1804–65) was appointed P.M.O. Scutari in place of Dr Menzies, but he lasted only a few weeks before being invalided home, to be succeeded for a few days by Dr Robert Lawson, who gave way to Dr Cumming.

46 Brigadier General Lord William Paulet (1804–93) was appointed to the command "on the Bosphorus, at Gallipoli, & the Dardanelles" by Lord Raglan in succession to Major Sillery, who had neither the rank nor the authority for the position he held.

47 Admiral Grey.

3
To use and be used

Just as Florence Nightingale had been willing to set aside her own maturing plans in October 1854 to respond to the challenge of Scutari, so three months later she again prepared to change course. She reacted instinctively to the circumstances of the moment. By January 1855 she perceived a new and "far greater question" than the settling of disaffected women. There were others to do that. But there was apparently no one to undertake the essential and most urgent task of reforming the administration of the hospitals.

Many now recognised the need. Lord Stratford was but one representative voice when he wrote to Lord Raglan on 14th December:

It is really time that some radical cure should be applied to the tendency which appears from some cause or other to exist towards getting things in a mess or deadlock. I have been slow to admit much of what now presses irresistibly on my conviction as to the mischief arising from want of unity, foresight, and proper feeling – I grieve to say it – in some quarters where no such deficiency ought to be.[1]

But while many were now recognising the truth, few were able or willing to offer a solution; even fewer had the capacity to carry through radical reform.

The three main sources of Florence Nightingale's power were, first, her authority from the government, explicitly conferred by Sidney Herbert as essential "in a service where official rank carries so much weight"; to this was added the immense weight of personal popularity which had grown up since her fame had been broadcast in the popular press.[2] And now to these was added a third. Those men who perceived the need for reform, were willing to attempt it, but were limited by their own lack of influence, turned to her as their mouthpiece and executor. She became the focal point of a powerful force for reform. She never hesitated either to use anyone who could further the attainment of a desired end, or to let herself be used.[3]

In a series of long, detailed and often repetitious private letters to Sidney Herbert, written over the next two months when the emergency in the hospitals was at its height, Florence Nightingale not only analysed the causes of the present disaster but formulated and developed a comprehensive scheme for administering the hospitals, for purveying, feeding, clothing the inmates, for raising and training an efficient corps of hospital orderlies, and for improving the training and standing of the medical officers. The repetitions serve to illustrate the development and expansion of her ideas – and underline the spontaneity of her responses.

The government, first in the person of Sidney Herbert, then, following him, Lord Panmure, made valiant attempts to carry out many of the suggested reforms during the early months of 1855, but their efforts were directed to patching up the existing system, and fell far short of the root-and-branch reform which Miss Nightingale was coming to see as essential. This perception led to her determination to devote her life to ensuring the reformation of the entire system of army hospital administration and general welfare after the end of the war. A study of the contents of the report of the Royal Commission on the Sanitary Condition of the Army, published in 1858, shows how closely the proposals contained in it correspond with the subjects covered in these letters.

To Sidney Herbert
Private
Barrack Hospital, Scutari
8th January 1855

Dear Mr. Herbert,

As the larger proportion of the Army (in which we are told that there are not two thousand sound men) is coming into Hospital – as there are therefore thousands of lives at stake – as, in a service where the future of the official servants is dependent upon the personal interest of one man, these cannot be expected to peril that future by getting themselves shelved as innovators, I feel that this is no time for compliments or false shame – & that you will never hear the whole truth, troublesome as it is, except from one independent of promotion.

I will just add that this letter I have been asked to write by the best men here. It is no result of an indefinite feeling of feminine compassion. But it is the well weighed conclusion of men of experience here, who see no provision made for the horrible emergency at this moment standing over us, yet who, if they represented it themselves, would obtain nothing but their own ruin.

I *beseech* you to keep this letter to yourself, while making the enquiries to which it may lead you.

The Commission has done nothing [4] – probably its powers were limited to enquiry – Cumming has done nothing. Lord Wm. Paulet has done nothing.

Lord Stratford, absorbed in politics, does not know the circumstances. [5] Lord Wm. Paulet knows them, but partially. Menzies knows them & will not tell them. Wreford knows them & is stupified. The Medical Officers, if they were to betray them, would have it "reported personally & professionally to their disadvantage."

Lord Wm. Paulet, & Dr. Forrest the new Medical Head, I see, are *desperate*.

As your official servant, you will say that I ought to have reported these things before. But I did not wish to be made a spy. I thought it better if the remedy could be brought quietly – & I thought the Commission was to bring it. But matters are worse than they were two months ago & will be worse two months hence than they are now.

The Medical Men are pulled up by the Senior Med*l*. Authorities for receiving ward-furniture & food from & being purveyed by *me* – & therefore, like naughty children, pretend to ignore that their Requisitions go in to me instead of to the Purveyor & leave me to be rebuked for over-facility.[6]

I subjoin (A) a rough estimate of what has been given out by me during *one* month – *the whole at the "requisitions" of the Medical Men* all of which I have by me (merely in order to substantiate the facts of the destitution of these Hospitals). Since the 17*th* December, we have received 3400 sick, & I have made no sum total as yet of what has been done for these new-comers by us – excepting for one Corridor which I enclose (B)

I then   The Purveying is *nil* – that is the whole truth – beyond bedding, bread, meat, cold water, fuel. Beyond the boiling en masse in the great coppers of Gen*l*. kitchen, the meat is not cooked, the water is not boiled except what is done in my subsidiary kitchens. My schedule will shew what I have purveyed. I have refused to go on purveying for the third Hospital, the Sultan's Serail – the demands upon me there having been begun with twelve hundred articles, including shirts, the first night of our occupying it. I refer you to a List of what was *not* in store & to a copy of one requisition upon me – sent last letter.

II The extraordinary circumstance of a whole army having been ordered to abandon its kits, as was done when we landed our men before Alma, has been overlooked entirely in all our system. The fact is that I am now clothing the British Army. The sick were re-embarked at Balaclava for these Hospitals, without resuming their kits, also half-naked besides. And when discharged from here, they carry off, small blame to them! even my knives & forks – shirts, of course, & Hospital clothing also. The men who were sent to Abydos as Convalescents, were sent *in their Hospital dresses,* or they must have gone naked. The consequence is that not one single Hospital dress is now left in Store – & I have substituted Turkish dressing gowns from Stamboul.* To purvey this Hospital is like pouring water into a sieve

*3 bales in the passage are marked Hospital Gowns, but have not yet been "*sat upon.*"[7]

– & will be, till Regimental stores have been sent out from England enough to clothe the naked & re-fill the kit.

I have requisitions for *Uniform trowsers,* for each & all of the articles of a kit sent in to me.

We have not yet heard of boots being sent out – the men come into Hospital half shod.

In a time of such calamity, unparalleled in the history, I believe, of calamity, I have a little compassion left even for the wretched Purveyor, swamped amid demands he never expected.

But I have no compassion for the men who would rather see hundreds of lives lost than waive one scruple of the official conscience.

III The Hospital & Army stores come out in the same vessels – & up go our stores to Balaklava & down they never come again – or have not yet.

IV The total inefficiency of the Hospital Orderly System as now is.[8] The French have a permanent system of Orderlies, trained for the purpose, who do not re-enter the ranks. It is too late for us to organize this. But if the Convalescents, being good Orderlies, were not sent away to the Krimea as soon as they have learnt their work – if the Commander-in-Chief would call upon the Commanding Officer of each Regiment to select ten men from each as Hospital Orderlies to form a depot here (not young soldiers but men of good character) this would give some hope of organizing an efficient corps. Above all, that the class of Ward Masters I shall mention should be sent out from England.

We require

(I) An effective staff of Purveyors out from England – but, beyond this, (II) *a head* – some *one* with *authority* to mash up the departments into uniform & rapid action. He may as well stay at home unless he have power to modify the arrangements of departments, made expressly by Sir C. Trevelyan[9] with Mr. Wreford before he came away in May.

III we want Medical Officers

IV three Deputy Inspectors-General, (whereas we have only one)

viz. one for Barrack Hospital, hulk & Turkish Ship — one for General Hospital, Sultan's Serail & Koulalee, if we send sick there — one for Smyrna[10]

N.B. Smyrna must not be purveyed or Medical–Officered from here – or we shall be swamped at once.

It is obvious from what has been said in former lettes *who,* if there are two D[eput]y Insp[ector] Gen[era]ls made to these Hospitals, should be made Dy., Inspr. Genl. of this Barrack Hospl., past & present efficiency being considered.

V We want

Discharged Non-Commissioned Officers – not past the meridian of life – not the Ambulance Corps who all died of delirium tremens or Cholera – but the class of men employed as Ward-Masters of Military Prisons, or as

Barrack Serjeants – or Hospital Serjeants of the Guards who can be highly recommended. We want these men as Ward-Masters & Assistant Ward Masters, as Stewards. They must be under the orders of the Senior Medical Officer, removable by him, – they must be well paid so as to make it worth their while, say 5/- per day, 1st Class – 2/6 per day 2nd Class – for they must be superior men, not the rabble we have now. N.B. There are three Ward Masters to each Division of this Hospital – of which there are three containing 800 & odd sick in each.

The book of Hospital regulations, admirable in time of peace, contains nothing for a time of war, much less a time of war like this, unexampled for calamity.

The Hospital Serjeants are, of course, up in the Krimea with their Regiments, – & we have nothing but such raw Corporals & Serjeants as can be spared, new to their work to place in charge of the Divisions & Wards. And these Lord Raglan complains of our keeping.

We must have Hospital Serjeants, if there is to be the remotest hope of efficiency among the Orderlies here.

IV   The Orderlies ought to be well-paid – well fed – well housed. They are now over-worked, ill fed & under paid. The sickness & mortality among them is extraordinary – ten took sick in one Divison tonight. They have only 4d a day as Orderlies additional to their pay.

If the Patriotic Fund would give them 1/- per day additional, – query would not such money be much better employed than among the widows, some of which ladies marry within 6 weeks of their husbands' deaths?

I reserve my other suggestions to next page – & also all about the Commissariat & Purveying jealousies till next letter, barring this that we want a strong hand to mingle the Commissary & Purveyor departments, where absurdly disunited.

I had written a plan for the systematic organization of these Hospitals upon a principle of centralization – under which the component parts might be worked in unison. But, on re-consideration, deeming so great a change impracticable during the present heavy pressure of calamities here, I refrain from forwarding it, & substitute a sketch of a plan, by which great improvement might be made from within, without abandoning the forms under which the service is carried on –

I   That the Purveyor should be – *not* a shop-keeper dealing in articles for requisitions instead of for money but a paterfamilias who owns the Hospital furniture for the time being in the name of the Queen – that he should provide these Hospitals at once with the number of beds which they will contain (say 2500 Barrack Hospital)
            1000 General Hospital)
& with the amount of bedding, linen, Hospital clothing, utensils etc. etc. necessary for each bed.
E.g. let each bed have

3 shirts (1 on, 1 at wash & 1 for an emergency)
5 sheets (2 on, 2 at the wash & 1 for an emergency)
2 towels
2 prs. socks
1 pr. slippers
2 night caps
2 neck-handkerchiefs
1 Hospital suit
1 knife, fork, spoon
4 tin vessels of different sizes to hold the drink
                                         medicine
                                           soup
                                           wine
1 tin plate
1 wooden tray 18 inch by 12 to hang up behind the bed
1 urine pot
    etc. etc.
Let each ward have
4 tin pails for tea
2 wooden buckets
4 zinc wash hand basins
1 soup ladle
2 round towels
Coarse cloths for cleaning & rubbing utensils
Aprons for the Orderlies

That the non-commissioned Officer in charge of the wards should be made responsible for the linen – every evening giving up that which was dirty to the person appointed by the Purveyor, & receiving every morning sufficient clean linen to replace what had been used the day before.

That what the Patients break or spoil be stopped out of their pay – a Memorandum being sent to the Divisional Pay-Serjeant to that effect.

That a printed form should be filled up by the Ward-Masters of each Division each day, containing besides the usual entries

No. of Ward	Names of Orderlies	Names of Orderlies for the Day	Patients admitted	Patients Discharged or Died	Vacant Beds

so that every day the Medical Officers should know how many vacant beds they have at their disposal.

II That the patient cease to be a soldier & become a patient from the moment he cross the Hospital doors.

that he leaves his clothes, blanket & kit behind in a store-room for the purpose – whence it is taken away to the Pack-store an inventory being given him of such Articles – & of any money etc. which he may also leave if he choose –

that, unless in exceptional or moribund cases, he have a warm bath after which he has a clean shirt & Hospital suit given him & goes up to his bed or is carried upon a stretcher with *clean* blankets.

That, when the Patient leaves the Hospital, he leaves every article used in the Hospital behind & becomes a soldier again.

That, for the purpose, if from losing his kit or other cause, he came in without sufficient clothing or baggage, there should be depots for each Regiment – & stores sent out from England – & that the Quarter Master or Divisional Serjeant of the Regiment should provide each man with the necessary kit & clothing – such articles to be stopped out of his pay as are usually accounted against him. N.B. when a man has abandoned his kit by order of his Commanding Officer, the replacing such kit is not to be placed to his charge – but made against the Public.

III That the Orderlies should have an Orderly's ward-room in each Division, where they sleep – one Orderly for each ward being on duty for the day & one for the night – the Orderlies taking it in rotation.

that no orderly should eat or sleep in the wards.

that the Orderlies of each Division should have a mess-table, a kitchen & an orderly to cook.

that the Orderlies *on duty* have their meals together half an hour before the other Orderlies, who then leave the wards for their meals –

that the Orderlies have each a pint of porter per day

that Orderlies be appointed by the Purveyor (with Arabas) to supply as often as is required coal, charcoal, wood & water the Purveyor taking receipts from the cooks.

IV That the personal washing, whether it be done by contract or by the servants of the Hospital, be done according to a given principle, with machines & in the same place.

that the washing (1) of bedding (2) of personal linen (3) of surgical appendages, such as bandages etc. & of cleaning cloths be done in three different places – the former by a contractor.

V that the cooking be done not by drunken soldiers but by cooks – that the kitchens be multiplied or added to *& the cooked food inspected daily*. It is inspected now, but not really.

VI That the Ward Masters should report to the Purveyor any destruction or wearing out of ward-furniture with a view of having such article replaced.

that the Purveyor should appoint a sub-purveyor to investigate any requisition from the ward masters which appears inordinate or suspicious.

VII That the Inspector General should decide the model & number of each Hospital piece of furniture for each ward, sub division or Corridor. And inventories should be hung up in each Ward of the No. to be found there.

The Inspector General having determined the amount of utensils he thinks proper for the whole Hospital – & the proportional quantity for each ward – and inventories being made of that which exists in each ward – the deficit gives the total of stores to be procured from England or this country.

It appears that the above would relieve both the Purveyor & the Divisional Staff Surgeons – & leave each to the discharge of his more legitimate & important duties, while the checks & counter checks would be sufficient.

> Believe me, dear Mr. Herbert
> ever yours

P.S. I would put the Orderlies in a kind of uniform, red flannel shirts, aprons of brown strong coarse stuff & slippers. You must send out these things from England.

There has been some attempt at organization made with regard to the Transports to & fro Balaklava. You will be pleased to know that *Floating Hospitals* (four) have been arranged, which are appointed each with its Surgeon & Assistant Surgeon – *not to be dismantled* to bring our sick from Balaclava. This will work well. McGrigor is appointed the Inspector.

I re-open this letter to acknowledge yours of Xmas Eve just received – I deeply feel the kindness of it. I will act up to its directions & report to you a fuller answer on Thursday.

A List of articles suppled by F.N. on the requisitions of the Medical Officers to the Gen*l*. & B*k*. Hospitals during November & part of December.

Flannel shirts	2274
Cotton "	3216
Socks	1074
Drawers	472
Nightcaps	
Slippers	
Plates	In proportion
Tin cups	
Knives, forks & spoons	250
Wooden trays	86
Tables	24
Forms	48
Clocks	6
Operating Tables	2

For all other Articles, see proportion in (B)

B List of Articles supplied by F.N. on the requisitions of the Medical

Officers for Corridor D & Wards containing 519 sick between 19*th* Dec. (when they came in) & 31*st* Dec. [*This list shows similar but more comprehensive requirements for corridor D.*]

B.L. Add. Ms. 43393, f. 75 (*Cal. B. 4. A12, 24*)

This letter was supplemented by a further two dated 14th January and 22nd January, enlarging on the theme. Then, on the 28th, Miss Nightingale proposed the wholesale reform of the system of supply and preparation of food to the hospitals, in the course of which she described, with devastating irony, the present method of drawing and serving rations. In this case custom proved too strong for any immediate improvement to be made; the system was dictated by the regulations of the service and was therefore sacrosanct. A new regulation would be required to bone the meat, she was informed!

To Sidney Herbert

Barrack Hospital, Scutari
28th January 1855

Dear Mr. Herbert

As the Purveying seems likely to come to an end of itself, perhaps I shall not be guilty of the Murder of the Innocents, if I venture to suggest what may take the place of the venerable Wreford.

Cornelius Agrippa had a broomstick, which used to fetch water for his use. When the broomstick was cut in two by the axe of an unwary student, each end of the severed broom, catching up a pitcher, began fetching water with all its might.

Were the Purveyor here cut in three, we might conceive some hope of having not only water but food also & clothing fetched us.

Let there be three distinct offices instead of one indistinct one –

(1) to provide us with food
(2) with hospital furniture & clothing
(3) to keep the daily routine going

These are now the three offices of the unfortunate Purveyor – & none of them are performed.

But the Purveyor is *supposed* to be only the channel thro' which the Commissariat stores *pass*. Theoretically but not practically it is so. (For practically Wreford gets nothing thro' the Commissary, but employs a rascally contractor, Parry – whose accts. or no accounts will soon be found out).

Now, why should not the *Commissariat purvey* the Hospital with food? perform the whole of Purveyor's office, No.1? The practice of drawing *raw* rations, as here seen, seems invented on purpose to waste the time of as many Orderlies as possible, who stand at the Purveyor's Office from 4 to 9

A.M. drawing the patients' breakfasts, from 10 to 12, drawing their dinners – & to make the Patients' meals as late as possible – because it is impossible to get the diets, thus drawn, cooked before 3 or 4 o'clock. The scene of confusion, delay & disappointment, where all these raw diets are being weighed out, by twos & threes & fours, is impossible to conceive, unless one has seen it, as I have, day after day. And one must have been as I have, at all hours of the day & night, in this Hospital, to conceive the abuses of this want of system! raw meat, drawn too late to be cooked, standing all night in the wards etc. etc. etc.

Why should not the Commissariat send *at once* the amount of beef & mutton etc. etc. required, into the kitchens, without passing through this intermediate stage of drawing by Orderlies?

Let a Commissioned Officer reside here – let the Wardmaster make a total from the Diet Rolls of the Medical Men – so many hundred full diets – so many hundred half diets – so many hundred spoon diets & give it over to the Commissariat Officer the day before. The next day the *whole* quantity, the *total* of all Wardmasters' *totals*, is given into the kitchens direct. It should be all carved in the kitchens on hot plates & at meal times the Orderlies come to fetch it for the Patients – carry it thro' the wards, where an Officer tells it off to every bed, according to the Bed-ticket, on which he reads the Diet, hung up at every bed. The time & confusion thus saved w*d*. be incalculable. Punctuality is now impossible – the food is half raw – & often many hours after time. Some of the portions are all bone – whereas the meat should be boned in the kitchen, accord*g*. to the plan now proposed, & the portions there carved contain meat only. Pray consider this.

There might be, *besides,* an Extra Diet Kitchen to each Division – a teapot, issue of tea, sugar etc. to every *mess,* for which stores make the Ward-master responsible – arrow-root, beef tea etc. to be issued from the Extra Diet Kitchens.

But into these details it is needless to enter to you.

(2) The second office of the Purveyor *now* is to furnish *upon requisition,* the Hospital with utensils & clothing.

But let the Hospital be furnished at once, as has been already described in former letters. If 2000 beds have their appropriate complement of furniture & clothing, stationary & fixed. Whether these be originally provided by a Commissary or a Store-keeper, let those who are competent decide. The French appear to give as much too much power to their Commissariat, who are the real chiefs of their Hospitals, while the Medical Men are only their slaves, as we give too little.

But the Hospital being once furnished, & a store-keeper appointed to each division to supply wear & tear, let the Wardmasters be responsible. Let an inventory hang on the door of each ward of what *ought* to be found there – let the Wardmaster give up the dirty linen every night & receive the same quantity in clean linen every morning. Let the Patient shed his Hospital clothing like a snake when he goes out of Hospital, be inspected by the Quarter-Master, & receive, if necessary, from Quarter-Master's Store, what is requisite for his becoming a soldier again. While the next patient succeeds to his bed & its furniture.

(3)   The daily routine of the Hospital. This is now performed, or rather *not* performed, by the Purveyor. I am really cook, house-keeper, scavenger (I go about making the Orderlies empty huge tubs) washerwoman, general dealer, store-keeper. The Purveyor is supposed to do all this, but it is physically impossible. And the filth, & the disorder, & the neglect let those describe who saw it when we first came.

This is not time to palliate things. Poor Lord Wm. Paulett hides his head under his wing. Ly. Stratford plays the game of popularity – & Lord Stratford, angry that the negotiations for peace are carried on at Vienna & not by him, hardens his heart & shuts up his despatches.

While, of 54,000 men, 11,000 are fit for duty. And the rest, where are they?

While you are straining every nerve to know the truth, & bring the remedy, at the expense of knowing that which must break the heart, these people are refusing, some to tell you the truth, some to know it themselves.

I am not "playing a game to ruin poor Wreford," as I hear said every day – "Miss Nightingale is bent upon ruining that poor man." I could easily do that by simply stopping when my present stores are exhausted — & letting it then be seen what the Purveyor will do. But these poor soldiers must be thought of first – & as long as I can do them any good, I shall stay, & shall go on collecting & issuing as long as I can get money & have your licence to do so.

I have had much talk with Mr. Maxwell since the Commission came back. He entirely agrees with all this. He is doing his work well and energetically.

He will tell all this much better than I can tell it myself. And I will leave it to him to right these miserable Hospitals, & to do you justice by telling you the facts *you* are so generously anxious to hear, & *all here* are so ungenerously anxious to conceal. The Commission have written a letter to Lord Wm. Paulett, of suggestions, since they came back. But of this man nothing will come. We are expecting your clerks with anxiety.

I go on to No. (3)

Let us have a Hotel-keeper, a House-steward, who shall take the daily routine in charge – the cooking, washing & cleaning us – the superintending the house-keeping, in short – be responsible for the cleanliness of the wards, now done by one Medical Officer, Dr. McGrigor, by me, or by no-one, inspect the kitchens – the wash-houses – be what a housekeeper ought to be in a private Asylum.

With the French the "chef d'administration," the Commissary, as *we* should call him, is the master of the Orderlies. And the Medical Men just come in & prescribe, as London physicians do, & go away again. With us the Medical Officers are everything & have to do everything, however heterogeneous. The

French system is bad, because, tho' there may be 20 things down on the Carte for the Medical Man to choose his Patient's diet from, *nominally*, – the Chef d'Administration may have provided only two – & the Patient has no redress.

Whether, in any new plan, the House Steward have the command of the Orderlies, or the Medical Man, which I am incompetent to determine whichever it be, let us have a Governor of the Hospital. As it is a Military Hospital, a Mily. Head is probably necessary, as Governor.

I could give you pages full of illustrations, if I had time, or you – of Lord. Wm. Paulett, of the Embassy, the Medical Men. But I have none – except for two, one of Lord Wm. Paulett, one of how the Medical Army Education, acting on the Scotch temperament, tells.

(1) I furnished 450 men, going on board the Dunbar, Convalescents for Corfou, with shirts, socks, etc. etc. Ld. W. Paulett having been called upon in vain by me through the Medical Officers to furnish them from his stores. After they were on board, he sent two bales of shirts on board, — his theory therefore being that they should go naked from the Hosp*l*. to the ship. Of my 450 suits, which were of course intended to become permanent Hosp*l*. clothing, I got back 43 shirts – & these only by the energetic interference of Dr. McGrigor, who sent his Serjeant on board for them. This I mention for the sake of the principle, not for the sake of the 43 shirts. It is manifest that all system thus becomes impossible – & all those *duplicates* will be thrown overboard.

(2) I made Cruickshanks put into words his principle about the Nurses. (He is our Senior Medical Officer here). He volunteered to say that my best nurse, Mrs. Roberts, dressed wounds & fractures more skilfully than any of the Dressers or Assistant Surgeons. But that it was not a question of efficiency nor of the comfort of the Patients – but of the "regulations of the service" "that *officially* he should think it his duty to interfere, if he saw a nurse dressing sores, because it was contrary to the regulations of the service – tho' *privately* he might wink at it, for the sake of a Patient's life." What could I say?

But we are only a symptom of what is going on in the Krimea. We are only the *pulse* which marks the state of the army. But this is my business.

If you promote Dr. McGrigor, you will shew that you recognize a *principle* that of preferring Man's life to the "regulations of the service."

I have been examined by the Commission[12] & sent in my Returns by their desire.

The Sisters & Nurses are all placed
19 have, at different times, gone home
 8 to Balaklava, who I hope will come back. For it is a mistake.
16 to Koulalee
<u>41</u> here
84 independently of Miss Stanley who always said from the first she did
      not mean to stay above a limited time – of Mrs. Bracebridge & of me.

Could Mrs. Herbert think I was "jealous of Miss Stanley?" But that is, Oh! such a minor matter *here*.

I never look at the Times, but they tell me there is a religious war about poor me there, & that Mrs. Herbert has generously defended me – I do not know what I have done to be so dragged before the Public. But I am so glad that my God is not the God of the High Church or of the Low – that He is not a Romanist or an Anglican – or an Unitarian.

I don't believe he is even a Russian – tho' His events go strangely against us. N.B. a Greek once said to me on Salamis, I do believe God Almighty is an Englishman.

Ever yours, dear Mr. Herbert

We have not yet succeeded in getting rid of the depot, an essential measure for the good of this Hospital.

B.L. Add. Ms. 43393, f. 113 (*Cal.* B. 4. A14, 28).

Mary Stanley and those of her party who had not yet been settled at Scutari or Balaclava moved in to the recently opened General Hospital at Koulali on 28th January. Florence Nightingale resented the move. She was quite unable to believe that Mary Stanley had no wish to establish an opposition, though many of the ladies under her by now did. In spite of these difficulties, however, Miss Nightingale was still able to experience moments of spiritual uplift due to the absolute conviction that she was doing God's work.

To her mother

Scutari Hospitals
Private   1st February 1855

Dearest Mother
One word to say that we are all right & that God is worth working for – tho' troubles perplex, but not overwhelm, us on every side, of which not the least (to me) is M. Stanley's inexplicable conduct, but of this not a word. She has intrigued with the Embassy & set up an opposition, (why opposition?) Hosp*l.* at Kullali, of which I remain nominal Head.[13]

I will work for these miserable Hospitals as long as I have power to do so.

I will fight for God & the right, for they are worth fighting for, but not to be justly represented by men which they will never do.

We have *no* Cholera. Your mind seems sorely troubled about Chloride of Lime. Can you suppose that such a Scavenger as I am have not a sack of Chlor. of Lime at the corner of every Corridor & do not myself see to the Fatigue Parties cleansing out the places which require it? Alas! I am Purveyor, Scavenger, everything to these colossal calamities, as the Hospitals of Scutari will come to be called in History.

I *do* read your letters. I do *not* read the "Times."

> Ever yours, dearest people, which means a great deal,
> I assure you in a place when envies & emulations &
> official jealousies interfere with the lives of men

S. Herbert has borne me out gallantly in Commissariat reforms.

Claydon; copy, Wellcome (*Cal.* B, 4. B1. 30).

As the final sentence of the letter hints, Sidney Herbert was doing what he could to promote the reforms being urged by his many correspondents in the field. In her letter of 5th February, as in most of her letters to him, Miss Nightingale acknowledges his efforts.

But the tragedy continued as the ships poured in the cargoes of dying men, victims of the appalling conditions on the heights above Balaclava. "Our own correspondent" reported to *The Times* from Scutari:

No sooner have the staffs attached to [these vast establishments] worked up to a tolerable standard of comfort for their patients, than down comes a fresh multitude of sick, and all again is confusion. . .

The fact is, the whole British army is passing through the hospitals here.[14]

To Sidney Herbert

Scutari Hospital

PRIVATE   5th February 1855

Dear Mr. Herbert

Your orders have produced an essential difference – & all hands are called to work.

Mr. Milton [15] arrived on Saturday – Mr. Cumming was inducted into office yesterday – Lord William Paulett, tho' not exactly knowing how to begin, is quite alive to the necessity of beginning (to reform) – & we are all looking up & hoping that something will be done.

The Commission had fully intended to say & to do nothing – but Mr. Maxwell is now determined to be honest – & very proud he is of himself for being so. The thing having been partially laid open, he sees that it is best for him to go on, that the War Office is really anxious to know the truth, & having set out on the cruise of Honesty, he is now proceeding with full sails.

But alas! among all the men here, is there one really anxious for the good of the Hospitals, one who is not an insincere animal at the bottom, who is not thinking of going in with the winning side, which ever that is? I do believe that, of all those who have been concened in the fate of these miserable sick, you & I are the only ones who really cared for them.

Gen*l.* Jones sailed yesterday for the Crimea.

It was rather a blow to us his not taking the command here – for he is a man with a head on his shoulders, while Lord Wm. Paulet has none.

Some news-paper has said of me that I am the fourth woman (query old woman) that had had to do with the war. Who are the other three? Wreford is the first, Lord Wm. Paulet the second, & I must not say Lord Raglan the third old woman,[16] altho' the acts in the Crimea have been the same as if he had been one. We will substitute Dr. A. Smith.

I must not go out of my "spezerìa"[17] – but the Hospitals of Scutari are only the result of the want of transport in the Crimea, as consequence follows cause.

Had there been any body to draw the novel inference that after autumn comes winter, – that roads would be wanted to bring the provisions etc. from Balaklava to the camp, the sick from the camp to Balaklava – that forage is necessary to keep horses alive as well as men, & that where the forage is, there should the horses be also, Scutari would never have existed on the gigantic scale of calamity it does now. But we have kept our horses in camp, our forage at Balaklava & the horses have died in bringing up their own food. Better have kept them at Balaklava. The French lend their mules, 100 at a time, which are sleek & well fed, once or twice a week, to bring down our sick from camp. And this brings me back to my "shop." Yesterday, & the day before, the frost-bitten men, landed from the "Golden Fleece", exceeded in misery anything we have seen – they were *all* "*stretcher* cases" – & the mortality is frightful – thirty in the last twenty-four hours in this Hospital alone.[18] One day last week it was forty – & the number of burials from the Scutari Hosp*ls*. 72. We bury every twenty-four hours.

But it is easy to criticize. The thing is to suggest a remedy – & that, neither the Times nor anyone else here, seems to do.

I have before me now "Return of Articles in the Purveyor's Stores at the General *and* Barrack Hospitals, Scutari, 31st January 1855"

I take a few items at random

Cotton shirts	474
Bolster Cases	98
Bedpans	55
Hand Lamps	6
Tin plates	285
Water cans	37
Drinking cups	200
Hand Brooms	1
Hair Brooms	5
Mops	1
Flannel Shirts	3
Candlesticks	5
Scavengers' Baskets	6

Embarkation of the sick at Balaclava

Broken Lamps (sic)	4
Door Mats	1
Table knives	2
Packages of Nails	6
" Needles	1

Signed "Purveyor to the Forces"

In these Hospitals are 3600 men, exclusive of Orderlies & Depot. There is nothing like figures to be impressive.

On Thursday we filled up C Corridor with Patients – one half-side of this enormous building.

(We have received 4000 sick from the Crimea in the last fortnight)

I left off purveying for a single day – by advice. The next day all the patients of C Corridor were tipsy, having drunk their wine at a draught, because they had no vessels to keep it in. There was literally nothing in the Corridor but the beds the men lay upon – & the rations – I went to the Purveyor & asked him in presence of Cumming & another Staff Surgeon whether he had purveyed that Corridor or meant to do so. He said "he had neither purveyed it nor meant to do so – he could not" – this before these two witnesses. Before night I purveyed it from Stamboul. The Staff Surgeon of that division being sick the duty of receiving etc. the patients devolved upon me.

L*d*. Wm. Paulet has, after many refusals, consented to remove the depot & to build huts on the Esplanade for this purpose. The best thing he could do for us would be to take himself off – the next best thing is this. That the two "Mrs. Partingtons"[19] Dr. Andrew Smith & Mr. Wreford must go is, I suppose, essential.

The "Times" is playing a most unfortunate game. I am told it is always writing to prove that it has done everything – the Gov*t*. nothing. (N.B. I have never told McDonald anything). It never suggests any remedy, but simply says it supplies me with money. Even this is not true – as not above one half of the things supplied by me come from the "Times" fund. I am told it appropriates all.

But to the remedies. This Hospital, being the largest, might be made the best in the world – because, on the principles of Pol[itica]l Eco[nom]y, there might be division of labor – instead of one man, as in a Regimental Hospital, doing everything. I had infinitely rather be Steward of *this* Hosp*l*. than of Harley St. were the offices properly subdivided. I hope Mr. Milton will do this. Perhaps he has received instuctions from home to do so.

Next to the great reforms wanted in the Crimea, in the officering our army, in the Horse Guards, proved by this great Catastrophe to be needful – & in the Army Medical Board – what is most needed is system in purveying these Hosps. – viz the appointing three or more departments, call them what you will – one to feed us – let the Commissariat send the meat *in bulk* to the kitchens, being supplied the evening before with a Relevé of the Med*l*. Officers' Diet Rolls & let 9 oz. of cooked & boned meat be issued from the kitchens through the Orderlies to the Patients at a fixed hour – instead of 1 lb of uncooked meat *with* bone & gristle thro' the Purveyor's Stores, – occupying the whole day of hundreds of Orderlies to draw these raw diets which have afterwards to be taken to the kitchens – one patient getting all bone, another all gristle, a third all meat – & a sheep sometimes lying in the infected wards all night – skinned, cut up or not, as the case may be!!!

Let the second department furnish at once & clothe the Hosp*ls*. & a House Steward or store-keeper be appointed to supply the wear & tear merely.

Let the third department inspect the cooking, the washing, the cleaning us, i.e. the daily routine & the servants. And there should be a sub-department for each of these three things.

I am now fitting up some of the wards with cupboards and lock & key with the approval of Mr. Cumming, for the purpose of holding the matériel of the wards.

Mr. Cumming has given his adhesion, in a series of Propositions, which he has accepted, to most of these things. He is most kind & amenable.

All this is, of course, sacred to you.

I have no time for more. I really hope that your Orders are going to be carried out. You are very kind & generous & I am ever yours

The arrival of proper ward-masters, of the "Eagle", which is daily expected, will be everything to us.

Forty stationary Orderlies have already arrived.

Thank you very much

It would seem unnecessary to trouble you with the kitchen details on the other side. But Cumming etc. tell me it requires a new "regulation of the service" to "bone the meat" etc!!!

B.L. Add. Ms. 43393, f. 131 (*Cal.* B. 4. B1, 31).

To her mother

Scutari, February 5/55

Dearest Mother,

Pray tell Aunt Mai that my "Education" is not wasted upon me that I often think of what we said together – of the great reformers who have died of disappointment – & I find our principles hold good in time of trial, the anchor is firm. I say "I expected this – I will not die of disgust & disappointment." I have often thought in early life (how little I then expected Scutari) that I should throw my body in the breach, that I should bridge the chasm to reform, – that there must be an Originator, a Promulgator, an Executor to each Reformation, Christ said, I am the way *and* the truth *and* the life – in general, there is the way, (the thinker,) the truth, (the speaker), the life, (the actor), separate pesons to each great step – the originator perishes without credit & without success, the promulgator is ruined in pocket, the third suceeds. I remember thinking, So perish those who pioneer the way for Mankind. But they may perish, but I shall endure. I shall not break my heart of disappointment, though even mine own familiar friend turns against me. No, dearest Mother, I shall do nothing, the originator never does, but greater things than these shall others do – the Army shall be reformed, the Army Medical Board, the Military Hospitals – those three sinks of jobbery & official vice – & I have done all I hoped by representing these things

Unfinished ?
Claydon; copy, Wellcome (*Cal.* B. 4. B2, 32).

At the end of January Mr Roebuck, M.P. for Sheffield, had inaugurated a debate in the House of Commons on the conduct of the war which resulted in the the motion being carried 'That a select Committee be appointed to inquire into the condition of our Army before Sebastopol, and into the conduct of those Departments of the Government whose duty it has been to minister to the wants of that Army'. Lord Aberdeen resigned, and although initially willing to serve under Lord Palmerston, the incoming Prime Minister, loyalty to colleagues finally induced Sidney Herbert to resign his office.[20]

In the new administration the offices of Secretary for War and Secretary at War were united, with Lord Panmure being appointed to the post.

Miss Nightingale thus lost her confidant at the War Office. Nevertheless, for the next couple of months she continued to rely on Herbert's interest and support until her illness in May temporarily reduced her literary output. Although, as a matter of policy, Panmure and Benjamin Hawes were bent on carrying out the reforms begun by Sidney Herbert, Miss Nightingale never felt the same confidence in their support.

To Sidney Herbert

Barrack Hospital
12th February 1855

Dear Mr. Herbert

You are probably out of the turmoil by this time, as would I were, (no, I don't, while these 5000 poor fellows are at stake).

I am sorry for our sakes, no one will do the work as you have done, very glad for yours.

Hundreds of things I have to write about these Hospitals, & am half indignant at myself for writing about anything else. But, as I do not know whether you are "in" or "out" & as something must be said about the Nurses, I will give a few words of explanation.

Kulleli is not headquarters – the Barrack Hosp*l*. is.

I have, (while incurring the increased difficulty & the increased usefulness of living at Head Quarters) by strict subordination to the Authorities, & by avoiding all individual action, introduced a number of arrangements within the "regulations of the service", useful on a large scale but not interesting to individual ladies.

e.g. four Extra Diet Kitchens – of which the two which I administer, feed above 700 of the worst cases

furniture & clothing on the scale which I gave in my evidence before the Commission[21]

washing

bath-house

lock-up cupboards

   etc. etc.

This is not so amusing as pottering & messing about with little cookeries of individual Beef Teas for the poor sufferers personally. And my ladies do not at all like it.[22]

I acknowledge it.

At the same time, it is obvious that what I have done could not have been done, had I not worked with the Med*l*. Authorities & not in rivalry of them. The consequence is that Cumming & I work hand in hand,[23] & I have carried, thro' him, almost all that was possible under these awful difficulties. And he comes to me every evening.

Miss Stanley has taken the exactly opposite tack. She may be able to work it at Koulalee, if so, God speed her, say I more heartily than any one. I have done everything in my power to speed her, so help me God – tho' she does not think so.[24]

She writes me word that she wishes to have *all ladies* – & 12 or 14 more than she has now.

I sent Cumming over to Koulalee on purpose to investigate & hear her own story.

He reports as follows, (1) that, as this fearful rush cannot last, he thinks it unwise to have out more women, who will not arrive till it is over.

(2)   that, as he is to have a body of 900 Orderlies, he thinks more women not desirable (3) that the ladies at Koulalee walk about doing little but carrying note books in their hands.

I offer no opinion. If the Balaklava party does not come back, I may myself perhaps desire six more nurses, so many of mine have fever.

But the first word Mary Stanley said to me was that she did not mean to stay – she has repeated this in every letter I have from her. Her own party understood it when they came out.

If she staid, I think she might be safely trusted with any party she may wish to have. And I am sure I wish Koulalee to be managed as she, & she only, can manage it. But, if *she* does not stay, not one of the ladies whom she brought out, with all of whom I am now acquainted, (excepting two at Balaclava & one at Koulalee, whom she herself considers incapable as *heads*) is capable of managing it as Superintendent still less, of being trusted with an increased band.

I am about to urge them to establish an Extra Diet Kitchen at Koulalee.

I consider that, Miss Stanley gone, the ladies will quarrel, as they have already done, & Koulalee will break up – in all probability.

Thanks for your letter of 29*th*. I hail the plan of the Civil Hospital.[25] You cannot think that I should have anything to say against a civil band of Nurses accompanying the Surgeons. Thanks for the Marseilles plan.

You will hear from Miss Kinnaird of her plan of furnishing the Officers with nurses whom they can hire. Lord Napier has asked me about it. Cumming does not think it feasible. I do. But I cannot undertake it. My hands are full & I think it desirable to keep it quite separate for many reasons.

The Drs. of the General Hosp*l*. have remonstrated with me in writing in temperate but too true language about the second party of Nuns.

I fear they will have to go. I have said nothing as yet. They say the Nuns are inefficient, sombre, disliked – very unlike the Bermondsey Nuns. I know it is but too true. What is to be done?

Ever yours

B.L. Add. Ms. 43393, f. 146 (*Cal. B. 4. B3, 36*)

The Koulali hospitals had only been opened a fortnight when the first fruits of the "perverse imbroglio" arising from the arrival of Miss Stanley's party, and Miss Nightingale's unfortunate reaction, combined to justify her worst forebodings.

Religious dissensions, already surfacing in the Scutari hospitals, came to the fore almost at once. The nuns were accused of proselytism and Miss Nightingale was disposed to believe the charges. Mother Bridgeman consistently denied that she ever attempted to convert non-Catholics; her understanding with the War Office was that "we are not to enter upon the discussion of religious subjects with any patients other than those of our own faith. We have never done so."[26]

Dr R. J. O'Flaherty, writing to Father Moloney on 13th April, bears out Mother Bridgeman's good intentions, but:

From the beginning converts were numerous, though the Sisters, scrupulously observant of their contract, used no means to promote conversions save that of silent prayer and the legitimate influence of example. On all sides they removed prejudices and gained friends, it being generally admitted by eye-witnesses that though religion was the motive of all their actions, they drew no distinction of race or creed, and never took advantage of their position to promote what was regarded in official circles as 'Their iniquitous scheme of proselytism.'[27]

Dr Beatson, a Presbyterian, and the Rev. Mr Coney, a Church of England chaplain, were to give similar testimony on their behalf.[28] But conversions did occur, whatever the cause. Father Ronan triumphantly recorded, "In Koulali there were at least fifty added to the Church, and everyone received by me attributed his conversion, under God, to the Sisters of Mercy."[29]

The problem might have been resolved with good will, but good will was signally lacking on both sides.

To Sidney Herbert

Barrack Hospital, Scutari

PRIVATE   15th February 1855

Dear Mr. Herbert

I think it better to make a formal Memorandum of the causes of future discord here which I anticipate & cannot prevent. You will do what you like with it.

The ship has gone to sea without finding whether the shot fitted the guns. I. These causes of discord were carefully anticipated and prevented with the first party of R.C.s. With the greatest prudence & entire success, a treaty was made with the high contracting parties, their own Bishops. This was slurred over in the second case.

You know the difficulties which have already arisen. More recently, a charge of converting & rebaptizing before death has been made, reported by me to the Senior Chaplain, by him to the Commandant, by him to the Commander-in-Chief. I have exchanged the suspected nun.

So sure am I that, give them rope & they will hang themselves, – that I would, had I not been sincerely anxious for the R.C. cause, have let this matter drop, & *not* put them on their guard. A further enquiry has been dropped at my request. II There are other inherent defects, which will bring about evil – want of speciality in the heads – those of Kulleli & Balaklava, want of brains in her of Balaklava,[30] obstinate refusal to recognise the official status here, in Miss Stanley – & also she is going back.

I could not persuade her to ask the leave of the Inspector General on her first going to Kulleli, & did so myself in her presence. It was not till after repeated urging that she would write him a formal letter about more nurses at Kulleli – & then, not through me, as he requested – & not till after she had written to England for them.

Mrs Herbert will see that it is not the question whether I am "offended" or not, but it is a matter of business – who is the Colonel whom they are to obey? Miss Stanley states in writing to me "I do not believe they (the ladies) considered themselves under your authority till they were actually employed by you. The consignment to Dr. Cumming they thought decided this point."

"I told her (one of the ladies) on her asking the question that you had asked me whether the ladies considered themselves as still under your jurisdiction – I told her I had answered you that they *did not*."

90

"You know I clearly undestand that you have, in Lord William Paulet's presence, given up all jurisdiction over any other Hospitals but those at Scutari – & as I told you, my party have not considered themselves as subject to you till they actually went to Scutari".

Now, the party cannot be consigned to *no one* – it must be either to the Inspector General, or to the Superintendent of Nurses, or to Miss Stanley, who is going home.

But III – here follows the perverse imbroglio – they are "consigned to Cumming" & not to me. But I am to supply them with money & not Cumming. And they ride off upon Cumming to avoid submitting to me – & they ride off upon me to avoid writing an official letter to Cumming, who is expressly designated as the person to fix the No. of Nurses by my written instructions.

Having tried a third party, the Embassy, for money, they are forced to come back upon me, & claim the orders of the War Office, which don't exist.

This is the present web of cross-purposes.

It is absolutely necessary that you should put the thing at once in an official & a definite form, if it is to continue to exist.

In my past instructions, the principles were laid down, as also in your letter, & were accepted by the Medical Staff. The *extra work* was also accepted by them, viz. – my extra diets, purveying of utensils etc. ditto, purveying of clothing ditto. This was not acceptable to the Purveyor – but this is in course of regulation by the establishment of other extra diet kitchens, & by stores coming in to Purveyor. The purveying of *extra comforts* by us remains, & is accepted by Government, viz. by the principle of acceptance laid down by you in sending private goods & practised from Queen downwards. This must continue – & in proportion as the Purveyor is made to do his duty, may be defined & reduced.

There remains the Nursing. This must be at Scutari as defined & practised – let there be an augmentation of Nurses – *not* of ladies, Sisters or Nuns. As to Balaklava & Kulleli, I claim to nominate the personnel only, & to leave the detail to them, under the Medical Men, say the first & second in command. And to decide in the last resort as to sending away.

As to the future, I claim 1*st* to officer & work these Scutari Hospitals on my plan – the only one which experience teaches can be worked here.

2*nd* that Haida Pasha should be considered a Convalescent Hospital & not have Nurses.

3*rd* that Officers should have Nurses upon their own paying only – and that these Nurses should be organised by other sources than me.

But, if any other Orders come out, I, of course shall obey them, provided I am not responsible for details beyond the two hospitals of Scutari.

Balaklava may be fitted for Nurses alone – under two Superintendents whom they have.

As to Kulleli & Smyrna, if ladies & Nuns are to be sent, I have nothing to say to it – I can only do so as above – & they will have to work with the Medical Officers as they can. Dr. Cumming being against it in the General & future – Dr. Tice, the present Staff Surgeon of Kulleli, a R.C., being for it in the particular & present. The question should be decided after sufficient examination.

If you will interest yourself for Nurses versus Ladies, good. If not, will you defend me at Scutari & let me work my own plan? I cannot be responsible for any other. If you have changed your opinion about my judgment, please say so openly. Every man has a right to change his opinion if he fairly declares that he has done so. (Only do not leave me between "hawk & buzzard.")

The thing must be put at once in an official & a definite form. If we are to remain here during the War – see P.S.

Privately & to *you*, I protest emphatically, – now before it is too late, – against the Kulleli plan i.e. the lady plan.[31] It ends in nothing but spiritual flirtations between the ladies & the soldiers. I saw enough of that here – it pets the particular man – it gets nothing done in the general. Try & work a Civil Hospital with ladies & nuns – & you will soon find what I mean. The ladies quarrel among themselves. The Medical Men all laugh at their helplessness – but like to have them about for the sake of a little female society, which is natural, but not our object.

Half the Nurses whom you have sent me in the last lot are admirable, good plain homely useful bodies.

Miss Stanley has written to Cumming at last – & he considers me bound to send his answer to you which is as follows.

"Dear Miss Stanley

From my own observation & after due enquiry I regret that I am obliged to decline acceding to your request respecting any addition to the number of Lady Nurses, & I am inclined to think that, were your experience a little more lengthened, it would bring you to the same conclusion.

(signed) A Cumming"
Believe me, dear Mr. Herbert, ever yours

P.S. You must write me, please, about the General Question (I am not now referring to the particular one of Nurses) a letter which I can shew to Lord Wm. Paulet etc. besides the official one. The reason of this is that we find unwilling listeners, while you have willing ones – because what we have to say is troublesome.

B.L. Add. Ms. 43393, f. 154 (*Cal.* B. 4. B3, 37).

At last, on 19th February, Miss Nightingale was able to report a decline in the appalling mortality. Her sense of humour surfaced once more.

To Sidney Herbert

Barrack Hospital
Scutari
19th February 1855

PRIVATE

Dear Mr. Herbert

The last few days have made a marked improvement in the health of the patients – whereas, in the first 8 days of February we buried 506 from the Hospitals of Scutari alone, on the 9th day 72 – during the last twenty-four hours we have lost only ten (out of twenty-one hundred in this Hospital) – only thirty (out of the whole of the Hospitals of the Bosphorus). It is not much more than ½ per cent. But fever among the Medical Men & Women is increasing. I shall have to send several home.

The Presbyterians in Scotland are anxious to send out Nurses. They tell me they have communicated with the W. Office. I object to the principal of sending out any one, qua sectarian, not qua nurse. But this having already been done in the case of the R.C.s etc., I do not see how the Presbyterians can be refused. And therefore let six trained Nurses be sent out, if you think fit – of whom let two-thirds be Presbyterians. But I must bar these fat drunken old dames.[32] Above 14 stone we will not have – the provision of bed-stead is not strong enough. Three were nearly swamped in a caique whom Mr. Bracebridge was conducting to the ship for Balaclava. And, had he not walked with the fear of the police before his eyes, he might easily have swamped them whole.

A Board must be appointed in London to enquire into the qualifications of the new six, with a Sub-Commission of Enquiry in Edinburgh – & they must come up to London to be looked at.

I hope & trust some plan will be carried out as to establishing a system in purveying, tho' nothing has been done as yet, & our position remains as urgent as before.

E.g. I received a Requisition from the Medical Officers at Balaklava for shirts, barley etc. – I went to the Purveyor, as I always do, to give him a chance (Dr. Reid, the Physician to the Rail-road,[33] was going on to Balaklava by the "Candidate" & had called with an offer to take any thing). The Purveyor answered 1*st* that he had no shirts. "Yes," I said, "You have received 27,000 by the Eagle, landed four days ago." 2*nd* that he could not unpack them without a Board – to which I answered that on every bale I had seen the No. within marked – & he could send one or two bales making a Mem*m*. for the Board. 3*rd* that they were at the Gen*l*. Hosp*l*. & he could not get an order in time. It ended by his accepting my offer to send a bale of my shirts, which he might replace to me afterwards. They have no cotton shirts & no means of washing at Balaklava.

By the same "Candidate" from England arrived an invaluable re-inforcement of twenty-four carpenters. These men I had to find with knives,

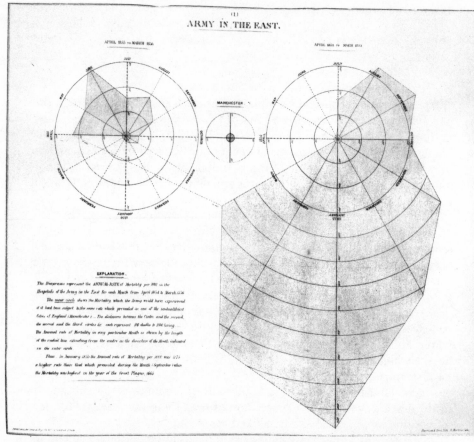

Mortality in the army in the East, April 1854–March 1856. This 'coxcomb,' as Florence Nightingale called these diagrams, demonstrated the extent of the disaster that overtook the army in the months of November 1854 to March 1855. In January 1855, when the mortality reached its peak, the annual rate was 1174 per 1,000. F.N. was a pioneer in these graphic methods of statistical presentation. The following explanation of the diagram appeared with the original:

"The Diagrams represent the ANNUAL RATE of Mortality per 1000 in the Hospitals of the Army in the East for each Month from April 1854 to March 1856.

"The *inner circle* shows the Mortality which the Army would have experienced if it had been subject to the same rate which prevailed in one of the unhealthiest Cities of England (Manchester). The distances between the Centre and the second, the second and the third circles &c. each represent 100 deaths to 1000 living. The Annual rate of Mortality in any particular Month is shown by the length of the radial line extending from the centre in the direction of the Month indicated on the outer circle.

"Thus: In January 1855 the Annual rate of Mortality per 1000 was 1174: a higher rate than that which prevailed during the Month (September) when the Mortality was highest in the year of the Great Plague, 1665."

forks & spoons, in default of the Purveyor, who had in his possession 7500 knives & forks from the "Eagle", & who besides, would not provide them with rations, unless the Officer of Engineers wrote "urgent" & asked it "as a favor".

It seems as if these people, Ambassador, Purveyor, Commandant, Director-General were struck with blindness.

The Carpenters brought out "monkeys" with them (for driving in the piles of our pier) & these have, as usual, gone on to Balaklava, being packed in hold of ship.

I think it matters little whether a vain, silly, swearing old man, like Wreford, is kept "in" or "out". But it matters much whether the principle of *necessitated concealment* is consecrated by keeping "in" Dr. Andrew Smith – it matters much whether our Embassy at Constantinople is to continue to be the laughing-stock of Europe, & the principle consecrated (in the person of Lord Stratford) of making diplomacy – *not* the protection of his country men, *not* correlative assistance to the war the business of his Ambassador-ship. Here has that old man been four months with the British Army perishing within sight of his windows. He has been over once for 1½ hour during those four months when I forced him into the wards.

[Two sentences here heavily scrawled out in black ink.]

And *he* is dissipated in business which does not exist & intriguing in politics which are no longer at Constantinople. What have the French been doing? They have now ten Hospitals in Constantinople, while the British position is nil. Within the last week *they*, the French, have taken the last available building, (a large building in the neighbourhood of St. Sophia) for 3,000,000 fr. *and* the Russian Embassy. We have nothing. I will send you a plan of their position on the other side. What is an Ambassador for? Is not this trifling with the sufferings of the British Army?

The French have received 6000 sick within the last 17 days. They are preparing for 5000 more.

I think the tendency of things here will be, as the season gets on, to keep our Sick & Wounded at Balaklava, where we are erecting huts now for 800 men, – & therefore, as soon as some system has been established here, – some plan of cooking, washing & purveying, & clothing, – & as soon as the pressure here is a little diminished, I shall go up to Balaklava with washing machines, made by the carpenters just sent out from those here, with cooking stoves etc. – and try & do the same thing there I have done here – & establish some Hospitals system if you approve.

Finally, the "Times" man, McDonald, goes home today. Would it not be a wise & a politic thing if you were to send for him & see him? He is on the whole a fair, but an incautious man. But you are one who wish to know the truth & I believe he would tell you the truth.

Believe me dear Mr. Herbert ever yours

The Ambassador is "en grand" exactly what Wreford is "en petit." The latter refuses blankets at 19/-, which the French buy up at 20/-. The Ambassador refuses to obtain buildings for the British, which the French instantly lay hold of.[34] I regret now that I did not lay down £12,000, (which we might easily have raised in the city), for the building near Sta.Sophia F2 Ecole de la Médicine – a grand structure, still unfinished.

Please don't let the "Times"'s injudicious interference counter-balance what we have said about McGrigor,[35] the only Dr. who has attempted reform here. Of course, he must be in Dr. A Smith's black books, as one of the disturbing forces.

B.L. Add. Ms. 43393, f. 164 (*Cal.* B. 4. B3, 38).

With the slackening of the emergency Miss Nightingale began to look around for other worthy causes aimed at promoting the general welfare of the army. One of the first and most far-reaching, and possibly one of the few schemes she did originate (though even in this she referred to the "ablest Staff Surgeon") was the establishment of an army medical school at the seat of war.[36] Mr Bracebridge had remarked on the extreme youth of the assistant surgeons,[37] many of whom were straight out of medical school. This letter, written on 22nd February, shows how early Miss Nightingale proposed the scheme which was to be a first step towards the reform of the Army Medical Department and the founding of the Army Medical School at Chatham in 1860.[38]

To Sidney Herbert

Barrack Hospital, Scutari
22nd February 1855

My dear Mr. Herbert

Very many thanks for your kindness to these hospitals, – for your kindness in allowing me to go on worrying you about them even after you have exchanged these worries for others – for your promise of still standing our protector in this terrible great work, & of allowing me to write unreservedly to you.

I do not see that our position decreases, alas! in urgency. You have done all you could, but the Personnel is wanting here to carry out your intentions.[39] Ld. William Paulet is not Mr. Herbert nor even his child George – & the heads once flattened in the savage boards (much worse than those of Indian women of the Army & Army Medical Staff discipline) become for life old children.

I One thing which we much require might be easily done. This is the formation of a Medical School at Scutari. We have lost the finest opportunity for advancing the cause of Medicine & erecting it into a science which will probably ever be afforded. There is here no operating room, no dissecting room, post mortem examinations are seldom made & then in the dead-house – (the ablest Staff Surgeon here told me that he considered that he had killed hundreds of men owing to the absence of these) no statistics are kept as to between what ages most deaths occur, as to modes of treatment, appearances of the body after death etc. etc. etc. & all the innumerable & more important points which contribute to making Therapeutics a means of saving life & not, as it is here, a formal duty. Our registration generally is so lamentably defective that often the only record kept is – *a man (sic) died* – on such a day.

There is a Kiosk on the Esplanade before the Barrack Hospital, rejected by the Quarter Master for his stores, which I have asked for & obtained as a School of Medicine. It is not used now for any purpose – £300 or £400 (which I would willingly give) would put it in a state of repair.

The young Surgeons here are first-rate Anatomists, as good, I dare say, as any in London, but miserable Pathologists – morbid Anatomy is almost unknown & the science of healing unpractised. At the request & according to the plan of the First Class Staff Surgeons, I gave them some expensive operating & dissecting tables, & I learn from these that they have pulled off the legs & burnt them as fire-wood.[40]

The Kiosk is not over looked & is in every way calculated for the purpose I have named. The Medical teaching duties could not be carried on efficiently with a less staff than two lecturers on Physiology & Pathology, & one lecturer on Anatomy, who will be employed in preparing the subject for demonstration, & performing operations for the information of the Juniors. If they could thus be interested in their profession (let alone in humanity) much vice would be checked, besides saving, in future, many hundreds of lives.

II The French have now all the available buildings on the other side, viz. eleven, including one on Prince's Island. They can now hold Constantinople. We have lost the opportunity of forming a Hospital on that side. Let us at least get a footing on the Seraglio Point, & make a convalescent institution there – there is every advantage on that side (of *market, landing* etc.) none on this. On the Seraglio Point the French have now, besides the Ecole de Médecine above, the Tunisian Barracks, which they occupied on Sunday 19*th*, & huts which accommodate 1080 men. I enclose a copy of a note to our Ambassador – which I have ventured (with some misgivings) to write to him.

I send you our Statistics of accommodation.

Barrack Hospital	1913
General Hospital	1018
Haida Pasha	500
Koulalee	1177
Stable	63
Smyrna	850
Abydos	400
"Turkish Hulk"	520
"Bombay"	256
	6697

We pick up the ships, as they go through the Bosphorus, & relieve them of their worst cases, sending the best on to Smyrna

Barracks for 2000 are about to be erected which during	convalescent
the summer will accommodate	1000
Stables at Koulalee	600
Riding-School	200
	8497

I will only add about the Medical Lecturers, if they are sent out by Govt. that they must bring *with them* all their microscopic & scientific apparatus.

We have heard of Mr. Stafford's foolish speeches to you, & also of his foolish speech in the House about Dr. McGrigor, which would have put us in a still more awkward position.[41] HIs promotion will put down the extensive jealousy (from Ld. W. Paulet down-wards) against a man who has disturbed the repose of this old system & its secrecy.

Miss Stanley is going home at the end of the month – leaving Koulalee without a head. She says that none of her, the second, party will do for a head there. No one of the first party would either.[42] The head of the Sellons is gone to Balaklava – nor would she do, were Balaklava given up.

I will send you Miss Stanley's letter, in which she does not recommend Miss Emily Anderson,[43] nor any one else, for Koulalee.

Under these circumstances, the lesser evil is to have out a head from England – to accompany the Presbyterian nurses.

We have drawn on Sir John Kirkland for £1500 & spent, as by account sent last post, £1243. This includes £400 for Miss Stanley, payment & credit, before receiving your letter empowering us to draw on the Purveyor for the second Party, which we will do in future.

Mr. Maxwell is going home this week. I hope you will see him & hear more of our true state from him.

Believe me, dear Mr. Herbert, ever yours

B.L. Add. Ms. 43393, f. 173 (*Cal.* B. 4. B5, 40).

Superficially things appeared to be improving, but while the system remained as before Miss Nightingale feared for the future.

To Sidney Herbert

Barrack Hospital
Scutari
26th February 1855

Dear Mr. Herbert,

Mr. Maxwell, your Commissioner, returns home today. I hope you will see him. He will give you a very fair account of things. He has taken the "Sick & Wounded" as he would a brief, but he will do it honestly & efficiently & then he will forget it & think no more about it, except as talk for a dinner-party.

However he *is* an effective organ – & therefore I leave to him the exposé of our situation, & will not write this post.

What the Commission was about for two months, we cannot conceive* – but latterly they have done their work well – & made many valuable suggestions which it remains for Cumming to carry out.

Mr. Milton has done nothing – but recommend a Band of Music for the Patients, games etc.

The French are making enormous preparations for sick – preparing 13,000 beds. I send you an extract from "La Presse d'Orient". I went over their new huts on Saturday, on the Seraglio Point, containing 1080 men – & with Lévi, their Inspector General, a man of immense power & intellect, I am to go over their Hospitals on Tuesday. The French send back *no* convalescents to the Crimea whence they only return (sick).

I seem to be always complaining. But all our arrangements continue to be of the Elizabethan era. The summer will soon be here & then we shall cry, as we did when winter came, who'd have thought it? Here is the hot weather.

Cumming with all his slowness, official narrow-mindedness, & timidity, *may* do something – responsibility & improvements being forced upon him. But Ld. Wm. Paulet, though highly estimable as a gentleman & a soldier, is an utterly unimproveable character quoad his official duties here.[44]

He feels himself a fish out of water, shrinks from every new difficulty, & those who may chance to bring it before him. If he does anything it is at the suggestion of A or B, overcoming for the moment his vis inertiae. In despair, he puts aside the difficulties of the Purveying etc. – & of the Medical Staff –

*We suppose that it was obtained from the D. of Newcastle by Dr. A. Smith to plaster over the Medical Men – & finding that impracticable, in the third month it did its duty, as far as you will see. Dr. Spence went up to the Krimea to make an apology to Dr. Hall for the existence of the Commission.

& restricts himself to trifling military details – & to gossiping with the Embassy. Even the roads round this building, the Barrack-yard & soldiers' barracks are in as miserable a state as ever.

Very many thanks for all your letters, which are more than kind.

Believe me ever yours

B.L. Add. Ms. 43393, f. 180 (*Cal. B. 4. B5, 41*).

On 5th March, after retailing difficulties connected with Miss Stanley's religious beliefs, Miss Nightingale enlarged on the lack of any real progress in the hospitals. She spelt out at some length her firm belief that the present troubles in the hospitals were a question of reform or no reform.

To Sidney Herbert

[5th March 1855]

[*Mrs Herbert's annotation:* "First part about Monument gone to the Queen"]

The Chapel might be done by Private subscription the Monument ought to come out of Public Funds.

And now I must bother you about a "row" at the Embassy, which you can read or not read, as you like – but which I am desired to inform you of.

Lady Stratford sent for Mr. Sabin, the Senior Chaplain here, over to the Embassy last week on other business. She then exposed Miss Stanley's grievances to him "au long et au large." Mr. Sabin was led on (little by little) to tell Lady Stratford that Miss Stanley had "grossly imposed upon her" & farther that he had reason to believe from putting two & two together, & from accounts which he received *from home* that Miss Stanley was only waiting to become a R. Catholic & was playing the game of the R. Catholics at Koulalee – that Dr. Tice who never shewed any great love for the Nurses at the General Hospital was encouraging the Nuns at Koulalee, being himself a R. Catholic – etc. etc. Lady Stratford was greatly alarmed – "why did you not tell this before?" & "don't tell Lord Stratford" being her chief ideas – to which Mr. Sabin replied "he was very sorry, but he had already told Lord Stratford."

Now, observe, dear Mr. Herbert, this bother is none of my making. I have kept strict honor with Lady Stratford, as also with Mr. Cumming about Mary Stanley's religious opinions – I could easily have defeated her representations by "telling of her" as the children say – and Mrs. Herbert will think that I have. But people out here do not require us at home to tell them "things" – & Koulalee has excited suspicions, without me or in spite of me. Cumming asked the question one day in my room whether Miss Stanley were not a R.C. & I put it off, in order that he might not say he heard it from me. Thus it stands now, & much harm will it do us. But let us bide our time. In the Summer, we shall, alas! have plenty of fighting, & then they will find out they must have more nurses. In the mean time, I am sorry to bother you with these miseries, & do not wish you to do anything. I have merely put you "au fait."

The whole Medical World is furious at the promotion of Dr. McGrigor – as they know he is junior, & don't admit that he is better than others in their ranks, they consider it an injustice to the fair hopes of all in the service. As they do not take a distinction between reform & no reform, (nursing element included), it is no wonder they think so. As the Doctors have enlisted Lord William Paulet in this belief, he, looking at nothing but military etiquette, of course will state the same opinion. He too sees no difference between reform & non-reform & will not go into the details of the facts. The end will be that Cumming will give in to the wish &, as I anticipate, plan of punishing McGrigor for his promotion by sending him either to Mitylene or the Crimea. This I gather from a conversation with Ld. William & others. From the same sources & my own observation, for I see Cumming daily, I find that he does nothing without the instigation of Dr. *Lawson*,[45] who has been second in command ever since Forrest took sick. Lawson then, altho' under the ban of L*d*. Raglan, has reigned supreme here for more than five weeks. I shall make no further remark about him than that he is a fossil of the pure old Red Sandstone. We shall get no reform out of him at all events. This is only one instance, as Mr. Milton will prove to be another, that the people here will try the strength of the old system with the smallest apparent emendations against Government reforms & rapidity in action – & this with a tenacity of purpose & a cohesion of individuals which you are not likely to give them credit for. Dr. McGrigor, as a Divisional Staff Surgeon, has carried out in his Divison, all the reforms as detailed in the Commission – in the other Divisions they are not carried out – though the old system may be well administered. These narrow-minded individuals would only consider my interference as that of a partisan – & therefore, as they can't value my argument, I don't like to exert what they would call impertinent & uncalled for interference. If Dr. McGrigor is sent to the Krimea, the authorities will plume themselves upon putting the thing into a more decent form upon the old system – & upon arresting the course of a hazardous reformer – leaving the orders of the War Office to be acted upon another time by those who choose to run the RISK.

As we stand, Cumming will evidently not carry out the views of his own Commission. If it is thought well to press them, it must evidently be done by stringent orders to Commandant, as a super-medical power. As for Dr. Andrew Smith & his injunctions, diluted as they come by his own opinions, I place no reliance on them – I have reckoned up all the Staff Surgeons here, & weighed them each in my mind, & I see nobody that will aid in carrying out the recommendations of the Commission but two, Dr. McGrigor, & Dr. Laing, (a *2nd* Class Staff Surgeon & Junior Commissioner).

Only let us have some system & force somebody to act upon it, whatever it is.

I say all this savagery because of the non-success of your unwearied efforts for the good of these poor Hospitals.

Believe me
dear Mr. Herbert
ever yours

We look to your protection the same as if you were still at the War Office, & only hope that you may not get half the torment at the Colonies which you have had among the Osmanlis.

B.L. Add. Ms. 43393, f. 183. (*Cal.* B. 4. B6, 44)

Occasionally some incident or scene awoke in Miss Nightingale strong emotions and feelings of homesickness. In 1850 she had rescued a little owl on the Parthenon. She called it Athena and took it home, where it survived until the eve of her departure for the Crimea.

To her family

Scutari
5th March 1855

Dear people

I saw Athena last night. She came to see me. I was walking home late from the Gen*l*. Hosp*l*. round the cliff, my favourite way, & looking, I really believe for the first time, at the view – the sea glassy calm & of the purest sapphire blue – the sky one dark deep blue – one solitary bright star rising above Constantinople – our whole fleet standing with sails idly spread to catch the breeze which was none – including a large fleet of Sardinians carrying up Sardinian troops [46] – the domes & minarets of Constantinople sharply standing out against the bright gold of the sunset, the transparent opal of the distant hills (a colour one never sees but in the East) which stretch below Olympus always snowy & on the other side the Sea of Marmora when Athena came along the cliff quite to my feet, rose upon her tiptoes, bowed several times, made her long melancholy cry, & fled away – like the shade of Ajax – I assure you my tears followed her.

On Wednesday 28th Feb., we had the sharp shock of an earth quake. It is indescribable. One does not feel the least frightened, but I felt quite convinced our old towers must come down. Two hundred patients jumped out of bed & ran into the Main Guard – two jumped out of window – some got out of bed who cd. not get in again. When next we looked across to the other side, two minarets of Constantiniple had disappeared. Half Brusa is in ruins, & the acc[oun]ts of killed & wounded there, where statistics are none, vary from 3000 to 8000. One man here with comp[oun]d fracture seriously injured himself by scuttling out of bed. We have had several slight shocks since.

Please pay £5 (which torment me) due to Harley St. for board of self & Mrs. Clarke from Michaelmas till the day of our going, *and* my £5 5 Sub*n*. for 1855.   Ever yours

Claydon; copy, Wellcome (*Cal.* B. 4. B7, 46).

A few days later Miss Nightingale again wrote home, this time commanding Parthe to be active in the matter of erecting a momument in the cemetery at Scutari. Her thoughs were never far from the "colossal tragedy" enacted at Scutari, and for many years she continued to identify with the fallen.

To Parthenope
[Scutari, 8th March 1855]

My dearest   I hope you are doing something about the Monument. The people here want to have a Cross – they do not see that immediately will arise the question, Greek or Latin Cross – that we cannot have our own Cross in a country where all Xtians are Greeks – still less can we have the Greek Cross – besides the ill grace of our setting up a Cross at all who are fighting for the Crescent. But these people cannot be made to see this. I should like Trajan's column – or Themistocles' *broken* column, only that nobody would see the sentiment of it.[47]

The whole of this gigantic misfortune has been like a Greek tragedy – it has been like the fates pursuing us – every thing that has been done has been a failure & nobody knows the reason why – the Gods have punished with blindness some past sin & visited the innocent with the consequences – for "our God is a jealous God" & how like the Greek & the Jewish Mythology!

But this great tragedy must now, one would think, be near its close.

Please put yourself *at once* in communication, dear Pop, with the Chaplain-General Gleig, to get us working drawings for our Public Monument & Private Chapel in the British burial ground now to be enclosed on cliff looking over Sea of Marmora – first ascertaining from Herberts whether Queen wishes to interfere. If she has no commands, set to work at once. I should like "Wingless Victory" for Chapel – one single solitary column for monument to greet first our ships coming up the Sea of Marmora. It is such a position – high o'er the cliffs we shall save in vain. I should have liked the Temple of Sunium – but a miniature never does – & they want a Cross.

I have told Herberts & Chaplain General you will put yourself in communication with him. *Let us live* at least in our dead. Five thousand & odd brave bearts sleep there – three thousand, alas! dead in Jan. & Feb. alone – here.

But what of that? *they* are not there – But, for once, even I wish to keep their remembrance on earth – for *we* have been the Thermopylae of this desperate struggle, when Raglan & cold & famine have been the Persians, our own destroyers – *We* have endured in brave Grecian silence. *Let* the "Times" avenge us. I do not care. We have folded our mantles about our faces & died in silence without complaining. No one can say *we* have complained.

And for myself, I have done my duty. I have identified my fate with that of the heroic dead, & whatever lies these sordid exploiteurs of human misery spread about us these officials, there is a right & a God to fight for & our fight has been worth fighting. I do not despair – nor complain – It has been a great cause.

We cannot yet believe in the death of the Emperor, [48] telegraphed from Bucharest yesterday – though it is believed at the Embassy – it is so like the dénouement of a Novel – too good to be true – how rarely do the fates of Nations hang upon the life of an individual & how rarely does that individual die in time to be of any use.

ever thine

Please date your letters.

Claydon; copy, Wellcome (*Cal.* B. 4. B7, 47)

Now that Sidney Herbert was no longer in office Miss Nightingale had been compelled to approach his successor, Lord Panmure, on 5th March in connection with the accounts of Mary Stanley and her party. She had also requested to be "distinctly instructed what authority I am deemed to have over the Scutari Hospitals, as regards the Sisters & Nurses generally – as well as over the Hospital at Balaclava & those at Koulalee. And in what way I am to be provided with means to meet their expences current & extra . . ."[49] She had repeatedly asserted that she could not manage more than the Scutari hospitals, and Panmure, after consultation with Sidney Herbert, prepared to take her at her word. Mr Herbert intimated the new order in a long letter dated 5th March:

I found that his [Lord Panmure's] wish was to separate the different hospitals so far as the nursing is concerned, now that there are so many and each so distant from the original establishments at Scutari, which were the only ones in existence when the first arrangements were made. He thinks this multiplication of hospitals at some miles' distance makes any real supervision from Scutari impossible, and gives you, therefore, a responsibility without corresponding powers. But he feared to make any change, lest you should think it implied a want of confidence in you or a want of appreciation of the great services you have rendered and are rendering . . . I told him that you were not a person to take offence at such an arrangement, which would leave you unfettered, and with undiminished powers in the two principal hospitals which have been the theatre of your exertions, and in which you are so much interested. What is more, I feel certain that it will be by far the best arrangement for you, and relieve you of the greatest of all anxieties, namely, the responsibility for actions which are not yours, and for people in whom you have not implicit confidence and who are too far off to be really under your supervision. You will, therefore, carry on your own system at the two hospitals at Scutari, supported by Dr. Cumming.[50]

On the question of the purveying, about which Miss Nightingale had never ceased to complain, Herbert was now equally forthright:

My advice to you . . . is that you should altogether give up purveying. It would, of course, be necessary to give them some days' notice, but they ought to be made to do that for which they are paid, and for which ample resources are placed at their disposal, and be held responsible for any failure. . .

Panmure talked this matter over with me, and quite agreed that the Purveyor ought to be forced to do his whole duty.[51]

But this instruction Miss Nightingale felt quite unable to obey, as she explained in a somewhat desperate letter – the last she was to write to Herbert for several months.

To Sidney Herbert

Barrack Hospital
Scutari
18th March 1855

Very many thanks, my dear Mr. Herbert, for your very kind interest in our grievous misfortunes & difficulties.

1st as to purveying. It is very well to say "leave off purveying," while they leave Wreford in office – while Lord W. Paulet, & Mr. Milton make it their business to bolster up that poor little old man. When I tell you that Lord W. Paulet & the Principal Medical Officer of the General Hospital each proposed to me to purvey the Purveyor privately – that I asked Mr. Maxwell's legal opinion what I should do in this matter, & that he answerd, "make them put that proposal in writing" – which they never would do. I think I have said enough to prove that saying "leave off purveying" to F. Nightingale & making Mr. Wreford purvey are two distinct things. What I have done I shall continue doing which is, when I see things deficient – to make the Medical Officer make requisition upon the Purveyor, if said requisition is uncomplied with, never till then, to send it in to me. You will see by my evidence before the Comm*n*. that I have, in no single instance but that of Arrow-Root, complied with a requisition without first ascertaining this point – viz. whether the Purveyor intended to comply with it.

But all this does not touch the main point. The Purveyor *has now* plenty of stores by the Eagle. Is he, or is he not to equip the wards with the complements of clothing & utensils necessary for each bed, as recommended by your Commission & approved, long since, at home? Is Ld. W. Paulet, or is he not to equip each man, as he goes out of Hospital, from Regimental Stores? All this is talked of & promised twice a week, but never done. Ld. W. Paulet *partially* clothes his men. Dr. McGrigor did equip one whole Division with the *complement* of necessary stores in each ward. And Cumming, urged by Wreford, ordered it to be taken out again. I am weary of this hopeless work. Sir John McNeill & Col. Tulloch [52] added, in vain, their potent recommendation to that of your Commission – & both have left me notes in writing to that effect.

Private 2nd As to the nuns, I have got over the case at Koulalee by a little letter-writing and objurgation & apologetic denial from the priest.

3rd As to Koulalee, I rejoice at your decision – about the separation.

My arrangement has been to fix the stations of all the second party, & to leave the internal management of Koulalee to Miss Stanley. Though she & the Nuns have tormented me with changes as to Sisters & Nurses, we have had no dispute. She has managed as she pleased, & in the great pressure of fever, of course wanted more. I know they have very loose rules among themselves. But I shall not interfere more than absolutely necessary till the new Sup*t.* comes. It will save me a world of trouble & fruitless anxiety to leave her to manage them, going to the Purveyor for supplies. I hope it will not be found more troublesome at home. I should be relieved of the arrangements of sending home & housing here previous to sending home (a terrible incubus & corrupter of my nurses) the sick and incompetent, which Miss Stanley has left me to do, merely saying what she wished without justifying reasons. That ladies, nuns & nurses may be made to work together, if faithful to their duties, we have proved. But I have found the ladies as wanting as the Nurses & more ignorant in professional matters. It is ony by perseverance that they can be made efficient.

Koulali has had	10 nuns
	6 ladies
	<u>6</u> nurses
	22

The state when Miss Stanley leaves will be

	10 nuns
1 *or* 2	ladies
1 *or* <u>2</u>	nurses
	14

As to Balaklava, you say nothing. If you see no radical objection, I should like to keep it *for the present* & if the war continues, to give it up to another Head, *when I have arranged it.* I shall not fight for the dependence of my Colonies, as England did for America. Balaklava shall be independent as soon as she is arranged.

My reasons for this are,

1st I look upon it as of the first importance to arrange the washing & an extra diet kitchen – & I do not think this will be done without me. I should like to go up & do this. 2nd The Superior of the Sellonites, who was Sup*t*. up there, has lost her head & her health, & returned yesterday with Harriet Erskine, the other Sellonite Sister there. They are going back to England, by their own desire. Miss Shaw Stewart [53] remains in charge. Miss Clough [54] has gone, without making it known to anyone, & absconded to the Hospital of the Highland Brigade on the Balaklava Heights, in conjunction with Sir Colin Campbell, & means to manage it. She must be a funny fellow, she, of the Highland Heights.

If Mrs. Herbert sends out Mrs. Sawtell, Mr. Sabin's sister, to whom I have written & who will apply to her, (Mr. Sabin is our Sen*r*. Chaplain) as Sup*t*. she might take my place here for a time, while I go to Balaklava. I would then enfranchise it, when ready.

Mr. Sabin is very anxious to have his Sister out, & I wish much to have her – at all events, she might find employment at the General Hospital *here*, where Miss Tebbutt,[55] now Superintendent, is quite incompetent – & has besides fallen under the Chaplain's displeasure for Socinianism[56] – of which genus we have two.

With regard to higher matters, the French say "Nous n'avons pas pris Sévastopol, il est vrai: mais nous avons pris Constantinople: nous avons toujours gagné quelque chose."

Lord Stratford never shows at all now. Lady Stratford has sent her Manufacturer of Beds etc. to Wreford with an unexamined Account of £8500 for Koulalee – which, after *swearing* a good deal, he has finished by paying, by Ld. W. Paulet's order. The accounts will never be examined, as far as we know, but Koulalee has been amply supplied. Mr. Wreford's boy-Purveyor there fell sick of a fever without apparent injury to his business. As Miss Stanley says, Lady Stratford has "the care of the place" – this does not seem to include the care of the money. I rejoice at success in purveying, whether it be done by an Ambassadress, a Purveyor, a Major Powell, or a simple poor persecuted individual. But "one man may steal a horse while" etc. the proverb is somewhat musty.[57]

A great deal has been said of our "self-sacrifice", "heroism," so forth. The real humiliation, the real hardship of this place, dear Mr.Herbert, is that we have to do with men who are neither gentlemen, nor men of education, nor even men of business, nor men of feeling, whose only object is to keep themselves out of blame, who will neither make use of others, nor can be made use of – the sole idea of the Pureyor being to make a waste book into a ledger (Mr. Milton included) – of the Military Authorities, that the soldier is a rascal (too often true) & must be *kept down* (Lord W. Paulet inclusive) – of the Surgeons "not to contribute in any manner by any requisitions to justify any statements which have been promulgated." This candid confession I copy verbatim from a letter to myself of one of the *Principal* Medical Officers, dated 14 March 1855.

I am so glad you are out of office, though VERY sorry for our country, because I can now have no shame in telling you sincerely, provided you still keep up your interest in us, of the dirt of this nest of official vice. And, of course, you will be listened to at home as much as if you were *in* office.

(1) The Eagle has now been arrived three weeks. And no use whatever has been made of her stores. Cumming says they have not yet been "sat upon". (2) The Sanitary Commission [58] is really doing something, & has set to work burying dead dogs & white washing infected walls, two prolific causes of fever. Ld. W. Paulet looks out of his window & sends word to us to remove four pieces of white paper (sic) at the corner of our store, while five dead dogs lay all of a row in the principal thorough fare from the Hospital to the wharf. A Liverpool Inspector of Nuisances has been left us to do what we should have done long ago. (3) Three times a week Lord W. Paulet tells us that he is going to remove the Depot. And this is made a reason for the incredible state of the Barrack here. The men lie on the ground with a single blanket – not undressed. In the Crimea they have a rum ration. In India an arrack ration. Here they have nothing but water, pronounced unhealthy by the Sanitarians. In fact, it looks like barley water what we drink. The consequence is they go into the town & buy all sorts of Greek abominations. Yet we have nowhere else to discharge our Convalescents to – & they generally return to us into Hospital in 24 hours.

Farewell, dear Mr. Herbert
Yours ever

P.S.

On re-reading your letter, I see you say "that I have attached too much importance to the second party being consigned to Cumming." It is they who have done this, not I. In fact I have it in Miss Stanley's hand writing "that they considered their consignment to Cumming decided this point" viz. of their "*not* being under my authority" – & "that she had told them that she had told me *that they considered* it so."

One thing more. The Eagle's stores, if not dispensed according to the system indicated, viz. so much to each bed, & thus made *stationary* Hospital furniture, will just go as all the other stores have gone, like water thro' a sieve.

No one has felt more strongly than I have done all that you say about the Purveying. I have represented it twice as sharply as you have – I have stated myself to be only an unprincipled expedient. When I see the wards equipped with the quantum of furniture & clothing approved & signed by your Commission, (with the Inspector General at its head) approved by the second Commission, Sir John McNeill & Col. Tulloch, who both *wrote* their opinion to me to this effect, approved by most of the Staff Surgeons & Deputy Inspectors here, then & not till then I will leave off Purveying. It is a matter very easily settled. The test has been approved by every competent & official judge here. And when Mr. Wreford has complied with it, be sure I will not purvey a moment longer. In the mean time, the Surgeons, if they do their duty, will make requisitions. And if Mr. Wreford will not answer them, why should not I?

It would rejoice you to see the decrease of sickness in Hospital. (Medical Men, Nurses & Civilians are suffering more than before). But the morning State of Sick today in all the Hospitals of the Bosphorus (including Kulleli, Scutari & ships) was 2 under 4000. On the 15*th* we buried 3

16*th*	none
17*th*	22
18*th*	12

We have never been so low since Inkerman.

P.P.S.

There are now twenty-six women & twenty-six babies (all under three months old) whom, on the principle of the Gauls, who took their women with them to encourage them to the combat, see Caesar, we have taken with us here to encourage us to the fight. But the women of the Gauls shouted & howled, I suppose, on the field – whereas these shout & howl in Corridor A to the disgrace of my decent door – around which they cluster to receive Mr. Bracebridge's teas & flannel petticoats – Mr. Bracebridge's twenty-six wives are the curse of the Hospital. Please send out the passage about the Allob*roges* or Allobrog*i*, I don't remember which, as a reason for Ld. W. Paulet to allege for their stay here – where they "deal destruction" not round the world but round the barracks.

The "Times" has gone throughout upon a fallacy. It has always supposed itself to supply all that I have distributed in these Hospitals – whereas it has not supplied more than half – I have had private funds at my disposal – from which I have drawn, but in all & every case, as you know, only according to Requisition from Medical Officers.

I am very much obliged to the War Office for passing our second Account of £1200 & odd.

You speak about transferring my "agent" to Wreford, if a good one. The fact is, Mr. Wreford has the very best of agents in Black. But he has only been stirred up to use him by my ordering things via Black, which I have always instructed Black to offer Mr. Wreford, (in order to give the Purveyor fair play) when they were landed on this side, not even saying that they were for me. And Wreford has almost invariably taken them, shewing thus that they were needed, tho' taking them out of jealousy, as he generally divined whom they were for.

If Wreford were judicious, he might make a great deal more use of Black than he does. But the same petty jealousy prevents him employing him as he might do.

B.L. Add. Ms. 43393, f. 192 (*Cal.* B. 4. B9, 52).

Sidney Herbert had written that Miss Nightingale "had attached too much importance to the second party being consigned to Cumming." But, quite apart from this having exacerbated the personal trouble between herself and Mary Stanley and other ladies, serious questions of financial accountability and responsibility were involved. From the beginning she had had the administering of government funds in respect of the payment of the nurses' wages, and general expenses. In addition she had been authorised to expend further sums as necessary on behalf of the inmates of the hospitals under her control. Besides which, she had access to private funds for the provision of comforts for the sick and wounded. She was also able to call upon the *Times* commissioners for various needs. In all these complicated accountings she was helped by Mr Bracebridge for as long as he was with her.

Florence Nightingale was herself extraordinarily meticulous in the way she accounted for every penny expended by herself and her party throughout the war, and from time to time she published detailed accounts. But others connected with her were less so. She was on the one hand accused of not releasing goods intended for the sick and wounded where wanted, and the accusers took it on themselves to distribute articles lavishly. On the other she was accused of over-facility.

The new Secretary for War and his deputy, Mr Hawes, were not as inclined as Herbert to give her a free rein. Something of the difficulty of her situation may be gathered from the draft of a letter written on behalf of Lord Panmure on 22nd March 1855, which ends on a distinctly minatory note:

. . . . It may be hoped now that the Hospitals are more regularly and systematically supplied with every Article necessary for the Subsistence & Comfort of the Patients, that there will be gradually less occasion for any extraordinary expenditure and that you will be able to exercise your benevolent interference in their behalf as actively as heretofore by ordering the Supply of what you consider proper through the Prin[cipal] Medical Officer whose orders the Purveyor must execute.[59]

. . . .I am in conclusion directed to request you will clearly understand that in requiring from you the details of the manner in which the funds entrusted to you have been disbursed the S. at War is only performing an indisputable duty to Parliament, before whom he is required to lay an Annual Account, in much detail, of the particulars of the Expenditure of all sums voted by the House of Commons for the Military Services under his control.[60]

Under this new regime, without the comfort and support of her old friend, Miss Nightingale was now compelled to do business with the deputy Secretary at War, Mr Hawes, whom she found decidedly less sympathetic.

On 2nd April she formally resigned Koulali.

To Benjamin Hawes

Barrack Hospital
Scutari
2nd April 1855

Sir

I have the honor to request that, for the reasons subjoined, you will be pleased to dissever my duties as "Superintendent of Nurses in the British Hospitals in Turkey" from those of the Superintendent of the greater & lesser Hospital at Koulalee – & also to modify the only instruction I have received, viz. providing the Sisters at Koulalee with money etc. by orders on the Purveyor General at Scutari – in order that the Superintendent of Koulale may be independent of me & that I should be in no ways responsible for the conduct and expenditure of those Sisters.

I am bound to trouble you with my reasons for the above request, which are – Miss Stanley leaves Constantinople for England today. I have hitherto arranged with her the distribution of those she brought with her, & in obedience to the instructions, supplied her with means. Among the eight nurses sent out, who arrived here on 27th March, was one destined for the Superintendency of Koulale.[61] I sent her immediately on her arrival, at Miss Stanley's request, to Koulalee, & after 24 hours, Miss Stanley sent her back to me writing that she did not consider her adapted for the situation. It appears, from letters received by the Ambassadress, that a party of twenty five Sisters & Nurses are immediately to be expected to arrive at Koulale with a Superintendent. As indefinite relations, with Koulale, under these circumstances, are exceedingly perplexing, I have resolved upon making the above request, which I take the liberty of pressing upon your immediate attention.

I had requested in my letter in March last, that the number of eighteen Nurses should be sent to make up the number for this & that Hospital respectively – for Koulalee to twenty-five & for Scutari to forty to fifty, according to the number of Invalids.

It appears that the opinions of the authorities at home as to the relative proportions of Sisters, Ladies & Nurses as well as to numbers are different from mine.

I need not, however, say any more on that subject than that I heartily wish that each experiment at Koulale & Smyrna may have the success hoped for.

I remain, Sir,
Your obedt. Servt.

P.S. The eight Nurses, including the Presbyterians, forwarded by the War Office to this Hospital, arrived here on the 27*th* of March in good health. Assuming the Ambassadress's intelligence to be true (of the expected arrival of the twenty five at Koulale) I presume that the eighteen which I requested to serve in both places, including the eight now arrived, will not be sent, as I have now no room for them.

P.R.O. WO 43/963, f. 205 (*Cal.* omitted).

The new nurses sent out by Mrs Herbert and Lady Canning proved no more reliable than the previous ones, in spite of rigorous selection. The temptations inherent in the situation of the hospitals, set in what was in effect a vast transit camp on the outskirts of an exciting foreign city, frequently proved too much for the self-discipline of women of limited education and sheltered experience. Miss Nightingale felt she had to deal summarily with the worst offenders. But she was not always as severe as the letter to Lizzie Herbert of 16th April suggests. Her "end of term" notes on nurses show she kept many weaker sisters if she thought they could be redeemed. Only those she regarded as unreclaimable were sent packing.

To Mrs Herbert

Bk Hospl, Scutari
16th April 1855

Dearest

I am so sorry to be obliged to tell you that Thompson & Anderson, two of the Presbyterian Nurses from Edinburgh, went out drinking with an orderly on Saturday night. Anderson was brought back dead drunk. But Thompson I believe to be the most hardened offender. This was such a catastrophe that there was nothing to be done but to pack them off to England *directly* – & accordingly they sail this morning by the Gottenburg. It is a great disappointment, as they were hard-working good-natured women. I sent them to the Genl. Hospl. & alas! I find that, under any guardianship less watchful than mine, I can hardly depend on any Nurse. Yet no one else is of any use.

Only one week's wages was due to them, which I have not given them, of course, as by rights they ought not to have a free passage home. There were *no* extenuating circumstances. Should they come to you to have their fares paid down to Edinbro', you will perhaps extend that as a matter of mercy, but pray do no more. They were engaged on March 9. You paid them the first month. I discharge them on April 16.

I think the other five promise well. I like Sinclair[62] particularly. Miss Wear is gone to Balaclava, Miss Stanley rejected her at Koulale. I fear she is too eccentric to be of real use.

Will you tell Mr. Herbert that Milton has with-drawn his paper, requiring me to sell the Free Gifts,[63] with an apology, compelled, I believe, by Ld. W. Paulet – & that since Mr. Herbert's letter, to him he has been much less red-tapy. Ever yours

B.L. Add. Ms. 43396, f. 30. (*Cal.* B. 4. B10, 58).

Writing home, Florence lamented her many troubles. Even those devoted friends, Mr and Mrs Bracebridge, were preparing to desert her.

To her family

Scutari Hospital
22nd April 1855

My dearest people

When the Bracebridges go away, it will be raison de plus for me to stay – otherwise this Hospital will become the bear-garden which Kullali & Smyrna are – where the ladies come out to get married – where the nurses come out to get drunk. Alas! the only question with me is not whether shall I come away? but shall I be able to hold the reins single-handed? Hitherto, amid severe disappointments it has remained a comfort to me to be able to feel, No woman's virtue has been wrecked through me – on the contrary, I have been able to take back some drunkards from other Hospitals and reform them. At the Barrack Hospital we have had not one flirtation, not one drinker – not one quarrel. And many a sinner has said to me, If I had been with you, this would not have happened.

At the General Hospital, where I do not live, though it is under my superintendence, all I can do is to watch – & dismiss the miscreant – a very unsatisfactory mode of government.

At Balaklava when the world thinks everything so successful, I don't know that any thing could have happened much worse – than Miss Clough's absconding – than the nurses' drunkenness, one of whom I have had to take back, since which she has been always sober – than the Mother Eldress losing her money, her head & her health. She actually lost the whole of the money I gave her, for the Hospital expences, save £1. She thinks it possible Miss Clough stole it. But does not say this, of course.

We are founding a new Hospital on the heights where the old Genoese fort is outside of Balaklava.[64] And I am going up this week to take & to settle nurses there.

Do you see how little prospect there is of my coming home at present, alas? Unless the W. Office makes the whole thing so repugnant to the spirit of it (by sending out its forty to Smyrna, who are a laughing stock to the Officers, and its hundred to Dr. Parkes's[65] new Civil Hospital,) that I say, No, it is more in consonance with the spirit of the thing for me to retire with the children God has given me than for me to stay.

Thanks for the dear little box, just arrived. But the umbrella I have never had. So send us this year's Nos. [Finished at top of first page] of Household Words. I want to read "North & South".[66] It rests me. No one sends us any but such old Nos. You sent us up to December. And I read them.

Complete but without formal ending or signature.
Claydon; copy, Wellcome (*Cal*. B. 4. B12, 65).

Miss Nightingale now set about educating Mr Hawes in her opinions on the position of female nurses in military hospitals. In a careful letter written on

1st May she gave details of the three different systems in force in the hospitals of the East, and explained her preferences. She hoped to persuade him to limit the numbers about to be sent out to the Civil Hospital at Renkioi. She feared for her own experiment if women went wild in other establishments.

To Benjamin Hawes, M.P.

Barrack Hospital
Scutari
1st May 1855

Dear Sir

With regard to the general Nurse-question in the East, it is divided into a three fold system.

viz. mine of ladies, nuns, nurses, – the latter in a large majority.

that of Smyrna – the same, with the omission of nuns & augmentation of ladies

that of Koulale – consisting of nuns, ladies & nurses – the paid nurses being in smaller proportion to the whole.

I maintain the opinion that, for Military Hospitals, under present circumstances, – where a large number of convalescents, unfit as yet for duty, must always be mixed with the Patients – the whole number of female Nurses should be small. Reckoning about 3 or even 2½ per hundred of *really* sick – & allowing one third of the whole number of Patients to be convalescent (and the proportion is now, happily, nearer two-thirds – out of 1100 Patients here we have not 100 in bed) this will give 25–30 nurses for 1500 Patients, allowing 500 to be convalescent.

II that the chief elements should be *paid* nurses

III that, as there are so many R. Catholic soldiers, there should be R. Catholic Sisters – (as also there *may* be Protestant Sisters). *And*, as there are Scotch soldiers, there should be Scotch nurses. But all should be chosen as qualified Nurses, whether Sisters or not, & as far as may be, *practically experienced*.

Great waste of money, of health & many other inconveniences have followed want of care in selection &, I may add, want of *special* knowledge in the selectors, as well as want of assiduity in testing recommendations.

As to the Smyrna plan, I fear that the large proportion of ladies & the formation of two distinct classes (one inferior to the other), may not succeed. Ladies are with difficulty to be found, whose qualities, experience & health fit them for the task.

It may be feared that more may be attempted for the solace & indulgence of the soldiers than can be carried out or be adviseable, considering his discipline, his past & future career. But, with a civil Medical Staff, it may be more easy than with the Military Medical Staff.

As to Koulali, it will, I fear, be found that, however well managed the Female Department may be, the numbers are greater than the requirements – & that the Military Medical staff may not like the interference of the female nursing element to so great an extent as it must be there employed.

As Miss Stanley had the entire interior management of Koulale, I cannot say how she specially arranged the R. Catholic Sisters. The sickness disarranged everything, – & now that this is abated, & the whole number of Sisters & Nurses made up to about 43 for 500 Patients, — (the present number), the application will be tested. The capacity of that Hospital (or rather the three adjacent ones at Koulale) will be about 1600.

Dr. Parkes has told me that he has positive instructions to erect huts for 1000 Patients – see Memo. HE wishes for 40 females to attend upon these, & I hear that 100 are coming.

Having great fears for the result of his difficulties – & knowing that Hospitals have been erected for 1000 at Balaclava & augmented at Koulale by 500 & at Smyrna by 500 since Smyrna was fixed upon /see Memo./ – & that the sick have diminished to

In Barrack Hosp. Scutari	1100
General " "	450
Palace " "	250
Smyrna	450
Koulale	500
	2750

(Leaving room at Koulale, Scutari & Smyrna for 1800 to 2000) – I would deprecate a *positive order*, & ask that Dr. Parkes may have *permission* to erect huts for 500 sick only, *if he sees fit.*

Secondly, as to the females – that they should, by no means, exceed forty for these 500 (a far larger proportion than I think necessary) & that no more than twenty should come at first.

Without entering into discussion as to the priciples of female Nursing & the proportions of the *classes* of females, it is obvious that, as *far* the greater part are wholly undisciplined, *numbers* make arrangements & management more difficult. Forty women, living closely packed in narrow quarters under new discipline & in a barrack – women too whose tempers & habits are unknown – present *great obstacles* to *management*. Those who send them should well consider what are the circumstances – & what the cost & hardship of sending *women* home who may not suit the work – & what the consequent result of working with *bad tools.*

The latent opposition of the Army Surgeon can only be augmented & stimulated, if he be annoyed by too great numbers, by inefficient people (as to nursing) & by indefinite rules. And both the female Superintendent & the Medical Chief of the Hospitals may be employed in soothing acerbities & smoothing difficulties which might have been wholly avoided.

What I fear is this (of which there are already incipient indications) viz. that the whole system of female Nursing in Military Hospitals may be brought into ridicule & disrepute, if it be not restricted in the numbers placed together & be not guarded by definite rules under these new circumstances – as existing at this date, viz. 1st May.

Believe me, dear Sir

Yours truly

Memo. According to the French proportion of extra numbers to 1000 sick, there would be 250

100	soldiers
50	orderlies
50	nurses
50	cooks, porters etc.

Increase (after decision on Smyrna) of Hospital room

Smyrna ⎰ huts promised 200 Koulale new buildings ⎱
⎱ Lazaret for   300   800 less ⎰
  convalescents   500   300 disused buildings
                               500

P.R.O. WO 43/963, f. 222 (*Cal.* B. 4. B13, 67).

Notes

1 Lane Poole, p. 390.

2 An article headed "Who is Mrs. Nightingale?" in the *Examiner*, 28th October 1854, p. 682 col. c, and reprinted in *The Times*, 30th October 1854, p. 7 col. c, in particular formed the basis of the popular image of Florence Nightingale at the time. (Cook, I, p. 164).

3 That F.N.'s was only one voice among many clamouring for reforms is apparent from the close correspondence of her letters with, for example, the letters of General Escourt to Sidney Herbert (Stanmore, I, p. 285–92); the letters of Sidney Godolphin Osborne to Sidney Herbert, and his book, *Scutari and its Hospitals*, 1855; the letters from J. C. Macdonald (Our own correspondent) to *The Times*, under the heading of 'The Sick and Wounded Fund'; and particularly the recommendations of the Hospitals Commission, whose report was published in March 1855 – indeed, F.N. is quoted throughout the text, clearly demonstrating the influence her evidence had on the commissioners.

4 The purpose of the commission, which had been appointed at the instigation of Dr Andrew Smith himself, was merely to establish facts; it was not empowered to take any action and could not alter existing arrangements.

5 F.N. was less than just to the ambassador. He too was frustrated by the Medical Department's refusal to admit any deficiency. He had written to Raglan as early as 16th November 1854: "The great obvious want is that of a Head – of someone to represent you, to inspire respect, and to decide uncertain questions without hesitation as to responsibility." (Lane Poole, p. 382).

6 Stuart to Dr John Hall, 28th March 1855, paid tribute to Wreford's "practical knowledge [which] led to the Hospitals here being supplied during the late fearful crises with every *necessary Article* required for the Patients, – and altho'

many a time we have been put to a shift and come somewhat *short* there has . . . *never been a want*: – altho' we refused to touch, or have anything to do with *The Times Fund* . . ." (B.L. Add. Ms. 39867, f. 13.)

7 One of the major causes of delay and confusion was the regulation which provided that, in the case of every bale or box of goods, a board consisting of three officers should be convened to "sit upon them." i.e. to check that the bale contained the goods specified. Until this formality had been completed, the contents could not be released. On one occasion the Apothecary at Balaclava released to Miss Nightingale three bales of old linen, merely noting this information on the requisition. Dr Hall ordered that a board be convened, with the comment on the Apothecary's note that "this was too laconic for an official document." (Hall Papers, R.A.M.C. Historical Museum, Aldershot.)

8 Sidney Herbert was already working towards the reform of the Orderly Corps. Herbert to Andrew Smith, 24th December 1854: "I would say that all the authorities concur as to the entire failure of the system of hospital orderlies. All press for the substitution of a permanent establishment devoted to this work, and to this only. I think we should lose no time in creating such an establishment, and should immediately look out for persons who would undertake the duties of ward-master, orderlies etc. There is no necessity for their now being soldiers any more than there is for the purveyors and the commissariat being soldiers." (Stanmore, I, p. 366). Smith had himself made suggestions for the formation of a properly constituted Hospital Corps but, as in the case of so many of his recommendations, was frustrated by Horse Guards. (Kirby, *Sir Andrew Smith*, p. 293). The results were as he had foreseen. Some attempts were now made to remedy the deficiency; a Medical Staff Corps was formed in June 1855, to be replaced two years later by the Army Hospital Corps. But the training of orderlies was only put on a satisfactory basis during the colonial wars of the 1880s.

9 Sir Charles Edward Trevelyan (1807–86). As Assistant Secretary to the Treasury, Trevelyan had been responsible for the arrangements for F.N.'s party in the East. In later years she maintained a voluminous correspondence with him on Indian matters.

10 The hospital at Smyrna, consisting of an old army barracks, was opened in February to take the overflow from Scutari. It was taken over by civilian doctors under Dr Meyer, who had accompanied Mary Stanley's party, in March 1855, and a staff of nurses sent out by Lady Canning. These never came under F.N.'s jurisdiction. (John Shepherd, "The civil hospitals in the Crimea (1855–1856)," *Proceedings of the Royal Society of Medicine*, 1966, 59, pp. 199–204.)

11 The Patriotic Fund was set up on 13th October 1854 to look after the widows and orphans of soldiers who died in the war.

12 "List of the principal Articles of Hospital Furniture, etc. supplied by F. Nightingale, on the Requisitions of the Medical Officers, to the Hospitals of Scutari, from 10th November 1854 to 15th February 1855." *Report upon the State of the Hospitals . . . in the Crimea and Scutari, Parliamentary Papers*, 1854–55, 30, p. 35.

13 Mary Stanley strenuously denied this charge: "I set up no opposition plan of nursing at Koulalee to Flo's. I simply obeyed the directions of the medical men under whom we were placed. I am not responsible for their orders being different from those of the Scutari Drs." (M.S. to Parthe, 15 May [1855], Nightingale papers, Claydon.)

14   *The Times*, 24th January 1855, p. 7, col. a.

15   John Milton (1820–80) entered the War Office in 1840. He was sent out to Constantinople in January 1855 as Purveyor, with "two intelligent clerks to enable him to act under Mr. Wreford and give him all the assistance he can in the organization of his department, after which he will proceed to Balaclava on a similar errand." (S.H. to Duke of Newcastle, 3rd January 1855, Stanmore, I, p. 386). A few months later Milton reported to Herbert, "I am happy to say that the hospitals are now in a most satisfactory state . . . The Purveyor's stores are amply provided in, I may almost say, everything . . . For cleanliness, sweetness of bedding, goodness of food – in fact every requisite of a well arranged hospital . . . these hospitals are now perfect models." (Stanmore, I, p. 411). F.N. considered he "dealt only in white wash." Milton for his part championed Dr Hall against F.N.

16   George Lawson wrote to his brother in April, "The feeling here is that he [the Commander in Chief] is a kind-hearted old woman, paying respect thus to his private and domestic qualities, but not saying much for him in his public capacity as head of a large army." (V. Bonham-Carter, *George Lawson*, p. 170).

17   *Spezeria,* derived from *spezie,* spice, usually means a druggist dealing in herbal medicines, or a grocery shop. F.N. here uses the word to mean her own area of special interest or knowledge, rather akin to the English idiom "talking shop."

18   At this time, the period of greatest mortality, Scutari was receiving the victims of the terrible trench duty before Sebastopol. William Howard Russell wrote one of his most dramatic and moving despatches about these men, seen on the road down to Balaclava on 23rd January: "There was a white frost on the night of the 22nd January, and the next morning the thermometer was at 42. A large number of sick and, I feared dying men, were sent into Balaklava on the 23rd on French mule litters and a few of our bât horses. They formed one of the most ghastly processions that ever poet imagined. Many of these men were all but dead. With closed eyes, open mouths, and ghastly attenuated faces, they were borne along two and two, the thick stream of breath visible in the frosty air alone showing they were still alive. One figure was a horror – a corpse, stone dead, strapped upright in its seat, its legs hanging stiffly down, the eyes staring wide open, the teeth set on the protruding tongue, the head and body nodding with frightful mockery of life at each stride of the mule over the broken road. No doubt the man died on his way down to the harbour. Another man I saw with the raw flesh and skin hanging from his fingers, naked bones of which protruded into the cold air, undressed and uncovered. That was a case of frost-bite, I presume. Possibly the hand had been dressed, but the bandages might have dropped off. All the sick in the mule litters seemed alike on the verge of the grave." (Nicholas Bentley, ed., *Russell's Despatches from the Crimea,* 1970, p. 160.)

19   In his speech on the defeat of the Reform Bill in 1831 Sydney Smith compared the attempts of the House of Lords to stop the progress of reform to the efforts of Mrs Partington, who lived close to the beach at Sidmouth, to keep out the Atlantic with a mop when a great storm in 1824 caused a flood in that town. (*Concise Oxford Dictionary of English Literature*).

20   Stanmore, I, pp. 251–69.

21   "List of the principal Articles of Hospital Furniture, etc. supplied by F. Nightingale, on the Requisitions of the Medical Officers, to the Hospitals of Scutari, from 10th November 1854 to 15th February 1855," *Report upon the State of the*

Hospitals of the British Army in the Crimea and Scutari, Parliamentary Papers, 1854–1855, 30, p. 25.

22 The point of view of the ladies of Koulali was presented by Fanny Taylor in her book: "It was very hard work, after Dr Cumming's order had been issued, to pace the corridor and hear perhaps, the low voice of a fever patient, 'Give me a drink for the love of God,' and to have none to give ... or to see the look of disappointment on the faces of those to whom we had been accustomed to give the beef-tea. The assistant surgeons were very sorry they said for the alteration, but they had no power to help – their duty was only to obey. On one occasion an assistant surgeon told us that Dr Cumming had threatened to arrest him for having allowed a man too many extras on the diet roll. Amid all the confusion and distress of Scutari hospital, military discipline was never lost sight of, and an infringement of one of the smallest observances was worse than letting twenty men die from neglect!" (*Eastern Hospitals*, I, pp. 82–3.)

23 Cumming replaced Dr Forrest as P.M.O. at Scutari when the Hospitals Commisson on which he had sat had completed its Report. F.N. became increasingly disenchanted with his performance.

24 Although F.N. was enraged by the unsolicited arrival of Mary Stanley's party, and refused to receive them officially, there were several happy meetings between the old friends according to Mary Stanley's own account. In a letter to Parthe dated 11th January she tells of just such an occasion: "Don't fret for us, we shall all light on our legs. I wish you could have seen Flo & me yesterday holding council over the affairs of the nation, laughing in fits at the ludicrous points. She had been overdone the day before – but was out & about yesterday. Don't be afraid for our mutual affection, it will more than survive. I wish you to see in my own hand these facts. You know there is much I cannot understand, but I take it on trust." But after Mary Stanley took over the nursing of Koulali the relationship deteriorated. She had not meant to stay, and only did so from the best of motives – she felt obliged to see her party satisfactorily settled. But she professed herself unable to see the justification for many of F.N.'s actions at the time, and therefore was unable to carry out whole heartedly her scheme of nursing at Koulali. She was moreover prepared to let the stronger-willed and more experienced Mother Bridgeman assume control. But the relationship between Mary and F.N. only finally broke down after the former's return to England, when she became the centre of all disaffection and led the party which tried to bring an action for libel against F.N.

25 As a result of the pressure on the Army Medical Department's resources created by the emergency of January and February, the government decided to employ a number of civilian doctors. Two additional hospitals, at Smyrna and Renkioi, were therefore established in March and October 1855, staffed entirely by civilian doctors and nurses. (John Shepherd, "The civil hospitals in the Crimea (1855–1856)." *Proceedings of the Royal Society of Medicine*, 1966, 59, pp. 199–204.)

26 Bolster, p. 159.

27 Bolster, p. 130.

28 Dr G. S. Beatson to Dr Hall, 15th November 1855: "... I can bear testimony that on every occasion their attention to the sick was unremitting, while they seemed always studious to carry out, and not to deviate from the instructions of the Medical Officers in charge of the patients. I have heard a loose assertion that their object and aim was to proselytize, but while their attention to protestants and men of their own persuasion seemed equal, I know of no instance in which the above assertion was even attempted to be established. I am myself a protestant – a Scotch Presbyterian – and cannot therefore be supposed to bear this testimony from any religious sympathy or bias; I do so merely from a sense of justice to these estimable women, believing that Christian Charity and benevolence are the motives that influence them . . ." (B.L. Add. Ms. 39867, f. 65) And the Rev. Thomas Coney to Dr Hall, 7th December 1855: ". . . my duties brought me in daily contact with the larger number of those Roman Cath. Sisters of Mercy who are now attached to the Gen. Hospital, Balaclava, and that during that period nothing ever came under my observation to induce me to attach the least credit to rumours which were then afloat of their bent in proselytism. If any effort had been made by them with that object in view it could have hardly escaped my notice. With regard to the care and attention paid by them to the sick in Hospital I have never seen the slightest approach to any line of demarcation being drawn by them between the Roman Cath: & our own communion, or that of the Presbyterians. On the contrary it has always struck me, from the kindness I saw displayed by them towards all alike, how much they seemed to strive to bury any differences of faith which might exist amongst those to whom they were called upon to minister in the universal love they shewed to all." (Hall Papers, Box 14 FC09/6, R.A.M.C. Historical Museum, Aldershot.)

29 Sir Shane Leslie, "Forgotten passages in the life of Florence Nightingale." *Dublin Review*, 1917, *161*, pp. 179–98

30 Miss Emma Langston, Mother Eldress, a Sellonite who came out with Miss Stanley's party, was Superintendent of Nursing at the General Hospital, Balaclava, at this time. F.N. complained of her lack of control on several occasions. She was also to be indicted in the Purveyor's Confidential Report, December 1855. (see appendix)

31 S. G. Osborne likewise doubted whether ladies should be employed in nursing duties, but for rather different reasons: "There are many offices about the sick and wounded which the surgeons would at once require, and with reason, of a hired hospital nurse, which nothing could induce them to ask of a 'sister'. I am also satisfied this is no field of usefulness proper for young English women . . . I have little doubt but that the majority [of Ladies who had been engaged in the work] would agree with me, that very much of it had been better left, had it been possible, to trained paid nurses; and that there would have still remained a large field of more fitting usefulness for the zeal of unpaid volunteers." (*Scutari and its Hospitals*, ch. 4.)

32 The fatness of the nurses was noted by others; George Lawson on the nurses sent to Balaclava in January 1855: "Eight nurses have been sent up to the Hospital at Balaclava, fine matronly fat-looking women, with waists I will not say how large, in fact almost straight up and down, such as one looks at with pleasure in a London hospital. They will, I am sure, prove invaluable, and do more real good than 30 clumsy soldiers employed as hospital orderlies, who have no interest in the patients . . ." (V. Bonham Carter, ed. *George Lawson*, p. 163.)

33 In January 1855 navvies were brought out from England to construct a railroad linking Balaclava with Headquarters on the heights above. By March the track was laid and supplies were moving steadily up to the army in camp before Sebastopol.

34 The French were far better at dealing with the local population and living off local resources than the British. (Hibbert, p. 18.)

35   Dr McGrigor was mentioned favourably by name on several occasions in *The Times;* 9th January p. 7, col. e, despatch dated 28th December: McGrigor "has more than any medical officer here of his standing shown himself disposed to set aside the narrow ideas of a peace establishment, and to look alone to the comfort and welfare of the soldiers in hospital." In the same despatch Dr Hall was castigated for the state of the transports. On 29th January, p. 10, col. a, McGrigor was again praised for "rising superior to narrow prejudices, and affording a fair field for the labours of the nurses and the usefulness of the Fund." As McGrigor was already the object of unfavourable notice by his superiors, this constant praise was indeed singularly injudicious.

36   Dr Peter Pincoffs, who came out to Scutari in April and was closely associated with the medical school built as a result of F.N.'s representation to Herbert, described it in his book after the war: "With the splendid dissecting-room built under the direction of the civil pathological commission, with the numerous and excellent instruments, microscopes, chemical apparatus etc. so liberally provided by Government (at the suggestion of Miss Nightingale and under the superintendence of Sir James Clark), with a Pathologist of superior attainments and industry stationary at Scutari, what advantages might not have been secured for the junior members of the profession" but, according to Pincoffs, once again the jealousy of the senior members of the Army Medical Department brought a good idea to naught. (*Experiences* . . . , p. 55.)

37   8th November 1854, Stanmore, I, p. 345.

38   Stanmore, II, p. 366.

39   In a long letter to the Duke of Newcastle, dated 3rd January 1855, Sidney Herbert detailed the arrangements he was making to effect many and significant reforms to the organisation and purveying in the hospitals of the East. (Stanmore, I, pp. 382–8.) He also instructed Dr Cumming to "communicate to Lord W. Paulet at once any alterations which you think necessary – without waiting for the completion of your report or for reference home. He has full powers to obtain, buy, hire, or erect whatever is necessary." (Stanmore, I, p. 388.) And in a letter to Lord William Paulet himself, of 18th January, the commandant was authorised to do what was necessary whatever the cost: Herbert added significantly, "Pray recollect that you have full power to send home anyone whose inefficiency is marring the public service." Paulet did what he could, but the disaster of December and January was overwhelming. On 7th January he informed Herbert of what he had done, was trying to do, and the difficulties that beset him: "The immense and constant influx of sick coming here almost prevent me putting things upon a system, whereby I might ensure economy and regularity. Since December 17th, about three weeks, we have disembarked and admitted 3,400 sick. One day we had 72 deaths and burials, but the average lately has been about 40 per diem. The men arrive with hardly any clothes, some with nothing but a blanket, and covered with vermin. There are now 4,500 sick; and above 700 just arrived, and not disembarked . . ." and so on. (Stanmore, I, pp. 390–2)

40   Fuel was short, and the young surgeons were conscienceless. Greig cheerfully recorded how he and his companions tore the shutters from the windows of their lodgings. (R.A.M.C. Historical Museum, Aldershot.)

41   F.N. is probably referring to August Stafford's speech to the House of Commons in the debate on the Roebuck motion, 29th January 1855. (Hansard, *Parliamentary Debates,* 3rd series, vol. 136.)

42   Miss Stanley was Superintendent of the Barrack Hospital, Koulali; Miss Amy Huggett was nominal head of the General Hospital, over Rev. Mother Bridgeman, but Miss H. was completely overshadowed by the latter.

43 Miss Emily Anderson, who came out with Mary Stanley, was appointed Superintendent of the General Hospital, Scutari, under F.N. herself, until she became ill and had to go home. Miss Stanley was also to reject Miss Margaret Weare, who came on from Smyrna specifically to take over at Koulali. Miss Weare was then sent to Balaclava, where she caused F.N. a great deal of trouble through her determination to establish herself independently. So perhaps F.N.'s assertions about the troublesomeness, not to say uselessness, of the ladies were justified.

44 Lord William Paulet's letters to Sidney Herbet were decidedly more optimistic in tone than F.N.'s and, as Lord Stanmore has pointed out, may be said to form their complement. "If Lord William dwells almost exclusively on the improvements effected, Miss Nightingale as exclusively dwells on the evils still existing. Read together, they probably convey a fairer impression of the existing state of Scutari than would be obtained from the letters of either taken alone." (Stanmore, I, p. 404.) Lord William represented those conservative forces who wished to see the existing system working reasonably, without any drastic change, while F.N. represented those who were working for root-and-branch reform. Their viewpoints were incompatible.

45 Dr Robert Lawson (1815–94), Deputy Inspector General, had been censured by Lord Raglan in December 1854 for the state of the sick and wounded on board the *Avon*. He was not in fact P.M.O. at Balaclava at the time, and so was in no way responsible, but F.N. believed the reports and was extremely indignant when he was appointed P.M.O. at Scutari for the few days between Forrest leaving and Cumming taking over. Lawson remained on in a subordinate position. Peter Pincoffs considered him one of the most deserving and efficient officers in the army. (*Experiences . . .* , p. 43.) By the end F.N. herself gave some signs of having revised her poor opinion of him.

46 Cavour, Prime Minister of Piedmont since 1852, was at this time looking for European allies in the possible forthcoming struggle against Austria, and although without a direct interest in the Crimean conflict offered a contingent of 15,000 Sardinian troops to the British and French allies. The French, who had little difficulty replacing their casualties, were not particularly interested, but the British, who had had a smaller force in the first place, were finding it difficult to replace their losses and gratefully accepted the offer. It was hoped the Italian contingent would do something to redress the imbalance between the opposing forces.

47 The monument erected in 1857 was an obelisk designed by Baron Marochetti, and with an inscription composed by Macaulay: "To the memory of the British soldiers and sailors, who during the years 1854 and 1855 died far from their country in defence of the liberties of Europe this monument is erected by the gratitude of Queen Victoria and her people 1857." (Lady Alicia Blackwood, *A Narrative of a Residence on the Bosphorus throughout the Crimean War,* London, 1881, p. 45.) A representation of the monument, and its inscription, is embossed on the cover of Lady Alicia's *Narrative*.

48 Czar Nicholas I died on 2nd March 1855. The British hoped for a change of policy on the part of his successor which might bring about a peace on acceptable terms, but Alexander II was unable to extricate himself. So the war dragged on.

49 F.N. to Panmure, 5th March 1855, P.R.O. WO 43/963, f. 199.

50 Stanmore, I. p. 413.

51 Stanmore, I. p. 414.

52 Sir John McNeill (1795–1883) and Colonel Alexander Tulloch (1803–64) were despatched to the East in February 1855 with a commission to enquire into the supplies of the British army in the Crimea. The resulting report, published in two parts, the first in July 1855 and the second in January 1856, sparked off a bitter and long-running controversy.

53 Jane Catherine Shaw Stewart (d. 1905, unmarried sister of Sir Michael Shaw Stewart, sixth Baronet; *Burke*, 1915.) F.N. generally, but not always, referred to her as "Mrs." – a courtesy title also applied to Rev. Mother Bridgeman. One of the few ladies with previous experience of hospital nursing, Miss Shaw Stewart went out to Constantinople with Mary Stanley's party, and took upon herself the washing for the party, before volunteering to go up to Balaclava under Miss Langston in January 1855. When Miss Langston left, Mrs Shaw Stewart took over the superintendency of the General Hospital; in April she moved to the newly opened Castle Hospital. F.N. found her one of her most reliable and loyal lieutenants in the East: "I cannot tell you . . . how good and sterling Mrs. Stewart is. Unwise, provoking & mad as she is, it is such a relief to come to something which is above, entirely above, all that is mean & petty & selfish & frivolous & low into a higher & purer atmosphere, into truth & generosity that she is like my bright tossing sea & stormy Castle top – here – compared with the funereal Eastern beauties of Scutari – where lie the whitening bones & rotting carcases of thousands under the opal skies & trim cypresses of that luxuriant climate." (Fragment of letter to her family, 28th October 1855, Nightingale papers, Claydon). In the spring of 1856, when she imagined herself to be dying, F.N. advised General Storks that Mrs Shaw Stewart should succeed her (Cook, I, 294). In her end-of-term report (No. IV, Nurses & Ladies returning June 26/56) F.N. wrote of her in very much the same terms as of Rev. Mother Bermondsey: "Mrs. Shaw Stewart – 17 months in the Crimea of which 15 months successively Superintendent of the General, Castle & Left Wing L.T. Corps Hospitals in the Crimea – I should fear to offend this lady, were I to say what my opinion of her is. Without her, our Crimean work would have come to grief. Without her judgment, her devotion, her unselfish consistent looking to the one great end, viz. the carrying out the work as a *whole,* without her untiring zeal, her watchful care of the nurses, her accuracy in all trusts & accounts, her truth – in one word, her faithfulness to the work as a whole, laying aside the desire (inherent in all vain & weak minds) that it should be observed how much more good she was doing in her own particular Hospital than others were – Without *all* her qualities, I believe that our Crimean work could not have withstood the insidious petty persecution, the laying of traps, the open opposition which it has received. Her praise & her reward are in higher hands than mine." (B.L. Add. Ms. 43402, f. 19.) After the war F.N. used her influence to have Mrs Stewart admitted to St Thomas's Hospital for further training and experience, and wrote to General Péllissier seeking permission for her to visit French hospitals. F.N. considered her the only woman capable of superintending the army nurses, and one of Sidney Herbert's last letters was to Mrs Stewart thanking her for having at last agreed to undertake this work. (Stanmore, II, p. 438.) She remained in this post until her turbulent relations with the authorities led to her enforced resignation in 1868. Relations between her and F.N. never really recovered from the offence F.N. inflicted in autumn 1857, when she wrote that she would never be able to see Mrs Shaw Stewart again, because of her great weakness. Even so, F.N. supported her through her difficulties with the authorities at Woolwich and Netley during all the years of her troubled superintendency.

54   Miss Clough was one of Mary Stanley's ladies who volunteered to go to Balaclava in January 1855. In March she went off to take charge of a regimental hospital with the Highland Brigade under Sir Colin Campbell for sentimental reasons. She died on 23rd September 1855 of "prolonged fevers and diarrhoea." (R. Roxburgh. "Miss Nightingale and Miss Clough," *Victorian Studies*, 1969, *13*, pp. 71–89; Anne Summers, "Pride and prejudice: ladies and nurses in the Crimean War," *History Workshop*, 1983, No. 16, pp. 33–56.)

55   Miss Tebbutt, one of Miss Stanley's ladies, took over the superintendence of the General Hospital, Scutari, when Miss Emily Anderson fell ill, and remained in that post for the duration of the war. She caused some trouble by becoming embroiled in the sectarian bickerings which were particularly rife in the General Hospital; the Church of England chaplain tried to force her dismissal, but F.N. refused, and the War Office likewise would not countenance such a move. But F.N. would not have been sorry to lose her. In report III – "Nurses and Ladies returning June 24/56" — F.N. wrote, "Though not exactly fitted for a Supt., still less for a Nurse, this lady's persevering and anxious care of the Nurses' morals & her devotion to the work deserve the gratitude of all. She has been Supt. of the General Hospital Scutari, since Feb./55 till the Hospital broke up." (B.L. Add. Ms. 43402, f.16.)

56   The Socinians, a sect founded in the sixteenth century, denied the divinity of Christ.

57   One man may steal a horse while another may not look over a hedge.

58   The Sanitary Commission, consisting of Dr John Sutherland, Dr Hector Gavin and Robert Rawlinson, arrived at Scutari in March 1855. Unlike the Hospitals Commission, which was instructed only to "inquire," the Sanitary Commission was issued with forceful instructions to act: "It is important that you be deeply impressed with the necessity of not resting content with an order, but that you see instantly, by yourselves or your agents, to the commencement of the work, and to its superintendence day by day until it is finished." (*Report . . . of the Proceedings of the Sanitary Commission dispatched to the Seat of War in the East, 1855–56*, London, 1875. *Parliamentary Papers*, 1875, 9, p. 241. Instructions, p.3)

59   The relationship between Purveyor and Medical Officer was not at all so clear to those in the field. It was reported to the Roebuck Committee: "The duties of Dr. Menzies were further obstructed by a conflict of authority with the purveyor, who claimed to act independently, under the instructions of the Secretary-at-War." (*Fifth Report of Select Committee on the Army before Sebastopol, Parliamentary Papers*, 1854–55, lxiii, p. 20.) And Dr Andrew Smith's evidence: "I cannot exactly describe what my position is in reference to the purveying department. At times I am told that I have full power over him; at other times I am told that I have not power, but that I must refer to the War Office; the consequence is, I cannot tell you exactly what my position in reference to the the purveyor is." (*Second Report of Select Committee on the Army before Sebastopol; ibid*, answer to question 8031.)

60   P.R.O. WO 43/963, f. 201.

61   Miss Margaret A. Wear was one of the party of forty ladies and nurses sent by the War Office to Smyrna to nurse the new Civil Hospital under the superintendence of Dr John Meyer. Sidney Herbert informed F.N. on 5th March 1855, "Dr. Meyer will, after trial, pick out the lady whom he thinks most fitted to act as head at Kullali to succeed Miss Stanley. Liz. thinks it will be either Mrs. Munro,

Miss Winthrop, or Miss Wear .... The nurses of course independent of you."
(Stanmore, I, p. 413.) It is not clear whether Miss Wear ever served at Smyrna; she
and one other seem to have arrived at Scutari at the same time as the six
Presbyterians mentioned by Herbert in the same letter. In any event, Miss Stanley
sent her back to F.N. as unsuitable. She then went up to Balaclava, where she took
over the General Hospital when Mrs Shaw Stewart moved to the Castle. Perhaps
because she had been destined for the Civil Hospital and relative independence in the
first place, Miss Wear never accepted F.N.'s authority, and was a constant source of
trouble in the Crimea, allying herself with Dr Hall, and championing the Irish nuns.
F.N. was never happy with Miss Wear as superintendent and on several occasions
tried to recall her to Scutari, without avail. In her end-of-term report, on the nurses
and ladies returning on 15th June 1856, F.N. described Miss Wear as "a devoted,
untiring and most kind and conscientious Nurse. But from habitual inaccuracy of
thought & expression, unfit for a Superintendent." (B.L. Add. Ms. 43402, f. 10.)
This stern judgement would seem to be borne out, at least to some extent, by Miss
Wear's letters to Dr Hall (see ch. 5) and, ironically, by Fitzgerald's Confidential
Report (see appendix).

62   In yet another disappointment, Anne Sinclair was dismissed for drunkenness
shortly after. (F.N. to Lady Cranworth, 10th February 1856, B.L. Add. Ms. 43397,
f. 85.)

63   Milton had had the "unparalled impertinence" to suggest that the free gifts
should be sold off. F.N. pointed out the impossibility of doing this in the strongest
terms in a letter to Sidney Herbert, not included in this selection (B.L. Add. Ms.
43393, f. 205.)

64   The Castle Hospital. Mrs Shaw Stewart moved from the General Hospital to
superintend the nursing of the new hospital.

65   The new Civil Hospital at Renkioi, designed by Isambard Kingdom Brunel in
prefabricated sections, was not completed until October. According to Shepherd the
nursing staff consisted of twenty paid nurses and five ladies for 500 beds. By the time
the hospital was ready the main pressure was over and the hospital accommodated
only 1,321 patients through its short existence. No cases were sent after February
1856. (John Shepherd, "The civil hospitals in the Crimea (1855–1856)." *Proceedings of the Royal Society of Medicine,* 1966, 59, 199–204.) The medical superintendent of the Renkioi hospital, Dr Edmund Parkes (1819–76), F.R.S., became a
firm and long-standing ally of F.N. In 1860 she secured his appointment as Professor
of Hygiene at the new Army Medical School set up at Fort Pitt. (See also Sir
Zachary Cope, *Florence Nightingale and the Doctors,* London, 1958.)

66   *North and South,* by Elizabeth Gaskell, was largely written at Lea Hurst. Mrs
Gaskell was an old friend of the Nightingales and knew F.N. well; she was evidently
somewhat chilled by her. (J. A. V. Chapple, *Elizabeth Gaskell, a Portrait in Letters,*
Manchester University Press.)

4

Balaclava: illness and convalescence

To her family

Black Sea
5th May 1855

Poor old Flo steaming up the Bosphorus & across the Black Sea with four Nurses, two Cooks & a boy to Crim Tartary (to over-haul the Regimental Hospitals) in the "Robert Lowe" or Robert Slow (for an uncommon slow coach she is) taking back 420 of her Patients, a draught of convalescents returning to their Regiments to be shot at again. A "mother in Israel", old Fliedner called me – a mother in the Coldstreams is the more appropriate appellation.

What suggestions do the above ideas make to you in Embley drawing-room? Stranger ones perhaps than to me – who, on the 5th May, year of disgrace 1855, year of my age 35, having been at Scutari this day six months, am, in sympathy with God, fulfilling the purpose I came into the world for.

What the disappointments of the conclusion of these six months are, no one can tell. But I am not dead, but alive. What the horrors of war are, no one can imagine, they are not wounds & blood & fever, spotted & low, & dysentery chronic & acute, cold & heat & famine. They are intoxication, *drunken* brutality, demoralization & disorder on the part of the inferior – jealousies, meanness, indifference, *selfish* brutality on the part of the superior. I believe indeed & am told by admirable officers in the service, that our Depot & Barrack at Scutari – in which to live for six months has been death, is a disgrace to the service & our Commandant the worst officer in the service, (had & solicited for by Ld. Stratford because he would have a man of rank). But our Scutari staff, military & medical, content themselves with saying that the English soldier *must* be drunk & not one thing is done to prevent him. Nothing has been done but by us. We have established a reading room for the Convalescents, which is well attended. And the conduct of the soldiers to us is uniformly good. I believe that we have been *the most efficient* – perhaps the only – means there of restoring discipline –

instead of destroying it, as I have been accused of. They are much more respectful to me than they are to their own officers. But it makes me cry to think that all these 6 months we might have had a trained schoolmaster & that I was told it was quite impossible – that, in the Indian army, effectual & successful measures are taken to prevent intoxication & disorganization, & that here, under Lord W. Paulet's very windows, the Convalescents are brought in emphatically *dead* drunk, for they die of it, & he looks on with composure & says to me "You are spoiling those brutes". The men are so glad to read, so glad to give me their money to keep or to send home to their mothers or wives.[1] But I am obliged to do this in secret.

On the 1st May, by the most extreme exertions, our Washing house opened, which might just as well have been done on the 1st November six months ago.

I am in hopes of organizing some washing & cooking for the Regimental Hospitals – & am going up with Soyer,[2] dollies & steaming apparatus for this purpose for more than for any other. Mr. Bracebridge goes with us. Mrs. B. keeps the bear-garden at Scutari. Four vessels of Sardinian troops go up with us – one vessel, the Argo, with Artillery & horses, ditto – but went aground in the Bosphorus & could not get her off.

I have more & more reason to believe that this is the kingdom of hell – but I as much believe that this is to be made the kingdom of heaven.

Beware of Lady Stratford

yours ever

P.S. [*written on inside of flap of envelope*] There is some Cholera in Camp, but not much. I want very much to hear how Blanch[3] is. I was very much disappointed that Aunt Mai did not write. I heard it through a common newspaper, till I had a note from Mama.

Claydon; copy, Wellcome (*Cal.* B. 4. B13, 68).

Thus, in jaunty mood, Florence Nightingale set out to bring order to the hospitals of the Crimea. A staff had already been sent up to the General Hospital in January under Miss Emma Langston, Mother Eldress, the Superior of the Sellonites. Then in April Miss Jane Shaw Stewart, who had gone up in January with the first party, took over the newly opened Castle Hospital on the Genoese Heights above Balaclava. The relationship of these ladies to Miss Nightingale, and indeed her right to be present in the Crimea at all, were open to question. She had opposed the sending of the first party under Miss Langston in the first place, and only reluctantly withdrew her opposition when it was clear that Lord Raglan wished it. But she continued to consider it "a mistake," and reports of the behaviour of the nurses under Miss Langston caused her a great deal of worry.

In her letter of 18th March to Sidney Herbert Miss Nightingale had written, "As to Balaklava, you say nothing. If you see no radical objection, I should like to keep it *for the present.*" But in fact in his letter of 5th March to which that was a reply her jurisdiction appeared to be limited to the Scutari hospitals, at least by implication: it was Lord Panmure's wish "to separate the different hospitals . . . now that there are so many and each so distant from the original establishments at Scutari . . ."

Certainly Dr Hall, Inspector General of Hospitals and head of the Medical Department in the East, chose to believe that she had no authority in the Crimea. And there is no evidence that Miss Nightingale ever thought of consulting Dr Hall either as to the disposition of nurses or as to the advisability of coming up herself. Perhaps she interpreted her Instructions[4] as meaning that she should consult the Principal Medical Officer of each individual hospital where there were nurses. In any case, what was once again a potentially difficult situation was not helped by a remarkable lack of tact on the part of Florence Nightingale in her dealings with Dr Hall.

She did, however, succeed in gathering about her the usual group of admirers, who again were the reformers. They included some powerful and influential men, the two commissioners appointed to enquire into the supply of the army, Dr John McNeill and Colonel Alexander Tulloch; the sanitary commissioners, Dr John Sutherland and Mr Robert Rawlinson; and a number of doctors who were disaffected under the present system. She remained anathema to the conservative elements in the Medical Department, who ranged themselves with Dr Hall to resist any change in the established order.

After five days visiting and inspecting the hospitals, Miss Nightingale again wrote to Hawes urging that no more female nurses be sent out.

To Benjamin Hawes, M.P.

Balaclava
10th May 1855

Dear Sir

Having now had the opportunity of examining myself into the condition of the Sick & Wounded here & hearing the opinion of the Medical Officers here, I hope you will allow me to trouble you with a few words about Female Nurses.

I arrived here a week ago with three of my Scutari Nurses, (as we had then every probability of having wounded immediately) – in order to re-inforce the eight Nurses whom I had previously sent here – to serve in the General Hopsital, – now containing about 200 sick – &, recently, in the Castle Hospital or Sanitarium, now containing about 110 wounded & 80 sick. The prospect of wounded is now indefinitely postponed. But, even in the case of any great & sudden emergency, there would be no lack of nurses – as I could spare any number from Scutari, for whom accommodation, in wooden huts or otherwise, could be made here – at least, twenty could be spared 50 being my present number at Scutari & Balaklava of whom I have at this moment

39	at Scutari
11	Balaklava
50	

It has been now announced as Lord Raglan's intention to keep his wounded, should there be unfortunately such, in the Crimea – .& to provide accommodation for them here – to the extent of about 2500*

I would earnestly deprecate the sending out any more "female troops" at present – for any of the existing Hospitals – I would point out that the number is far too large under existing circumstances, – the proportion of Convalescents being, I am thankful to say, in every Hospital from 1/3 to 9/10. The attendance of females upon Convalescents is obviously objectionable. I could work the Scutari Hospitals *at present* better with twenty than with forty Nurses. And I am informed by the Principal Medical Officer of Balaclava[5] that he considers 10–12 Nurses here, at present, amply sufficient – I have therefore, a reserve of twenty for a battle or an assault, whom I could bring up from Scutari at any moment. The health of the Army is admirable. We have a few cases of fever only, a few of Cholera.

To place women in the *Regimental* Hospitals could, of course, never be contemplated or permitted.

But, as there has been much irresponsible action in this matter of sending out Female Nurses to the Army – action too upon *partial* information,[6] – I have thought it desirable to express strongly to you an opinion founded upon present circumstances – & supported by all the Army Medical Officers.

> I remain, Sir,
> your obedt. servt.

P.R.O. WO 43/963, f. 225 (*Cal.* B. 4. B14, 70).

Her visit to the Crimea made a deep impression on Miss Nightingale. It was the first time she had come in contact with the troops about their normal business, and it reinforced the sympathy she had gained from dealing with them as patients. She sent Parthe a vivid impression of the camp, and the emotions watching it had roused in her. The letter breaks off after a few pages, clearly unfinished. Perhaps it was at this moment that the fever struck her.

*to the extent of viz. 700 sanitarium   1060–1590 Regimental huts besides
200 General Hospl. the huts about to be erected at
620 Transports   Monastery St. George

To Parthenope   10th May 1855

My dearest   My days at Balaklava have been so busy as you may suppose. I have made a tour of inspection of Regimental Hosp*ls*. in camp – besides re-organizing the two Hospitals under our care, which were terribly "seedy" – Nurses all in confusion.

The camp is very striking – more so than any one can imagine or describe. Between 150,000–200,000 men in a space of 20 square miles all obeying one impulse, engaged in one work – it is very affecting. But to me the most affecting sight was to see them mustering & forming at sun-down for the trenches – where they will be for 24 hours without returning. From those trenches 30 will never return. Yet they volunteer, press forward for the trenches. When I consider what the work has been this winter, what the hardships, I am surprised – not that the army has suffered so much but – that there is any army left at all, not that we have had so many through our hands at Scutari, but that we have not had all as Sir John McNeill says. Fancy working 5 nights out of 7 in the trenches, fancy being 36 hours in them at a stretch – as they were, all December, lying down or half lying down – often 48 hours without food but *raw* salt pork sprinkled with sugar – & their rum & biscuits – nothing hot – because the *exhausted* soldier *could not* collect his own fuel, as he was expected, to cook his own ration. And fancy, thro' all this, the army preserving their courage & patience – as they have done – & being now eager, the old ones more than the young ones, to be led even into the trenches.[7] There was something sublime in the spectacle. The brave 39th, whose Regimental Hospitals are the best I have ever seen, turned out & gave Florence Nightingale three times three, as I rode away. There was nothing empty in that cheer nor in the heart which received it. I took it as a true expression of true sympathy – the sweetest I have ever had. I took it as a full reward of all I have gone through. I promised my God that I would not die of disgust or disappointment, if he would let me go through this. In all that has been said against & for me, no one soul has appreciated what I was really doing, none but the honest cheer of the brave 39th.

Nothing which the "Times" has said has been exaggerated of Hardship.

Sir John McNeill[8] is the man I like the best of all who have come out. He has dragged Commissary General out of the mud. He has done wonders. Every body now has their fresh meat 3 times a week, their fresh bread from Constantinople about as often.

It was a wonderful sight looking down upon Sevastopol – the shell whizzing right & left. I send you a Miniè bullet[9] I picked up on the ground which was ploughed with shot & shell – & some little flowers. For this is the most flowery place you can imagine – a beautiful little red Tormentilla [sic] which I don't know, yellow Jessamine & every kind of low flowering shrub. A Serjt. of the 97th picked me a nosegay. I once saved Serjt. —'s life by finding him at 12 o'clock at night lying – wounds undressed – in our Hosp*l.* with a bullet in his eye & a fractured skull. And I pulled a stray Surgeon out of bed to take the bullet out. But you must not tell this story. For I gave evidence against the missing Surgeon – & have never been forgiven.

Sir John McNeill whom you must not quote, it was who told me that it was . . .

Claydon; copy, Wellcome (*Cal.* B. 4. C1, 71).

The exact date on which Florence Nightingale fell ill with the Crimean fever seems to be unknown. She was taken to a hut of the Castle Hospital, where she was nursed with devoted care by Mrs Roberts, the nurse from St Thomas's Hospital, to whom she owed her life, as she was always afterwards to maintain.

She left the Crimea on the 5th June,[10] escorted by Mr and Mrs Bracebridge, but it was more than a month after her last letter to Parthe before she was able to write a shaky note to her family, reassuring them that she was now recovering and back at Scutari.

To her family

Scutari
18th June 1855

This comes, dearest people, to inform you that I think much & often of you, which is not necessary & that you are too anxious, which is necessary.

The "baptism of fire", what words those are! must baptize all those who would be "Saviours" of mankind, whether from intellectual, physical, but most of all from moral error.

We are daily expecting the wind-up of our affairs in the Crimea, so long promised us, now, it seems, actually impending.

You may fancy what it cost me to leave Balaklava at such a time. But the Drs. were peremptory & Σ came to fetch me. I think seeing her did me more good than all their blisters.

I am gaining strength every day but suffering from a compound fracture of the intellect.

I think my handwriting does the Drs. credit.

Yours ever, in sickness as in health

I wish you would write your thanks to Mrs. Roberts who nursed me to her own injury as if I had been her only child.

Alas & yet not alas that I should not see Aunt Hannah[11] again.

Claydon; copy, Wellcome (*Cal.* B. 4. C2, 75).

It was ironic that Miss Nightingale should have been writing about the "wind-up of our affairs in the Crimea" on the day of the unsuccessful assault on the Malakoff, which was planned to precede the final attack on

Sebastopol itself. Once again the hospitals of the Crimea filled with wounded. A week later, on 25th June, Lord Raglan died, either from a broken heart at this failure or from cholera. Florence Nightingale, who greatly respected him as a gentleman, if not as a soldier, provided a fitting epitaph:

To her family

Scutari, 5th July 1855

Dearest people   You are too good. Your letters have given me so much pleasure & helped to cure me more than anything.

I have been sent to Therapia for a few days where Mrs. Roberts & I had a ward in the Naval Hospital to ourselves with the most glorious view in the world & I am come back much stronger.

Many thanks for what you have done for the little boys, which glads our hearts to hear – i.e. mine & Hawkins.

I enclose you a dismal note of poor Ann Clark's. I wish you could take her as a servant or find her a place. She is discreet above her years, active, obliging, clean, has a good notion of linen & needlework – & did for me as much as two servants. She is a good scholar, stupid & affectionate. Many a time she has stood between me & her Aunt's indiscretions – never repeating anything – & always contented. I wish I could do something for her. She wd. make a good housemaid.

Lord Raglan's death thunderstruck us – (1) There is but one voice among the soldiery. "Now we shall take Sevastopol." (2) It was impossible not to love him for his kind & gentle courtesy. I did. But I shd. think his death an equal gain to himself & us – to himself, because a good man has been taken from the evil to come – to us, because few perhaps could have done worse for us than he has done. If I might tell the real history of the 18*th*!

A private letter was read to me about his illness – from a medical man in camp. The Diarrhoea was slight – but he was so depressed by our defeat of Waterloo Day, the more by reason of his apparent equanimity, which never failed, that he sank rapidly without sufficient physical reason. It was *not* Cholera. Peace be with him & with his hecatomb of twenty thousand men. With regard to my returning home, the idea is too pleasant – it is too good for me. How can I? If Miss N. goes to England, says my troop, she will never come back – & all my best, Rev*d*. Mother & her crew, Roberts, Polidori, Hawkins & several nurses, Robbins etc. have announced their intention of not staying if I go. This is not so selfish as it at first appears. With so many jarring elements, without a central authority, they wd. not be able to do any good here.

Yours till Doomsday i' th' afternoon

With what longing love I think of our hilltop where you now are you cannot think.

The letter ends at the top of the first page.
Claydon; copy, Wellcome.

Meanwhile, to cheer her up, Parthenope wrote and had printed the story of *The life and death of Athena, an owlet from the Parthenon.*

To Parthenope

Scutari
9th July 1855

Dearest I cannot tell you how the record of Athena's little life & death affected us all. It is worth while to have died to be so remembered. Curious instinct! A little terrier rat-catcher, sent us by Mr. Herbert, the most engaging of all animals, except Athena, was so aware that we were reading about something we loved more than it, that it never ceased whining & howling & caressing & fidgetting while the book of Athena's exploits was being read.

My own effigy & praises were less welcome. I do not affect indifference towards *real* sympathy – but I have felt painfully, the more painfully since I have had time to hear of it, the éclat which has been given to this adventure. The small still beginning, the simple hardship, the silent & *gradual* struggle upwards – these are the climate in which an enterprise really thrives & grows – time has not altered our Saviour's lesson on that point – which has been learnt successively by all reformers, down to Fliedner, from *their own experience*. The vanity & frivolity which the éclat thrown upon this affair has called forth – which seemed to animate all Miss Stanley's party, of whom now scarce a wreck remains, (except that good old mad Shaw Stewart, who escaped it all,) has done us unmitigated harm, & brought ruin to (perhaps) the most promising enterprise that ever set sail from England. Our own old party which began its work in hardship, toil, struggle, poverty & obscurity has done better than any other, & I, like a Tory, am now trying to get back to all my first regulations.

Dr. Sutherland[12] has given it as his opinion that "to go to England is neither necessary nor advantageous for" me. He says that it would be too great a strain upon me. He says that Switzerland would be best & Therapia next best – Balaclava not for two months.

I believe I am going to Prinkipò, the capital of Princes' Islands for a couple of days with Σ & then must decide what I really ought to do – feeling that, if I go, all this will fall to pieces.

Yours ever, whatever betides

Claydon; copy, Wellcome (*Cal.* B. 4. C3, 79).

Florence Nightingale has been accused by many of being censorious and ungenerous towards almost all who came in contact with her in the East. Certainly she expected a great deal of her subordinates. But she was unstinting in her praise where she felt praise was due. Her tributes to Rev.

Mother Bermondsey, Mrs Shaw Stewart, Mrs Roberts, Mrs Drake and many others are often in the nature of panegyrics. The following letter to Mrs Herbert contains a glowing tribute to another, invalided home with broken health.

To Mrs Herbert

Scutari

11th July 1855

Dearest Lizzy

Mrs. Noble, who has just left us, I am sorry to say, with broken health, & advised to return home (from the Westminster Hosp*l.* she came) deserves, if any one ever did, a year's salary from the War Office. I told her that I would recommend her to you for this – 1*st* because she has been one of our best, kindest, most proper, most skilful Surgical Nurses – in the two Hospitals of Balaclava successively – 2*nd* because she has contracted a complaint from which I fear her perfect recovery is doubtful. I have a real attachment for her. Of all Miss Stanley's party she, Mrs. Shaw Stewart! & Mrs. Robbins (from Birmingham) have turned out the best.

Robertson,[13] the new Purveyor, works wonderfully. It is awful to think what, had he come sooner, & Wreford been displaced sooner, might have been spared. He has furnished & stored the Hospital with every possible needful. But, till Lord Wm. Paulet, the Commandant, & Cumming, the Ins*r.* Gen*l.* are removed, I am not afraid of saying that no attempt even at a real system which will prevent a recurrence of our calamitous winter, should the press of sick recur, will be made. I do not fear saying this, now; you are out of office. The D. of Newcastle is here, to whom I have told pretty nearly the whole truth. Had the broad sketch of your Government been carried out by the officials here, all would have been well. But it was not. Could we have had Gen*l.* Jones, vice Ld. W. Paulet, as Commandant, Dr. Sutherland as Medical Chief, vice Cumming, & Robertson as Purveyor then vice Wreford, nothing of what has happened would have happened. But there is hardly a man here excepting Robertson, who is not diametrically opposed in feeling & action to the Govt., the Houses of Parl*t.*, the Queen & the country. They are hopeless. NOW, the great diminution of numbers, the magnificent profusion of matériel, a very active & efficient Purveyor make things march & we look well. But there is not the shadow of real improvement in system. All are just as much wedded to everything that was done in the Peninsular War as ever. But the sinner of all was Wreford – & he being absent, things *look* better. If I could outlive Cumming & Ld. W. here I might live to see what my soul longs for & really I think we deserve this. Now I will say what I would not, except under this pressure, & what I would not, if you were in office have said – what I will never say to anyone else. *We* pulled this Hospital through for 4 months & without us, it would have come to a stand-still.[14] That time may & very likely will come again next winter, should there be another press of sick, anything like the last, should there be a less active Purveyor or should he be thwarted in his endeavours, which I know has been already so much the case that he has threatened to resign.

Since I wrote this, Lord W. Paulet has told me that he will very likely be ordered up to the front. God grant his successor may do something for us.

ever yours

The direction of Mrs. Noble, should you give her a year's salary, as you proposed for those with broken health, is

Mary Noble
at Mr. Flexon's
15 Buckstone St.
Mile End
Newtown.

Will you thank Mr. Herbert very much for a most kind letter which I received from him at Balaclava? It was truly kind. I hope he is recovering.

B.L. Add. Ms. 43396, f. 35 (*Cal*. B. 4. C3, 80).

On 14th July Miss Nightingale committed another serious error which was to lead her into a new set of difficulties as harassing as those she had experienced as a result of refusing to accept Miss Stanley's party nine months previously: she suggested to Dr Hall that she should withdraw the nurses from the General Hospital at Balaclava. She was in fact anxious to remove Miss Wear[15] from the superintendency of the General Hospital, as she considered that lady unsuited to be a superintendent in any situation, as well as being disloyal to herself.

To Dr John Hall[16]

Scutari, Barrack Hospital
14th July 1855

My dear Sir

Having unfortunately been deprived of the services of several Nurses at the General Hospital, Balaclava, since my departure on 5th June – and, as the season of the year must add to the heat & discomfort of the Hospital & therefore act injuriously upon the Superintendent & Nurses who remain, I have reluctantly formed the opinion that it would be right to withdraw my Nurses from the General Hospital, at least, till October

I therefore hasten to apply to you for advice on this subject – & trust that you will have the goodness as soon as possible to examine the question of the Nurses at the General Hosp*l*.

I have an additional reason for applying to you from the report which prevails that you are about to decide upon restricting the use of these buildings & huts to that of a mere refuge for the sick in transit from the Camp to Scutari & England.

Should you advise me to act upon this opinion, it will become a farther question whether any Nurses could be sent to your Sanitarium at the Monastery, supposing that not to become a Hospital for Convalescents only. It is a recognised rule with me not to send Nurses to such.

Besides this, as my numbers are so restricted, and as I have determined not to have any Nurses out from England during the hot weather, it would probably at once be wisest to concentrate those who remain at Balaclava upon the Castle Hospital.

I beg to thank you for your kindness during my illness. Though I am not able to walk much in the Hospitals I am beginning to enter again into the business. The wounded are doing well. One man only has been landed from the Tasmania who sails tonight.

I beg to remain, dear Sir,

Yours sincerely

I send a copy of the above to Dr. Hadley

Since writing this, a letter from Miss Wear informs me that you may perhaps send her & her nurses to the Monastery. May I request that you will not come to this determination without previously consulting me. As we cannot undertake another Hosp*l*. without consideration – & there may be circumstances impossible now to detail which would prevent it.

B.L. Add. Ms. 39867, f. 17 (*Cal*. B. 4. C4, 81.)

Dr Hall replied curtly, "I had no intention whatever of sending the nurses to the new Hospital Establishment at the Monastery . . . "[17] This may have been the truth in July, but within two months Miss Wear persuaded him to let her undertake the Monastery, thereby enlisting his support in her own rebellion. He now seized the opportunity to put Miss Nightingale in the wrong, writing that he needed to retain nurses at the General Hospital, but offering to obtain them elsewhere – a proposition Miss Nightingale, anxious for her authority in the Crimea, could not possibly agree to. She accordingly wrote back:

To Dr Hall

Barrack Hospital, Scutari

24th July 1855

My dear Sir,

I am obliged by your letter of July 20, received yesterday. I am sorry to find that you have such good reason for retaining the General Hospital for general purposes. Upon my proposition you remark "that, if two Nurses could be kept there, it would be a convenience" – but that if I wish "to withdraw them altogether," you "will make some other arrangement for the sick."

I feel that I cannot do otherwise than at once accede to your proposition – and I will write to Miss Wear accordingly – that she may remain with one nurse.

It is obvious that, if two only are retained, they must undertake a less amount of personal labor. Their duties must resemble more those of the French Sisters of Charity, who overlook the linen, & extra Diets of the Patients, – & see that their cleanliness & smaller comforts are attended to.

I am very much obliged for the other details of your letter. I hope that your health will be preserved for the most important objects of carrying out the centralization of the service.

I beg to remain, dear Sir,
Yours truly

I am grateful for your kind interest about my health & am glad to say that I am able to take a portion of my duties in the Hospitals.

B.L. Add. Ms. 39867, f. 22 (*Cal.* B. 4. C5, 87).

This exchange represented the opening salvo in what was to develop into a full-scale and long-drawn-out war. For the moment, however, with Miss Nightingale convalescing at Scutari, an uneasy truce was maintained between the Inspector General and the Lady Superintendent of the Nursing Establishment.

On 28th July the Bracebridges left, several months after their time was up, deeply regretted by Miss Nightingale, who paid extravagant but moving tribute to Mrs Bracebridge in particular:

For nine months she has been the moving power by which these hospitals were made to go at all – & no one can tell what she has been to me – more than my Egeria – almost my Holy Ghost. I have kept them two months after their time, which I shall never cease to regret – though regret be unphilosophical – & more, impertinent. With Mr. Bracebridge goes the only man of sense & feeling & the only man but one of business in these miserable Hospitals.[18]

By the beginning of August Miss Nightingale was still not fully recovered, but she was beginning to pick up the threads of her work, and her mind was as active and far-ranging as ever. The opening of the letter she wrote to her friends ten days after their departure suggests she was suffering from depression. Officers whom she had formerly regarded as beyond reproach were now found to be incompetent or drunk. What is more likely is that this dissatisfaction was a reflection of her own state of mind. Now that the fearful emergency which had fuelled her energy was over, the hospitals were in excellent order, and men who had laboured to exhaustion to bring about this improvement were inclined to take a well deserved rest. So the depression natural to the convalescent state was probably exaggerated by feelings of redundancy.

But Florence Nightingale could not rest. And in this, one of the longest letters she wrote from the Crimea, she gave free rein to her restless intellect, ranging over a wide field – the physical and moral salvation of the army.

To Mr and Mrs Bracebridge

Scutari
7th August 1855

My dearest friends

I have so much to write to you about that is really important & no time to write it in.

I am like one in a Greek tragedy where all is *fated* to ruin & struggle is useless. I think this tragedy greater far than any of Aeschylus & I feel like Prometheus bound to the rock, against which every thing is going to wreck – the rock of ignorance, incompetency & ill-will. For McGregor is incompetent, Lord Wm. is ignorant & Robertson is drunk. Everybody deteriorates in this place – & deterioration is the most tragic of all denouements & Robertson, whom I looked to as our plank of salvation came to me the other day in a state which I thought was the pangs of despised love or of drink. And I afterwards found from private information it was brandy. He has only been three hours in the place during the whole of the past week, the rest being spent at Koulali. I have sent for him twice a day for seven days upon very particular business concerning his own Linen Stores & he has never been to be found. Now he has the Cholera which is better – & I am going to him. Lord Wm. goes to England next week.

If I could have condescended to make these men in love with me, it wd. have been better. But that I could not do.

I (*Caffè*)

By dint of Pincoffs,[19] & me & the incessant exertion of money, the Coffee-house was opened yesterday. I advanced others £150 – & sent them hams, butter, brandy, tea-urn, tent, prints, a band, newspapers etc. for the opening day when everything was gratis. I went, though I could hardly stand, because I did not choose the Nurses to go without me. I was cheered, of course, & my health drunk when my Uncle[20] answered, to my great humiliation. There was some good speaking, but the best was from a common Serjeant, who proposed the health of the Chaplains, Protestant & Catholic.

I brought the Nurses of both Hospitals away in twenty minutes, which nothing but my going myself could have done. The sympathy of these honest fellows is like the Chorus in the Greek tragedy, always the best part.

I am sorry to say that Pincoffs hurts Valerio's proud feelings so much that that worthy professes he only stays for love of me, & I am afraid he will go at last. I am always adjusting quarrels. They settled the list of prices without consulting him, the most absurd prices. I made a new List, which was accepted by the Committee, or I think they never could have sold anything. Shore & Pincoffs are the only men who take the least interest, & Shore knows nothing of business, – & Pincoffs is too worrying. I wish you could have staid over the opening of the Caffè, I am afraid we shall have more trouble.

II (Huts)

But to business. I dislike writing this next excessively – because it is not my business – & one does not like reminding & teasing the Government to do that which it may have done already. But the existence of the army next winter depends upon it. And so please to consider that you must never change your shirt till this is done. The Isabelle Linen will be the consequence.

I understand, from all the Officers who come down & from Lord William himself that there is not a single Regiment hutted – that, if they are not hutted before winter, the same misfortunes will befal us which befell us last winter.

I understand that the Officers sometimes ask for huts for themselves, & are told that there they are at Balaclava, which is true, if they can bring them up to camp – which they cannot, because they are too heavy.*

The only Reg*t*. which was hutted, was the 39th, you know, & those huts have been converted into a General Hosp*l*.

I hear there are seven miles of huts coming out for the HORSES. But even this is doubtful.

Secondly, all competent authorities suppose that we shall be before Sevastopol another winter.

III (Trenches) If so, & if this trenches' work still goes on, as they seem to suppose it will, unless we have a trenches' dress, we shall have a repetition of what you only who saw our last winter's work, of taking off frost-bitten feet, can imagine. There must be a trenches' dress – I would propose a light flexible material of Gutta Percha or some thing of the kind to draw over the feet & fasten with a strap in front so as to accommodate all feet – & to draw up to the thigh – fastening round the waist. Gloves or gauntlets lined with fur, to prevent frostbitten hands – and *ears,* to fall down over the ears.

Anyone accustomed to the business could invent a dress better than I – but there must be a dress, with water proof coat, (*that* matters little how it is made). It was not the excessive cold, but the wet, the evaporation which cut off our men's hands & feet last winter. And the sights I saw then only the Surgeons can tell who will not tell. The men ought to march down to the trenches in their usual boots, mits & dress, carrying the light trenches' dress with them, put it on not over, but *instead of* their usual dress, & put on their

---

*It takes 40 horses to bring one up to camp – & the Railroad won't or can't be used, because it is more than preoccupied with carrying Commissariat stores.

own dry dress again when they come out. The trenches dress should be solid enough to rush out of the trenches in, if necessary. I do not understand these things but that a dress should be invented & sent out by those who do, is absolutely necessary to save life.

Pray see to this. I will never cease bothering about it.

It may have been done already – but, if not, the health of the army is at stake.

Bakewell,[21] the Surgeon in the front who wrote the letter in the Times about the Regimental Hospital, has been dismissed the Service – discharged for his letter. I have not seen the man, because I thought him a wrong headed mortal when he was at the General Hosp*l*. here, 6 months ago, & I have enemies enough without Quixotizing. But I believe his letter was correct.

IV *(Hospitals in front)*

I will tell you why. Last week came down the "Wm. Jackson" from Balaclava with wounded Invalids for England. Her crew deserted & she has been detained here now a week in consequence & is still here, with 3 wounded Officers & 98 wounded Privates all on board – most of them amputation cases – shoulder-joints & high up in the thigh. Three who were dying were brought in here – two of these are since dead. I was horrified & scandalized by the condition of these. One with a broken jaw (by a shell) had a wound in the back of the head, another in the breast – & the whole of the back of the neck excoriated (not from the enemy's shell but) from the matter coming from the wound in the face having been allowed to run down & accumulate till the flesh was eaten away & the bone laid bare. They were brought in here after 9 o'clock at night. Mrs. Roberts dressed the wound in my presence & was two hours cleaning away the accumulated filth. The man said "Thank you" when he could hardly speak. Afterwards he became delirious & died in three days. They were all too far gone to gather from them clearly where they came from. But I think the Jaw-man came from the Hospital in the front.

There was no fault here. Dr. Summers was upon the spot immediately – so were restoratives – & I was allowed to send in Isinglass flavor*d*. with Wine from us for the dying. And if the Dressers were not forthcoming, so much the better.

The whole story is to me in⌣omprehensible – & had I not seen it, I would not have believed it – how they were sent home at all in such a state (the death of one, I can have no doubt, was occasioned by moving him – it was a wound in the leg, nearly healed, with inflammation of the absorbents) & how they were so neglected. The Jaw case must have been the result of the neglect of two or three weeks, not of that merely of the voyage, which was remarkably short. I have written to Mrs. Stewart to learn whether any came from her Hospital. Oh that they would send us to the Hospital in the front. But while a drunken isolated Miss Clough receives not only toleration but sanction, I should be considered mad if I were to offer to undertake the General Hosp*l*. in the front with a regular body of women.

V *(Nuns)*

Now for the Nuns at the Gen*l*. Hosp*l*. I have at last compelled them to send in the List of Names of those whom they "instruct". This is their own word, though the W.O. despatch says expressly they are not to instruct. I think I told you that they are appointed as *Nurses* to three out of the six Divisions of the Hospital.

The other three Divisions they have distributed among themselves to "instruct". When I wrote to them, they simply sent me the names of these three Divisions, making up thus the whole Hospital under R. Catholic care. I answered that I "was sure they would allow me to smile" at such a way of informing me what they were doing, & ended by saying, which was suggested to me by my Rev*d*. Mother, that I took for granted they only went to Patients in an advanced state of disease (i.e. in Corridors *not* their own) & that they sent the Convalescents to the priests to instruct. I knew well that they were principally seen in the two Convalescent Corridors – & that the gossip of the *lay* Sister with Orderlies & Convalescents in the Corridors was the talk of the whole Hospital.

I suppose they found themselves in the wrong, for the next day came the long requested list. *One* Sister had in the one Divison (& that *not* her own except religiously), which Division is one sixth of the Hospital, FORTY-NINE names!! I thought this peculiar – & wrote to them to come at last & see me. The Rev*d*. Brickbat had never thought fit to come near me since I was ill, tho' I sent her the £5 to do so. They came – & I asked them what the proportion of R.C.s among the Patients was. They said at once, one fourth. How then, said I, can there be forty-nine R.C.s for you to instruct in one sixth of a Hospital, which has not contained for four months above 400 patients, generally little more than 300? (I forgot to tell you that I had made enquiry – & found that, in one Sister's list, in the *whole* Division, there were only two in bed – in another only six – & these, it seems to me obvious, are the only ones to whom women should go).

Oh! said the Sister directly, I "instruct" the Orderlies & *that* makes up so large a number, together with the Convalescents.

I asked her whether she did not think such should go to the Priest & that we women were for the sick.

No, she said, it was no use "instructing" the Sick – it was only the well that it was any use to go to.

Now I thoroughly believe in the conscientiousness of these women, though they never cease to bother me – they have been intriguing again with Robertson about their Room & their Door & about building & knocking down & partitioning for them – till I have been obliged to speak to the latter – Sister Elizabeth having actually told me that I need not trouble myself – for that the females at Koulali & Robertson would settle it all.

Still I believe Sister Elizabeth & her nuns to be thoroughly conscientious (the Lay Sister is nothing but a gossip – & I have been obliged to remove her from her wards). I believe that they don't like forcing their "instructions" upon Orderlies, but that *they* are ordered to do it.

The question with me is not at all that of R. Catholicism v. Protestantism – not at all a religious question. It is that every body laughs at them, excepting those who cry. My Rev*d*. Mother cannot bear their doing it – says that she never remembers its being allowed, even in Ireland, in Convents – that she would feel it most awkward to have to do it. The question with me is, – we are sent out to nurse in a Military Hosp*l*. Is it desirable, is it not calculated to bring ridicule upon the whole thing, for women & young women, be they veiled or be they not, to stand about Corridors talking to knots of Orderlies or Convalescents upon religious subjects or any others? – I would have dismissed any Nurse who talked as their Lay Sister does.

I must premise that S. Elizabeth & I are on the most friendly terms – & that all this passes in the guise of mere question & answer. Also, with Robertson I get on admirably when I see him.

I have complaints innumerable from the Gen. Hosp. where they are always quarrelling. Some are trivial. Three, I think, are authenticated.

A poor dying R. Catholic had fallen asleep after many days & nights of utter sleeplessness. The nun came in, & the nurse said, He is asleep. She passed on without taking any notice & woke him. This was in a ward where the Nun was not nursing.

A controversial Periodical called the "Lamp", which puts the Ch. of England in a very ridiculous point of view, is distributed (N.B. I believe the Protestants have religiously adhered to *their* promise *not* to distribute any controversy). And is read aloud by a R.C. Orderly in a Corridor not his own to a knot of laughing Orderlies, when the Protestant Sister comes by.

In one case a boy was persuaded not to eat after he had been confessed & communicated. The boy was not dying & ultimately lived some time, after he had been compelled to eat.

Father Molony & Lyas are at their tricks again – & I believe that both Lawfield & Sanson are only waiting to take places in Scutari for their new masters to promise that they will frank them home when they like to go which they cannot obtain.

I am glad you are gone. The weather here has been atrocious. Heat like a steam-bath. Tropical thunder & lightning & tropical rains. If we could but catch it. But the poor washermen come to me with the cry of "No water" & Gordon does nothing. Meanwhile the Hospital is flooded & our quarters too. I hope you have not forgotten "Times" & "Illustrated News" for Caffè, which I supply at present, but cannot go on.

I have anticipated the operations of Nature by shaving my head, & I find it a great comfort in this weather to be able to wash my head twice a day.

142

The letters from "heartbroken friends at home" have begun again – friends who want to know whether a man who died in Feby. (a time when we were never in from the wards till near twelve o'clock) "appeared to have any desire to be saved & left a Savings Bank Book for £20". I am desired to give the minutest particulars of what he thought & did not think at 6 months' distance of time to a "praying Mother & a father who has feared God many years." Curiously enough, I remember this man – tho' at that time we were losing from fifty to seventy a day.

Some publishers write to me to ask to publish my Crimean experience.

VI (Sending money home)

Some sharp men here when they bring their money to send home say that you allowed them 1/- to £1 & when they gave you £5 5s, their wives received £5 10. They want to know whether I shall do the same. Pray tell me what I am to do, if this is the case now.

The Allobroges are dreadful & come round poor Revd. Mother, but they don't inspire me at all with their howls. There was one Allobrog came to me howling for mourning for her husband just dead of the Cholera & I found Ly. Alicia had given her mourning complete a week ago.

The work in the Linen Stores has grown tremendously. I have been obliged to put on four Nurses & two Nuns and a half besides two Orderlies, for it was really wearing Revd. Mother & the women out this weather.

VII (Nurses)

I have been making great reforms – changed all the Nurses wards all round to break off acquaintances which I accidentally found out were coming to bad. One or two had already gone a long way – & Mrs. Tainton fell sick in consequence. We have been much more respectable since.

Sanson is a dreadful mischief maker, I have found out. So much for St. John's house. It has worked me nothing but mischief, excepting poor Drake.[22] Lawfield behaves perfectly well. But I expect every day to hear of her going.

Hawkins has been sober two whole days – the result of my having locked up the Brandy in our sitting-room in the closet in the kitchen & keeping the key. But she never wants *now* to clean the sitting room, nor ever offers to do anything – tho' she protested the very day after you went away she was always ready to clean. I have changed her wards & broken off her acquaintances.

Howse, I am afraid, is getting drunk. Clark & Tainton, the two most troublesome ones, are luckily in bed.

VIII (Officers Nurses)

Do pray try & make Koulali into an Officer's Hospl. They want Nurses. Now the ladies there have learnt to nurse a little & have learnt to flirt a little, both requisites for doing the business to the Officers' satsifaction. It seems to me Koulali is the very place for an Officers' Hospl., instead of plaguing me for Nurses. We have, by this Morning's state, 101 Officers sick, of whom *not one* in bed, & every one has a servant. Do you think I will give them Nurses? Hang me if I do! They are sick, q[uer]y, of the Krimea?

Ly. Canning's Nurses under Mrs. Willoughby Moore[23] are just arriving, Ld. Wm. says.

M. Vido has never shewn since he was paid his wages – the coolest thing he has done yet.

Antonio reigns triumphant.

Can any good thing come out of the Embassy?

The greatest compliment I have had paid to me was by the Vice-Consul at Missolonghi who said that Lord Raglan was dead which was bad – but that Miss Nightingale was going to be married, which was worse.

Now, please remember that I say this about the *Hutting & Trenches' clothing* in every letter, though I never write again.

We are filling the Corridors again. Our numbers are increasing. They are emptying the Hospitals in the front, which looks like business & on the Genoese heights. Soyer & Dumont are gone up. The Patients here don't like Soyer's cookery, in whom I believe, nearly so well as ours, & I hear nothing but complaints. But I will not reopen our kitchens yet. Robertson is falling into the same habits of indecision as Wreford. Lemons, vinegar, lime-juice, he will not make up his mind to buy. So I have bought a cargo of Lemons from Messina & Messrs Barton's Vinegar, or the Hospitals would have come off minus – I think this is the Hospital & the Grave Yard of all the Virtues, which do all fall sick here. Also, they have left off purveying the Sheds with Stationery & say they have none – so I have begun again.

Pray do not forget a print of Inkermann, of the Queen etc. etc. & a map of the Krimea etc. for the Caffè.

Pray don't forget us

The thing I should like best if you would send me would be a good Novel – not fashionable – like Mrs. Gaskell's "North & South," which also you might send us in its whole Edition. (I have read it in Household Words) – for the Reading Room. When I lie down, which I never do, I think of all the things to be done & they start me up again. If I had a good Novel, perhaps I should not think of them.

Mr. Sabin is ill & gone home. He is no loss to me, tho' he was the best of the Chaplains. I like Dr. Blackwood however, if he would not come & read the Times in my room. Only think of that Lawless being our Senior Chaplain. I don't think the Greek tragedy ever turned out a character like him.

Everybody is going home to England but the Bashi-Bazouki & me. A child in England, hearing we wanted reinforcements, has sent me his wooden soldier without an arm.

Will somebody kindly write to Sir James Clark & to Mr. Bowman & say that I wish to thank them very much for their kind advice, which, so far from annoying me, touched & pleased me very much that they should think of me – but that my Medical adviser, Dr. Sutherland, thought it best that I should not return to England. Should Σ come back, I will make a little tour to Brusa in November.

I enclose letters from two very different men, the flowery Purveyor of Balaclava & the surly P.M.O. of Scutari, in answer to two questions of Mr. Bracebridge's.

We have had several horses killed & several men struck down but not killed by the lightning. Every one says they never remember such.

The joke here is that Genl. Simpson[24] does not speak French & cannot write English. There is no good news from the Krimea.

I have just heard that Mrs. Willoughby Moore, the widow of the Europa, is *on her way* out with the Officers' Nurses. I don't know whom she is to nurse. But she is a very proper age for it.

I have had a disagreeable business with Tainton. She made love to a man, an Orderly, who turned out to be a married man. I first said that she & a nun were to be together in the wards – she rebelled, hoping that I would take of the unwelcome restraint – and I then removed her altogether off her wards, which she expected so little & was vexed at so much that she fell sick. I have not told her that I know it. But, as all the Nurses know, I fear she must go back to England.

I do not wish to discuss those trivial instances of R.C. empiètement which I have told you with R.C. Bishops who always get the best of it. But the great question as to whether the Nuns are to wander about "instructing" Convalescents & Orderlies strikes at the very root.

9th

Lothian Nicholson [25] came yesterday & goes to the Krimea today. He looks well & in good spirits tho' his face is blistered with heat. I was so very glad to see him. He gave me a cruel account of dear Aunt Hannah's sufferings. If she still lives, ask her to send a message, tell her how I have thought of her & loved her & how I shall miss her being on earth. I should have liked to have seen her again. The old are so much better than the young. If she is still living, tell her why I have not written. If not, it does not signify. She will understand.

If Aunt Mai does come out, what a pity she did not come with Lothian. I really think it is doubtful now whether she had better take the trouble. I may be gone to B'clava before she is well here now. Is it worth her making the exertion? I shall go up at the end of this month probably to the Krim.

Oh if you had seen the flood! The water pouring into our Quarters like a spout. The Corridor between our Quarters & the Main Guard impassable – (the rain continued 24 hours) I, catching sight of a Hospital Orderly, making telegraphic signs to him to go to Dr. McGrigor & get an Order for a fatigue party & tubs for us. The Depot thoroughly flooded out. I had sent our Orderlies to "Rag and Famish" to rescue our stores. But my telegraph succeeded.

I have got another Athena. Shall I keep him?

Claydon; copy, Wellcome (*Cal.* B. 4. C7, 92).

On 27th August she wrote to the Bracebridges again, a vividly dramatic account of a fire which destroyed a whole area of Constantinople.

To the Bracebridges

27th August 1855

The beautiful Kadikoi was burnt to the ground last night. Did you ever see a town on fire? It is impossible to conceive it. No one knows any thing definite this morng. It is said 200 houses & some women & children were burnt. I believe & trust the latter is exaggerated. The fire began at one & was all out by 4½ A.M. The terrible & malignant rapidity of the spread of fire in these wooden houses is what one fancies one conceived but does not.

There was not a breath of wind stirring. The full moon lay cold & bright on the glassy blue sea in the Bosphorus. While Marmora & the fleeces in the sky were all one hue of flame. With all the stillness, it spread & in one hour the whole of Kadikoi was one sheet of blazing red. There was not a sound but the occasional howling of dogs. The silence was awful. I thought Oriental fatalism was a novelist's myth now. But Scutari was as quiet as if nothing were the matter. A few men saunterd out smoking their pipes. "Sonst nichts" – I shall make a subscription here & if many poor have suffered, I will let you know. But probably the Greek merchants in London will subscribe or do something of their own accord. I shall propose here that every man shall subscribe a day's pay, which they can well afford. Lord W. Paulet was absent & is not come back yet. So he is not to blame. Clarke, who is sick & I were sleeping up at the House. She woke me & said, that the Barrack Hosp*l*. was on fire. I soon saw it was not that. But I thought it was the Cavalry Barracks & I scudded faster than I thought my legs cd. carry me to the Barrack Hosp*l*. in case the alarm was not given to get out the fire engine. It was not – tho' many men were standing outside at the Main Guard. In a moment, a fatigue party came up at "pas de course" from the Depot & dragged away the fire engine. But you might just as well have played upon the sun. We know so few particulars that I am afraid to blame. But there seemed no attempt to blow up houses. It began at the farthest extremity from the sea & licked on till it reached the sea – in one long line. A blazing whirlwind of orange smoke which might be a mile high, for any calculation one can make. Had there been wind, one cannot think where it would have stopped.

Question V. The Nuns cannot go to B'clava without the Rev*d*. Mother & I cannot spare her from the Linen Stores here & she is satisfied of the great good she does.

Incomplete? R.A.M.C. Museum, Aldershot (*Cal.* omitted).

On 8th September the Russians withdrew from Sebastopol, leaving the town open to occupation by the allied forces. Beyond heralding the beginning of the end of the war, this momentous event made little impression on or difference to the lives of the medical and nursing establishments.

Florence Nightingingale was now ready to resume the reins of office. The second phase of her service in the East was about to begin.

She was able to feel that, with reservations, the experiment on which she had embarked just under twelve months ago had been a success. At the beginning of December she prepared her official report on the year's activities in the Nursing Department. She was able to record, "It is obvious that the experiment of sending Nurses to the East has been eminently successful, and that the supplying trained instruments to the hands of the Medical Officers has saved much valuable life and remedied many deficiencies."[26]

Notes

1   F.N. is frequently credited with having started the idea of sending money home on behalf of the troops, and Cook has an interesting section on her "Money Order Office" (I, p. 278), but Sidney Godolphin Osborne recorded having sent home odd sums on behalf of the sick and wounded with whom he came in contact during his six weeks at Scutari during November and December 1854. (*Scutari and its Hospitals*, 1855, ch. 3.)

2   Alexis Benoit Soyer (1809–59), the famous French chef of the Reform Club, volunteered to serve in the Crimea at his own expense. He revised the dietaries at Scutari and Balaclava and, in co-operation with F.N. and some of the medical staff, undertook the victualling of the hospitals. In 1857, shortly before his death, he described his experiences in *Soyer's Culinary Campaign, being Historical Reminiscences of the late War, the plain Art of Cookery for Military and Civil Institutions, the Army, Navy, Public, etc.*, London, 1857.

3   Blanche Smith, daughter of Uncle Sam and Aunt Mai, married Arthur Hugh Clough in June 1854.

4   Sidney Herbert's instructions of 20th Oct. 1854 (p. 23) ordered F.N. at that time only to "place yourself at once, in communiction with the Chief Army Medical Officer of the Hospital at Scutari, under whose orders and directions, you will carry on the duties of your appointment." Dr Hall chose to interpret this as meaning she should have no jurisdiction at all in the Crimea.

5   Dr Arthur Anderson, P.M.O. General Hospital, Balaclava, was regarded as an ally.

6   Benjamin Hawes evidently showed this letter to Lady Canning, for in a note dated 25th May she warmly defended the sending out of more nurses: "I perceive from Miss Nightingale's letter to you that there has been what she calls 'irresponsible action' in the matter of sending out nurses. I cannot help recalling to yr. recollection that not *one* has been sent without the express sanction of Ld. Panmure. I do not think any regret is to be felt at what has hitherto been done &, that for a time with a *minimum* of sick and wounded there should be a few more nurses than are actually [needed], is surely better than the previous state of things in which they were so cruelly over-worked & so many sick hardly attended to – & this *happy* state of things is hardly to be expected to last." (P.R.O. WO 43/963, f. 227.)

7   Part of this letter was sent to the Queen, and was quoted by Sir Theodore Martin in his *Life of His Royal Highness the Prince Consort*, London, 1874–80, vol. III, p. 214.

8   Sir John McNeill (1795–1883) started life as a doctor in the East India Co.'s medical service but later was employed in diplomatic missions in the East. With Colonel Tulloch he was responsible for inquiring into the breakdown of supplies in the Crimea. F.N. conceived a great admiration for Sir John, which by the end of the war was warmly reciprocated. In the years immediately after her return she came to depend on him a great deal, particularly during the difficult months in which she was fighting for the Royal Commission appointed to inquire into the sanitary condition of the army.

9   The Minié bullet and the rifled musket had been invented in France in 1847. It was adopted by the British army about a year before the death of the Duke of Wellington in 1852. This innovation was encouraged by Sidney Herbert, then Secretary at War, and it led to the development of the Enfield rifle. It was regarded as a revolutionary weapon. "A greater gap lies between it [the Minié rifle] and the 'Brown Bess' of former days than between any later military rifle and itself." (Stanmore, I, p. 1770.)

10   This date was given in F.N.'s own letter of 14th July, p. 204.

11   Aunt Hannah Nicholson, the sister of George Thomas Nicholson of Waverly, was not really an aunt of F.N., but she had been greatly influenced by "Aunt Hannah," who offered her spiritual comfort at a time of great distress in her youth. (Cook, I, pp. 46–7.)

12   Dr John Sutherland (1808–91) arrived at Scutari in March 1855 as a member of the three-man Sanitary Commission, which according to F.N. saved the British army in the East almost alone. Dr Sutherland became a lifelong friend of F.N., who was perpetually irritated by him but depended on his help and advice a great deal, especially in sanitary matters. For an account of their relationship see Cope, *F.N. and the Doctors*, ch. 2.

13   James Scott Robertson (d. 1895), appointed Purveyor in Chief to the Army on 7th April 1855 in place of the "swearing old man" Wreford. He did not long remain in favour with F.N. On 7th Aug. she was accusing him of drunkenness. And he committed the unforgivable sin (in her eyes) of championing the Irish nuns.

14   S. G. Osborne and Augustus Stafford certainly thought that F.N.'s nurses pulled the hospital through. S.G.O.: "I do not think it is possible to measure the real difficulties of the work Miss Nightingale has done, and its peculiarly horrible nature.

Every day brought some new complication of misery, to be somehow unravelled by the power ruling in the sisters' tower. Each day had its peculiar trial to one who had taken such a load of responsibility in an untried field, and with a staff of her own sex, all new to it . . . Miss Nightingale . . . in my opinion is the one individual, who in this whole unhappy war, has shown more than any other, what real energy guided by good sense can do, to meet the calls of sudden emergency." (*Scutari and its Hospitals,* ch. 4.) Stafford: "Success more complete had never attended human effort than that which resulted from [sending out female nurses]. They could scarcely realise, without personally seeing it, the heartfelt gratitude of the soldiers to these noble ladies, or the amount of misery they had relieved, or the degree of comfort – he might say joy – they had diffused: and it was impossible to do justice, not only to the kindness of heart, but to the clever judgment, ready intelligence and experience displayed by the distinguished lady to whom this difficult mission had been entrusted. If Scutari was not altogether as we could wish it to be, it was because of the inadequate powers confided to Miss Nightingale; and if the Government did not stand by her and her devoted band, and repel unfounded and ungenerous attacks made upon them – if it did not consult their wishes and yield to their superior judgment in many respects – it would deserve the execration of the public." (Speech in the Commons, 29th Jan. 1855. Hansard, *Parliamentary Debates,* 3rd series, vol. 136.)

15   Although Miss Wear had been recruited as a superintendent (p.124 note 61) F.N. never considered her suitable for such a position. For although "This lady is a devoted, untiring and most kind Nurse . . . from habitual inaccuracy of thought & expression & from want of habits of business or order [she] is totally unfit for a Superintendent." (Report No. 11, 15th June [1856], B.L. Add. Ms. 43402, f. 10.) And according to the Purveyor's Confidential Report which was to cause such trouble (see appendix) Miss Wear's practice of devoting her attentions to the Sardinian officers (she evidently spoke Italian) aroused great jealousy among the British sick and wounded.

16   John Hall, M.D. (1795–1866), Inspector General, was the Chief Medical Officer in the East. He was summoned from India by Dr Andrew Smith at the outbreak of the war to take charge of the Medical Department. F.N. regarded him as the epitome of the system which brought about the disaster. He regarded her as an adventuress, and did not hesitate to say so publicly.

17   B.L. Add. Ms. 93867, f. 20.

18   F.N. to her family, 28th July 1855, Nightingale papers, Claydon; copy Wellcome.

19   Dr. Peter Pincoffs (1816–72) arrived in Constantinople at the end of April 1855 as a civil physician attached to Scutari. He established a small medical school at Pera in which F.N. was deeply interested. She had suggested such a scheme to Sidney Herbert in February 1855. After the war Pincoffs consulted F.N. during the preparation of his book *Experiences of a Civilian in Eastern Military Hospitals, with Observations on the English, French and other Departments,* London, 1857. F.N. in turn enlisted his help and sought his advice in the preparation of her *Notes on Matters affecting the Health . . .of the British Army.* She also attempted to secure him the post of physician to the embassy in Constantinople, but it went to someone else.

20   It would appear from this and a couple of other references that Uncle Sam went out to Scutari acompanied by his son Shore for some short period. Uncle Sam undertook some of the financial work that Bracebridge had previously done. In

September his wife, Aunt Mai, went out to replace Mrs Bracebridge as F.N.'s companion and secretary. She remained to the end.

21 R. Hall Bakewell's letter, signed M.R.C.S., L.S.A., appeared in *The Times* of 5th July, p. 7, col. e. After condemning the lack of preparation for the reception of the wounded after the battle for Sebastopol, he launched into a general attack on the organisation of the Medical Department: "I will only say this, that as long as you have a system by which one man discovers a deficiency, and has to report it to a superior, the superior makes a requisition which has to be approved by his superior, and perhaps a second, and the requisition is sent to an official who may or may not comply with it – as long as medical officers have to make requisitions for candles, soap, brushes, and things of that kind, as long, in fact, as the army medical system continues the preposterous and rotten thing it is, so long must you look for results similar to or worse than those I have described." Court-martial proceedings were instituted and Bakewell was dismissed the service without being heard, on the grounds that he had attacked the Medical Department and it was the department that was being tried. The court further found that everything in the hospital had been as perfect as humanity could wish.

22 Mrs Elizabeth Drake, who had come out with F.N. in November 1854, died on 9th August at Balaclava. Her death when she was convalescent shocked F.N. immoderately. Through the second half of August she was engaged in the proper disposal of Mrs Drake's letters, money and box, entailing correspondence with the Rev. C. P. Shepherd of St John's House (G.L.R.O. HI/ST/NC.3/SU 35, 36, 37, 38). F.N. erected a small cross in the cemetery in remembrance of her (Cook, I, p. 262.)

23 Mrs Willoughby Moore (1798–1855), widow of Captain Willoughby Moore, who lost his life on board the *Europa,* which went down on the way to the Crimea. Mrs. Moore organised the nursing of the officers until she died in November 1855.

24 Sir James Simpson (1798–1855), despatched to the Crimea as Chief of Staff by Lord Panmure to report on the staff direct to the Minister for War. After the death of Lord Raglan he was appointed Commander in Chief temporarily. He felt unable to deal with the allies and asked to be relaced by "a General of distinction." (Hibbert, p. 298.) He was succeeded by General Codrington on 11th November.

25 Lothian Nicholson (1827–93), son of George Thomas Nicholson and F.N.'s aunt Anne. Lothian went on to enjoy a distinguished military career. In 1877 he was promoted major–general; in 1887 he was awarded the K.C.B.

26 List of Nurses and Sisters who have ceased to be employed in the Hospitals of Scutari and Balaclava, November 30, 1855, Wellcome Institute.

5
The "papal aggression"

By September Miss Nightingale was back in the swing of hospital routine, as she informed her old patroness from Harley Street, Lady Canning,[1] one of the ladies now engaged in selecting nurses for the hospitals of the East. While evidently concerned to justify her own role as superintendent, mediating between nurses and medical authorities, Miss Nightingale also showed in this letter a sensitive understanding for the comfort and welfare of individual nurses under her care which seemed to be lacking on her first arrival. Many of the principles enunciated here were to be carried over into her prescriptions for all those future training schools which were to stem from the one which opened at St Thomas's Hospital in 1860.

To Lady Canning

Scutari Barrack Hospital
9th September 1855

My dear Lady Canning
    I have been waiting only for an hour to thank you very, very much for your most kind letter & to answer the questions contained in it. I have been driven by over-work more than usually of late from the sudden death (by Cholera) of my excellent Matron,[2] who managed the Linen Stores for 1200 Patients & the Hospital Furniture & from the illness of my Assistant at the same time.
    I never doubted the sympathy of the Queen for her poor soldiers, & consequently for all those who tried to do them good. Indeed the fellow-feeling at home with these poor fellows has throughout been a great help in their sufferings. And to be assured of the Queen's sympathy was the highest pleasure to them. We feel it the more because on all hands we hear of the pains & the interest she takes in informing herself of all that concerns them.
    It seems as if I had been negligent in accounting for the use of the £200 which Col. Phipps desired me to lay out for the Queen in any comfort which it might seem well for her to give. But I have not. The only use I have as yet made of it was to purchase a tent for the Convalescents to air themselves

151

under, which cost £21. Soldiers are strange beings & it seemed desirable that they should have to thank their Queen for something which they did not consider their right. To spend her money in Arrow Roots & socks would not have attracted their attention. At this time too we are amply supplied with every kind of store, very different from what it was when we first came out. Tobacco is, above all, the luxury which the soldier most enjoys – & far be it from me to grudge it him in this miserable war. Still it is not exactly a *Queen's* present. But I look forward to a time next winter, when we shall be less fashionable in all human probability than we are now, when England will be tired of us – & the Queen's kindness will be well applied & fully appreciated by the soldier.

Question I

It struck me when I read the agreement signed by the Civil Nurses that the last paragraph would not do for a Military Hosp*l*. Because the Nurses there must not be placed under the *immediate* direction of the Principal Medical Officer. In Civil Hospitals, the Medical Officer is accustomed to the direction of women – & may be trusted with it – in Military Hosp*ls*. not. Bind the *Superintendent* by every tie of signed agreement & of honor to strict obedience to her Medical Chief. (I think it has been the defect of Koulale that this has not been done). But let all his orders to the Nurses go through her. I mean, of course, not with regard to the medical management of the Patients, but with regard to the placing and discipline of the Nurses. I have never had the slightest difficulty about this – the Medical Men always coming to me & saying, "I want such & such assistance" – and I always informing them of any exchange or removal of Nurses – & consulting them. But I would never have undertaken the Superintendency with that condition that the Nurses consider themselves "under the direction of the Principal Medical Officer". *I* am under his direciton. *They* are under mine.

I will give two instances just to explain that my meaning is, to attain not insubordination to the Doctors, but a power of explaining to the Doctors.

It has continually happened to me, especially at B'clava, to be asked for a Nurse to attend an Officer where there was *no possibility* for the woman to retire day or night for even a moment – & where it was too far for her to return to her Hospital. And this request has been made by an old married Doctor & a father. In one instance, the Principal Medical Officer of B'clava, when I pointed this out to him, immediately gave up his own room for the Nurse to retire to at certain hours – shewing that it was not indifference but inadvertence. In another instance though, – similarly with the first instance – the house was crowded with men, (viz. Officers, servants & doctors etc.) & there was not a cranny where a woman could go unseen, – yet, though three of the men were Chaplains & the sick man nursed was a Chaplain, it was only by going myself & turning out an Officer's Servant & providing for him elsewhere that I could secure a corner for my poor Nurse – whose Patient required her constantly. These are the things which deaden women's feeling of morality & make them take to drinking & worse – if the Superintendent is not continually on the alert.

The other case which makes me "stickle" for the Superintendent being the first in authority over the Nurses was that of a Nurse whom I removed from her wards on account of an intrigue in which she was slightly to blame & removal was all that was necessary. In the anger of the moment, she said she thought she had been only accountable to the Medical Officer. She immediately repented, saw the justice of the removal & was forgiven. But a Medical Officer would neither have discovered nor removed her for this – & she could have quoted her agreement to prove that she was chiefly responsible to him.

Under these circumstances, therefore, I must suggest that the form of Agreement should bind Nurses to obedience to their Superintendent, the Superintendent to the Principal Medical Officer by another Form signed by *her*. But, if the Medical Officer conveys his orders, in the first place, to the Nurse, the Superintendent can only interfere in the second place. And there will be continual quarrelling, which there never has been in the four Hospitals under my charge.

Question II

With regard to the wages, a sliding scale is absolutely necessary. At what rate it shall begin I cannot decide. Because I have no doubt that the excitement which has been made about us in England has raised our price – I will only remark that the *lowest* description of Nurses I have had were a Mrs. Gibson who came out at 18/- in the 2nd. party, a Mrs. Whitehead who came out at 18/- in the same party & who has not yet returned home, because she has broken her leg, – a Mrs. Thompson, & Mrs. Anderson who came out at 18/- each by the 3rd party & returned drunk in 3 weeks, a Mrs. Holmes of the same party, who *was* a woman of bad character, but whom I have kept, because I believe she has really been shocked into reform here – also at 18/- a Mrs. Clarke, from Oxford, of the 4th party, who came out at 16/- & several others, whose names I will not give, because they are not likely to trouble you. These all came out at 18/- whereas some of the most respectable women were of the first party, who all came out at 10/-. I do not think their having children to settle has anything to do with the Government question of providing good & respectable Nurses for their soldiers. But I am not aware, as I have already said, of the present state of feeling in England – & think that your sliding scale may be a necessary one viz. 14/- a week for 3 months, to be then raised to 18/- & after a year to 20/-.

I have not had a single Nurse yet, either at high or at low wages, whom I could place in a situation of responsibility, excepting Mrs. Roberts & Mrs. Walford, (the latter I found out here & she is the poor woman just dead of Cholera).

I think a mistake has arisen that a Nurse out of a Surgical Ward means a Surgical Nurse. The *nurse* out of a surgical ward is nothing but a

153

maid-of-all-work. She scours, washes the Patients, makes the beds, sometimes the poultices etc. Mrs. Orton, of the 4th party, who came out as a Surgical Nurse from Bartholomew's, is scarcely fit for a maid-of-all-work. She came out at 16/-. But she is such a good creature, though silly & vulgar, that I employ her in the Linen Stores under direction.

I send you the first Agreement & first Certificate which I think, after all, were the best.

Question III   I see no objection to the "Drink" rule being left out. Because it is different at different Hospitals. But, without the rule against Presents, no discipline could be maintained. I have had no difficulty in enforcing it. I *know* of many instances where the Nurses have refused money & have never told me so themselves. I *know* of only one instance where money was accepted & that was by an unprincipled woman, Mrs. Lyas, of the 2nd party, whom I was about to dismiss, & who has procured heself a situation as Governess!! in an Armenian family by the agency of the R.C. Priest. Experience connected with this woman leads me to the suggestion that it is desirable *never* to send out R.C. *Nurses,* who will always be borne scatheless by their Priests – through any misconduct – & *never* to pay their wages, or any portion of their wages, in any other way excepting thro' the Superintendent. This woman sets all at defiance, has carried off all her new summer clothing, endeavours to seduce away the other Nurses, because I had no check over her – her wages having been paid in London by the W. Office. She sent me word, when she ran away, that she was sure of her wages without me. And she has completely deluded that unlucky Lawfield, of St. John's, whom she converted.

We require, if you please, a large number of new Badges. Ours are worn out & we have not time to work them. Mrs. Bracebridge has the pattern.

I think it undesirable that the Nurses should be allowed to take with them their own outer clothing. It will be a constant struggle to prevent their wearing it.

I would suggest that, if Nurses choose to wear white Petticoats & white stockings, it should be made a condition that they put them *out* to wash at their own expense. Grey Twill would do very well for petticoats. I have sent for some to Malta.

The rule about wearing the regulation dress applies *particularly* to when they are *out of* Hospital – & therefore the rule as it is written about this is not explicit enough. I have myself heard one soldier address another, "Don't yo speak to her'n! don't yo know that's one of Miss Nightingale's." The necessity of distinguishing them *at once* from camp-followers is particularly obvious when they are *not* engaged in Hospital work.

I think the rule about receiving wages should be – quarterly.

I hope the additional rules I sent home by Mrs. Bracebridge will be adopted – especially that about their accepting no other situation out here. People in the East will take a servant, or even a Governess, with no character whatsoever.

The rule about remitting Nurses' wages thro' the Paymaster is undesirable for two reasons – 1st the extreme delay. It is stated "in the same way as soldiers' remittances." The delay in making these is so well known that the soldiers are in the habit of remitting by me to England in small sums of 20/- or 30/- a *weekly* amount of (now) not less than £150. It is stated that "the Genl. Agent will, in due course, issue the same." The "*due course*" is one of many months.

2nd the Nurses should be dependent on the Superintendent for their wages – entirely – as she alone can know their deserts.

The Exhortation to the Nurses is excellent. But something might be added. In the rule (4th) about the walking, we are obliged to arrange that they should not go out for exercise excepting with a superintendent, as when two or even three were together, the soldiers would make appointments to meet them – for we have here the misery of a depot. On the other hand, I have been obliged to waive the rule that two must always be together in the wards. It cannot be always maintained.

The 5th viz. the instructions of the W. Office respecting religious intercourse to Lord W. Paulet has been so completely misunderstood by the R.C.s that it has been, in fact, my principal difficulty – & the less publicity which is given to it the better. The R.C.s who, before, were quite amenable, have chosen to construe the rule that "they are not to enter upon the discussion of religious subjects with any Patients other than those of their own faith" to mean – therefore with *all* of their own faith – & the 2nd party of Nuns, who came out now wander over the whole Hospital out of Nursing hours, not confining themselves to their own wards nor even to Patients, but "instructing" (it is their own word) groups of Orderlies & Convalescents in the Corridors – doing the work each of ten Chaplains – & bringing ridicule upon the whole thing, while they quote the words of the W[ar] Office, which indeed seem to have been left intentionally vague, & to bear this construction.

(1) Aprons may "well be served out like Towels". But it is better for the Nurses that each should have her own towels, aprons etc. as some tear & destroy so much more than others – & the tidy ones ought not to be called upon to succeed to the others' patches or rents.

(2) Etnas[3] etc. are very useful

(3) A good stock of needles, cottons etc. etc. would be eminently acceptable to me. I am constantly "emptied out" – as we give a small stock to each Patient returning to the Krimea. He cannot drink cottons. Buttons may be sent us by the million & used gratefully.

I will send back the Lists of the clothing which the Nurses *have had*. I have not yet got in those from the Krimea which has caused my delay.

We are truly grateful to you for all you have done for us. I am very anxious that Mrs. Bracebridge should be the person to approve the Nurses sent by Lady Cranworth & that none should come without her approbation – because she knows so exactly what we want.

Death & illness & misconduct have thinned our ranks & I now require

2 Matrons for the Linen Stores

one at each of the two Scutari Hospitals. For we have now undertaken the whole of these immense Stores. There are four Divisional Stores to this Hospital only – & each man has now his clean shirt twice a week or oftener & his clean sheets once a week or oftener. These Matrons will have nothing to do with nursing.[4]

1 Housekeeper – who will exercise control over the Nurses IN the Quarters – not in the wards – she too has nothing to do with nursing.

2 steady elderly healthy Maids of all work – willing to go to B'clava, if necessary.

4 Nurses – who must also be willing to go to B'clava, if necessary.

I cannot sufficiently say how much I feel all the trouble you have taken with us – nor how great I feel your loss will be to us. Believe me, dear Lady Canning, most truly & gratefully yours

P.S.

Many, many thanks for your kind enquiries after my health, which is as much improved, I believe, as I can expect in the time. I have most seriously considered the kind wishes of my friends that I should leave this place for a time. But I believe those about me come to the conclusion that, on the whole, it was best that I should remain here.

Can you pardon this long letter, which I have not time to make shorter, written among interruptions & business of all kinds?

There are of the many good wishes, which will follow you to your command in India, [5] none more *fervent, at least,* than ours. I do not know how you will look upon the exile from England. But I cannot help rejoicing at your going to so responsible & important a post.

Many thanks for your encouraging words upon mine.

Leeds Record Office HAR/LdC 177/Z2 (*Cal.* B. 4. C12, 103).

Ever since the spring the numbers of sick and wounded in hospital had been diminishing. Lord Raglan had decided that any new wounded resulting from the prolonged siege should be kept until convalescent in the hospitals in the Crimea, which, with the opening of the Castle Hospital in April 1855, were able to accommodate about 2,500.[6] Those that remained on the Bosphorus were being concentrated on Scutari. By August there was little serious work for the nurses in Koulali. Mother Bridgeman and her nuns were faced with the prospect of returning home to Ireland or removing back to Scutari, where they would once more be under the jurisdiction of Miss Nightingale, which was by no means acceptable to them. Mother Bridgeman had been ordered by her superiors in Dublin to remain at her post as long as she possibly could.[7]

In this awkward situation she decided to offer her services to Dr Hall in the Crimea, where the hospitals were still full. On 2nd September she therefore addressed Dr Hall through the Rev. S. Woollett:

...As we have left our Convent homes for this work of Mercy, I am anxious to extend the sphere of our usefulness as far as possible, especially now that so few other than Convalescents are sent down to the Bosphorus.

Indeed it seems as if we are hardly doing the work for which we came so far ....

and she went on:

It may be well to add that I would not undertake again to *work with Miss Nightingale*, as I learned while I was at the Barrack Hospital Scutari, *how very DIFFERENT from ours*, are Miss Nightingale's views of nursing, hospital arrangements etc. etc.

But if the Authorities wish to appoint a Secular Lady Superintendent I have not the least objection to work in the Crimea as here with the Protestant Lady Superintendent with whom I now act.[8]

This was just the chance Dr Hall needed to be rid of Miss Nightingale and her nurses. Referring back to her letter of 14th July, and without telling her of this latest offer, he invited Miss Nightingale to recall her few nurses from the General Hospital, Balaclava, and she replied on 21st September:

To Dr John Hall

Barrack Hospital, Scutari

PRIVATE   21st September 1855

My dear Sir,

I accede immediately to your desire & opinion that the female Element should be withdrawn from the General Hospital of Balaclava.

I believe that my opinion entirely coincides with yours.

I have written to Miss Wear *conveying your Orders*, & wishing our party to be withdrawn by the beginning of October.

I thank you for your kind words about the use which the Nurses have been of.

I am glad to break up the establishment at Balaclava for more reasons than one.

I am intending to come up to the Crimea myself very shortly, when I shall have the pleasure of seeing you.

I *hope*, with you, that there will be peace, more than I expect it. Still the having Sebastopol is great gain.

I thank you most sincerely for your kind letter & remain,

my dear Sir
most truly yours

Will you inform Dr. Hadley, who has always been most kind to me & mine, of the conclusion which you have come to about the General Hospital & that it will be immediately carried into effect? – May I ask you, should Miss Wear request you to appoint her to some other position in the Camp, not to give her any answer till you have heard from me, as I have very particular reasons for making this request which is, of course, in the strictest confidence to you *only*. I have no reason to suppose, however, that Miss Wear is about to make any such request, nor would I put such an idea into her head as being possible.

B.L. Add. Ms. 39867, f. 28 (*Cal.* omitted).

This letter was used by Dr Hall to claim that Miss Nightingale had resigned the General Hospital at Balaclava on 1st October, a claim that was to be repeated by several authors[9] but was always strenuously denied by Miss Nightingale herself.

To Mother Bridgeman Dr Hall replied on 27th September:

> . . . .It was necessary to make reference to Miss Nightingale regarding Miss Wear and the two nurses whom she allowed to remain at my request when she had made up her mind to withdraw them altogether from the General Hospital at Balaklava.
>
> Your kind offer of service afforded me an opportunity of allowing her to relieve those kind and useful people, of whom I cannot speak too highly, from this bondage.[10]

On the same day Dr Hall wrote again to Miss Nightingale, paying tribute to Miss Wear's usefulness, and admitting that he had had another offer of assistance, but still not informing her that it was from the nuns:

> My note to you was written under an impression that it was your desire to withdraw your nurses altogether from the General Hospital at Balaclava and as an unexpected offer of assistance was made to me I thought it would be meeting your views, and afford you an opportunity of relieving those whom you had so considerately kept at my solicitation . . . .[11]

It was left to Mother Bridgeman to convey the unwelcome news to Miss Nightingale, which she did at the beginning of October when she gave notice of her intention to withdraw the four nuns who had been employed at the General Hospital, Scutari, since the previous December.

Miss Nightingale at once complained to the ambassador that

> the Sisters who had engaged themselves personally to me for the work of the Hospitals under my direct charge are offered, accepted and ordered elsewhere, with only an ex post facto communication to me that they are going, when the arrangements that they shall depart in less than a week are made.

Your Excellency will see 1st) That it is impossible for me to obey the instructions of the War Office under these circumstances. 2nd) That it would be impossible to conduct any Institution whatever with such conditions . . .[12]

When called upon by General Storks[13] for an explanation, Mother Bridgeman replied on 7th October:

. . . When the War Office sent us fifteen Sisters out nearly a year since, Miss Nightingale refused to accept more than five Sisters, intimating that the remaining ten might return home, or in short, do what they pleased.

After passing a month between the Sisters of Charity at Galata and at Therapia, *unemployed,* Koulali was opened and the Sisters found work there. In the meantime I had a letter from Mr. Sidney Herbert authorising me to find work where we could, or return home. I suppose you are already aware that Miss Nightingale has no authority over Koulali nor over anyone in it.

. . . Only four of mine are at Scutari: therefore over these four, *and only these,* has Miss Nightingale even a shadow of authority. I always considered myself and the Sisters free to withdraw from the work whenever we should deem it expedient. I believe we owe Miss Nightingale obedience merely in nursing details while we remain in a hospital under her control.[14]

General Storks, who was a firm adherent of Miss Nightingale, decided with her that the best solution would be for her to accompany the Sisters to the Crimea, thus preserving some semblance of her authority. The whole party left Scutari on 9th October and arrived at Balaclava on the 13th.

On 15th October Miss Nightingale addressed a long, tangled letter to Dr Hall recapulating the events leading up to this "papal aggression," as she was to call the episode, adapting a phrase current among Protestants outraged by the restoration of the Catholic hierarchy in Britain, and quoting the relevant documents in the case. This time she did resign the General Hospital, saying she had prayed the War Office to be relieved of the General Hospital under exisiting arrangements.

To Dr John Hall

Castle Hospital, Balaclava
15th October 1855

PRIVATE

My dear Sir

Will you allow me to recapitulate to you the statement which has this day been made by me the subject of a communication to the War Office – & which I fear is likely to assume a (somewhat *perhaps* undue) importance in the eyes of our brethren in England?

After referring

(1) to my Instructions from the War Office, dated October 19, 1854, by which the duties of "selection", of "distribution", & the "power of discharge or dismissal" of the "female Nursing Establishments for the

Hospitals of the British Army serving in the East" were imposed upon me.

(2)   to the Dispatch dated War Office, 8th September 1855, 15565/193 of which the following is an Extract

Madam
   . . . I am to add that Lord Panmure requests that you will consider what steps should be taken to make the service of those already attached to the Hospitals in the East most available at such points & for such situations as may happen to require further aid at any particular time or under unforeseen circumstances.

(signed) B. Hawes

Miss Nightingale
Scutari

(3)   to the Certificate of appointment of all those who came out "to act as Nurses under my orders" including the R. Catholic Sisters of Mercy

(4)   to the Dispatch dated War Office 14th July 1855, 15565/138

"that Lord Panmure considers that the proper course regarding the superintendence & control of the Nurses & Sisters would be for Miss Nightingale to select a Superintendent at each of the Stations of Balaclava & Scutari, who, in her absence from such station, whether from illness or any other cause, should assume the control & direction of the Nurses & Sisters, under the orders of the Principal Medical Officer in the Station.

"This arrangement, while vesting in Miss Nightingale full authority over the Nurses at either station, while she is residing there, will relieve her from the responsibility of controlling parties at a distance, over whom she is thereby prevented from exercising an immediate supervision."

(signed) B. Hawes

(5)   to my Instructions from the War Office given verbally (in an interview between the Duke of Newcastle, Mr. Herbert, & Dr. Andrew Smith & myself) in London, October 20, 1854, the day before I left England – & repeated in January, 1855 – by which I was enjoined to fix the proportion of R. Catholics in the "female nursing Establishments in the British Military Hospitals in the East" at not more than *one third*.

I have stated that,

In September, 1855, Mrs. Bridgeman, the Superior of the R. Catholic Sisters of Mercy who came out to serve under my orders in December, 1854, & were stationed partly at the General Hospital of Scutari which is immediately under my care, – partly at that of Koulali (which was, at my request, placed by the War Office more immediately under the orders of the General Officer commanding in the Bosphorus by instructions dated "War Office, April 20, 1855") offered the services of herself & Sisters, without the knowledge & consent of this General Officer or my own, to you, which you accepted for the General Hospital, Balaclava – after that you had written to me, (referring to a letter of mine, dated some months previous, proposing to withdraw the Nurses then there, a proposition at that time negatived by you) – desiring that this proposition should now be carried into effect which I acceded to.

that Mrs. Bridgeman *then* wrote to me withdrawing the whole of her Sisters at Scutari & Koulali, & announcing this withdrawal for the beginning of the ensuing week.

that I immediately communicated with our Ambassador, who gave it as his opinion that I should be "fully justified in calling upon Mrs. Bridgeman not to undertake her intended voyage & upon Dr. Hall not to receive her at Balaclava without" my "consent & permission" – & that I "should be entitled to the support of Brigadier General Storks & Rear Admiral Grey in giving effect to" my "determination."

that, conceiving it to be injudicious to take such a measure – & thus produce a breach between the R. Catholic & Protestant elements, I consulted with Br. Genl. Storks, the General Officer Commanding in the Bosphorus, & came to the determination to bring Mrs. Bridgeman & her Sisters, amounting in number to thirteen, to Balaclava myself.

that, finding you of opinion that it was better for the arrangement to stand – viz. that the General Hospital at Balaklava should be served by R. Catholic Sisters alone, because the Patients in that Hospital at present consist chiefly of R. Catholics, Jews, Turks, infidels & heretics – & referring to my instructions from the W. Office placing me "under the direction of the Chief Army Medical Officer in Turkey or elsewhere in the East" I considered it to be my duty to acquiesce in your arrangements.

but that, finding this arrangement to be at variance both with my Instructions from the War Office relative to placing one third at most of R. Catholic Nurses in any Military Hospital & with my own judgment – & finding also that it was your desire to follow the wishes of the R. Catholic Superior, Mrs. Bridgeman, which, being taken by you, were found to be, as was most natural, that her authority should be independent of my control, – I have now prayed to be relieved by the War Office of my responsibility relative to the female Nursing in the General Hospital, Balaclava, under the exisiting arrangements.

I have added that you have stated in a verbal conference with me that it is your intention

(1)   that no Nurses or Sisters shall be admitted into any of the other British Military Hospitals in the East, without my knowledge & consent

(2)   that – seeing that all the Sisters, be they R. Catholics or Protestants, who have come out to the Hospitals of the British Army of the East, have come as *Nurses* only

seeing that the small number of Sisters & Nurses assigned by you to the other Military Hospitals in the Crimea has prevented the due admixture of one-third R. Catholic sisters there – these having always declined to go, when I proposed it to them, to any Hospital in parties of less than five. [15]

the R. Catholic Sisters, now at the General Hospital, Balaclava, shall not be allowed to visit any of the other Hospitals in the Crimea – such visiting inferring the character of missionaries & not of *Nurses*, for the reasons above stated – & being more fitly done by their own priests.

> I beg to remain, dear Sir
> Yours sincerely & faithfully

B.L. Add. Ms. 39867, f. 44 (*Cal.* omitted).

Dr Hall continued to maintain that Florence Nightingale had no jurisdiction in the Crimea and to encourage the nurses and nuns there to flout her authority. On 27th November Miss Nightingale forwarded a despatch from the War Office that, she felt, clinched the matter. But Dr Hall was equally convinced it proved *his* case. Against a sentence which read:

Lord Panmure considers that Mrs. Bridgeman was not justified in removing except by your consent, any of the Nurses engaged under your [i.e. F.N.'s] control in the Hospitals at Scutari, nor in offering the services of herself & the Roman Catholic Sisters at Kululi to *the Principal Medical Officer in the Crimea without having previously obtained the consent and sanction of the Secretary at War*

Dr Hall noted in the margin:

Note . . . clearly showing that Lord Panmure did not consider Miss N.'s authority to extend beyond the nuns employed in the Gen*l*. Hosp*l*. at Scutari under her orders.[16]

The authorities at home were not impressed by Dr Hall's repeated assertions of ignorance of Miss Nightingale's position. In an internal memorandum written by Mr Hawes a few months later he stated:

. . . Dr. Hall knew & knew officially that Miss Nightingale had general superintendence of the Ladies & Nurses in the East. Lord Panmure's reply to the correspondence between Dr. Hall, Miss N. and Lord Stratford de Redcliffe was sent to him & that clearly conveyed the authority Miss N. claimed in addition to which Miss N. acts under the original authority given by Mr. Sidney Herbert & subsequently confirmed by Lord Panmure.[17]

Dr Hall was to discover the following March in the most public and mortifying circumstances that Miss Nightingale did indeed have the support of the authorities.

Meanwhile Miss Wear, whose "misdemeanours . . . were the original cause of my wishing to withdraw her,"[18] had no intention of returning to Miss Nightingale's fold if she could possibly avoid it, and asked Dr Hall to transfer her to the Monastery. He had already denied to Miss Nightingale any intention of placing nurses at that hospital, but he now granted Miss Wear's request, and on 1st October Miss Wear thanked him for his permission:

Miss Nightingale I consider wishes me to feel myself from *this* day entirely released from all obligation to her and her orders I therefore Sir place my services completely at your disposal and henceforth wish to obey *only* your orders and recognize you only as my superior, therefore whenever you desire I shall be ready to go to the Monastery at a very few hours' notice.[19]

Dr Hall had won this round, as F.N. acknowledged in a note to Aunt Mai, holding the fort at Scutari:

To Aunt Mai

[Castle Hospital, Balaclava, mid October 1855]

You know that Dr. Hall has palmed Miss Wear on me by appointing her to the Monastery – then writes me word that neither is her hut ready then nor likely to be & that all the sick are gone – & that she had better not stay at the General Hosp*l*. Really, Dr. Hall is so clever, it is almost a pleasure to contemplate such cleverness, even at one's own expence. But was there ever such a fix? I don't choose to give up the Monastery now, because it may be another trap to put the Brickbat's Nuns in there – & therefore I must have Wear squabbling with Mrs. Stewart here till I can send her to the Monastery.

I have no one to send with her. For all my soldiers' wives have failed me. And I have no intention of entrusting her with more Nurses. And yet she must have two women with her, in order to prevent her from Cloughing it or Nun-ning it.

P.S. Do not say *to any one* that *any of the Nurses* were concerned in Salisbury's robbery.[20] I have been sifting the evidence *& I really can find none* – not even against Wheatstone.

Claydon; copy, Wellcome (*Cal.* B. 4. D9, 138).

Amidst the harassments involving the rebellious nuns and disobedient nurses, Miss Nightingale managed to maintain her interest in the broader aspects of army sanitary reform, and on 18th October adressed a letter to General Sir Richard Airey [21] suggesting certain sanitary improvements which might be made at the Castle Hospital if it was to be habitable during the coming winter.

For once she was able to mention the name of the medical officer on whose behalf she made the request.

To Lieutenant General Sir Richard Airey

Castle Hospital, Balaklava

PRIVATE   18th October 1855

Sir

Will you allow me to take you at your word, & may I venture to trouble you with a few suggestions which, IF they are practicable, & IF this Hospital is to be continued through the winter, (so as to make the expense desirable) would contribute to the healthiness & comfort of the Patients?

(1)   Water Closets to each ward – with drain – two portable engines to

163

flush them from the sea – & shoot to debouch the refuse into the sea – for which there is a good place. It might have a common flap – & be 3 ft. by 1½ ft. in dimensions.

A bath for each ward might be included with no great additional expence, if this experiment were tried.

There is a portable Engine at Renkioi to spare & tank which they would let us have.*

(2)   To bore for spring-water or to bore the rock. But better Geologists than I say that we might go down one hundred yards without finding water.

If this be the case, the rain-water might be collected – & with half-a-dozen rum puncheons, half filled with pebbles, charcoal etc., filters would soon be made. But this should be done immediately.

(3)   A hut for a Reading Room for Convalescents. These sit swearing & smoking outside the huts, whereas, if there were a hut furnished with books, newspapers & stationery, the better kind of men would sit there to read & write. At least so we have found at Scutari. There must be a Non-Commissioned Officer in charge – & chairs & tables.

Dr. Matthew [22] the Principal Medical Officer here, empowers me to say that, having now sixty vacant beds, he could give up a hut, holding fifteen beds, for the purpose, if authorized to do so. And, should there be a fresh influx of wounded, there is nothing to do but to move out the tables & move in the beds.

I would supply the rest

(4)   to "jump" a hole to drain off the water from the ice in the ice-house in the Castle ruin.

(5)   to make all the huts weather-tight – for which will be necessary

   I to roof them with felt or tin
   II to hold down the roofs with iron hoops
   III to prop up the walls.

I am no Engineer, as you will perceive. I have only talked with the Principal Surgeon here, Dr. Matthew, who authorizes me to use his name in all these propositions – & with a foreman of Mr. Dogue's who appears to be a practical intelligent man & assures me that they are all *feasible* – I do not venture to express an opinion, but only to lay them before you, as our Chief.

I beg to remain Sir, Your obedt. Servt.

B.L. Add. Ms. 39867, f. 48 (*Cal.* omitted).

General Airey forwarded the letter to Dr Hall, whose comment on it was brief: "19 October 1855 Miss Nightingale about visiting the Camp Hosp*l.*, and sundry improvements at the Castle Hospital – not very practicable."

*If a well could be sunk, there would be no occasion for the Portable Engines to flush the water-closets.

But it would appear from her letter to Mrs Herbert of 17th November that some at least of her suggestions were carried out.

Aunt Mai Smith had now, since September, taken over the management of Miss Nightingale's household at Scutari in place of Mrs Bracebridge. Aunt Mai had always been very close to her niece. Since early childhood she had shielded and supported her in the face of the family's disapproval, she had promoted her education, and encouraged her to pursue her vocation. Now she had left her own husband and family to help at Scutari.

To Aunt Mai Smith

Castle Hospital
Balaclava
19th October 1855

I have been appointed a twelvemonth today. And what a twelvemonth of dirt it has been – of experience which would sadden not a life but an eternity. Who has ever had a sadder experience? Christ was betrayed by one. But my cause has been betrayed by everyone – ruined, betrayed, destroyed by everyone alas! One may truly say excepting Mrs. Roberts, *Revd. Mother, first,* & Mrs. Stewart. All the rest, Wear, Clough, Salisbury, Stanley et id genus omne, where are they? And Mrs. Stewart is more than half mad.[23] A cause which is supported by a mad woman & twenty fools must be a falling house.

I never expected that the Bracebridges would come back & therefore your information was not such a shock to me as it would have been three months ago.

Also, I find much less difficulty in getting on here without him than with him. A woman obtains that from military courtesy, (if she does not shock either their habits of business or their caste prejudices,) which a man, who pitted the Civilian against the Military element & the females against the Doctors, partly from temper, partly from policy, effectually hindered.

I am in the midst of water closets, [deleted by another hand] reading rooms, boring for water, – felting huts for the winter, binding down roofs with strong iron against the wind & building Extra Diet Kitchens – Soyer is still here.

Dr. Hall is dead against me, justly provoked, but not by me. He descends to every meanness to make my position more difficult.

Generals Airey & Barnard [24] are very kind to me.

This is only a preface to what I want to say. You have given me a lift over my most difficult time. God bless you. But it would make me quite miserable for you to spend your winter here. I should be always thinking that they wanted you at home. I shd. never have a moment's peace in your society.

I have not the least expectation of returning home. I am quite determined, Deo volente & the War Office, to remain with our Army as long as that Army is carrying on war, & as long consequently as it has General

Hospitals. All here expect what they call "a good rattling campaign" next summer – whether that campaign will be here or on the Danube who can tell? In the latter case, the General Hospitals would be at Varna. As long as there is work to do, I shall stay & do it, if I can. I do not understand the arguments which are used against this. What can I do better in England? As General Airey said to me, the Civilians can understand nothing at all of what we are about. Why, it would take five months to move this army if peace were made today. Tomorrow we expect an attack. This winter it is true we shall have no trenches. But we shall have a very sickly winter in all probability. What better can I do in England? There I might have as many hundred patients as here I shall have thousands, UNDER WHATEVER circumstances. Every where we have to organize kitchens, baths, linen stores, washing.

I hear Soyer called a "humbug" because he leaves work half-done & goes to something else, while that goes to ruin, which is true, & I hear myself called a humbug, because, after a year of the hardest work, the thing is only just organized & I will not leave it.

To leave a work which one has undertaken, in order to try something else which sounds better, is a dangerous experiment, at best. But I leave that which is succeeding to fly to something I know not what.

It is quite true that Drs. Hall & Hadley sent for a List of Vessels going home & chose one, the Jura, which was NOT going to stop at Scutari, *because* it was *not* going to stop at Scutari – & put me on board of her for England (when I was ill here before). And that Mr. Bracebridge & Lord Ward took me out, at the risk of my life – to save my going to England, though unconscious at the time that it was *intended*.

I do not intend to go home while the war lasts. And I am sure that the impatience to get you home will tend very much to entreaties & *supposed conviction* that it would be better for me to come home. You cannot stay long enough to bring me home. Do please go before the winter. I do not mean now, or till I come back to Scutari, but before the very bad weather. Tell them that you will.

There is not a hut, not a stove, not a provision for winter come out yet.

I have written to Dr. Blackwood negativing Mr. Hadow's proposition.

Let Horsfield have the ½ pint (the same as Vickery) daily. Between ourselves it is a pint they have – & Robert ½ pint. But, if Vickery is content with ½ pint, so much the better.

Yours for ever

B.L. Add. Ms. 45793, f. 106 (*Cal.* B. 4. D4, 119).

In much the same vein she wrote to her mother five days later:

To her mother

Castle Hospital
Balaclava
24th October 1855

Here have I been three weeks, my dearest Mother, & I wish you could see me in the most poetic spot in the world, looking out upon the old Genoese Castle – upon peak upon peak in the cold moonlight or in the red glow of the autumnal sunset – for the nights are hard frost & listening to the everlasting roll of the sea at the foot of the steep cliff, some 490 ft. high upon which our hut is perched & thinking of the everlasting patience of God, (as typified by that eternal roll,) which endures for tens of thousands of years, that we may "work out our own salvation," which is the only way He sees by which we can become like Him, while my patience is weary at the end of one twelvemonth, (which is now completed) by the ill-will, incompetence, ignorance & bigotry, with with I have to keep up one slow, weary, melancholy round of opposition, varied only with occasional flashes of more vehement hatred & active ill-doing.

Alas! Who has not betrayed us in our cause but Revd. Mother, Mrs. Shaw Stewart & Mrs. Roberts?

Yet my name is dear to me – it has won the goodwill of the humble hardworking part of my countrymen.

But oh! What a tale I should have to tell of selfishness, conventionalism & malice.

Well! I am too busy to attack or to defend – & am in the midst of extra diet kitchens, baths, linen-stores, shoots, reading rooms, stoves, boring for water, felting huts for winter etc. etc. etc.

What this winter shall bring forth who can tell?

The name of the Chersonese sounds musical in British ears & sweet in sound to mine from that of Howard, which it commemorates.

Ever yours

Claydon; copy, Wellcome (*Cal.* B. 4. D6, 126).

Friends at home were ready with offers of help. Some whom Miss Nightingale remembered as having shared her convictions or supported her aspirations in the past she enlisted in her service now. One such was Richard Dawes, Dean of Hereford, [25] educational reformer, to whom she described something of her hopes for improving the lot and reforming the character of the soldier.

Copy in Parthenope's hand of letter to
Richard Dawes, Dean of Hereford

Castle Hospital
Balaclava
24th October 1855

My dear kind friend (if you will allow me to call you so), let me thank you, first of all for your pleasant words of remembrance of me. For kind words are more precious than people in England can tell, out here in Crim Tartary, among the strange faces & stranger doings of the camp.

If I have seen little of Mrs. Mitchell it is because the pressure of business is so great that we have not time even to speak of home.

We are now here for the winter, & though the road making is so heavy just now that the men say they "wish Sevastopol were not taken & that they were again in the trenches," yet there is no doubt but that we are here for an idle, a drunken & a sickly winter. The men are not in good condition whatever may be said, & the whole army gets drunk whenever it gets paid.

Yet there are many ripe for something better, & there are many remedies against drunkenness, if our rulers would but use them. But few will.

Three men, a Chaplain, a Lord & a Surgeon, would however I know give lectures to the men in the evening, if they had but diagrams, in a Regimental hut where some Non-Commissioned Officers have been persuaded to come to practise their reading & writing. And another man, a Commanding Officer, is intent upon having a school for the Privates. During the siege of course little could be done, but now is the time.

I often hear of kind friends at home asking what they can do with wisdom for us. The best thing they can do for us is to give us something more tempting than rum & water, or rum without water. I have often been told by Commanding Officers that the only conversation which can be overheard among the men, is about the comparative merits of rums.
We want   Copy-books
            Pens & Ink

Chambers Educational Series or some Reading Books which will enable us not to use the Bible as a text book, & not to offend the priests, one third of the army being R. Catholic.

Diagrams (of the simplest kind) large, to use at Lectures, which will illustrate the Elements of Astronomy & the Amery [?]
            Natural History
            the Mechanical Powers
            the Elements of Physiology
            Stratification of the Earth
                etc. etc.

But you know a great deal better than I do what Diagrams to recommend.

Mr. Best had some which I think came from a Society connected with the Xtian Knowledge.

The only books which the men will read besides Parlour Libraries & Railway novels, are, Shakespear illustrated by Kenny Meadows, & Milton illustrated by Martin & Darby a small copy about 7d. Kingsley's Sermons (they liked "Brave Words" very much).
            Ryles Tracts & Parkers
            All the Illustrated Newspapers,
            Household Words
            Chambers Miscellany

Pilgrim's Progress   Adams & Munro's [?] Allegories

The men read aloud, very badly. But some of the Officers would read Shakespeare aloud to them in the winter, if we had him. And one of the Chaplains is anxious to get up some acting, not Shakespeare of course, but Box & Cox or such sort of acting Plays if we had them.

I will undertake to apply everything of this kind, which may be sent out to us, in Regiments where they shall not be used to light the men's pipes.

There is as much difference between Regiments where the Commanding Officer the Chaplain or the Officers are or are not inactive as between Croats & Coldstream Guards.

A very intelligent Sergeant of the Coldstreams told me that he thought the Russian the most ignorant & best soldier in the world excepting the English.

I wish you could persuade the War Office to send us out a trained School-master to Scutari, one who could even give Trigonometrical Lessons to the Officers if they would take them. At Scutari where there will be a Dépot for months, one could always be useful. I wrote for one in May. But he never came. And then I was ill.

I do not think that it would be worth while to have a trained Schoolmaster up in the Crimea, because the Army may be moving again in Feb. or March. And there are very good non-Commissioned Officers who will act as Schoolmasters.

I know that I need not apologise for thus trespassing upon your time because you live only to do us good. And the poor soldier may well come within the number of your children. For he is a sad silly child. He boasts now that the whole of his extra Pay is "to go into his body," which has (as he says, & as is sadly true) "been badly put upon."

If you can do anything for us will you send the account to my Father, if you will kindly take so much trouble, & he will settle it for me.

> With kindest regards to Mrs. Dawes
> ever yours gratefully

Claydon; copy, Wellcome (*Cal.* B. 4. D6, 127).

The ill feeling that had been developing between Florence Nightingale and Mary Stanley ever since the latter's arrival the previous December finally reached a climax in the autumn of 1855 when Miss Nightingale discovered that Miss Stanley had taken Miss Salisbury, dismissed for theft, under her wing, and was now engaged in trying to get up a libel case against Miss Nightingale over the matter.

Furthermore, in a letter to Aunt Mai, Miss Nightingale wrote that she had heard

that Miss Stanley, *on her voyage OUT*, said that "she had never been intimate with me," that "she only knew me *on matters of business*." Alas! how this last year has lowered my estimate of characters. Miss Stanley also accused me of love of power, of a tendency to R. Catholicism!!!! tho' she said she knew me little, of want of religious principle etc. etc. etc. to her companions before she ever arrived at Constantinople. Oh! woman! woman![26]

The accusation that Miss Nightingale had "a tendency to R. Catholicism" was particularly ironic. It was Miss Stanley who was converted to that faith before she left Constantinople.

To her family

Castle Hospital
Balaclava
28th October 1855

I declined being God mother, to the child of my best friends, the Sidney Herberts, (who were so good as to ask me), – *because of* not making a solemn promise where one has neither the power nor the right to perform it. It is a well meant farce which one ought not to play in. So I cannot be the godmother now – tho' I am pleased & more than pleased to be remembered (out in Crim Tartary) at my dear own home. If they like to name the child[27] after one who has struggled thro' & suffered disappointment & disgust such as I am fain to think falls to the lot of few, (*can* fall, I should hope, to *very* few,) I shall be pleased. It will not make the poor child be like me. And I would not augur it such a fate.

Don't think I regret – never for one moment during this whole twelvemonth – I always thanked God that He sent me out.

I cannot tell you *how* much to distrust Miss Stanley. I have never known it till now. She is false to the very back-bone. Her treachery began *before* she ever saw me at Scutari, *before* she arrived at Constantinople. I have always defended her, pitied her, allowed for her *till lately*. Now I tell you, distrust her, you will find out some day why, there is not a villain in a French play more false than she. I can hardly believe it with the proof of it in black & white before my eyes. What can have made the daughter of that upright sterling truthful woman, – the sister of that silly, scrupulous, conscientious simple man, such a clever reckless intriguer? Is it the Jesuits?

I cannot tell you, at the same time, how good & sterling Mrs. Stewart is. Unwise, provoking & mad as she is, it is such a relief to come to something which is above, entirely above, all that is mean & petty & selfish & frivolous & low into a higher & purer atmosphere, into truth & generosity that she is like my bright tossing sea & stormy Castle top – here – compared with the funereal Eastern beauties of Scutari – where lie the whitening bones of rotting carcases of thousands under the opal skies & trim cypresses of the luxuriant climate.

Incomplete. Claydon; copy, Wellcome (*Cal.* B. 4. D7, 131).

During her six weeks in the Crimea this October and November Miss Nightingale was unable to dissociate herself from the detailed daily running of the Scutari hospitals. Sidney Godolphin Osborne had accused her of "too great love of management."[28] But Aunt Mai was new to the work, and perhaps, remembering some of the mistakes Mrs Bracebridge had made, especially in the distribution of the Free Gifts, Miss Nightingale was fretted by the fear that her well ordered world would become a bear garden in her absence. She never completely trusted her lieutenants, except Rev. Mother Clare of Bermondsey and Mrs Shaw Stewart, now at the Castle Hospital.

So a constant stream of extremely detailed instructions on nursing and household matters poured down upon Aunt Mai. Many of these notes, undated, have become fragmented, separated from their beginnings or ends. In fact it is doubtful whether there was a coherent sequence. On one occasion she apologised to Aunt Mai for contradicting herself. On another she asked her to apologise to Mother Bermondsey for her rudeness in issuing *her* with instructions in this way. A few of the more striking fragments have been included here, illustrating Miss Nightingale's way of life, her inmost thoughts and multitudinous concerns, at this time.

In the midst of all the other harassing concerns she was not infrequently asked by anxious relatives to fulfil one of the functions now performed by the Red Cross – that is, to trace "missing" men. She did her best in such cases.

To Aunt Mai Smith

C.H. B'clava
3rd November 1855

Would you, please, find out about the enclosed man, T. Ward, 93rd, Highrs., whose fate seems very mysterious & let me have back the enclosed Mem[orandu]m at all events.

Nurse Grundy, who will come to you by the "Cleopatra", leaves me with no cause of dissatisfaction on my part – & to my great regret. She is to be allowed to see Mrs. Parker. But her going home, with passage paid by me, is to be *no* precedent for the others – as I consider going home because they are tired of the place, a thoughtless breach of duty to the country & the W. Office who pay for them. And I shall never sanction it by paying their passage home. Grundy goes home because she has heard from her brother *here* bad news of her children. Please let Miss Tebbutt tell Parker this.

I don't think you could have done otherwise than let Mrs. Edgar go. For the utmost we could have *obliged* her to do would have been to give us a month's warning. But the arguments are worth nothing. I have no more to do with Mrs. Fairbrough's have a drunken servant or no servant at all than with the Emperor of Oude having drunken servants. Mrs. F. is only out here upon sufferance. In no army in the world, excepting ours, it is even suffered. Whereas *we* are out with a distinct commission from the Queen. And I have the right to provide ourselves first with servants & no one else. When I first came out, I used to be expected to find the Officers' wives with Nurses,

Monthly Nurses, Quarters & servants. But I soon put a stop to that. Koulali & Miss Wear have gone on doing it. And great has been the kudos & great the damage they have gained by it. I wish the Wives were at Astrachan. For *they* have no business here & they take their husbands off *their* business.

Ever yrs.

I am *very* sorry about the Barrack Hosp*l*. Please tell me which Corridor *we* keep for the Hospl.

In a note appended at the bottom Aunt Mai comments, "I have no scruple at having agreed to Mrs. Edgar's going to be servant with Mrs. Fairbrough. Mrs. E. was servant at Genl. Hospital but Miss Tebbutt told me she was really not wanted: that they had so few sick so little to do." Claydon; copy, Wellcome (*Cal.* B. 4. D10, 143).

Miss Nightingale was not averse to indulging in camp gossip, as many of her letters to her family testify. She enjoyed the company of the great and famous: "It was a great thing to be well with the great men to keep down the insolence of the underlings."[29]

To her father

C.H. B'clava
14th November 1855

The expedition to Kaffa [30] is counter-manded – & Lothian remains here for the winter. I saw him today, looking & calling himself much better – & in ten days he blows up the famous Dockyards of Sevastopol, to replace all which city with its fleet, as they were, would cost the Russians £300,000,000 – three hundred millions, for fear you should not be able to count my noughts. Yet what is that to have done? after all. Far better have made Sevastopol a free port under our protection. Lothian is probably Major by this time & is much disappointed not to have Kaffa & a Colonelcy.

The Camp gossip here is that the Codrington [31] appointment is only a warming-pan – & that Gen*l*. Wyndham, [32] Chief of the Staff, is to have the honor of next year's campaign, at Nicholaieff, with the Command in Chief.

Though the whole camp is as cautious as Ladies of the Bed-chamber, none scruple now to say, Gen*l*. Simpson being gone, that the whole failure of the Redan rests with him – that, had the Highland Brigade with the Third Division to support them, led the attack, we could not have failed, with the loss indeed of *three times the men*, to have carried the Redan & all before us, taken the little Redan & all the Russian army in flank & all but annihilated it.

Sir John Hall is going back to his rupees in India with a K.C.B. ship.[33] It is like the lifting of a great incubus – & every body seems to breathe more freely. Now I think something may be done in the Crimea. I feel as if my hands were untied.

Dr. Hall's *probable* departure makes my stay here as long as the War much more certain. I do not think he would ever have made me desert my post nor by rendering what I could do little, make me give up the little I could do. But,

Sir John Hall, M.D., K.C.B., F.R.C.S.

though I hope experience has long since caused me to cease either to hope or to fear, but simply to act & to trust, I do, though I may be most excessively mistaken, expect great reforms from the absence of this incubus.

The dirt he has walked thro' in opposing & thinking to sting me is wonderful. For he really is an able & efficient officer – with a head square like Napoleon's & as vain – as inclined to dirty tricks as that great ruffian. Dr. Hall has actually stooped, as I know from authority that cannot be doubted, to tell the Nurses I have sent to the Crimea that they may take off their Badges, that they may cease to consider themselves as under my authority & that he will provide. If they will desert me, he will pay them. It is fact, that poor Miss Clough deserted upon this fiction, engaged a man & his wife whom she always called her "servants", with this understanding, & after her death, left them, (Dr. Hall's tender mercies having failed & he refusing to send in their claim for wages) to me & General Cameron to pay out of our own pockets as it was impossible for me to send in such a claim to Government.

I should like to have, please, a Cuckoo Clock sent out for this Hospital as a present for Mrs. Stewart. Please, send it to me at Scutari. *It must make a noise* – not a little silvery voice like mine.   Yours for ever

PRIVATE

Lord Raglan, in his last visit to me, asked me "if my father liked my coming out." I said with pride my father is not as other men are, he thinks that daughters should serve their country as well as sons – he brought me up to think so – he has no sons – & therefore he has sacrificed me to my country – & told me to come home with my shield on upon it. He does not think, (as I once heard a father & a very good & clever father say,) "The girls are all I could wish – very happy, very attentive to me, & very amusing." He thinks that God sent women, as well as men, into the world to be something more than "happy", "attentive" & "amusing". "Happy & *dull*", *religion* is said to make us – "happy & *amusing*" *social life* is supposed to make us – but my father's religious & social ethics make us strive to be the pioneers of the human race & let "happiness" & "amusement" take care of themselves.

Claydon; copy, Wellcome (*Cal*. B. 4. D14, 152).

On 16th November Florence again wrote to Aunt Mai about the disposition of nurses and household servants. Aunt Mai had evidently criticised her attitude to nursing sick officers, for here she was at some pains to justify her position. She was always impatient of the expectation of special privileges in those of higher rank. The episode of the officers' toast was to rouse her to repetitive rage during the following winter and spring.

To Aunt Mai Smith   C.H. B'clava
                                                   16th November 1855
Mrs. Brownlow[34] Please read the enclosed to Mrs. Brownlow & let her come up with one of the Household Servants as soon as possible – the Laundress &

other Household Servant remaining now at the House to fill Mrs. Brownlow's & Greek's place – with Laxton as Chef – acknowledged.

If Mrs. Little or any one else be already engaged, she may wait till Mrs. Brownlow's month here be out – & then she may still come up. Mrs. Little will probably come on her own book – in spite of me.

Mrs. B. & the Household Serv*t*. are for the Monastery.

Officers Nursing About the Officers, I must have misexpressed myself – for the facts of the Officers' Nursing are not at all as you think them.

I have never declined to Nurse any Officer. I have declined uniformly to send them Nurses – to take away a woman from nursing 100 men to sit or lie the 24 hours in an Officer's room, as *they* wished. But, *in* the Hospitals, Barrack and General, where ever we were sent for, whether to Military, Medical or Ecclesiastical Officer, Mrs. Roberts & I have always gone. I have farther found everything that was necessary. And few have died without me or Mrs. Roberts – & few have recovered without acknowledging us. But I have always nursed an Officer like a Private – that is, visiting him at necessary times. If he did not choose to be nursed in that way, he was not nursed at all.

Farther, I kept an organized corps of Soldiers' wives (respectable women) all of whom, but one, are now gone home (& are indeed no longer wanted), to nurse the Officers, Military, Medical & Ecclesiastical, *out of* the Hospitals, Barrack & General, at my own expence. These were inspected & visited by me. Also I once took a sick Officer into my own house & many times into the Barrack Hosp*l*.

At these two Hospitals of *B'clava,* we have, farther, done the whole cooking for the sick & wounded officers, Mil[itar]y, Med[ica]l, & Ecc[lesiastica]l, ever since we have been established, & nursed them with *Nurses*, in-doors & out, the same as I have done at Scutari with myself, Roberts & soldiers' wives. It has not answered, as I will at some time expose, but so it is.

Farther, there is not an egg, nor a piece of butter, nor of jelly, nor Eau de Cologne, which has not been provided at Mrs. Stewart's or my private expence at this Hospital for the sick & wounded Officers ever since its Establishment – & we have, as stated, done their whole cooking & nursing.

Farther, I have, in individual severe cases, given a Nurse, both here & at Scutari, *to sit up.*

Here we have so spoilt the sick & wounded Officers that they complained to the Commander in Chief, (because I would not bake their toast for *twenty four hours*), of my "ill treatment".

It cannot therefore be said that I do not nurse officers. God knows I have enemies enough. Please therefore find some other excuse for me with Mrs. Shrubb, who has, however, put "My Nursing" already in the Times Advertisement of Deaths.

Bracebridges   I do not think Mr. Bracebridge intends to return & (to tell you the truth) *he could not,* (after his Lecture as reported in the "Times") without greatly injuring the work. He is too clever a man to have said that (I cannot enter into it at length) had he *intended* to return. It has set all the Medical Staff in the Crimea in a blaze & besides being utterly untrue, it was not our business to say it. And, if you read my letter to him, you will see that I have told him so. Did I, by the bye send you that letter of mine to him?[35]

But, in short, his coming back now would be a hindrance instead of a help.

I cannot bear to cut off my own right-hand by signifying anything of this kind to them – & thereby to kill myself with my own hand. But I leave the facts with you to make use or not of it as you like.

Dr. Hall, my chief, burrows & burrows away the ground from under me. The whole of the Wear, *Clough* & Bridgeman rebellions were *his* organizing. You little knew the man when you tried to interpret his conduct in the Clough affair. He has done *much* worse things.

House Rent   If the Turk Landlord comes again, tell him that he knows perfectly well that I have his Receipt for the rent of his house which I paid up to January – & also that I have the refusal of the house after that – & that I mean to keep it for another three months.

Don't be daunted by him. He comes about every 6 weeks. I say this & he goes away again.

But as for giving him 2500 piastres a month, I won't give him 1000 pi. which is what I gave before.

Many thanks for all you say & do.

I do not quite understand the distribution of the Nurses. There is one Nurse & three half-nurses in C. And why should Mrs. Clarke & Mrs. Hawkins the two suspicious one, be in C at all? It does not do to have different Nurses working in the same ward. Please confine these two, at least, to A & I. The system of Nurses *following* their patients is one fraught with mischief.

Yours for ever

Claydon; copy, Wellcome (*Cal.* B. 4. E1, 154).

On 17th November Miss Nightingale wrote to Mrs Herbert, acknowledging a magnificent donation to the Nightingale Fund, and recapitulating her grievances against Dr Hall. The letter was really meant for Mr Herbert, whose help and advice she felt in need of in her effort to re-establish her position with the authorities after her recent troubles with Dr Hall and the nuns.

To Mrs Herbert

Castle Hospital
Balaclava
17th November 1855

My dearest Lizzie

Many thanks for the £1000 information from Wellington N. Zealand. It is a magnificent tribute from our Colonies – & comes to cheer one's spirits with its kindness, after all the dirt one has to wade thro' here – & the wreck of characters this Crimean War has made.

Now I am going to do a little "dirty work" myself.

It did very much for our peculiar work the having, as our friends, the great men – Lord Raglan, Gen. Estcourt, & the departure of Sir Richard Airey have been great losses to *our* cause. The man who was born Lord Fitzroy Somerset would naturally not be above interesting himself in Hospital matters & a parcel of women – while the man who was born James Simpson would essentially think it infradig. Again, a word from the Quarter Master General was quite enough to expedite the Extra Diet Kitchen, the draining, flushing, reading-huts for Convalescents etc. etc.

Dr. Hall does not think it beneath him to broil me slowly upon the fires of my own Extra Diet Kitchen – & to give out that we are private adventurers & to be treated as such.

Remember, please, that this is quite private, that I do not wish to complain of Dr. Hall, who is an able & efficient officer in some ways – & that I think he has been justly provoked by Mr. Bracebridge's "Lecture" in the "Times" about English medical treatment – with which I utterly dissent both as to its truth, & as to the propriety of saying it, were it true. The French Physicians utterly disown it.

I believe that Dr. Hall is going to India. So that what I say now I say quite generally, & only give a particular instance to shew what I mean.

It is this.

In April I undertook this Hospital – & from that time to this we have cooked *all* the Extra Diets for 500–600 Patients & the *whole* Diets for all the wounded Officers by ourselves in a shed – & till I came up this time, (tho' I sent up a French man-cook,[36] to whom I give £100 per ann., in July,) I could not get an Extra Diet Kitchen built promised me in May, till I came to do it myself viz. in October. During the whole of this time, every egg, every bit of butter, jelly, all of Eau de Cologne which the sick Officers have had have been provided out of Mrs. Shaw Stewart's or my private pockets. On Nov. 4, I opened my Extra Diet Kitchen – but, for 24 hours, I would not bake the Officer's toast in this kitchen, because it disconcerted the Extra Diets for 550 Patients. In those 24 hours, the Officers made a complaint to Head Quarters of our "ill-treatment" in re. toast. And Dr. Hall, with the PMO of Balaclava, came down in their wrath & reprimanded the – Cook's Orderly! Whereupon Mrs. Shaw Stewart wrote Dr. Hall a civil formal letter, "requesting that his orders & reprimands might be given to her," in order that the business might be properly done. Dr. Hall then published to his inferior Officers that the ladies at the Castle Hospital meant to throw off all subordination to the Medical Officers – & that this was the reason he had brought the Nuns to the General Hospital, Balaclava.* He also wrote to Mrs. Stewart that it was his duty to care for the Officers as well as for the men – his paternal care having begun for their toast & them on Nov. 7, while he had never enquired how they had been provided for at all since April 25. So that they have perhaps profited more by Mrs. Stewart's & my maternal care than by Dr. Hall's paternal one, which never could be persuaded to issue eggs – or any other comfort, till the Purveyor-in-Chief came up himself.

These things are nothing excepting in as much as they thwart the work.

And, if Mr. Herbert saw no impropriety in it, – whose judgement will be far better in this matter than mine, – a private letter from some high authority to the Commander-in-Chief or Chief of the Staff to the effect that this work is not a silly display of feminine sensibilities but an authorized set of tools – provided to the hand of the Medical Officers to supply extra diets, cleanliness, clean linen & Hospital Comforts to the Patients – might greatly further these objects – by enabling us to obtain the "de quoi".

If Mr. Herbert thinks it better not, I am content to work on sottomano, building my Extra Diet Kitchens etc. myself. PLEASE don't say anything about our having provided these things at private expence.

The Irish Catholic rebellion & establishment of the thirteen Irish nuns on an independent footing at Balaclava is what I have been expecting all along – & only wonder it did not take place before. It is the old story. Ever since the days of Queen Elizabeth the chafing against secular supremacy, especially English, on the part of the R. Catholic Irish. I am very sorry for it. For I think it is fraught with mischief. For these Irish nuns are dead against us. I mean England – the way their priests talk is odious. The proportion of R. Catholics & of Irish has increased inconceivably in the army since the late Recruits. Had we more Nuns, it would be very desirable, to diminish disaffection. But *just not* the Irish ones. The wisest thing the W. Office could now do would be to send out a few more of the Bermondsey Nuns† to join those already at Scutari & counter balance the influence of the *Irish* ones, who hate their soberer Sisters with the mortal hatred which, I believe, only Nuns & Household Servants CAN feel towards each other.

It reminds me of the Butler who said "I am sure, my Lady, you must have observed, your Ladyship, that for six months I have not repeated after your Ladyship the "Forgive us our trespasses etc." in the Lord's Prayer because I could not forgive Mrs. Baker (the Housekeeper) nor will I, my Lady, & by

*He has since announced this officially. F.N. 26/2/56
†This has been done F.N. 21/1/56 [37]

the same token it is now six months since I have spoken to her in the House-keeper's Room."

Dearest Lizzie, do not trouble yourself in this matter, if you think it better not. You don't suppose the impertinence of vulgar officials troubles us much – we get the things done all the same, only a little more slowly. When we have the support at Head Quarters, matters advance faster, that is all. During six months, the Castle Hospital, always the *principal* & now the *only* general Hospital in the Crimea, which has always had more than double the number of Patients of any other Crimean Hospital, has had scarcely any thing done for it in the way of all the Engineering necessities of a Hospital. This is the statement of its own P.M.O. But, you know, it would ruin him to say so.

The real grievance against us is that we are independent of promotion & therefore of the displeasure of our chiefs – that we have no prospects to injure – & that, although subordinate to these Medical Chiefs in office, we are superior to them in influence & in the chance of being heard at home. It is an anomalous position. But so is War, to us English, anomalous.

God bless you
Thank you
Ever yours

B.L. Add. Ms. 43396, f. 40 (*Cal.* B. 4. E1, 155).

For some reason she decided not to send this letter at the time but only forwarded it with her letter to Mr Herbert of 20th February 1856, when her anger with Dr Hall reached its climax.

A few days later the news that cholera had broken out again at Scutari sent her urgently back to Constantinople, leaving the question of her jurisdiction in the Crimea unresolved.

From Scutari she attempted to exert some contol over the rebellious Miss Wear.

To Miss Wear

B.H. Scutari
17th November 1855

My dear Miss Wear

You will receive this week Mrs. Brownlow (& baby!) & a house-hold servant, Mrs. Nisbett. I hope therefore that all is ready at the Monastery – I will write to you with particulars about them.

Hitherto you have nursed & not superintended. Let me remind you that, while we must all admire & respect your devoted efforts as a Nurse – & none appreciate them more than myself – I must again allude to the fact that it was not as a Nurse but as a Superintendent that I placed you, acting for the Government, at the General Hospital at Balaclava – & that our duties in this latter office are far more responsible, painful & difficult than in the former one.

Mrs. Brownlow comes to you temporarily only. I trust you will like Mrs. Nisbett.

Believe me ever yours truly & gratefully

B.L. Add. Ms. 39867, f. 71 (*Cal.* omitted).

A fortnight later she attempted to persuade Miss Wear of the necessity of keeping accurate returns of the Free Gifts. Miss Nightingale claimed that Koulali had been broken up because the ladies would give out articles of diet not on the diet rolls. Smyrna too had closed. In both places, she asserted, the ladies had proved unmanageable:

Depend upon it that our only duty, & safety resides in close obedience to Requisitions, & that sooner or later should our obedience fail we shall be justly punished. I have never wished to render anything but this close obedience – not one article in the Hospitals of Scutari or in the Castle Hospital of Balaklava has been given except in answer to Requisitions, either of diet, of clothing, or of medical comforts.

Pray my dear Miss Wear let me feel that, in you I have a Superintendent as judicious as she is zealous. The medical authorities will be as glad to trip you up hereafter as they have been in other quarters. You see you have been already reported to poor Lord Raglan as having made Requisitions for Eau de Cologne of which he informed me – tho' I know that you had never had it before you informed me of this.[38]

Then, three days later, on 14th December, Miss Nightingale demanded to know how it was she had received two nurses from Smyrna sent apparently at the request of Miss Wear.[39]

Miss Wear promptly forwarded the correspondence to Dr Hall with a note showing clearly where her allegiance lay.

I beg to enclose letters all received last night from Miss Nightingale, she had better not send any more of her people here, unless *you* wish it, as there is not any necessity for them and I almost regret having anyone beyond Mrs. Brownlow of whom I have every reason to approve . . .

I am very happy and comfortable here and I am only anxious to retain *your* approbation and have *as little* correspondence with Scutari as may be.[40]

The problem caused by the appearance of two Smyrna nurses at Scutari assumed quite disproportionate dimensions. Dr Hall had written to Miss Wear that though he considered her request for such assistance reasonable, it would be better not to have them.[41] But the Purveyor, Mr Fitzgerald, had then, apparently in collusion with Miss Wear, written to the Superintendent of Smyrna requesting two of her redundant nurses, who arrived not at Balaclava but at Scutari. Miss Nightingale employed them — from humanity, as she was to explain to Lady Cranworth — but used the incident to demand of Mr Hawes that her position in the Crimea be clarified.[43]

To Lady Cranworth

Scutari
Barrack Hospital
22nd December 1855

Dear Lady Cranworth

In reply to your very kind letter of Dec. 10,

1. The War Office have consented to send out three Nuns of the Bermondsey (English) "Sisters of Mercy" – a very prudent measure, I think, combining, as Lord Panmure may be reasonably supposed to do, the wisdom of the serpent with the gentleness, is it?, of the dove.

2. My other serpent & dove, the General Commanding here, – M. General Storks, – has abolished the Palace Hospital filling it with troops – & placed the sick Officers at the General Hospital Scutari under my tender mercies, which I have graciously consented to exercise upon the following conditions, which have all been granted: I that the sick Officers should be upon a Diet Roll, similarly tho' not similar to the sick Privates   II that they should be served by the Orderlies and not by servants   III that we should nurse only serious cases & not toddle about doing odd jobs among the "Polloi". The Officers are now comfortably ensconced under these regulations, which they do not discern as coming from my heavy hand, at the General Hospital here. Of poor Mrs. Moore's 4 nurses, 1 is dead, 1 gone home, 2 I have taken, very fit women for the purpose.

3.   Koulali is extinct – turned into a barrack for our German Legion – & we have taken all the Patients – & I all the Ladies & Nurses I could – from thence – viz. 10. One (I had taken 11) was invalided home at the crisis of engagement.

Of these, 2 ladies & 3 nurses are at the General Hospital, Scutari, – 1 is at the Barrack Hospital, Scutari, – 2 I have sent up to my two Hospitals at Balaclava – 1 Lady & 1 nurse are at my House in Scutari.

As *Lady*-Sisters, it is supposed, "*may do anything!*" i.e. marry gentlemen who stay in their houses, & themselves stay in the houses of unmarried gentlemen, I thought it prudent to let a few of the Koulali Ladies go home, whom I felt I could not reduce to my merciless working rules. They will soon re-appear here as the wives of their respective husbands. Please do not betray me in this piece of diplomacy – meant only for yourself.

4.   I have two Smyrna Nurses (*by mistake*). I have kept them here at this Hospital – as I feared they would desire more liberty than I could give. I think them very promising. Dr. Hall (Ins*p*. Gen*l*. of Hosp*ls*.) sent for them ("*by mistake*") to the Crimea. I am going to make it a subject of a letter to the War Office. But the poor women must not suffer. They are what they ought to be (quite).

With regard to Miss Salisbury's case, the General Commanding here & myself can give a statement, which must crush all future patronising of her case on the part of any but partisans. But what must we call those who, knowing the circumstances viz. that she was *proved* to be guilty of embezzlement, *suspected* of something worse, have taken up such a case?

The Cholera has subsided, thank God.

I do not share the anticipations of those who think we shall not have a sickly winter. But, happily, it cannot be anything like last winter, for the trench-work is over. Could our English officials, however, but see the roads in the Crimea. One General Officer tells me he thinks "locomotion" is not much more easy than last year.

Miss Morton [44] is better, tho' still at my house. Her goodness makes her invaluable. Believe me yours gratefully & faithfully

B.L. Add. Ms. 43397, f. 71. (*Cal.* B. 4. E6, 173).

At the beginning of January Miss Nightingale's interrupted correspondence with Sidney Herbert was resumed in connection with the disposition of the Nightingale Fund.

Since her illness various schemes to recognise her work had been considered. These came to fruition on 29th November, when a public meeting was held in Willis's Rooms in London "to give expression to a general feeling that the services of Miss Nightingale in the hospitals of the East demand the grateful recognition of the British public." Many of her most influential friends were present. Mr Herbert was elected honorary secretary with Mr S. C. Hall. It was decided to set up a fund to enable her to establish an institute for the training, sustenance and protection of nurses, paid and unpaid. Herbert sent a copy of the resolution, to which Miss Nightingale made two replies, formal and private. In the formal letter, for the council, she acknowledged the sympathy and confidence shown her by the originators of this scheme.

Exposed as I am to be misinterpreted and misunderstood, in a field of action in which the work is new, complicated, and distant from many who sit in judgment upon it, − it is indeed an abiding support to have such sympathy and such appreciation brought home to me in the midst of labour and difficulties all but overpowering. I must add, however, that my present work is such as I would never desert for any other, so long as I see room to believe that what I may do here is unfinished. May I then, beg you to express to the Committee that I accept their proposal, provided I may do so on their understanding of this great uncertainty as to when it will be possible for me to carry it out?[45]

In her second, private letter to Herbert she elaborated the reasons for her inability to do anything now, and enunciated the principles which dictated her present course, and which formed the philosophic base for the future.

The main guard entrance to the Barrack hospital, Scutari, showing a loaded *araba* drawn by two oxen in the foreground. Water-colour sketch by Anne Morton in spring 1856

Florence Nightingale's room in her house at Scutari Water-colour sketch by Anne Morton in spring 1856

Typed copy of letter to Sidney Herbert

Scutari
6th January 1856

My dear Mr. Herbert

I have written a letter as you desired, in order to relieve you from Trouble & responsibility which are a bad reward for all your kindness & confidence in this matter.

But I would far rather leave the naming of the Council in your Hands, & should you see anything injudicious in what I have said, I shall be grateful to you to make any alterations, which I sanction before hand.

I confess that I do not see what a Council has to do till I *return*, die, *break up*, (so as to leave a conviction of my never being able to act) *or else begin to act in London*. It seems rather a case for Trustees now as I see specified by you – & I hope that you will take the trouble, always great but not ungrateful of acting as my Trustee.

Believe me to be ever most gratefully yours

P.S. The confidence which you & the Subscribers to this Fund have shewn me has been so generous & extraordinary that it is perhaps hardly necessary for me to allude to a very natural letter which I am told has appeared in the "Times", to the effect that I must furnish a Prospectus of what I am going to do before I can expect to have *money* subscribed to do it. I think this perfectly reasonable, if I originally had asked for the money, which, of course I did not. But to furnish a cut & dried Prospectus of my Plans, when I cannot look forward a month, much less a year, is what I would not if I could, & I could not if I would! I would not if I could, because everything which succeeds is not the production of a Scheme, of Rules & Regulations made beforehand, but of a mind observing & adapting itself to wants & events. I could not if I would, because it is simply impossible to find, – time in the midst of one overpowering work to digest & concoct another – & if it could be done, it would be simply bad & to be hereafter altered or destroyed. St. Vincent de Paul, who, I am told is quoted in this letter, *began* with one Lady & four Peasant girls – & no scheme at all. *That* was made *afterwards*.

B.L. Add. Ms. 43393, f. 209 (*Cal. B. 4. E9*, 184).

Miss Nightingale did, however, nominate a council of nine: C. H. Bracebridge, Dr William Bowman, Sir James Clark, Sidney Herbert, Richard Dawes, Sir Joshua Jebb, H. Bence Jones, Sir John McNeill and the Earl of Ellesmere. Five trustees were appointed to invest the money raised, which amounted to more than £44,000: Sidney Herbert, Richard Monckton Milnes, Lord Monteagle, C. H. Bracebridge and Edward Marjoribanks. When it became evident in 1859 that Miss Nightingale would never be able to engage personally in the work for which the fund had been established a sub-committee consisting of Sidney Herbert, Sir John McNeill, Sir James Clark, William Bowman and Sir Joshua Jebb, with A. H. Clough as secretary, was appointed to negotiate the setting up of the Nightingale Training School at St. Thomas's Hospital, [46] where "the very good Matron [Mrs Wardroper] and a sensible Resident Officer, Mr. Whitfield, already had a great idea of raising the nurses."[47]

Another of Miss Nightingale's harassing functions was that of savings banker to the troops and nurses who wished to remit money home. Sidney Godolphin Osborne had begun this service during his six weeks at Scutari[48] during the winter of 1854–55, and Miss Nightingale appears to have continued the work through much of 1855, with the assistance of Mr Bracebridge. By the autumn large sums were being handled every week, so that when Uncle Sam Smith offered to manage the business at the English end Miss Nightingale was only too thankful to accept his offer. After the war she was frequently to complain about the complication of her accounts.

To Uncle Sam Smith

Scutari, B. Hospital
6th January 1856

Dear Uncle Sam

As you are so kind as to say that you will undertake my Money Concerns, tho' I really think you hardly know what you have thereby offered, I send you the First Fruits in a week's Money Orders for soldiers & women.

They are individually in not such small sums as usual.

The (under £5) sums I pay by P.O. Orders & the larger ones in any way your prudence directs. I enclose a Cheque for £248 – the overplus of £1.6.0* I have allowed for the price of P.O. Orders.

Harry Carter or Parthe will, I am sure, help you.

And Harry Carter must, I believe, be a man of business.[49] For I can assure you that the boxes he has sent me are the only ones which have not cost me hours of unnecessary labor. Because he has given me Invoices of the contents of each box, announcements of the same per "Ossian" – & Bills of Lading. One of his Boxes per "Ossian" is still missing. But, as I had the Bill of Lading, I could claim it – & shall presently get it from Balaclava. Otherwise I could really state that the things which go astray & are lost – & the things which I have to search for all over the two sides the Bosphorus make the time lost to me not worth the contents of the Package. The Nurses' Clothing sent out by Ly. Canning & Mrs. Bracebridge (which arrived here 6 weeks ago) has not all turned up yet.

I feel like a culprit in detaining your wife, my dear Aunt Mai. And I am sure you must look upon me as such.

---

* I shall be too glad to give £6.6. or £8.8.0 (whichever you think proper) to the Clerks at Glyn's for their former trouble about small cheques.

With regard to the Sums for Savings Banks herein inclosed, those for the *Atherstone* Savings Bank Mr. Bracebridge will pay in & there is an enquiry for one "Book" at the *Bloomsbury* Savings Bank for a sum £10 of which he paid in – which must be made of him. The Sums for the *Oxford* Savings Banks must be sent to Miss Felicia Skene

18 Beaumont Street

Oxford

who manages those matters there

Signature missing. B.L. Add. Ms. 45792, f. 1 (*Cal.* B. 4. E10, 185).

Notes

1   Charlotte Stuart, eldest daughter of Lord Stuart de Rothesay, wife of Charles John Earl Canning. Lady Canning had been one of the Committee of Management of the Harley Street Institution when F.N. was Superintendent. She became involved in the recruitment of nurses for the War Office in the spring of 1855. F.N. reported regularly to her on the progress of her protégées during 1855 and 1856, a correspondence which continued until Lady Canning's death in 1861.

2   Mrs Walford, whom F.N. recruited in the East.

3   An Etna was a container in which a small quantity of liquid could be heated by burning spirit.

4   F.N. made a clear distinction between the Superintendent, who directed the nursing on the wards, and the Matron, a superior housekeeper who looked after the linen and other hospital stores. The Housekeeper, "who will exercise control over the Nurses in the quarters," is the obvious forerunner of the Home Sister whom F.N. was to have appointed at St. Thomas's Training School to look after the welfare of the nurses.

5   Lord Canning was appointed Governor General of India at the end of 1855. He took up the post on 29th February 1856.

6   F.N. to Benjamin Hawes, 10th May 1855, p. 128.

7   Dr Delany to Mother Bridgeman, 25th January 1854: "You will . . . retain your post until it is manifest to all men that you abandon it only through necessity; and I recommend therefore that you continue to give the services of such Sisters as may be required . . . always provided that the Religious form a community under their own Superior." (Bolster, p. 125.)

8   B.L. Add. Ms. 39867, f. 28.

9   Taylor, *Eastern Hospitals* . . ., p. 164; Bolster, pp. 199, 202.

10   B.L. Add. Ms. 39867, f. 28v.

11   B.L. Add. Ms. 39867, f. 36.

12   F.N. to Lord Stratford [?3rd October 1855], copy, Nightingale papers, Claydon; copy Wellcome.

13   General (Sir) Henry Knight Storks (1811–74) succeeded Lord William Paulet to the command of the British establishments in Turkey, from the Bosphorus to Smyrna, in August 1855. At Scutari he was soon established as an admirer and ally of F.N. She, in turn, had him appointed a member of the Royal Commission on the sanitary condition of the army in 1857. They corresponded on matters

concerning the welfare of the men for many years. In the controversy over the transfer of the nuns to Balaclava, General Storks was firmly on F.N.'s side. J. Scott Robertson, writing to Dr Hall in February, mentioned that "I had too, a battle with [Lefroy] & Gen*l*. Storks regarding certain statements made about them, but I fancy the feeling in that quarter is adverse & fixed." (Hall papers, box 14 FC09/7, R.A.M.C. Historical Museum, Aldershot.)

14 Bolster, p. 201.

15 F.N.'s own practice in the future, when trained staffs were being sent out from St Thomas's, was to insist that whole staffs should go, five or six in a group. She may well have learnt from the experience of dealing with Mother Bridgeman the strength of such groups.

16 B.L. Add. Ms. 39867, f. 69v.

17 P.R.O. WO/43/963, f. 335v.

18 F.N. to her family, mid October 1855, Nightingale papers, Claydon.

19 Miss Wear to Dr Hall, 1st Oct 1855, B.L. Add. Ms. 39867, f. 37

20 Charlotte Salisbury, who had been for eleven years governess with the family of Mr Wood, consul at Patras, went to Scutari in June 1855 when F.N. was ill and Mrs Bracebridge was in charge of the stores. Miss Salisbury was entrusted with the issue of the Free Gifts in the stores when the Bracebridges left. Her engagement was ended on 27th September when F.N. and General Storks became convinced of her dishonesty in the distribution of the stores. She was sent home to England on 1st October. Back home she vigorously protested her innocence of the charges brought against her and attempted, with the support of Mary Stanley and other disaffected parties, to get up an action for libel against F.N. The action failed, and on 15th February 1856 Benjamin Hawes wrote to Miss Salisbury to inform her that Lord Panmure, having received the fullest explanation from General Storks, Miss Nightingale and the Rev. Dr Blackwood, was of the opinion that her dismissal was right and necessary. (Documents of the case, Nightingale papers, Claydon; copy Wellcome.)

21 Sir Richard Airey (1803–81), Quartermaster General, was at this time regarded by F.N. as a "friend" and he seems in this instance to have forwarded the engineering works that she wanted in spite of Dr Hall's view that they were not practicable. (F.N. to Elizabeth Herbert, 17th November 1855, p. 177) But after the appearance of the McNeill–Tulloch report which indicted Airey as one of those responsible for the failure of the supplies in the Crimea, and therefore responsible for so much death and suffering, she changed her opinion of him. But she would have given up her father in such a cause, as she was to say.

22 F.N. must have been particularly impressed by Dr Matthew, for, although he does not appear frequently in her correspondence, she went to extraordinary lengths after his death in 1865 to help his widow and children. In November 1866 she urged that Mrs Matthew be treated in the same way as women widowed during the war, even though she was not actually married until after it, as Surgeon Major Matthew had certainly contracted his fatal illness in the course of his Crimean service. (B.L. Add. Ms. 45800, f. 14.)

23 F.N. was not the only person to regard Mrs Shaw Stewart as mad. Dr George Lawson sent home a graphic description of her behaviour: "One of our nurses is a Miss Stuart . . . The lady is, I am sure, perfectly mad . . . She will persist in sitting up nearly every night with the worst fever cases, does her work also by day,

and takes her rest by snatches of sleep, seldom removes her clothes, but when she is craved to take a little rest, wraps herself up in a cloak and lies down on the ground. She has already had an attack of erysipelas, and if she continues in her foolish ways, will probably get an attack of fever." (V. Bonham Carter, ed., *George Lawson*, p. 164)

24   General Sir Henry William Barnard (1799–1857), Chief of Staff; commanded 2nd Division of the army in the Crimea.

25   Richard Dawes, Dean of Hereford (1793–1867) worked to improve the education of the middle and lower classes; he established large and well organised schools at Hereford and Ledbury.

26   F.N. to Aunt Mai Smith, 28th Oct. 1855.

27   This probably refers to the birth of a baby to Blanche and A. H. Clough. One of their two daughters was called Florence.

28   S. G. Osborne, *Scutari and its Hospitals*, ch. 4.

29   F.N. to ? Aunt Mai, 11th November 1855, Nightingale papers, Claydon.

30   The circumstances surrounding the expedition to Kaffa were typical of the chaos that afflicted the whole Crimean campaign. Twelve thousand men were embarked to take Kaffa, a port where the Russians landed stores, but at the last minute the French were recalled, so the whole enterprise had to be cancelled. (George McMunn, *The Crimea in Perspective,* London, 1935.)

31   Sir William John Codrington (1804–84), K.C.B., took over from Sir James Simpson as Commander in Chief, though many were surprised that Sir Colin Campbell did not succeed to that position.

32   Sir Charles Ash Wyndham (or Windham) (1810–70), Assistant Quartermaster General of 4th Division, 1854–56. He recorded his experiences in *The Crimean Diary and Letters of Lieut. General Sir Charles Ash Windham, K.C.B.,* London, 1897.

33   This rumour was untrue. Dr Hall was awarded the K.C.B. in February 1855 and never returned to India.

34   Among Dr Hall's papers (box 14, FC09/14, R.A.M.C. Historical Museum, Aldershot) is a copy of a letter from F.N. summoning Mrs Brownlow to the Crimea to look after Miss Wear. Her baby's name is mentioned – Bessie, who was the model for the chapter on "Minding Baby" in F.N.'s *Notes on Nursing for the Labouring Classes*, 1861. In her "end-of-term report" to the War Office (Report No. 1, 15th June, 1856) F.N. makes special mention of Mrs Brownlow's good services: "Though this person is not strictly one of H.My.'s Nurses, being the wife of a Pay Serjeant of the Coldstream Guards, & having been originally taken into my house at Scutari because she had a very young infant, yet from her 18 months' service, her invariable sobriety, respectability, & honesty, her industrious habits & really superior conduct, she deserves to be classed as one of those who have done good service having washed, cooked Extra Diets, & kept my house in Scutari for Sick Nurses during the whole campaign." (B.L. Add. Ms. 43402, f. 12.) And again in the Register of Military Nurses (G.L.R.O.) it was noted that Mrs. B. was not engaged as a nurse, but was "highly remarkable for invariable sobriety, respectability, honesty, her industrious habits, and really superior conduct: one who has done good service."

35   In a public lecture which was reported at length in *The Times*, 16th October 1855, p. 5, col. f, Bracebridge made various exaggerated claims for F.N.'s achievements at Scutari — "When they first made their appearance at Scutari there

was neither kitchen, coals, nor candles – nothing in fact but the naked walls"— and attacked the Medical Department for, among other things, failures in treatment: "As a proof of the obstinacy of the English Medical Department, he [Bracebridge] might mention that they continued to pursue the old system of treatment, notwithstanding the advice of the French physicians. From this cause alone, not taking into account the climate, many persons perished who might have been saved had it not been for these prejudices . . ." "He had a word or two to say in dispraise of some of the medical gentlemen. He would not mention names, but, though one of them was of superior rank, his deeds were far from being superior. He actually took the butter from the poor sick men and threw it away. This butter had been given them by Miss Nightingale, ordered by the medical men or purchased by themselves. The excuse which he made for this heartless action was most frivolous. The men, he said, ought not to have butter, as it was against medical etiquette . . ." In a letter to *The Times*, 20th October, p. 8, col. f, Bracebridge claimed to have been misrepresented in several instances. Be that as it may, F.N. was furious. She wrote a stinging rebuke on 4th November, the letter here referred to, a copy of part of which is preserved among the Nightingale papers at Claydon; a typed copy is in the B.L. Add. Ms. 43397, f. 171. However, while F.N. undoubtedly and with justification felt at the time that Bracebridge had seriously undermined her position – it gave Dr Hall the opportunity to pour scorn on herself and her supporters – she nevertheless never ceased to acknowledge her debt to both Bracebridge and more particularly to his wife.

36   This French man cook is probably to be identified with "Dumont", who is mentioned in several of the notes to Aunt Mai. It was not Soyer, who went to the Crimea as an independent agent.

37   Three Sisters arrived most opportunely to join F.N. in the Crimea in April 1856.

38   Copy in Dr Hall's hand of letter from F.N. to Miss Wear, 11th December 1855, B.L. Add. Ms. 39867, f. 75.

39   Copy in Dr Hall's hand of letter from F.N. to Miss Wear, 14th December 1855, B.L. Add. Ms. 39867, f. 76.

40   Miss Wear to Dr Hall, 21st December 1855, B.L. Add. Ms. 39867, f. 73.

41   Hall papers, box 14 FCO9/2, R.A.M.C. Historical Museum, Aldershot.

42   Miss Wear to Dr Hall, 9th November 1855, B.L. Add. Ms. 39867, f. 63.

43   F.N. to Benjamin Hawes, 7th January 1856, P.R.O. WO 43/963.

44   Miss Ann Ward Morton (1806–65) was one of the ladies sent out under Lady Canning's auspices. F.N. recorded the following encomium on her in her final report, No. IV: "Miss Morton, Lady Matron: last come out, but not least useful, – in the constant good influence exerted by her over the Nurses, in her unfailing desire to teach them & train them to good – in her willingness to take any work which offered to be most useful – & which only her physical want of strength prevented her carrying out more fully – I have the deepest obligations to her for her faithfulness to the work, for her tender care of the workers." During spring 1856, when the pressure on the hospital had relaxed somewhat, Miss Morton made a series of coloured sketches of the interior of Scutari and its environs. These were lent to the R.A.M.C. library in 1966, and photos and prints were made which are on display in the museum at Aldershot. The sketchbook was discovered By Miss Morton's great-nephew, Derick Ashley, who wrote an interesting short article about his aunt's work in Scutari for *St John Review*, 1966, 39, 25.

45   Cook, I, p. 271.

46   Lucy Seymer, *Florence Nightingale's Nurses, the Nightingale Training School, 1860–1960,* London, 1960, gives details of the composition of the council and trust, and negotiations with St Thomas's Hospital for the establishment of the Nightingale Training School.

47   B.L. Add. Ms. 45792, f. 68

48   Sidney Godolphin Osborne, *Scutari and its Hospitals.*

49   Henry Bonham Carter (1827–1921). So impressed with his business acumen was F.N. that she appointed him Secretary to the Nightingale Fund Council in 1861 on the death of Clough, the first secretary. He continued in that post until 1914.

6
The "confidential report"

In January 1856 the struggle between Dr Hall and Miss Nightingale reached a climax. Towards the end of December 1855 the Deputy Purveyor in Chief in the Crimea, David Fitzgerald,[1] submitted to Dr Hall a "Confidential Report on the Nursing, since its introduction to the Crimea on 23rd January 1855," prepared apparently at the request of Colonel J. H. Lefroy,[2] Lord Panmure's Confidential Adviser in Scientific Matters. The contents of the report soon became widely known in medical and military circles, and before long to Miss Nightingale herself. But officially she was unable to obtain a copy of the "confidential" document. In it the Purveyor criticised the nurses for lack of discipline, for drunkenness and for insubordination. He alleged that several, whom he mentioned by name, had been sent home for various more or less serious offences.

Considering that Miss Nightingale had been against sending nurses to Balaclava at that time – January 1855 – and that she had herself on several occasions lamented Miss Langston's lax superintendence and the lack of discipline among the nurses, it might be considered that her reaction to the Purveyor's report was excessive. Unfortunately several of those impugned could be shown to have been criticised quite unfairly.

Mrs Noble, one of those allegedly dismissed for misbehaviour, had been recommended for a year's extra pay.[3] Mrs Lawfield, whose behaviour Miss Nightingale had had occasion to reprove from time to time, remained in the East until July 1856, one of only seventeen who did stay throughout the whole period.

Fitzgerald's criticism that Miss Wear favoured the Sardinian officers, to the neglect of the British soldiery, might have been expected to strike a sympathetic chord with Miss Nightingale, who never ceased to deplore Miss Wear's superintendence; by the same token it ought to have embarrassed Dr Hall, who had insisted on retaining and supporting her in that post purely to irritate Miss Nightingale.

But Fitzgerald's greatest sin, in Miss Nightingale's eyes, was his uncritical enthusiasm for the Irish nuns under Mrs Bridgeman. And finally he had had the supreme audacity to attack Miss Nightingale herself, though not by name, and to dispute her claim to overall authority in the Crimea.

In an "energetic denunciation," nearly as long as the Confidential Report itself, to her new friend Colonel Lefroy, Miss Nightingale disputed Fitzgerald's facts and assertions paragraph by paragraph – proving, incidentally, that she had seen the document. In fact, Colonel Lefroy had himself shown her a copy.[4]

To Lieutenant Colonel Lefroy

11th January 1856

Sir

I have carefully considered the letter of Dr. Hall of Dec. 28/55, a copy of which you have placed in my hands – &, as in several particulars, I am compelled to differ in opinion with him, I will state, for the information of the War Office, the grounds upon which I do so.

Dr. Hall states that the number of Nurses at present employed in the General Hospital at Balaclava is not more than sufficient for proper attendance on the number of sick there. On this point, I have to say that Dr. Hall himself stated to me that four (or at most six) nuns were sufficient for that Establishment, in which opinion I concurred. The number there at present is twelve. And Dr. Hall's own expression to me on this point was "I have been innocently floated into this – I expected four & I have thirteen."[*5]

Dr. Hall now says that the small number of Nurses employed during the summer was "a source of grumbling, jealousy & discontent among the sick." It was in October that he stated to me his opinion that four were enough – & as the average had been always above that number, I must leave it to himself to reconcile the contradiction. Indeed I have a letter from him, in which he states, in reply to one of mine, that Miss Wear & even two would be sufficient.

As to the alleged "grumbling and discontent" on the part of the sick soldiers for insufficient & preferential nursing, I must express my strong doubts as to the fact.

I think I can shew the War Office that these doubts are well founded, as it is evident that Dr. Hall's information is derived from the document, which he immediately after quotes, & to which I must refer at considerable length; I mean the "Purveyor's statement," annexed by Dr. Hall to his letter.

Relying on the "Purveyor's Statement", Dr. Hall reminds the Government that the Nuns, whom he calls "Sisters of Charity", but who are really Nuns, are the least expensive Nurses who can be employed – & on this, & other grounds, he seems to intimate that they ought to be exclusively employed in Military Hospitals.

*One has since died.

The value of the Purveyor's statement will presently appear – and, with respect to this general opinion of Dr. Hall's I would here mention that Dr. Cumming, also Inspector General of Hospitals, & who had observed the system & its working in these Hospitals, repeatedly expressed to myself his judgment that Nurses were much preferable – & ought, at all events, to be the preponderating element. I suppose I need not say that such is my own opinion.

But, even admitting that Nurses were required at Balaclava & that Nuns were preferable, Dr. Hall knew perfectly well that he had only to apply to me for whatever number or quality he required, which I beg to submit to the War Office would have been the PROPER & regular course.

And now, Sir, for this "Purveyor's Statement" – so firmly relied upon by Dr. Hall – but which I cannot consider otherwise than as a tissue of unfounded assertions, wilful perversions &, in some instances, malicious & scandalous libels.

I do not mean these for mere hard words – as I shall now proceed to shew – paragraph by paragraph

This gentleman says

1.2   "Arrangement was in its infancy – & no fixed appointment appeared to have been assigned to the Nurses, each attending at pleasure thro' the wards."

This is false. I have at this moment before me my first Superintendent's Report from Balaclava, sent to me at my desire (Miss Emma Langston's) & containing, with the No. of each ward, the name of the Nurse assigned to it – including even the hours of the *watches*, especially the Night-watches, as fixed by the Medical Officers themselves. At *no* time did the Nurses "attend at pleasure through the wards."

2.3   The Superintendence was never, at any time, given to Miss Clough, as Mr. Fitzgerald asserts.

It is difficult to rebut so vague a statement as that "insubordination & discontent were manifested among the Nurses." I can only state that Mrs. Shaw Stewart (the Superintendent at the General Hospital, Balaclava & now at the Castle Hospital, Balaclava) has been always a most valued, trustworthy & trusted local Superintendent. And, if I am unfit to judge of the competency of a Sub-Superintendent, I am unfit to fulfil the duties assigned to me by the War Office.

Nurse Gibson was undoubtedly drunk, & I recalled her on that account.

Again, "discontent prevailed", is an unsupported assertion, which, I am hardly called upon, I think, to answer.

Mrs. Shaw Stewart's moral control over the Nurses has been always most remarkable – &, even in the cases where, unfortunately, Nurses have been found wanting & dismissed, they have never breathed a word against *her*.

With regard to the withdrawal of Miss Clough, since dead, the circumstances are briefly these – as stated by herself in writing. She came out *with the*

intention of joining the 79th Highlanders (owing to a romantic senti-
mentalism to which, the poor woman being dead, it is not necessary farther
to allude) & of remaining at my Hospital at Balaclava, as one of H. My's
Nurses, only so long as to learn the Extra Diet Cooking therein practised by
us. She then left without giving any notice of her intention. I heard from Dr.
Hall himself his disapprobation of this step – & I learnt, with extreme
surprise, that *her* Requisitions upon the Purveyor were answered – she
having no more authority from the War Office to draw upon the Purveyor
than any other lady who might come out, unauthorized, from England.

Miss Clough did endeavour to induce some of the Nurses, especially
Gibson & Disney, to follow her – promising that they should continue to
receive the same rate of wages as that given by myself. But these persons
had, at least, the worldly wisdom to ask, "Who is to pay us?" and, receiving
no satisfactory answer, declined. Miss Clough was attended only by a
woman of the 42nd Highlanders & her husband, whom she called her
servants – & to whom she promised wages through Dr. Hall. But Dr. Hall
declining to put them, subsequently, on the list of Gov*t*. servants, their
wages were paid, after Miss Clough's death, out of the private pockets of
Br. General Cameron & of myself. I have never heard this proceeding of
Miss Clough, in establishing herself on the Highland Heights, characterized,
by the Crimean authorities, either Military or Medical, as anything but a
"mad freak" – & not at all as the result of "disgust" or "discontent". It is
but right to poor Miss Clough to add that she spoke of Mrs. Shaw Stewart,
who nursed her in her last hours at our Castle Hospital, with the utmost
respect, not only *then* but always.

3.   With regard to the "superseding" of Mrs. Stewart, alledged by Mr.
Fitzgerald – it was at that Lady's own request that I sent up another
Superintendent, Miss Wear, to the General Hospital, Balaclava. Mrs.
Stewart, in consequence of a written Requisition to me from Dr. Anderson,
then Principal Medical Officer at Balaclava, for her services at the then
newly-established Castle Hospital, was transferred to that Hospital by me,
with one nurse & one Extra Cook. The number was increased within a
fortnight, also at Dr. Anderson's Requisition, by myself & three Nurses
joining the above.

4.   This is one of the paragraphs which I have not hesitated to describe as
a malicious & scandalous libel against the good name of five (not only
innocent & respectable but) most excellent & devoted women. Mrs. Davies,
Mrs. Noble & Mrs. Tuffill were invalided home by the advice of Dr. Hall
himself & of Dr. Anderson with broken health – broken by their unremitting devotion to their duty. One of them is now dying. They were three of
the best Nurses I ever knew. To their high merits all the Medical Officers,
under whom they have served, have given their testimony in very remarkable terms. It is enough, however, to state that *the gentleman himself* who
signs this "Confidential Report" with his name ("Confidential", I presume,

because never meant to be seen by those who could alone refute his base & cruel slander) stated to me, in the presence of Miss Wear, & several other witnesses, his opinion, which was confirmed by Dr. Hall himself, that Mrs. Davies (one of the women stigmatized in his Report) – "for her *unparalleled* services (sic) ought to receive a pension from the Government, & that she was worth twice the wages" which I paid her.

N.B. I recommended two of these women (accused *by name* of misconduct by Mr. Fitzgerald) for a year's wages to the War Office after their return, which they received. Others for a lesser sum. And two received each the sum of £25 out of our own pockets, which is merely mentioned by me to shew how highly they were valued in public & in private.

It appears almost superfluous, after exposing this deliberate falsehood, to examine all the others in the gentleman's "Confidential Report."

Mrs. Lawfield is *not "gone home" at all*, but is with me at this present time & is a woman of faultless character.

Mrs. Sandhouse went home with no aspersion whatever upon her character, but simply because, in a place where the most efficient nursing is required, I did not consider her so efficient as others. She nursed one of my Lady-Nurses, Miss Emily Anderson, through a severe illness, & was offered a present for her services by Sir Charles Anderson, which, as I learnt from *himself*, she honourably declined.

5. I feel compelled to call attention to this passage which, although not so mischievous as others, because the names are not all specified, is, if possible, more basely, because more consciously, false. "Scandal", as this gentleman justly says, "ascribed faults . . ." Whence this scandal originated now appears. It was my unpleasant duty in November/55 at Balaclava (for the sake of at once repressing this false report, utterly groundless as it was, & of clearing the characters of Dr. Jephson, 1st Dragoon Guards, who was justly indignant & intended an appeal to the Commander of the Forces, – as well as those of two most innocent and excellent women) to appeal to Dr. Hall & Dr. Hadley, now Principal Medical Officer at Balaclava, & to confront the accused with the accusers. The result was, as Dr. Hall & Dr. Hadley had anticipated, to prove the charge not only utterly without foundation but absolutely impossible under the circumstances for all three – of which I had evidence ready to produce before the Commander of the Forces, had it been necessary. The two women, whom Mr. Fitzgerald represents as "dismissed," had been *previously* invalided home. It was the false accusation which was "dismissed". And this, the lie which was raked up only to be proved a lie, is now called in by Mr. Fitzgerald as an Auxiliary to his array of charges.

Were it not for the sake of clearing the reputations of these women, thus unjustly & *secretly* accused, (depriving them of the power of defending themselves), by a "Confidential" enemy, from the filth cast upon them by this gentleman, I could hardly reconcile myself to wading through it.

6.   I am weary of these calumnies. But, for truth's sake, I have to state the real circumstances, tortured by Mr. Fitzgerald into "threats used by a Nurse against Miss Wear's life." Miss Wear, whilst delirious from fever, conceived the very common delusion that the Nurse, attending on her, was intending to poison her. The Medical Officer, Dr. Matthew, changed the Nurse, in order to pacify this state of excitement. He informed me, subsequently, of the reason (I was not at Balaclava at the time) treating it as a fancy of delirium. As, however, it did not disappear, but continued in dislike of the Nurse, I removed her – that is to say, she accompanied a sick Officer home who believed, as I do, his life to have been saved by her services. I have no knowledge of any other foundation whatever, for the Purveyor's story.

Thus far the charges are specific. And thus far I have answerd them specifically. To the long tissue of vague allegations & unsupported inferences which follows what can be said?

I would simply observe in reply

1.   that Dr. Hall openly expressed his satisfaction with Miss Wear's treatment of the Sardinian Officers in our Hospital – & even when, for reasons which made me not quite satisfied with Miss Wear as a Superintendent, I expressed to him a doubt as to whether she should remain or not, he alledged her usefulness in these foreign cases as one reason, among others, for retaining her services.

2.   In answer to the Purveyor's complaint of there being too few Nurses, I beg to call attention to this circumstance. The number of Nurses, in any Hospital, has always been fixed by the Medical Officer himself. The following clause was drawn up in pursuance of my Instructions dated Jan. 21/55 – "A written requisition for Nurses must be forwarded to" me "from the Medical Officer in charge of any Hospital, to be confirmed by the Inspector-General of Hospitals."

I appeal to the correspondence between Dr. Hall, the Inspector General & myself, & between Dr. Anderson, P.M.O. of Balaclava & myself, relative to the appointments, withdrawals & numbers of Nurses, of which the Purveyor is now complaining, for the truth of this assertion. When the thirteen Nuns went to Balaclava, Dr. Hall himself stated to me that he had "expected three or *four*," & that "*four* were enough," & that he had been "innocently floated into it" viz. the number of thirteen, a number he had "neither required nor expected." This I have already mentioned in commenting upon Dr. Hall's letter, who seems to echo the Purveyor's complaint. I would also add that, at the Castle Hospital, Balaclava, 500–600 Patients have been attended by 5–7 Nurses – the number considered sufficient by the Medical Officers – while the General Hospital at Balaclava contains only 250 patients, of whom a large number were convalescents, to be attended by 13 Nuns – the Patients also being not *all* Roman Catholics, as need hardly be added.

3. I would call attention to the passage "it should be the duty of a Superintendent to obey the Instructions of the Hospital Authorities & not to criticize or contravene them" in Mr. Fitzgerald's Report, – where he draws the distinction between the relative merits of Nuns & Protestants, as Hospital Attendants – & state merely the fact.

I   that all my Local Superintendents have had strict written Rules from me, which they have as strictly carried out, to issue no article of food or of clothing whatever to Patients, excepting in answer to the Diet Rolls & written Requisitions of the Medical Officer in charge.

II   that the system of Koulali, whence Mrs. Bridgeman came to Bala-clava, & her own at Balaclava, have been to issue Extras etc. at their own discretion to Patients, *without* Requisition from the Medical Officers.

III   It was on this very account that the Nursing Establishment at Koulali was broken up as a whole. They resigned, on account of the P.M.O. at Koulali insisting on extra Articles of Diet, given by the Ladies, being inserted in the Diet Rolls. He found the expenditure & consumption enormous. They declared that this destroyed their usefulness, resigned, & their resignation was accepted.[6]

I draw from these facts two conclusions. 1. that the only system by which Female Nursing Establishments can be made of permanent use is that of issuing every Article, whether of food or of clothing, upon the written Requisitions *only* of the Medical Officer in charge.

2. that the preference here given to Mrs. Bridgeman's Nuns, on account of their subordination to the Medical Officers, is a fiction invented to support a Roman Catholic theory, & not only without foundation, but *in direct opposition* to the truth.

I may add that, while the "ad libitum" distribution of Extras was permitted to no one under my charge – their regular administration even, in answer to the Diet Rolls of the Medical Officers, has been always confined to Nuns & Ladies in the Hospitals under my care, for the very obvious reason of their superior education ensuring the necessary accuracy.

At the Castle Hospital, Balaclava, Mrs. Shaw Stewart always superin-tends the issuing of the Extras herself, & always according to this rule.

I am, therefore, apprehensive lest the remark, made by Mr. Fitzgerald, must be applied in the inverse sense of that in which he intended it viz. that the subordination to the Medical Officers which he *so justly* admires, is found among the Nuns & Ladies under my charge, *& not among Mrs. Bridgeman's Nuns.* I am farther confirmed in this observation by the remark, made to me in October last at Balaclava by *Mr. Fitzgerald himself,* complaining that the Purveyor-in-Chief had allowed the system among these Nuns at Koulali of giving Extras without Requisitions – & that he "wished it might not be introduced with themselves at Balaclava," – & he farther stated, in terms of unqualified approbation, his sense of the superiority of my system of absolute subordination to the Diet Rolls.

I am here forcibly reminded of a piece of advice once given me by an old Irish woman. "Don't quarrel with a certain character. For he can lie & you cannot."

With regard to the "Court of Investigation" story, I am wholly at a loss to what it refers, unless it be the following. I informed Dr. Hall that, in the General Hospital at Balaclava, the dead were occasionally buried without the corpse having been viewed by the Orderly Medical Officer, or the death verified save by a nurse or an Orderly. His answer was "An Orderly might as well *admit* Patients." He accepted the information & remedied the irregularity.

Mr. Fitzgerald's concluding flourish, Page 7, I confess myself unable to understand, either as to its construction or its meaning – & therefore to answer it I subjoin this "morceau" –

"Lady Nurses – of the disposition & experience of Miss Stewart & Miss Wear, would be equally useful as the Sisters, if the pride & will & independence of action of former years could be silenced and humble obedience connect & maintain an amicable union between large numbers. Experience shews the preponderance of the former conditions, and the transitory nature of new, – negative & contradictory obligations of subordination & obedience." (*sic*)

The Tables of Comparative Expenditure I can assert to be false, a number of the Requisitions having been verified by myself.[7]

At the Castle Hospital, from the time of my undertaking it in April up to the present moment, we have cooked & issued the whole of the Diets of the Wounded Officers, the whole of the Extras for the Wounded Men. A part of these were derived from our Requisitions upon the Purveyor, here quoted – a part from my own private stores. But the principal Articles in the Purveyor's table of Expenditure for Nurses at the Castle Hospital were solely for Patients, viz.

Arrow Root	£7	14	0
Brandy	3	4	0
Port Wine	3	12	0
Sherrry	1	10	0
	16	0	0

Nurses Expenditure			
as estimated by Purveyor	£40	5	0
Deduct	£16	0	0
Actual Expenditure	£24	5	0

as proved by me, F.N.

For the Port Wine which is drunk by the Nurses, & solely when they are on the Sick List, is furnished entirely by myself, as well as a part of the Port Wine drunk by the Sick Officers & Men.

Compare the Port Wine Expenditure stated by the Purveyor himself to be for the Nuns, at the General Hospital, Balaclava – viz. per month

$$£9 \quad 0 \quad 0$$

It is difficult to account for an Official falsifying a Report in a manner so easily contradicted, except by remembering that it is headed by him "Confidential". And it is difficult to me to think it necessary to continue taking it to pieces thus item by item, after such an exposure of its untrustworthiness.

If I am, however, to do so, I will mention two more items.

The allowance of drink to the Nurses in all the Hospitals under my charge has always been

      1½   pints Porter per diem

or { 1   pint Porter &

      1   glass Marsala

or { 1   pint Porter &

      1   oz Brandy

This was given in writing to Miss Wear at the General Hospital, Balaclava, on May 10 1855, authorized by Dr. Anderson, & copied by the then Principal Medical Officer of that Hospital – where, as well as at the Castle Hospital, it became the settled allowance – never deviated from except in cases of sickness – and in the case, correctly stated by the Purveyor, of one Nurse Brooks, dismissed by me on that account & Miss Wear was requested never to allow it again. Even in her case, it was my wine she drank & not the Purveyor's.

It may be as well to state here, in reply to the Purveyor's sweeping generality as to our expense to the Government that the Wine & Brandy for the Extras – distributed from our Extra Diet Kitchens and for the consumption of our own Nurses – (issued however solely *according to Medical Requsition,* as above stated) has not been at the expense of Government *at all* but at our own. This is the case *in toto* as to our central Establishment, the Barrack Hospital, Scutari – *in part* as I have explained, as to the other Hospitals under my charge. The statement has already appeared in the "Blue Book on the Crimean & Scutari Hospitals" & will appear in print up to the present time.[8]

The Expenditure of the General Hospital in June does & did appear to me excessive. And I can only state that, when, upon my mentioning to Dr. Hall that I feared Miss Wear was incompetent as a Superintendent & notwithstanding her devotion & kindness, had not the necessary control over the Nurses, – & proposing therefore to recal her, which I did in writing to him, he not only negatived that proposition, but, in spite of my written remonstrance & without my knowledge, appointed her to the Monastery

Hospital and sent for two Nurses for her from Smyrna, also without my knowledge. And I, as a concession to the interference of my Principal Medical Authority, against which, however, I must in future protest, retained her in authority at that Hospital.

I leave it to Dr. Hall to explain the discrepancy of his at once basing his conduct as to appointing the Nuns at the General Hospital upon the alledged defects of the previous system under Miss Wear, & compelling me, in deference to his request, to retain that Lady.

I must also deduct the item

Sherry   £15   2   6

which was for the *Patients,* from the Purveyor's estimate for the Expenditure of *Nurses* at the General Hospital in June. This farther reduces

	£68	0	10
deducting	15	2	6
to	£52	18	4

With regard to the Nuns now at the General Hospital, Balaclava, I myself, through Miss Wear, continued to draw their Requisitions during my stay at Balaclava. Their consumption during one day for twelve was

27 lbs meat
20 eggs
6 bottles Port Wine

besides Ham, Potatoes & Bread in proportion.

I must add that all Mrs. Stewart's Requisitions at the Castle Hospital are countersigned by the Principal Medical Officer – while those of Mrs. Bridgeman, at the General Hospital, by some unaccountable difference, are not so counter-signed.

The pay of the Nurses is wrongly stated, Mr. Fitzgerald not being cognisant of the facts. I have already stated them in my Report sent home to the War Office, a copy of which I furnished, Sir, to you.

I wish farther to state that Dr. Hall has expressed his satisfaction with the Nurses, not once but repeatedly to me, in writing & in conversation – mentioning some by name for efficiency & good conduct – especially some now stigmatized by Mr. Fitzgerald. He also made a special testimony of their usefulness in one of his Reports to the late Commander-in-Chief, Lord Raglan – to which he directed my attention when, in the month of November last, I asked him whether he were satisfied with them – the said Report having been published in the "Times".

And now, Sir, having, in compliance with your Requisition & for the information of the War Office, made the foregoing comments on the letter of Dr. Hall & the "Purveyor's Statement," (which, altho' styled a "*Confidential* Report," has been thus embodied in a letter, not, I presume, confidential but official) I must add that, on its own intrinsic merits, I should scarcely have considered the "Purveyor's Report" worthy of so much of my notice. And I cannot consider that a document of this kind, so adopted by Dr. Hall, either ought to be or can be regarded as of a really "confidential" character. On the contrary, I think I am entitled to be furnished by the War Office with a copy of Mr. Fitzgerald's Paper – as being necessary for me in case of any future Enquries in Parliament upon this subject.

At all events, I by no means wish that my present communication should be considered confidential in any similar sense.

I simply desire to see my system efficiently carried out – and, having been appointed Superintendent of Nurses in the Hospitals of the British Army serving in the East, by H. My's Govt., it was surely to me that "Confidential Reports" ought to have been made, whether by Dr. Hall or Mr. Fitzgerald. Indeed what the latter gentleman has to do with the matter, I cannot at all imagine – or how Dr. Hall can consider himself authorized to receive "Confidential Reports" of this character, & suppress them from me – while he relies upon them in his own official communication to the War Office.

I make this observation, irrespective of the still farther grievance that, in the present instance, this "Confidential Report" is utterly at variance not only with the truth but with the truth as viewed by both Dr. Hall & Mr. Fitzgerald, in their own communications with me.

On the subject of the Hospitals in the Crimea, let me add, Sir, that I find that the Inspector General, Dr. Hall, has not only appointed Mrs. Bridgeman & twelve Nuns to the General Hospital at Balaclava, – but has since, in conjuction with my Sup*t*. at the Monastery Hospital, Miss Wear, upon his & her authority, thro' Mr. Fitzgerald, without any reference to me, written for two Nurses from Smyrna for that Hospital viz. on October 29/55 when I was myself present in the Crimea.

I, therefore, must beg you to express to the War Office that I claim to be informed whether I am to continue to appoint the Nurses in the Hospitals under my Superintendence, as I have been instructed to do by the War Office.

If the War Office has since adopted the opinion of Mr. Fitzgerald that the "local Superintendents should be exclusively under the orders of the Principal Medical Officer of the Army or his subordinate local representative," meaning himself, it is necessary that such a change in the plan upon which I was instructed to act, when I was asked to assume this responsibility, should be notified to me. I will then take into consideration my future course.

I have followed my Instructions to the letter which, no less than my own judgment, placed me implicitly under the direction of the Medical

Authorities as to the treatment of the Patients, medical & dietetic. But the duties of "appointment" "distribution", "selection" etc. of the Nurses in the Military Hospitals were definitely committed to me.

If the War Department desire me to continue to exercise these functions entrusted to me by themselves, I must request that they will support me in doing so, by notifying to the Inspector General of Hospitals that he is to second & not to oppose me in the performance of my duties. The incessant difficulties arising from the want of such support consume my time & strength to the impediment of the work properly belonging to me.

I would, also, beg humbly to suggest to the War Department that my Instructions be communicated to the Commander of the Forces by the War Department itself.

I have the honor to be
Sir
your obedt. servt.

B.L. Add. Ms. 43397, f. 205 (*Cal.* B. 4. E11, 190).

Miss Nightingale was not alone in her indignation over the Confidential Report. On 21st January Mrs Shaw Stewart wrote to her, complaining about the substance of the report, and that it was no secret to the officials in the Crimea, though she, like Miss Nightingale, had been unable to see a copy. This Miss Nightingale copied and forwarded to Col. Lefroy under cover of a formal note from herself.

To Colonel Lefroy

Scutari
Barrack Hospital
28th January 1856

Sir

Having found that Mr. Fitzgerald's "Confidential Report" was "Confidential" only from myself, & has already ceased to be so in the Crimea, I have the honor to forward to you a Statement, written by my Superintendent, at the Castle Hospital, Balaclava – addressed to myself, – & to request that you will urge, as she desires, that a Copy of the Purveyor's "Confidential Report" be transmitted to her through me.

Whatever the Inspector-General of Hospitals in the Crimea may consider his duty as to allowing an Expenditure, considered by him excessive, to be continued for eight months by my Superintendents of Nurses in the Crimea, – without making any mention of it at all to the person, appointed by the War Office, – (namely, myself), – under whose control it was placed, – & then reporting it "*confidentially*" to the War Office – I consider it my duty, & have always made it my practice, rigidly to "*overhaul*" my Superintendents' expenditure & therefore I now furnish the enclosed Statement &

pray to be called upon to furnish any others which may be considered requisite for the elucidation of this point.

> I have the honor to be Sir,
> Your Obedt. servt.

P.R.O. WO 43/963, f. 310 (*Cal.* omitted).

Then followed a long extract copied from a letter of Mrs Shaw Stewart, written from the Castle Hospital, Balaclava, on 21st January 1856, in which Mrs Shaw Stewart disputed the Purveyor's returns and continued:
... 'You [F.N.] told me in May that the government desired to supply every thing (or nearly every thing) in the War-Hospitals, & to render unnecessary private gifts. With this tallied the orders I received very soon after I arrived here (April 25/55) to separate the Nurses' from the Patient's Requisitions ...

'As to the Nurses' consumption, *that*, I can prove as well as assert, from the Purveyor's own requisitions, *if the genuine papers are forthcoming, as I suppose they are*, to have been, throughout, rigidly moderate, for women of their own class. One reason, though not the principal, why I have been & am afraid of ladies, lay or ecclesiastical, coming here is that I know it would be difficult to satisfy them with our very plain frugality. No reduction can properly or economically (for there would be no economy in underfeeding or laying up women wanted for work) be made in their living. I respectfully submit that, here again it would be better to let the Queen maintain Her own Nurses – "overhauling" most rigidly the sub-Superintendent's draughts upon Her Stores in doing so ... I cannot but think that her Majesty should feed, light & warm Her Majesty's Nurses.

'Suffer me once more to ask you to procure for me Mr. Fitzgerald's "Confidential Report". I suspect some items may be more in my power to refute than even in yours ...

'*I have never drawn one lb. of Arrowroot for Nurses. Nor one bottle of Port. But I draw Port for the sick Officers, specifying it was for them, under the head of Nurses – & their loaves & meat went under the head of Nurses – by express Order – notwithstanding my objections to this jumble, which I repeated to the Purveyor-in-Chief when here & of which I told the PMO.* You will remember this – I have not the slightest fear of the most searching "over-hauling" of my expenditure, either for Nurses or Patients. Only let it be an "over-hauling," not a garbling, which, I suspect, Mr. Fitzgerald has done. Let me, I entreat of you, see his Report ....

'I believe this "Confidential Report" is no secret to some Officials here ... It is always better, for the sake of one's work, to know what is going on about it, more especially when, as now, others know."

P.R.O. WO 43/963, f. 312.

On the same day Miss Nightingale wrote another, informal letter to Colonel Lefroy, recapitulating the grievances of the last few months and fore-shadowing the fight she was going to make for a public enquiry into all aspects of the organisation and management of the hospitals and their supporting services. It is so similar to the one she had written to Mrs Herbert on 17th November 1855, but not yet sent, that it seems probable that Miss Nightingale copied some of that letter.

To Lieutenant Colonel Lefroy

Scutari
Barrack Hospl.
28th January 1856

My dear Sir

As I am somewhat bruised & battered with a fifteen months' war with enemies who "strike below the knee" – as, like the gentlemen in Cherry Chase, I am now fighting on my "stumps", I have ventured so far as to presume upon your kindness in writing you a private, though *not* a "confidential" letter, upon matters, on which we have conversed together & on which I really require some support.

I this day enclosed you officially a statement of my Supt., Mrs. Shaw Stewart, at the Castle Hosp. Balaclava, which forms an important Commentary upon the Purveyor's "confidential Statement," which, you will find, is by no means "Confidential" in the Crimea.

I should have wished to have made to you many statements, though not at all "confidential" ones – when you were here. But my Rule of Conduct has been – Let us not give them out by feeble driblets. Let us hope a time may come, when I shall speak them myself, & as a whole – *not* as complaints against individuals, but against a system.

I think it not true, & even, *could* I *truly* represent what is wrong, I think it injudicious to pitch upon or "pitch into" individuals, who cannot do better, instead of the system which places them where they are. To complain of that system now would be simply to displace myself. Let me modify & alleviate by my presence the evils of that system, live thro' & know them by experience, & then a time may come when I may represent them as they are.

Two or three *trifling* instances I must however trouble you with, not at all as matters of complaint but of information – to give a sense to what I have said – & because it appeared to me that those were under peculiar difficulties in obtaining *real* information in the Crimea – where it is almost impossible to do so – who have not been living in the midst of it.

1. In April, I undertook the Castle Hospital, Balaclava, a few days after it was opened – & from that time to this we have cooked *all* the Extra Diets for 500–600 Patients, (which was the number up to the middle of December,) & the *whole* Diets for all the Wounded Officers. These were cooked by a Nurse in a shed. Because the cooking in the General Kitchen

was so bad – and this was done at the request of the P.M.O. In May, I was promised that an Extra Diet Kitchen should be built, while I was there. In July I sent up a French man to cook, to whom I give £100 pr. ann., also at the request of the P.M.O. In the beginning of October, I went up again myself, & found no Extra Diet Kitchen built. I then had it done. During the whole of this time, all the eggs, butter, jelly (all the Eau de Cologne, *of course*), supplied to the Sick Officers was supplied by Mrs. Shaw Stewart or myself privately. On Nov. 4th I opened my Extra Diet Kitchen. But, for 24 hours, (or it might be, 26 hours), I did not bake the Officers' *toast* in this kitchen, because it interfered with the Extra Diets for 550 Patients.

In those 24 hours, the Officers made a complaint to *Headquarters*! of our ill-treatment "in re" toast. And Dr. Hall, with the P.M.O. of Balaclava, came down in their wrath & reprimanded the – Cook's Orderly! Mrs. Shaw Stewart wrote, with my consent, a short Official request to Dr. Hall "that his orders & reprimands might be given to *her*, in order that she, who had the responsibility, might see that his orders were obeyed." Dr. Hall then published to his inferior Officers that the ladies at the Castle Hosp*l*. meant "to throw off all subordination to the Medical Officers" & that this was the reason he had brought the Nuns to the General Hospital, Balaclava. To Mrs. Stewart he wrote that "it was his duty to care for the Officers as well as the men" – his paternal care for their toast & them having begun on Nov. 7/55, while he had never enquired how they had been provided for at all since April 25/55. So that the wounded have perhaps profited more by Mrs. Stewart's & my "Maternal cares" than by Dr. Hall's paternal ones – which never could be persuaded to issue eggs, or any other comfort, till the Purveyor-in-Chief went up to the Crimea in the latter end of September/55.

2. My two Superintendents, Mrs. Shaw Stewart & Miss Wear at the Castle & General Hospitals, Crimea, were informed that Dr. Hall had sent in a provision of Eau de Cologne if they would make Requisition for it for the Sick. Mrs. Stewart was too *sharp*, & did not fall into the trap, but simply said that she had enough of her own, & would never think of imposing on the Queen for such a luxury for the Sick. Miss Wear fell into the trap & made Requisition, which was refused. In the next "Times" I was shewn a paragraph "We learn from Dr. Hall that Requisitions are now made for the Hospitals for such Articles as Eau de Cologne, Apple Jelly, & Rose Water". Poor Lord Raglan also informed Mrs. Stewart that Dr. Hall had complained to him that we "had actually made Requisitions for the above Articles"!

3. The P.M.O., then in being, of one of the General Hospitals in the Crimea, informed Lord Raglan in our presence that the men had on clean shirts regularly twice a week – the fact being that they had not then had clean shirts for 28 days & those were of my giving.

4. During six months, the Castle Hospital, always the principal Hospital in the Crimea, which has generally had more than double the number of

Patients of any other Crimean Hospital, had scarcely anything done for it in the way of all the Engineering necessities of a Hospital. This is the statement of its own Principal Surgeon.

But Dr. Hall, as he told me himself, "*burked*" his "Reports." And that it "would interfere with his Promotion, were this known."

Again, I repeat, I say these things to you not to complain of Dr. Hall, who is an able & efficient Officer in many ways – & who, I think, has been justly provoked in many ways. Dr. Hall is indefatigable in *detailed* work, & wants only a governing system to work under. But he is wholly incapable of originating one. And we have no system for *General* Hospitals, in time of war.

Believe me, dear Sir
Yours very truly

Wellcome (*Cal.* B. 4. E14, 204).

Yet again Miss Nightingale was urged to do something about the Nightingale Fund, this time by Mr Bracebridge. Again she replied that she could do nothing at present, elaborating the arguments she had previously used to Mr Herbert at the beginning of January.

Copy of letter to Mr Bracebridge

Scutari
Barrack Hospital
31st January 1856

My dear Mr. Bracebridge

In reply to your letter requesting me "to give some sign" as to what I wish to have done with the money about to be raised under the name of the "Nightingale Fund" and as to what purpose it is to be devoted to I can only say

1. The people of England say to me by this subscription "We trust you – we wish you to do us a service." No love or confidence can be shown to a human being greater than this, and as such I accept gratefully & hopefully. I hope I shall never decline any work God and the people of England offer me. But 2. I have no plan at all. I am not new to these things. I am not without experience. And no fear presents itself more strongly to my mind, no certainty of failure more complete, than accompany the idea of beginning anything of the nature proposed to me – with a great demonstration, a vast preparation – a great man perhaps coming down to the Hospital to give the first "cup of cold water". People's expectations are highly wrought – they think some great thing will be accomplished in six months – altho' experience shows it is essentially the labour of centuries – they will be disappointed to see no apparent great change – and at the end of a twelve-month will feel as flat about it – as they do on a wedding day, at three o'clock, after the wedding breakfast is over. But, worse than this – the

fellow workers who would join me in a work which began with excitement, public demonstration, public popularity, would be those whom vanity, frivolity, or the love of excitement would bring – and these would, least of all, bring about the wonderful results which the public would be expecting – or rather the results would be very "wonderful" the other way. These are not theories, but experience. And if I have a plan in me, which is not battered out by the perpetual "wear & tear" of mind & body, I am now undergoing – it would be simply this – to take the poorest & least organized Hospital in London & putting myself in there – see what I could do, not touching the "Fund" perhaps for *years*, not till experience had shown how the Fund might be best available. This is not detracting from the value & importance of the "Fund" to the work – It will be *invaluable* as occasion arises.

I have hardly time to write this letter – much less to give the experience which wd. prove the deductions to be true. But I would only appeal to two recent instances –

1. My strength here lay in coming to Hospitals miserably disorganized – or rather *un*organized altogether, and in organizing them. Had I come to an Institution cut & dry, what could I have done to alter it?

2. The greater proportion of valuable fellow workers here, came out with the first party, notwithstanding the hurry of selection, – when the work was obscure – & laborious & laughed at – and the hardships great, and *not*, with a few priceless exceptions, with the subsequent parties – when the excitement and popularity were great – & love of glory, of gain, & curiosity, all on the alert. I have no objection to what I say thus in private to you, being repeated to those who have so kindly interested themselves in the "Nightingale Fund" – & sympathized in the work.

The first fruits of a long series (as I expect) of the brick & mortar plans of needy or philanthropic adventurers, who wish to get hold of the "Nightingale Fund" have already come in upon me. But I hope our inexorable Common Sense will not be taken in. One more instance and I have done.

Compare the gradual but complete success of Fliedner's at Kaiserswerth, with that of the magnificent & pompous "Bettanica" [?] at Berlin – whose excellent & simpleminded foundress was appalled by "the greatness thrust upon her" & which marred her work.

I therefore must decline making any plan whatever, even were I not overwhelmed at present, not with plans but work. At the same time – would I could say – which I cannot – "*how* much I feel the love & confidence of the people of England, in whose service as I have lived, so I shall die –

I am, dear Mr. Bracebridge
most truly yours

Claydon; copy, Wellcome (*Cal.* B. 4. E14, 205). B.L. Add. Ms. 43397, f. 179, another handwritten copy, with small differences of punctuation.

When the opportunity presented itself of acquiring an interesting and unusual gift for her mother, Miss Nightingale seized it.

To her mother

[Barrack Hospital, Scutari, 11th February 1856]

Dearest Mother

I send you by that kind Capt. Wright whom it always does me good to see, the life's work of a poor Turkish widow. I hope you will wear it for my sake. It will just suit you, & it is all *good Turkish*. As I never go over to the Bazars & as it was a mere chance her offering me this for sale, I snatched at it, thinking it a fitting garment for you. Mind you wear it. It is not at all too fine by candlelight. And you have the only one in the world – if that is a recommendation.

The drawings in the box are, I think, Mr. Bracebridge's, but if they are mine, they are yours. I don't think they are of much account.

Mind you make much of my good Capt. Wright

Yours ever

They call me the Sultana of the Bosphorus &, if I am, I think I have a right to insist upon the mother of the Sultana wearing a very fine gown.

Claydon; copy, Wellcome (*Cal*. B. 4. F2, 212).

A few weeks later she elaborated with a few lines of interpretation.

To her mother

[5th March 1856]

Dearest Mother

I have never had time to tell you that your gold robe is a Chap. of the Koran – the last, I believe – repeated
plus the words

God be with you

God protect you

May you live long in happiness –

Altho' you are in joy, remember the words of the Prophet –

This occurs several times.

When the people of England rise, as they did about the Corn-Laws, about these late Promotions, I shall believe in them. But now, what can we expect other than more Sir John Halls, more Sir Richard Aireys, more Lord Cardigans? We are just where we were. Those are rewarded for having *done* what the D. of Newcastle was turned out for having merely suffered to be done. Put not thy faith in peoples. Ever your loving child.

Claydon; copy, Wellcome (*Cal*. B. 4. F7, 230).

In the meanwhile there were moments of frivolity to be enjoyed when boxes arrived from friends in England with books and games for the troops.

To Parthenope

Scutari B.H.
18th February 1856

My dearest

In answer to Mrs. Robert Holland's enquiry about Evening Schools, she must understand that we have none other here – because, of course, *all* our Schools are for Adults – with the exception of one very small one for children – but, as all our children are born here, of course, I think this must be to teach them the bottle.[9]

We have now five first-rate schools here – one for the Cavalry – one for the Victoria Barracks – one the Garrison School, in a magnificent hut, built on purpose, where we have two school masters, lectures (entertaining) twice a week, Magic Lanthorn, very good singing classes, & *crowded* every night. The fourth School is for the Mounted Sappers the fifth for the Artillery at Galata Serai.

Everything which has been sent by you has come in handy for these. *Everything* has been snapped up. And I have been obliged to *insist* on a proper share for the Crimea – for which Govt. has done nothing.

However we have Lectures there, a Theatre where they are acting my or your Plays, a Reading Hut for each Regiment, etc. And I have sent them the Lion's share of the Diagrams etc. especially the Astronomical Diagrams & SLIDES. Mr. Somerville is thankful.

Two boxes from Mrs. Robert Holland have just come in per *Clyde* – the whole of which were instantly divided among the Schools here & in the Crimea. I sent up a large portion to the latter.

H.B.C.'s box also arrived "per Edecia" yesterday of Foot-Balls etc. – all distributed almost within the hour. Galata Serai had just broken its only Foot Ball & Officers & Men were [look]ing over the wall in blank dismay. But, when informed that Miss Nightingale kept every thing & among other things Foot Balls, a roar of laughter & three Cheers for Miss N. followed. "And *do* you think she keeps any Quoits?" Oh! you can make those out of horse-[hair] "But will she send Draughts & Dominoes?" Yes, boys, yes.

Everything has been used to the last box.

PRIVATE Pray do not think that I suppose Harry has done all the work. I know you worked yourselves off your legs. I only commended him for his great goodness in putting a List of Contents inside each box which does save such a world of trouble & waste. Please thank him for his last box, which was most acceptable, marked H.B.C. & tell him about the Foot Balls (Even the Senior Chaplain began to play, & please thank Mrs. Robt. Holland for her most useful Box.)

I have also received a Box *very good* dated January 4 (I know not how or whence) containing Stationery – Household Words – in weekly unbound Nos. – Diamond Testaments & Prayer Books – Wafers, Seals [. . .] etc. – Have you any knowledge of this? We cannot identify Boxes especially if they come out of the

209

Custom Ho. – when we do not even know by what vessel they came. And very few people condescend to give us any distinctive mark. Let every one put (inside) List of Contents & from whom they came – *besides* sending Bill of Lading. Mrs. R. Holland's box was perfect in these respects. But it did not come "per Severn". People often seem to think that their own identity is so strongly & mesmerically marked on their Box that I can tell whom Stationery bought at a shop and looking precisely like any other stationery bought at a shop comes from – Schools have two hours afternoon

two hours evening
& the men rush in.

God bless you, my well beloved. Your "Seggiola" came in Mrs. R. Holland's boxes – beautiful. But I saw no Chess or Games. There were plenty in H.B.C.'s box however. We have besides a Mutual Improvement Socy. for workmen. Is this what Mrs. Holland means? – which I have furnished *entirely* (with things from home) as Govt. does nothing for them. And they did it for themselves, brave fellows.

I got the bonnet – very nice. Thank you. God bless you again & again.

Ever yours

Claydon; copy, Wellcome (*Cal.* B. 4. F3, 214).

On 20th February Miss Nightingale was once again soliciting Mr Herbert's help and active intervention on her behalf in her battle with the Medical Department. She felt that the "Confidential Report" had seriously undermined her position, already shaken by the events of the previous months. When her own devoted friend Dr Sutherland pointed out the anomalies in her situation, she reached the conclusion that formal and authoritative definition of her position in General Orders was imperative. The government was coming to the same conclusion.

To Sidney Herbert

Scutari, Barrack Hospital
20th February 1856

Dear Mr Herbert,

I cannot thank you sufficiently for your kind letter.

But I am now about (not to acknowledge your interest for our future work but) to ask it for our present one.

The enclosed I wrote to Mrs. Herbert some months ago.[10] But I did not send it, partly because I did not like troubling you, partly because the "anything-for-a-quiet-life principle" seemed the pervading War Office rule of action.

I am now, however, fighting for the very existence of our work and whether Peace is to come or not, I desire, for the sake of that work, that it should be placed in "General Orders", so to speak, before the next move, whatever it is, takes place.

(1) Col. Lefroy, who has kindly allowed me to refer you to him, will inform you of the attempts which are being made to root us out of the Crimea, of Dr. Hall's official letter to him – of a Purveyor's "Confidential Report" against me.

Some other facts are known, perhaps, more to *you* than to any one else viz. that the second Edition of Nuns who came out in December /54, came (as the first did) with the express stipulation that they were to have no peculiar Chaplain to themselves, without which condition I would never have received them – that, in direct violation of the treaty, they had, first, the Revd. Mr. Ronan, & secondly the Revd. Mr. Wollett – as their own Director – which latter gentleman managed the affair of their taking possession of the General Hospital at Balaclava for them. Dr. Hall states this affair in the following manner – "that he had been placed in a painful position about the General Hospital at Balaclava – that, when Miss Nightingale's Nurses were to be removed, a gentleman (the priest above alluded to) called & offered the services of the Nuns, & that he, Dr. Hall, was induced to accept of them & that without any intention of offending any one."

(2) The Hospitals of the Land Transport Corps in the Crimea have been & are still the worst in the Camp. The Commanding Officer of the *Left* Wing was desirous that I should send them Nurses – the Medical Officer of the *Right* Wing was equally desirous – I had Nurses *and* Nuns able, ready and willing to go, & was prepared to go up with them myself.

Now arose this question, which is so much better stated by Dr. Sutherland in a letter to me, which he has allowed me to make use of, than I could do that I beg leave to quote it.

Balaclava Feb.4/56

"My dear Miss Nightingale

I have seen Dr. Hall & made the necessary enquiries of him & also of others.

The main question, as it appears to me respecting the Nurses in Hospitals in the Crimea, is one of "*responsibility*". The jurisdiction in the matter, inferred in the letter received from the War Department, is not, I conceive, sufficient of itself to enable you to claim the support of the Authorities here, for I am told that no official intimation as to your having any charge of the Hospital Nursing in the Crimea has been sent to Dr. Hall, a circumstance which I was not before aware of. And the *responsibility* hence rests officially with him.

I cannot conceal from myself that, such being the case, there is a disinclination to give you any further facilities than those you already have.

Under these circumstances, then, it appears to me that it would be adviseable to state the case fully to the War Department, & ask them to place you on a proper footing with the Authorities here. Until this be done, I would advise you not to press for the transference of any Nurses to the Land Transport Hospital at Karani.

In the event of a campaign in Asia & your desiring to go to any Hospital that may be formed at Trebizond or elsewhere, I would still advise you to have yourself placed in an official relation with the Military & Medical Authorities in the Army.

If this be done, everything will go smoothly, but I fear not otherwise.

In regard to the charges brought against your Nurses at the General Hospital by Mr. Fitzgerald (the Purveyor formerly alluded to) Dr. Hall stated that Mr. Fitzgerald* must be held personally responsible for the statements he made."

I am yours ever faithfully
(signed) John Sutherland

It is obvious that Dr. Hall's statement is only a subterfuge. But it is true viz. "that *he* had no official intimation from the War Office of the circumstances inferred in the W.O. letter to" me.

It is obvious that my usefulness is destroyed, my work prevented or hindered & precious time wasted by the uncertainty of the relations in which I am left with the Crimean Authorities.

To have the "jurisdiction", as Dr. Sutherland calls it, of all the Hospitals in & north of the Bosphorus, i.e. the power of placing Nurses in any of the present or future Hospitals with the sanction of the Military & Medical Authorities & the power of preventing that these latter should engage any Nurses or Ladies dismissed by or withdrawing from me in other Hospitals is essential to my usefulness – as also to have this signified, (not by myself but) by the War Department to the Military & Medical Authorities. And I would submit that, without this, the responsibilities conferred upon me & the work expected from me by the W[ar] Office are rendered impossible.

If I have served my country well, this is the reward I should wish – the power of continuing that service – of continuing it in Asia, should the war take us there – or of resuming it in any future war – which seems, alas! but too likely, if peace comes now.

Might I ask you, dear Mr. Herbert, to crown your enduring kindness to me by, if you see it desirable, conferring with Col. Lefroy in this matter & urging upon the War Department to *telegraph* my powers to the Military & Medical authorities in the Crimea & to myself? The Hospitals wait.

Believe me ever yours faithfully & gratefully

B.L. Add. Ms. 43393, f. 211 (*Cal.* B. 4. F3, 216).

---

*That Dr. Hall would throw overboard Mr. Fitzgerald in this matter I am not at all surprised to learn, I always expected it.

To *Sidney Herbert*

Scutari, Barrack Hospital
Private & Confidential   21st February 1856

Dear Mr. Herbert

It has been very strongly recommended to me to ask you, unless you see very cogent reasons to the contrary, to move at once in the House for the papers containing

1.   my original Instructions & Agreement

2.   the Dispatches which, subsequently, from time to time, entrusted to me certain duties & responsibilities.

3.   the Official Letter & "Confidential Report", recently received by Lt. Colonel Lefroy from Dr. Hall, & my Official Answer.

It has been represented to me that, did the House know how I am fettered & trampled upon by Red Tape, by Dr. Hall, & by insidious attacks of the above nature, it would require that the powers necessary to carry out the work entrusted to me by the War Office itself, necessary to give me effective means of usefulness, be signified to the Military & Medical Authorities in the Crimea.

Instead of this, the War Office gives me tinsel & plenty of empty praise which I do not want – and does *not* give me the real business-like efficient standing which I do want. It is doubtless difficult to define my jurisdiction. But the War Office sent me here. And surely it should not leave me to fight my own battle. I have given time, mind, health. Surely they should give me the footing which alone can effect their own objects. If they think I have not done my work well, let them recal me. But, if otherwise, let them not leave me to shift for myself, in an ever-recurring & exhausting struggle for every inch of that ground, secured to me by original agreement, but which agreement was never officially made known to the authorities.

I am sure that this is not the species of *fighting* which the country requires from us, nor which you required, in sending me out.

In a few weeks, there will be either War, when business will be all too pressing to attend to me, or peace when it will be said "We would have done what Miss Nightingale rightfully requires, but it is not now necessary." In either case, however, I desire to bring it to a point, *before* the advent of either – in the former, it being clear that I should be paralyzed without it – in the latter, I should stand better for whatever may betide in the future. This is the eleventh hour & it is now or never.

You could, if you think as we do here, see the papers I allude to, relative to the "Confidential Report", at Lord Cranworth's, to whom I have sent them.

For this is essentially, however unintentionally so, nevertheless bad treatment. And I am assured that the people of England would not suffer this with me nor with any one who has served them with love and judgment.

213

Especially, as all this is contrary to the Original Agreement, by which the Nursing in the "present or any future Hospitals that may be appointed for the accommodation of the Sick & Wounded of the British Army serving in the East" was definitely committed to me.

For these I have (and gladly) perilled life & home, & from these I am now, by an Official quibble, shut out as to effective usefulness.

I am certain that this is not what my country & you intended. And I am certain that, in this, you & my country would bear me out viz., in requiring definite powers & these *immediately*, (& these signified not only to me, which they have been, but to the Military & Medical Authorities) relative to the Hospitals of the Crimea or any future Hospitals in Asia.

To your judgment I leave all this—it being by so far better than mine as to how the thing is to be done, though we alone can judge of how much it requires to be done.

I scarcely apologise for troubling you, knowing that, in this, you are the father & I but the child of the work.

Supposing you think that the measure I propose savours too much of the servant complaining against her masters, may I hope that you will think for me as to what step should be taken to effect the same object in a more private manner?

Believe me to be
dear Mr. Herbert
ever yours faithfully & gratefully

Supposing, also, you think it better not to recur to original Instructions and Agreements, which are sometimes intentionally left vague or contradictory, let the "jurisdiction" I at present desire be put as a reward for past service. This lets the War Office off easy.

B.L. Add. Ms. 43393, f. 215 (*Cal.* B. 4. A3, 217).

Miss Nightingale's request was supported by Colonel Lefroy, who indicated a wider issue:

. . .Her claim appears to me indisputable, and I am persuaded that if it is once broken up into unconnected establishments, under no united system or control, the Protestant part certainly, and probably the whole, will soon disappear. The medical men are jealous of it. Dr. Hall would gladly upset it tomorrow, and he knows better than any one, that Miss Nightingale is its only anchor. A General Order recognising and defining her position would save her much annoyance and harassing correspondence: it is due , I think, to all she has done and sacrificed. Among other reasons for it, it will put a stop to any spirit of growing independence among those Ladies and nurses who are still under her, a spirit encouraged, with no friendly intention, in more than one quarter. If the Nightingale Institution is to bear any fruit to the Army she must be supported until it can do so.[11]

The War Office agreed. Panmure and Hawes wanted a strong central nursing authority on whom responsibility could be fixed. It was not "desirable that the Gov*t.* in any degree beyond what is inevitable took upon itself any responsibility for the conduct of the Ladies & Nurses – the more it rests upon Miss N. the better."[12] Accordingly, on 25th February Lord Panmure wrote to Sir William Codrington, the Commander in Chief, censuring Dr Hall's conduct in the matter of the Smyrna nurses and requesting him to publish Miss Nightingale's authority in his General Orders:

> . . . I have to direct that you will call the attention of Sir John Hall to the irregularity of this proceeding, and at the same time will guard against the recurrence by promulgating in your General Orders the rightful position of Miss Nightingale in reference to the distribution, situation and power of discharge, or dismissal of all nurses, and sisters, employed in the military hospitals of the Army.[13]

But she was refused an official copy of the Confidential Report and her old opponent, John Milton, strongly depreciated Colonel Lefroy's action in having shown it to her in the first place. Milton considered it was time to curb Miss Nightingale's pretensions to unlimited and almost irresponsible command over the nurses, and on 3rd March 1856 he submitted a memorandum urging reconsideration of the despatch censuring Dr Hall, now Sir John Hall, and summarising fairly enough the history of the troubles in the nursing department in the East. He recalled that Miss Nightingale had herself declined to be responsible for more than the Scutari hospitals, and in a Parthian shot he pointed out that the censure was not consistent with the recent honour bestowed on Dr Hall:

> . . . I would respectfully beg to be allowed to ask a reconsideration of that Despatch, at least of the wording of it, for the following reasons.
> 1. That it censures Sir John Hall for putting aside the authority of Miss Nightingale over Nurses in the Crimea, whereas it has never been intimated to him by the Government that any such authority had been conferred upon that Lady.
> 2. That Miss Nightingale's Instructions never gave her any such authority in the Crimea – the fact being that Miss Nightingale went to the Crimea without being authorized to do so – at the very time, indeed, that this Department was writing out to her that she was *not* to have any control over the Nurses in the Crimea.
> 3. That she herself put aside the theory of her having control over *all* the nurses in the East – in desiring to be relieved of all connexion with or control over those at Kululi – many of whom, after being made, by her own act, independent of her at Kululi, have gone to the Crimea, and remain independent of her there.
> 4. That the Smyrna Nurses – including the two now in question – were independent of her, by the orders of the Government itself – and like the Kululi nurses these two proceeded to the Crimea independent of her still.
> 5. That it will be perfectly easy to confer upon Miss Nightingale either new powers, or enlarged powers, or to add the Crimea to her sphere of control, by a General Order or by fresh Instructions, or by any other means – without it being at all necessary to accompany such measure with a reprimand of the Head of the Medical Department of the Army in the East.
> I am not (I beg to add) at all advocating that such extended powers should be granted to Miss Nightingale – in fact I apprehend that such a step will be very

probably the ruin of the Nursing system in the Army, especially if – as I gather from the Despatch – it is intended to endeavor to replace under her control the Roman Catholic nuns whom she herself dissevered from her when at Kululi, and who have resolved, as stated in the Report /440, to cease to serve as Nurses the moment Miss Nightingale's supremacy is reimposed upon them. I am now neither advocating nor combatting such extension of her powers: I am only begging for a re-consideration of that part of the Despatch which reprimands the Inspector General of the Army in the Crimea – that part is, I respectfully submit, unnecessary, as the object in view can be obtained without it – it is founded on an ex-parte statement, and condemns a man unheard – and it is liable to be considered inconsistent with the contemporary acts of the Government in decorating and defending Sir John Hall as has recently been the case.[14]

Sir Andrew Smith also protested at the government's action on the grounds that

. . . I have never been entrusted with a copy of the Instructions now requested, and until the present time I have considered that neither Miss Nightingale, nor any other person, had the power of admitting into, or employing any nurse in any of the Hospital Establishments, who was not in possession of a certificate signed by myself.

Upon the breaking up of the Hospital at Kulluli, Dr. Hall informed me that at the recommendation of the military Chaplain and the Principal Medical Officer, he had sanctioned the transfer to Balaklava of the Nurses who had been employed at the former Station, and that he took that step solely in consequence of the high character they had maintained, for attention, efficiency, and tractability.[15]

The War Office was by now thoroughly irritated by the whole affair and desired to bring the controversy to an end. Lord Panmure wrote to Hawes on 3rd March 1856 with finality:

I can only add to Mr. Milton's minute, that it must have been as patent to Sir J. Hall as to all the rest of the world, that Miss Nightingale alone has been the recognised Head of the Nursing system & he, as PMO in the Crimea shd. have been the last to interfere in the distribution of the Nurses without consulting her & that it should not by his Act now have become necessary to issue a Genl. Order as to Miss N.'s position which has hitherto been tacitly admitted & perfectly understood by all parties in the East except the Med. Officers. The step taken by Dr. Hall, & I gather from these papers that it was taken by him, appears to me so entirely calculated to break up the system and the control so absolutely necessary for carrying it on by encouraging a spirit of independence on the part of the Nurses, that I cannot say I consider the terms of these Despatches at all too strong. The Nurses shd. be taught to look to Miss N. as their Head & sole instructress, but if the PMO interferes in what is clearly her province, her authority must cease & the system become a failure . . .[16]

Sidney Herbert received Miss Nightingale's letters at the beginning of March and at once conferred with Colonel Lefroy, who had been the recipient of similar tirades on the subject of the Confidential Report. Both considered she expressed herself with unnecessary and unbecoming heat and, as good friends, did not hesitate to say so.

Herbert's letter accurately reflected the government's feeling on the subject. But, more than that, it was a fundamental expression of the special relationship between himself and Miss Nightingale. On several occasions he might well have taken offence at her immoderate outbursts in the course of their Crimean correspondence, but he never did. Most of his letters of this period have been lost, but Florence Nightingale's own testify again and again to the wisdom, the courtesy, the kindness of his replies, even when called on to censure her. Far from being the catspaw so often represented, he showed himself throughout the war to be the strong partner, able to withstand the storms of her frustrated fury.

Sidney Herbert to Florence Nightingale

49 Belgrave Square
6th March 1856

My dear Miss Nightingale

After receiving your two letters I saw Col. Lefroy and read Dr. Hall's & Mr. Fitzgerald's papers and your statement in answer to them. I was much pleased with Col. Lefroy who talked very sensibly and appears to have succeeded in effecting at the War Department very much what you wish, and what Dr. Hall's proceeding rendered necessary, if you are to maintain any order or discipline among your nurses – a despatch is gone out to Gen*l*. Codrington defining your position as Chief of the Nurses for the Hospitals in the East, apparently much in the same terms, as on your first appointment, wh. was at that time notified to Lord Raglan, but wh. notification not having been published, seems to have been unknown to his successor. This, I hope, will effect your object and meet your wishes. Lord Panmure objects to sending the order by Telegraph, but as it is on the road out, I hope the delay will not be such as to be prejudicial to you. So far one subject of your letter is disposed of without any intervention from me; but I may as well add that I observed to Col. Lefroy that in sending you out a copy of the order to Gen*l*. Codrington you ought to be told to give the necessary sub-instructions to your Deputies to place themselves immediately under the orders of the P.M.O. of each Hospital in which you have placed them in charge of nurses; just as you yourself are at Scutari or else where, as it w*d*. not do for a Medical Officer to be transmitting his directions to a nurse on the spot thro' you on the opposite shore of the Black Sea.

As regards the other matter, namely the moving in Parliament for the production of papers, I am decidedly against it as matters now stand. In the first place your object as to the definition & promulgation of your position & authority is obtained. Secondly it will always be time to produce papers in your vindication when you are attacked, and so long as there is no public attack upon you, you stand better than you w*d*. if publicly attacked and triumphantly defended. The highest praise & the highest proof of success wh. could be adduced to a mission like yours w*d*. be that it had been carried through without producing quarrel or attack. The papers the publication of wh. you suggest, would prove first that there is great doubt as to the value of the nurses in the eyes of the chief medical officer of the army, which, however unfounded your answer may shew it to be, would have weight with many people. Then, his testimony to the superiority of nuns, however unfounded, w*d*. to all time be claimed as conclusive by the R. Catholics. A controversy would be engendered, all who have been or who think themselves offended by or slighted by you would take up the one side & your friends the other. The Salisbury party, the Stanley party w*d*. of course take up the Hall & Fitzgerald view & press their particular cases and the public distracted, indolent, & weary would settle that it was a pack of women quarrelling among themselves, that it is six of one & half a dozen of the other & that everybody is equally to blame all round.

In the estimation of all thinking people who w*d*. give themselves the trouble to inquire, those who thus assail w*d*. sink low; but the unreflecting majority would by dividing the blame to save themselves trouble, lower you a good way towards their level.

Your position is best so long as no disputes, discussions, or difficulties appear. The longer you can maintain things so, the better. If you cannot i.e. if they publish or move in Parl*t*. (wh. they will *not* do, I think) it will then be quite time enough for you to occupy your next best position, w. is, tho' in a quarrel, to be in the right.

The House of Commons w*d*. I think be very indisposed to entertain anything on the matter from whatever side it might proceed & would not be well-disposed towards whoever first mooted it.

Lastly, tho' your answer to Mr. Fitzgerald appears to me to be complete, as I believe it does also to the War Department, I sh*d*. be sorry to see it published. – And now I am going to criticise and to scold you.

You have been overdone with your long anxious harassing work. You see jealousies & meannesses round you. You hear of onesided unfair & unjust reports made of your proceedings & of those under you. But you over-rate their importance, you attribute too much motive to them & you write upon them with an irritation & a vehemence which detracts very much from the weight wh. w*d*. otherwise attach to what you say – our friend Bracebridge writes & talks about a Popish Plot. I see in Fitzgerald's report nothing more than the unfair, biassed, special pleading report of a narrow-minded religionist. These are mis-representations & annoyances to which all persons in office, & you are in office, are exposed; a single flower of the sort from wh. the bed of roses on which Secretaries of State repose is made. The result of your over-estimating its value is that you write too warmly on it. The reader seeing the vehemence of your language w*d*. at once say: "This is written under great irritation & I must take its statements with suspicion;" and he chooses for himself what he put aside as the result of anger & perhaps puts aside just what you most rely upon in y*r*. statement.

You should disprove Mr. Fitzgerald's assertions not characterize them. If you satisfy the reader that his statements are unfounded he will supply the inference that M. F*d.* is a calumniator and his assertions libels or lies and he will be the more likely to do so because you do not; for your calmness will have inspired him with confidence in the accuracy of your statements.

You will have had McNeill & Tulloch's report.[17] It is a signal illustration of what I mean. There is not a hard word in it, nor an epithet, not an accusation, scarcely an animadversion, but this sobriety of tone has arrested the attention & conquered the confidence of the public & they have made the necessary inferences & pretty broad ones too. The fact is, the public like to have something left to their own imaginations & are much pleased with their own sagacity when they have found out what was too obvious to be missed. It is always wise too in a public document to *under*state your case. If on examination your case proves stronger than you stated it to be, you reap the whole advantage. If however, any part, however slight, is shaken, the credit of the whole is shaken with it. My moral is, that you must write more calmly, & not yourself accuse or attribute motives to those whose misstatements you may disprove & whose misconduct you may expose without either, and do it far more effectively too.

You will pardon this long sermon, for you know why I write it, and I do not think you did yourself justice in the tone of your answer to Mr. Fitzgerald . . .

God bless you, yr. sincerely

B.L. Add. Ms. 43393, f. 218.

Unfortunately this letter did not reach Miss Nightingale until she was back in the Crimea and engaged in the final desperate struggle with Sir John Hall and the Purveyor, and consequently in no mood to take Herbert's excellent advice to heart. Her immediate reaction verged on the hysterical.[18] In the long run, however, Herbert's letter appeared to bear fruit; her advice on Colonel Tulloch's long-running battle with the Chelsea Board was to have a very similar ring.[19]

Meanwhile Miss Nightingale was vigorously pursuing her own quarrels with the civil servants of the War Office. She was having particular difficulty with her accounts, as she wrote to Uncle Sam, who had the thankless task of helping her unravel their complexities.

To Uncle Sam Smith

Scutari B.H.
3rd March 1856

Dear Uncle Sam
1. I enclose a Treasury Bill for £500. I have another in my pocket, but which I think better to keep for an emergency.

By writing a most impertinent letter to the Purveyor in Chief, to be transmitted to the Examiner of Accounts in London, which is the only way I find at last to treat these people, I got by return of Mail £1100 of the £1500, which has been accumulating as due to me since June/'55. The quibble upon which it was withheld I have not time to tell.

I will not submit to the impertinence of these War Office Clerks, of whom one John Milton is the chief. If these cringing officials out here would keep as steady a tone, they would not be *made* to cringe *as they are*.

But how am I reminded of S. American Slavery in my official life. Could you but be one half hour behind the medical scenes as I am. In the list of medical C.B.s, I see but one name of those who nobly, humanely & stedfastly withstood the prince of Red Tape & inhuman routine, *Sir John* Hall.[20] With this one exception, all those who have been thus rewarded have been *Sambos & Quimbos to Legree*.[21] I cannot think that, if you knew the things that I know, have seen with these eyes & heard with these ears, you would think these words too strong. What honest man can ever care for official honours again. Life is so hopeless in official trammels – I doubt the Decline & Fall of the British Empire is at hand.

2.   I am so tired of that Talbot of Peterboro' who has written to Mr. Herbert, Mr. Bracebridge, (I believe to you) & to me about the £1 his son never gave me, drunk it, I suppose. *After* I had received four letters on the subject, I got hold of the son, who told me a very long story about it, gave me £1 which was transmitted same day by me to you. I wish you would tell this to any of the above who may ask you.

3.   The General Commg. & I have been both too busy this last week to look for (or *copy*) the *copy* in his possession of a letter of his to Mrs. Bridgeman, when she went up to Balaclava – which is a complete answer to the unworthy cavil made at the W. Office, as you state it to me, about "Miss Hutton having given her sanction to Mrs. Bridgeman's going." In that letter, the General Commanding (backed by the Ambassadress) informed Mrs. Bridgeman that "a great irregularity had been committed by her," that "his permission, which was the only one to ask, had never been asked," but that "he thought it best, at the stage at which matters had arrived, not to stop their passages to the Crimea as he otherwise would have done." These were as nearly as he & I can remember, his words. But I see so little use in dragging up all this history again that, had not this aggression been made by Dr. Hall (& even by the War Office) the *excuse & motive for farther aggression* & finally, as Dr. Sutherland states, for rooting me out of the Crimea, I should have taken no farther trouble of recapitulation. The General Commg. states that Miss Hutton never had or never exerted any authority over Mrs. Bridgeman at all.

Believe me ever yours faithfully and gratefully

Will you please send me out, as soon as may be, the Account paid by Papa for me for stoves etc. amounting to £160 & odd?

It is of course, impossible for me to arrange my Accounts at all till I know the items of this. Nor should I have known the sum but from you.

Half the stoves are going up to day to the Crimea, viz. 20 – Soyer having been directed to prosecute his operations there.

B.L. Add. Ms. 45792, f. 12 (*Cal*. B. 4. F6, 225).

The promotions and decorations announced in *The Times* on 6th February enraged Miss Nightingale as much as anything else that spring. Three days after her letter to Uncle Sam she wrote equally passionately to Colonel Lefroy, and movingly contrasted the fate of the common soldiery with the rewards enjoyed by their undeserving superiors.

To Lieutenant Colonel Lefroy

Scutari
Barrack Hospital
6th March 1856

My dear Sir

I beg to thank you very much for your letter of Feb. 18 & its enclosures. It makes me wish to keep a canteen, when, if ever, I am out of this.

I have never been able to join in the popular cry about the recklessness, sensuality, helplessness of the soldier. On the contrary I should say (& no woman perhaps has ever seen more of the manufacturing & agricultural classes of England than I have – before I came out here) that I have never seen so teachable & helpful a class as the Army generally.

Give them opportunity promptly & securely to send money home – & they will use it.

Give them a School & a Lecture & they will come to it.

Give them a book & a game & a Magic Lanthorn & they will leave off drinking.

Give them suffering & they will bear it.

Give them work & they will do it.

I had rather have to do with the Army generally than with any other class I have ever attempted to serve.

And I speak with the *intimate* experience of 18 months which I have had since I "joined the Army" – no woman (or man either) having seen them under such conditions.

And when I compare them with the Medical Staff Corps, the Land Transport Corps, the Army Works Corps, I am struck with the soldier's superiority as a moral & even as an intellectual being.

If Officers would but think thus of their men, how much might not be done for them.

But I should be sorry to have to give my experience of the former & (so-called) higher class.

With regard to what you kindly say of me, it will be of immense service to my work to have it officially recognised by the War Department, officially notified to the Commander of the Forces. This should have been done long ago – I have now the responsibility of REFUSING Nurses to Medical Officers, to Commanding Officers, to Chaplains who make requisition for them, prepare huts for them, are ready to receive them, because – Sir John Hall says that he has never been called upon to recognize me officially. This has been the case with the Hospitals of both wings of the Land Transport Corps – which have been & are still the worst in the Camp.

The private griefs of Hospitals are, however, now as nothing compared with those of the whole Army – that Army which was, but is no more.

In the presence of Sir John McNeill's cool, correct & dispassionate Report, I feel that what I have to say is worth nothing.

I am still in the state of chronic rage, like the "nigger" who, when he was to be flogged the second time, said "*Same* drunk, Massa, *same drunk*."

I gave my evidence before the Commission on the "Scutari & Crimean Hospitals" – & I being now one of the oldest inhabitants in Scutari & the Crimea, it had some value on that account.

I think I could tell even Sir J. McNeill some facts, having been more behind the scenes, especially the Medical Scenes, than even he has been.

But, if all were told, what would the "Scribes & Pharisees" be, compared to our British Scribes & P.s. The former, we are told, "devoured widows' houses", & put the "anise & cummin" into their own pockets.[22] But we have *made* the widows & put a great deal more than "anise & cummin" into the pockets of the widow-makers. Sir R. Airey, Col. Gordon, the two Cavalry Lords,[23] Sir John Hall, Mr. Fitzgerald et id genus omne – From this time forth can a K.C.B. ship or a promotion from Horse Guards or War Dept. ever be anything but a title of disgrace.

If you have friends among these men, so have I. But I would have given up my own father in such a cause.

England has never realised the eight thousand graves at Scutari, and more in the Crimea.

But I, who saw the men come down through all that long, long, dreadful winter (four thousand sick we received in seventeen days – Dec. 17/54 – Jan 3/55 – & of these we buried more than the half) without other covering than a dirty blanket & a pair of old Regimental trowsers, when we knew that the Stores were teeming with warm clothing – living skeletons, devoured with vermin, ulcerated, hopeless, speechless, dying like the Greeks, as they wrapped their heads in their blankets & spoke never a word, 70–80 we lost per diem on the Bosphorus alone up to Feb. 13/55 on which day we buried 85 in one grave without a Register – in that month there were 1000 more burials than deaths registered. Can we hear of the promotion of the men who caused this colossal calamity, we who saw it, without thinking, will the next thing be the "Decline & Fall of the" British "Empire?"

In the list of the Medical C.B.s, I see but one name among all those many deserving Medical Officers who boldly, at the cost of their own promotion, as it appears, withstood Red Tape, official routine & Dr. Hall, & procured, by one means or another, the necessaries for saving life among their men. With this one exception, all the Medical C.B.s are men of fourth or fifth rate capacity, who have won their little day by truckling to formalities & licking Dr. Hall's shoes.

Would that the men could speak who died of Cholera in the puddles of Kalamita Bay, when their zealous & active Medical Officers could not get a grain of medicine out of Dr. Hall, without a Requisition which they could not write.

The 1st Cl. Staff Surgeon who openly & to his face remonstrated with Dr. Hall on the occasion, I look for in vain in the list of Promotions & C.B.s

But the man who let the sick come down to Balaclava & gave no notice, so that they lay there for 3 hours together in the winter & could not be embarked, he is a C.B. [24] Tho' even Lord Raglan was frantic about that neglect.

After all we have done & all we have suffered, this is the glorious conclusion. At the end of two years, we leave off, having rewarded the authors of our great calamity – & hoped they would do the same next time.

And Lord Panmure gets up in the House of Lords, & with bated breath & whispering humbleness, begs the Cavalry Lords nor to be offended.

"The Lord never visits these parts" nor the Horse Guards nor the War Dep*t*. apparently. Or if He does, He has taken sides against us.

I should like not to deal in invective, with such a model of marble truth as Sir John McNeill's report before me. But he did not *see* these things – I did. And none, I believe, to this day, realize them.

I know & feel, personally, that several of these culprits, thus rewarded, are men of honor, conscience & capacity. But what of that?

If men are to be rewarded in the proportion of the harm they have done, let us proceed to business. I live in hopes to see Fitzgerald who, in his little way has done great things, in cutting off supplies from other Hospitals when his store was full, a Peer & hear Lord Panmure speak of "my noble friend." And Dr. Hall will be Baron Red-tape – how well that sounds! – & Andrew Smith must be a "Royal Highness" or "Lord Lieutenant of Ireland", at least.

Even in Sir J. McNeill's most admirable Report, the facts, as stated by Hall, about the "Linen" & "Lint" at Scutari are put, so as to convey an idea exactly contrary to the truth.

If the people of England would rise as they did this time last year, when they put the D[uke] of Newcastle out of office – they were very expeditious about that – & for what? – for ignorantly allowing the very things which the men who did them are now rewarded for doing – if England would now rise in like manner, we should have some hopes. But what can *this* end in

223

but in having more Sir R. Aireys & Sir J. Halls? See what the public feeling of England evaporated in – in "Free Gifts" among the women – their feeling found expression in flannel & old linen. Among the men, in turning out the D. of Newcastle who did not commit the murder.

In a matter where I am fortunately so out of the pale of promotion that I cannot be supposed to have preferrence or prejudice, I am unwilling to put forward one grievance which might seem to be personal.

But – a poor little acting Assistant Surgeon, named Bakewell, publicly writes a letter which was a true statement in some respects at least if not all, for which he loses his Commission & is dismissed the service, this being slander.

A Fitzgerald who *secretly* indites a malicious libel against a whole department of H. My.'s servants & causes it to be laid "confidentially" before the W.D. organ, is promoted to be Dep. Purveyor in Chief, with his back pay & all his little soul desires, over the heads of excellent & worthy seniors.

I make no apology for taking up your time with subjects about which I believe we must all be full.

Peace, I suppose, we must have whether we will or no. And is our next war to be conducted in like manner?

Believe me
very truly yours

B.L. Add. Ms. 43397, f. 217 (*Cal.* B. 4. F7, 232).

Maybe friends and relations did feel that she was overstating her case in the heat of the moment. She hastened to disabuse Uncle Sam. In her letter of 6th March, as in other letters written in a state of seething indignation, she showed herself feeling isolated and unsupported. In fact the support she got from the War Office, not only under Sidney Herbert but afterwards from Lord Panmure and Mr Hawes, who could easily have dropped her, is a testimony not only to the power of her popularity but to the fact that she was performing an indispensable public service, as Hawes himself had suggested.

To Uncle Sam Smith

Scutari
6th March 1856

Dear Uncle Sam

I am very anxious to correct a false impression, which seems to exist in your mind, that I have had a steady & consistent support from the War Office – that, such being the case, I kick against every prick – & am unduly impatient of opposition, inevitable in my or any situation, to my work.

The facts are exactly the reverse – I have never chosen to trouble the W.O. with my difficulties, because it has given me so feeble & treacherous support that I have always expected to hear it say "Could we not shelve Miss N? We daresay she does a great deal of good. But she quarrels with the authorities & we can't have that."

I have therefore fought my own battles – not only, as I can truly say unsupported by any official out here, with the exception of Gen*l*. Storks, so that I was amazed the other day at getting the loan of the little Gov*t*. tug for carrying goods – but exposed to every petty persecution, opposition & trickery that you can mention.

I have never had time to keep any records whatever except in the way of accounts. But I should have liked to have left some record of the way in which officials can torment & hinder a work.

And, as they now see, torment not only unmolested but rewarded, as every man who has been in any way instrumental in our great calamity, has received promotion or honours.

I will give you the slightest, pettiest instance of the hindrance which the pettiest official can make out here, if so minded.

When I came out, an order to furnish me with money was, of course, forwarded, from the W.O. to the Purveyors here. I have never availed myself of this to the amount of one farthing. On the contrary, they have been frequently in my debt to the amount of £1500. But the Senior Purveyor at Balaclava refuses to cash my Cheques, for no other reason discoverable than the love of petty annoyance & the hope of injuring my credit, in the minds of ignorant servants.

As I think it is a pity that he should have the pleasure of doing this, I now send up *cash* to the Crimea or take it.

Otherwise I could, of course, if I chose to complain, get an order to compel him not to refuse my Cheque.

This is the little Fitzgerald, who, after a course of successful villany, has like id genus omne, been promoted to be Dep*y*. Purveyor in Chief, with back pay & all his little soul desires. This is Dr. Hall's doing. But he is only one specimen of the promotions.

I do not like to use hard words. But I have no time to give the facts which would support them. But even to Sir J. McNeill's Report I could add a few facts which, if they were told (I being now one of the oldest inhabitants in Scutari & the Crimea) would make us feel that the times of the Scribes & Pharisees were nothing to these.

This little Fitzgerald has starved every Hospital when his store was full – & not, as it appears from ignorance, like some of the honourable men who have been our murderers, but from malice prepense.

I know that you think the credit of a wild imagination belongs to me. But I cannot but fancy that the W.O. is afraid of the Irish Brigade. And I know that Card. Wiseman, who is supposed, right or wrong, to have some influence over Hawes, has been busy in this matter.

A "sot" in the hands of "habiles méchans" can do much, as I know to my cost. And perhaps you do not know that Card. Wiseman has publicly, in his

Indults, noticed with praise Mrs. Bridgeman's Insurrection. Now Mrs. Bridgeman & Fitzgerald are one.

Fitzgerald topped up, with his *"Confidential"* Report against me – for which he is rewarded, – while a poor little Asst. Surgeon, for a true & public letter in the "Times", is dismissed the Service.

I assure you that our utter disgust at these latter promotions would tempt us, (the few honest men as I hope) to preach a Crusade against the Horse G*ds*. & War Dep*t*., feeling as we do now that not one step has been gained by our two years' fiery trial & that more Aireys, Cardigans, Halls & Fitzgeralds will be propagated for the next war.

Believe me
faithfully yours

B.L. Add. Ms. 45792, f. 17 (*Cal*. B. 4. F8, 233).

Notes

1   David Fitzgerald was appointed Deputy Purveyor in Chief in the East under J. Scott Robertson (which made Fitzgerald in effect Purveyor in Chief in the Crimea) on the recommendation of Dr Hall to Dr Andrew Smith (Smith to Hall, Hall papers, box 11, R.A.M.C. Historical Museum, Aldershot). He was entirely loyal to Dr Hall and jealous of his patron's interests in this dispute with F.N. His correspondence with Hall, which appears to have been preserved intact among the Hall papers in the R.A.M.C. Museum at Aldershot, suggests that his attitude towards F.N. was quite as malicious as she asserts; he must also have regarded her as a rival to his own position. The report is reproduced here in the appendix., p.298.

2   Colonel (Sir) John Henry Lefroy (1817–90) was sent out to Constantinople by Lord Panmure as his Confidential Adviser in Scientific Matters. His mission was to confer with General Storks on the condition of the hospital staff in the East, and on the accommodation of the sick at Scutari. There he formed a lasting friendship with F.N. Without his firm support in the battle with Dr Hall and the Purveyor, she might well have been shelved by the authorities. F.N. fully appreciated the part he played in securing her position and in 1864 acknowledged his "extreme kindness, judgment & tact to which, as I always gratefully acknowledged, I owed my position in the Crimea, which you & no one else, obtained for me." (F.N. to Lefroy, 25th Nov. 1864, B.L. Add. Ms. 43397, f. 271.) Lefroy believed in the principle of centralised control of the nursing department and considered F.N. the only person capable of heading such a department (P.R.O. WO 43/963, f. 329.)

3   F.N. to Mrs Herbert, 17th November 1855, p. 284.

4   F.N. to Lord Cranworth, 4th Feb. 1856, Nightingale papers, Claydon. Milton considered Lefroy's action most improper: "I must say that I do not think that reference at all justified his shewing to the party concerned a confidential Report, presuming that it was asked for by him as confidential, & obtained on that understanding." (P.R.O. WO 43/963, f. 339.)

5   As the thirteen nuns took the place of Miss Wear and two assistants, F.N. was probably right in asserting that Dr Hall had not expected so large a party. No

226

number was mentioned in the early correspondence. Only in her letter of 2nd October did Mother Bridgeman state her intention of bringing a party of twelve with her. (B.L. Add. Ms. 39867, f. 39.)

6   F.N.'s account of the causes of the break-up of the Koulali nursing is supported by Fanny Taylor's account. As the health of the patients improved, and requisitions upon the Purveyor became easier, Dr Humphrey gave the order that the old routine of the diet roll ought to be revived, i.e. signed requisitions to be provided for all extras. This caused some dismay among the ladies of Koulali. "The ladies' plans for nursing were upset, and they did not know what to do with themselves, so they assembled in the store-room looking very blank, and complaining to our superintendent. The lady in charge of the storeroom, who had been thinking of going home, now laughingly declared the matter was settled, for her work was done." (Frances M. Taylor, *Eastern Hospitals and English Nurses*, 2nd edn, London, 1856.)

7   Mrs Shaw Stewart also suggested that the Purveyor's accounts were cooked. (Letter to F.N., p. 203.)

8   (a) "Average Daily issue of Extra Diet Rolls of the Medical Officers, Barrack Hospital Scutari, from 13th January 1855 to 13th February," *Report on the State of the Hospitals in the Crimea and Scutari*, London, 1855, p. 41. (b) *Statements exhibiting the Voluntary Contributions received by Miss Nightingale for the Use of the British War Hospitals in the East . . . 1854, 1855, 1856.* London, 1857.

9   According to a memo by Bracebridge, a second Turkish house was taken for the women, under the organisation of Lady Alicia Blackwood. Several rooms were given over to sick and lying-in women and various other uses. "Subsequently a school was held here, for children who came with civilian artizans & non-commissioned officers sent out in the summer of 1855." ("Soldiers' Wives Widows & Children at Scutari," R.A.M.C. Historical Museum, Aldershot.) Lady Alicia described the school,which was supplied with copy-books, pens and other scholastic materials by F.N.(Lady Alicia Blackwood, *A Narrative . . .* , p. 81.)

10   F.N. to Mrs Herbert, 17th November 1855, B.L. Add. Ms. 43396, f. 40 (p. 177.)

11   J.H.L[efroy] to F. Peel, P.R.O. WO 43/963, f. 335.

12   Benjamin Hawes to F. Peel, 22nd January 1856, P.R.O. WO 43/963, f. 335.

13   Hall papers, box 14 FCO9/13, R.A.M.C. Historical Museum, Aldershot.

14   John Milton, 3rd March 1856, P.R.O. WO 43/963, f. 341.

15   Dr Andrew Smith to Benjamin Hawes, 29th February 1856, P.R.O. WO 43/963, f. 321.

16   P.R.O. WO 43/963, f. 342v.

17   *Report of the Commission of Inquiry into the Supplies of the British Army in the Crimea*, London, 1856. *Parliamentary Papers, 20. The Times* also reprinted the report almost verbatim through February.

18   F.N.'s reply to this letter was written on 3rd April 1856, p. 244.

19   A Board of General Officers was appointed "to inquire into Statements contained in the Report of Sir John McNeill and Colonel Tulloch . . ." This was popularly known as the Chelsea Board.

20   The list of promotions and decorations which so enraged F.N. was published in the *Gazette* on 5th February 1855 and reproduced in *The Times* on 6th February 1856, p. 7 cols. d–e. Dr Hall was honoured with the K.C.B. Five other doctors were

appointed Companions of the Order of the Bath, David Dumbreck, William Linton, John Forrest, Thomas Alexander, John Robert Taylor, Archibald Gordon, James Mouat. Dr Alexander must be the one F.N. means here. She had him appointed Director General of the reformed Army Medical Department in succession to Sir Andrew Smith.

21 Sambo and Quimbo were the brutalised minions of the slave owner Simon Legree, who beat Uncle Tom to death in Harriet Beecher Stowe's novel, *Uncle Tom's Cabin*, published in 1852.

22 Matthew 23, 14–23, "Woe unto you, Scribes and Pharisees, hypocrites! For ye devour your widows' houses, and for a pretence make long prayer . . . Woe unto you, Scribes and Pharisees, hypocrites! For ye pay tithe of mint and anise and cummin, and have omitted the weightier matters of the law, judgment, mercy, and faith . . ."

23 Lords Lucan and Cardigan. Together with Sir Richard Airey, Colonel Alexander Gordon and Commissary General Filder, they petitioned the Secretary of State for War to set up the board of enquiry (the Chelsea Board) into the *Report of the Commission on Supplies to the Army*.

24 Dr David Dumbreck was mentioned by name in one of Lord Raglan's General Orders censuring the Medical Department for not ensuring proper attention to the sick and wounded on their hideous journey down to Balaclava. (Hibbert, p. 214.)

7

In General Orders

On 16th March Miss Nightingale at last found herself "in General Orders":

It is notified, by desire of the Secretary of State for War, that Miss Nightingale is recognised by Her Majesty's Government as the General Superintendent of the Female Nursing Establishment of the Military Hospitals of the Army.

No Lady, or Sister, or Nurse is to be transferred from one Hospital to another, or introduced into any Hospital, without previous consultation with her.

There was, however, a significant proviso:

Her instructions . . . require her to have the approval of the Principal Medical Officer in her exercise of the responsibility thus invested in her.

The Principal Medical Officer will communicate with Miss Nightingale upon all subjects connected with the Female Nursing Establishment, and will give his directions through that Lady.[1]

But Miss Nightingale herself did not appear to recognise this as in any way restricting her absolute authority. Her 'consultation' with Sir John as to the disposition of nurses was minimal. His humiliation was complete, as he virtually acknowledged in a dignified remonstrance to Sir William Codrington on receiving Lord Panmure's censure through the Commander in Chief:

The position of Miss Nightingale will now be perfectly understood by the Medical Officers of the Army; but it is right I should add that until now I have never received from the authorities at home any official instructions defining her exact powers, and authority – as it was generally understood that her mission related solely to the Hospitals at Scutari; and until the present notification from the Secretary of State for War I should not have thought I was exceeding the authority of my position as head of the Medical Department of this Army, in appointing two nurses to a Military Hospital, on an emergency, but even that trifling act of authority I beg distinctly to state I have not exercised on the present occasion; and the only thing I can charge my memory with having done that would give even a color to this accusation is having, when Miss Wear was in tribulation about some one to accompany her to the Monastery, sanctioned the Purveyor's writing down to

Smyrna to enquire if two nurses could be obtained there – an answer was received by Mr. Fitzgerald in the negative. Subsequently, I understand, when the Smyrna Establishment was ordered to be reduced – that two nurses were sent up from there to Miss Nightingale at Scutari, but I am not answerable for that.

Having been censured by the Secretary of State for War on information that is not correct I request you will do me the honor to submit this my Explanation, which I trust will be satisfactory to his Lordship.[2]

Co-operation between Inspector General and Lady Superintendent became more and more difficult.

On the day she appeared in General Orders, Miss Nightingale set sail for the Crimea for the third time, in a spirit of slightly wary triumph graphically illustrated in the two letters she wrote to Colonel Lefroy and Uncle Sam as she was about to sail.

To Lieutenant Colonel Lefroy

Scutari
Barrack Hospital
16th March 1856

My dear Sir

Though I am just starting for the Crimea, & should have been there by this time, had it not been for the gale of wind which has caused our transports to put back, I must thank you for your kind letter of March 3, & for the act of justice to our work, which I am sure I owe to you.

My revered friend & patron, John Hall, K.C.B. has consented to my undertaking the two dirty & neglected "Land Transport Corps Hospitals," at the earnest request of the 1st Cl. Staff Surgeon[3] in charge, & I was on my way thither.

To find me in G.O. up there will be a great satisfaction to my numerous friends & patrons there, and (now I am serious) will greatly facilitate the work which the W.O. has given me to be done & will prevent an exhausting & ever-recurring struggle.

With regard to Dr. Hall's false report, if it is his, to the W.O., that I had "renounced all responsibility for Crimean Hospitals," I am perpetually reminded by him of O'Connell's aphorism, "It is a good lie, if it lasts four & twenty hours". But, if the W.O. would *think, this* could not last 24 minutes. The W.O. have, at this moment, before them Mrs. Shaw Stewart's letter to me. She is my Superintendent at the most considerable Hospital in the Crimea, the Castle Hospital, & she does not write to me as if I had nothing to do with them.[4] But the "Budget" is the grand thing, as we are told in the late discussion between Horse Guards, War Departmt. & House of Commons. And the W.O. will have in my "Bill" at Lady Day for two Hospitals in the Crimea, which I have had since the beginning, & now for four – leaving out the General Hospital at Balaclava.

So that question is at rest.

I cannot too much thank you for your kind interest in our work, nor express how much I feel this benefit, that you are good enough to give me your advice. But, in the matter of the R.C. Nuns, it is entirely in accordance with my opinion & constant line of conduct throughout. I receive the R.C. assistance here with open arms. "Revd. Mother" here is one of my very best helps. The W.O. send out, at my request, more Nuns to be under her. The "Bridgemans" at Balaclava, it is true, are the tools of an Irish faction. They have been always called here the "Brickbats". It is wise in the English Government to forward as much as possible the respectable & worthy R.C. work here. The French have greatly increased their influence by doing so. By strengthening the *Irish* R.C.s here, the Govt. raise up enemies to themselves – the Irish R.C.s hating the English Govt. as they do. But, in fear of the Irish Brigade, the Govt. pass over Fitzgerald's slanders, & Mrs. Bridgeman's insurrection.

I have always said that a R.C. can do everything which we cannot do, lie, steal, murder, slander, because we are afraid of the Roman Catholics. What an advantage it must be!

The incessant, unspeakably laborious struggle which I have had for 17 months will now be greatly saved me by the G.O. in question.

And you need not be afraid that I shall molest the "Brickbats". Above all, I am afraid of their resigning & making martyrs of themselves, which is their grand object. I shall interfere in no way whatever. That there should be none but R.C.s in any one Hospital is entirely contrary to my original Instructions from the W.O., & to common principle. But, in this instance, common prudence & feeling leave but one course open to me.

For, as a Superintendent of women, I cannot expose any woman, directly under my charge, to the slanders of a scoundrel like Fitzgerald (I really have looked in the Dic[tionar]y for another synonime for Fitzgerald, & have not been able to find one – being unwilling to use so hard a word) and therefore while *he* remains in Office of Balaclava, only I and the "Brickbats", whom he has taken under his Aegis, shall have anything to do with his Hospital proper.

Also, as a practical woman, I think it a pity to give Mr. Fitzgerald the pleasure either of refusing my Requisitions or of falsifying them to the W.O., I shall therefore take up everything with me which my Hospitals will want, leaving it to the Queen to supply such things only as bread & meat etc. which I cannot make.

Had this man been one of our persuasion, he would have been brought to a Court Martial. But it is enough for a man to be a Roman Catholic for the Govt. to say, "Oh! do pray be quiet, don't tell of his lies. Or you will bring the Roman Catholics down upon us."

Very well. I am content. I had at all events, much rather that Mr. Fitzgerald should speak ill of me, than that he should speak well.

I must say one thing more. We have heard, with the greatest astonishment in these Hospitals, of Mr. F. Peel's speech in the Ho. of Commons concerning the State of Health in the Crimea [5] & Dr. Hall's exposition of it, which tallies exactly with his letter to you, of which you were kind enough to give me a Copy, asserting that none but Convalescents were sent down to Scutari.

Upon my mentioning this to the Principal Medical Officer of this Hospital, he exclaimed, with genuine feeling, "What a devil of a story!"

The facts of the case are exactly the reverse. The Army in the Crimea is healthy, because all the bad Cases are sent down here. An acute case may, now & then, slip through their fingers, but, if a case does not recover quickly, immediately or as soon as possible it is sent down to Scutari. I do not know whether men with condensed lungs & ulcerated bowels who come down here to die are called by Sir John Hall "Convalescents." But nearly all the cases who do die here are from the Crimea – &, if it were not for these, Scutari would not have a death in a fortnight.

Thus far I would put into the "Times" if I were in the habit of being my "Own Correspondent." But what follows is strictly private. I said to the Dep. Inspector Gen*l*. of this Hospital, "And do you mean to allow these Statements (which, tho' not false, convey an impression absolutely the reverse of the truth), to pass?"

He said, "No: I shall write a Statement to the Army Medical Board at home – but it will never be heard of. And, if I were to write a Statement to Dr. Hall, I should only make him my enemy for life – & the enmity & not the truth would be the thing to appear."

So much for our rotten System.

Pray let me thank you again for your kind letter & believe me

My dear Sir
most faithfully & truly yours

B.L. Add. Ms. 43397, f. 223 (*Cal. B. 4. F10, 240.*)

To Uncle Sam Smith

Scutari
Barrack Hospital
16th March 1856

Dear Uncle Sam

I should have received your last letter in the *Crimea*, but that we have had such gales of wind that no Steamer could leave this port. Had the "Severn" & the "Medway" been able to sail, we should have been aboard taking up fourteen females to serve two new* L.T.C. Hospitals in the Crimea. We shall probably sail today.

I shall be very glad to find myself in "General Orders" there, as it will enable the work to be much better done, & without such an exhausting & ever-recurring struggle.

*Land Transport Corps.

And now about Fitzgerald – the Pur*v*r. at B'clava.

I have had a private & an official letter from Sir B. Hawes.

(What I am going to say I say without intending anything offensive either to him or to Lord Panmure, both of whom I respect, both have been uniformly kind to me. Both have now done a decisive though tardy, act of justice to the work in putting it into G.O.)

What the Government in these letters virtually asks me to do is to "let them off" – they say "pray say nothing about it."

I am not at all surprised that the Gov*t*. *is* very anxious to say nothing, but hush up the matter.* I have that confidence in British honesty that I think, were Fitzgerald's "confidential" slanders known, & the answer I could make to them, it would make a considerable disturbance.

But I can afford to be generous – & I am willing to "let" the Gov*t*. "off". Two practical consequences, however, I must, as a practical woman, cause to follow.
1.   I think it is a pity to give Mr. Fitzgerald the pleasure either of refusing my Requisitions (he is now Deputy Purveyor-in-Chief i.e. Purveyor-in-Chief in the *Crimea*) or of reporting them, or rather *not* them, home to the W.O. I shall therefore take up everything with me which my Hospitals will want, & leave the Queen to provide only meat, bread, porter, fuel & candle.
2.   I cannot, as a Superintendent of Women, expose any woman directly under my charge to come within the slanders of such a scoundrel (I do not wish to use hard words, but I have looked in Johnson in vain for another synonym to Fitzgerald) & therefore while he remains at Balaclava, only I & the Bridgeman Nuns whom he had taken under his Aegis, shall have anything to do with his Hospital proper. This is a matter of common prudence.

The Gov*t*. ask me to be silent. They refuse me a copy of Fitzgerald's Report (I would here remark that *I* was compelled to write my answer at a great disadvantage, without being able to confer with my Sup*ts*., or to shew them the charges, & I should be really glad to know with what part of my answer Sir B. Hawes "is not quite satisfied, as not meeting the exact point." I have no doubt there may be many such lacunes – & I should be glad to fill them up if I can).

The Gov*t*. wishes me to be silent. But will Fitzgerald be silent? He, of course, has a copy, if I have not, of his *secret* Report which is no "Secret" in the Crimea. You say "his lies" about the Nurses "are not believed by the very few who have seen them." But they have been both *seen* & *believed* by very *many* (in the Crimea).

If the Gov*t*. had the spirit of men, could they endure to put themselves in the power of such a scoundrel? Do you imagine that if Fitzgerald had not been a R. Catholic, he would not have been degraded instead of promoted, as he has been?

See the difference – A wretched little Acting Assistant Surgeon, by name "Bakewell", publishes a statement in the Times, a part, at least, of which every one knows to have been true, for which he loses his Commission & is

*which, if known, would be considerably the worse for them.

233

dismissed the service.

So that Bakewell's statement is slander because it is true, & Fitzgerald's is not slander, because it is false.

Again, Cardigan whose character in the Crimea is such that I will *not* look for a word in Johnson to be *his* synonime, obtained his Court of Appeal against Sir John McNeill.

And the Gov*t*. asks ME to be quiet. I will be quiet. Because, tho' Fitzgerald can starve me & slander me, I can do without him. But, if HE will be quiet is another question. The thing will come out, sooner or later, you may depend upon it. The R.C.s who, if they cannot use one side, will the other, will make use of it one way or another – against the Gov*t*.

If the Gov*t*. had had the spirit of men, they would have brought him to a Court Martial, or by an arbitrary exercise of power, dismissed him from his office. We hear of Courts Martial every month for much less flagrant offences.

It appears to me that the want of moral, & even of intellectual, perception in Sir John Hall is remarkable. The Gov*t*. cannot prevent *private* slander. But they *can* prevent *official* slander. But Sir John Hall presents a document as "confidential", & founds an official letter upon it. *He cannot make thus a double use of it* – to say nothing of the impropriety, is not this a want of perception that he does not see that he cannot do this, & that the Gov*t*. do not make him see that he cannot do it with impunity. We used to call this *corrupt* – & so I believe it would still be called, did it come out in the Ho. of Commons.

At all events, a Gov*t*. so weak cannot stand.

I have nothing more to say. I do not wish anything more to be done. But I have not the least objection to this, my opinion, being known.

I should have been in the Crimea before this even without my "General Orders", had it not been for the gale. But I am very glad that the Gov*t*. has put it in my power to do its own work. And I shall write to Sir B. Hawes to thank him.

The gist of the Official Dispatch which has been written to me is to allow me *unlimited extravagance,* in return for the Purveyor's calumnies, a power I shall *not* hasten to make use of Quam parvâ – the proverb is somewhat musty.

Finally, it is a matter of the utmost indifference to me whether Fitzgerald speaks ill or speaks well of me. Indeed, I think that you would rather prefer the former – he is a kind of *Squeers*, only lower & with a more sneaking flattery, & without the energetic barbarity of that celebrated master of Dotheboys *Hall*.[6]

But Sir John *Hall** is a more formidable enemy, as he could entirely paralyse my usefulness & frustrate the object of our being here.

Unless the Gov*t*. therefore have, with its curious system of double dispatches & official & private letters, given Sir J. Hall a private rap for *officializing* the Purveyor's slanders, I think it will find itself in a difficulty.

It appears to me that all sense of honesty in official life is gone.

---

*who is as completely his slave as that other Hall was of Squeers.

However, it is much the most dignified thing for my work for me to be quiet. And I am satisfied.

Believe me, dear Uncle Sam, in too great haste to be short

Yours very faithfully
& gratefully

B.L. Add. Ms. 45792, f. 20 (*Cal.* B. 4. F11, 241.)

Miss Nightingale arrived in the Crimea on 24th March and at once set about making her presence felt.

She could now have afforded to act generously, and it would have been politic to do so. But in her anger over the events of the past six months she appeared incapable of magnanimity. On 25th March she addressed Sir John Hall a somewhat arrogant letter:

To Sir John Hall

Balaclava
25th March 1856

My dear Sir

I beg to report to you

I.   that I arrived here yesterday per "Severn", bringing with me the first instalment of the Nurses appointed by you to the two L.T.C. Hospitals, whom I propose settling there tomorrow. The second detachment follows per "Ottawa"

2.   that, in consequence of the "General Order," replacing matters which regard the "Female Nursing in Military Hospitals" where they were before, I called upon Mrs. Bridgeman today at the General Hospital, Balaclava, to inform her that I purposed making no change there – your satisfaction with the arrangement, as at present existing there, having been expressed by yourself. She "referred the case" to you as to her "continuing her work in the Hospital when no longer independent."

I beg, therefore, to await your decision upon the subject, & to request that you will communicate it to me. I have only to add that Mrs. Bridgeman is but replaced under the same conditions as understood & acknowledged by her in writing (as by all the other Nuns) upon their coming out – to resign upon which account would make but a lame story.

& also that the "General Order" in question is as much an order to me as to any of my Nurses – & being such, I cannot discharge myself from the responsibility which the War Department saw fit to impose upon me.

3.   I would beg the favor of you to inform me whether you wish us to have our Requisitions at the L.T.C. Hospitals upon the Purveyor counter signed by the Principal Medical Officer – an arrangement I should myself prefer.

I beg to remain, dear Sir,
Yours faithfully

B.L. Add. Ms. 39867, f. 99 (*Cal.* omitted).

Sir John replied:

. . . .With regard to the nurses at the General Hospital at Balaclava the supervision of whom you state has been re-imposed on you by the War Department I take leave to observe that all doubt has now been removed by the General Order as to your relative positions and it is a question not for me, but for Mrs. Bridgeman herself to decide, – but in justice to her, and the Sisters under her orders I must state that they have given me the most perfect satisfaction by the quiet & efficient manner in which they have performed their duty since they have been employed there, and I should regret their departure.[7]

Mother Bridgeman held to the position that, since Miss Nightingale had refused to accept her and her nuns in the first place, she was released from her original contract of obedience to the Lady Superintendent. On her behalf the Purveyor informed Sir John on 27th March that

She wishes . . . that her remaining moves should be strictly limited to you – and distinctly to you – and exclusive of all interference or authoritative action in regard to her on the part of Miss N—— as it is solely to avoid the Recognition of such control that she has resolved in the painful alternative of resignation.[8]

In the circumstances Sir John could do nothing but accept the nuns' resignation. He wrote to his wife on the occasion:

I am quite prostrate as the General Order, procured by mendacity, has deprived me of the only real nurses we ever had; for Mrs. Bridgeman, a very superior and conscientious person, the Mother Superior of the Sisters of Charity, has positively refused to acknowledge Miss Nightingale's authority, and I cannot blame her after what is past, and they all go home on Saturday next. Thus the Government loses the free services of these estimable women, and the soldiers the benefit of their ministrations, to gratify Miss Nightingale.

I was told, when I declined to interfere, that right or wrong Miss Nightingale's powerful friends were powerful enough to carry her through. My reply was "so much the greater pity."[9]

It was not purely a matter of gratifying Miss Nightingale. The government, following the line indicated by Sidney Herbert in October 1854, a policy now confirmed by the War Office memoranda and the General Order, was determined to establish a strong central nursing authority. It was also seriously concerned by the sectarian aspects of the quarrel involving the nuns. The Secretary of State for War therefore, following Colonel Lefroy's advice, preferred to confirm Miss Nightingale's position as the supreme nursing authority.

Miss Nightingale pursued her struggle with Sir John Hall with unabated vigour. In the subsequent petty and undignified proceedings neither party could be considered to emerge with credit.

To Sir John Hall

Balaclava
31st March 1856

My dear Sir

With reference to a passage in your letter of March 26, referring to the "usage in Military Hospitals," a circumstance which has taken place induces me to offer an observation.

You state that you wish "all demands for the Sick to be made by the Medical Officer in charge, with the approval of his immediate superior."

It appears to me that this rule so far as it relates to Nurses and Superintendents is reasonable, and should be complied with, as has been done heretofore.

Personally, however, I have exercised the right of Requisition without such approval ever since I received my Instructions in October, 1854.

I am in the habit of doing so at Scutari, & have always hitherto done so in the Crimea. And my Requisitions for the sick have always been attended to.

But, on the 29th inst., I sent a Requisition to the Medical Store-keeper for 2 Graduated Glass Measures and 1 Gill Measure for the "Sisters of Mercy" at the Land Transport Corps. And it was refused, unless the counter-signature of yourself or Dr. Taylor were obtained.

It appears to me that the definite position, which I now occupy with regard to the Hospitals in the Crimea, cannot be considered to have deprived me of the above-mentioned right.

And I should therefore feel obliged by your giving the necessary Instructions.

Of course, when I leave the Crimea, the Requisitions will be sent for approval by the Superintendent in the manner pointed out in your letter.

I beg to remain
dear Sir
faithfully yours

B.L. Add. Ms. 39867, f.103 (*Cal.* omitted).

This amazingly arrogant and tactless letter is quite at variance with all those protestations of humility and obedience to the medical officers' orders that Miss Nightingale repeatedly made to Sidney Herbert, Colonel Lefroy and others. It provided Sir John with the opportunity to administer a well deserved and unanswerable snub:

2 April 1856

. . . I am not aware that any power or privilege you are invested with is at all infringed by this rule [that Requisitions for patients are to be made thro' the M.O.s] – certainly none that has ever been communicated to me, and until the Queen's Regulations for the management of army Hospitals are altered, I must, without wishing or intending any discourtesy to you, request that it may be observed.

You must, however, allow me to observe, my dear Madam, that the custom in the Hospital at Scutari is no guide to me, nor can I permit it to supersede the Queen's Regulations.

By the observance of this Regulation the comforts and welfare of the sick are in no way whatever interfered with, as it is the duty of the Medical Officer in charge to see that a needful supply of medical comforts is at all times on hand – but any suggestion of yours, will, I am quite sure, meet with that attention which it merits.

My own opinion of the duty of a nurse in a military, or any other Hospital is, that she should implicitly obey the instructions of the Medical attendant in the charge of any case or cases placed under her immediate care – . . . but initiating nothing of her own accord . . . besides it would be unfair to tax you with the administrative duties of the Hospital, and Medical department in addition to those of Superintendent of Nurses.[10]

Dr. Smith, on being informed of this latest brush, remarked that this went

. . . to prove the same thing namely only a certain kind of nurses are likely to prove useful in Hospitals particularly Military ones. I expected something from the Despatch to General Codrington. I foresaw the immediate efforts which would be made and I doubt not the results have proved unsatisfactory to even the supporters of universal domination . . .

I think you acted rightly in refusing the graduated measures & what could they be wanted for – if to distribute fluids surely the more ordinary vessel is the table spoon.[11]

while Fitzgerald's comment provided a perfect example of that petty and obstructive malice which had contributed to the Crimean *débâcle* in the first place:

I return the enclosed; it is a graphic delineation of the usurping & presuming views of the writer, — and nothing could be stronger as an evidence of the interference of her – and her superintendents, than the power she claims of disposing of public Stores for the sick.

Your reply is an admirable reproof, – all that could be desired in dignity and energy.

She will make another move – but unless it is done with her utmost caution and Cunning, she will involve herself and the Authorities in a discreditable dilemma; They cannot empower her to draw public Stores for the use of the Sick – without an abandonment of all principle . . .[12]

On 11th April the nuns left the General Hospital. Miss Nightingale, determined to retake the position from which she had retreated the previous October, immediately demanded that the keys to the store be handed over to her. Fitzgerald, equally determined to keep her out, tried to keep the keys out of her hands. He sent Dr Hall a hurried account of events as they developed:

. . . about 5 p.m. I met Miss N——. She stopped me – and questioned about the Keys; – at the time I had received one – that of the Store Room in the Extras Kitchen – . . . She was annoyed . . . She then asked for the Keys of the Quarters – I told her that as the Quarters had been given over by the P.M.O. – they were of course returned to him. . . about 7 p.m. Miss N—— called at the Hospital, – I was at Dinner – she asked for the Keys – and was referred to the Medical Officer – while in my Office she mentioned that she had seen Dr. Beatson – and that he had authorised her to resume the Nursing – as it could not be interrupted. She did so – and on return from Dinner – I found her in possession of the Extras Kitchen – with one of her Nurses; – she soon after by some means – got the Key of the Room adjoining surgery, which is now occupied by her Nurses. She next sent to me for the Key of the Store Room – but I informed her that I had given it over to the charge of the Officer in Purveying Charge of the Hospital. I next sent for Mr. Powell – told him to . . . keep the Key according to my first instruction to him – until you would authorize other parties to succeed to Nursing duties; – Mr. Powell understands me – and will obey.

I fear she has gained a point by the disingenuousness of Dr. Beatson – but if you will authorize my occupying the Huts – by bearer – I shall at once call on Dr. Huish to give me the Keys.

This may be done – as my Communications must reach you before Miss N—— can make any move on the Head Quarter direction.

She has gone far enough however – to violate the notorious Genl. Orders; unless – by equivocation – and ambidexterity – she invests Dr. B—— with the power of the P.M.O. of the Army of the Crimea.[13]

On 13th April Miss Nightingale herself informed Sir John of her successful invasion. She had, as the Purveyor wrote, ignored that part of the General Order which instructed her to "have the approval of the P.M.O. in her exercise of the responsibility invested in her." She probably considered the acquiesence of Dr Beatson[14] sufficient authorization.

Sir John Hall had reason to be annoyed, and informed her coldly:

As the army is on the eve of breaking up and vacating the Crimea, I regret I was not previously made acquainted with your intention of withdrawing nurses from Scutari where they will soon be more required than here. This unnecessary move may, I fear, have put them to inconvenience and the public to expense without any adequate advantage from the arrangement.[15]

Miss Nightingale next reverted to the question of supplies for the nurses. In her letter of 25th March the day after she arrived in the Crimea, she had asked whether Sir John wished her requisitions to be countersigned by the P.M.O.s; he had replied the following day, "All requisitions for the personal use of the nurses the Purveyor has orders to comply with at once on your, or any Superintendent's demand."[16]

But the Purveyor had informed Miss Nightingale that requisitions "*must be & always had been* . . . countersigned by the Principal Medical Officer."[17]

Meanwhile Miss Nightingale and Dr Taylor of the L.T.C. Hospital had together worked out a scheme for rationing the nurses on the same basis as the orderlies, an arrangement of which Dr Taylor informed Sir John on 28th March.[18] Hall's response was to issue another instruction to Fitzgerald to

give directions to the Purveyor's clerks to diet the Medical Staff Corps Orderlies, & nurses, employed in the Land Transport Hospitals in the usual way, and account for the same under its proper head in their returns. He will also give directions for Requisitions, from Miss Nightingale, or the Superintendent of the Nurses at the Land Transport Hospitals, for the *personal* use of the nurses to be complied with without further counter signature – but the articles so drawn must appear on the face of the Expenditure returns in a distinct shape. The dieting, & supplies of the nurses & orderlies is in no way to be mixed up with the issues to the sick.[19]

Fitzegerald responded:

I have the honor to acknowledge the receipt of your Memorandum of this date on a letter from 1st Class Staff Surgeon Dr Taylor of yesterday's date, submitting arrangements for your approval which have been agreed up in this Office the day previously, & to state that I have communicated your instructions to the Purveyor's Clerks attached to the Land Transport Corps, cancelling a recommendation I had given of having all Requisitions, for personal use of Nurses – or otherwise – approved by the Principal Medical Officer of each Hospital.[20]

At this stage Miss Nightingale had been in the Crimea for five days.

On 16th April she complained to Fitzgerald that the nurses of the Left Wing Hospital of the L.T.C. had received no rations for four days, and the Sisters of Mercy at the Right Wing none for seven days. The complaint was forwarded to Sir John Hall, who left his comments in the margin.

Copy of formal letter to David Fitzgerald, with Sir John Hall's comments (in the margin of the original, footnoted here)

General Hospital Balaclava
16th April 1856

Sir

In reply to your letter of yesterday's date relative to the Nurses being upon

1. "Hospital full diet," I beg to state that I am happy to accede to any arrangement which lends to the facilitation & accuracy of accounts & to the convenience of the Service.* I consented to it at the Land transport Corps – I consent to it here:-

2. I would however observe that it does *not* tend to *economy*, as my Requisitions will shew, which draw for about half the quantity of meat

---

*I understood this was Miss Nightingale's own wish. *J. Hall*

allowed by Hospital Full Diet, when drawn according to the *number* of Nurses.

3. Also that it does not tend to *simplicity* of accounts, as it requires one drawing for Diets & another for Extras for Nurses.

4. I would also wish to leave on record the fact that the Nurses at the Left Wing L.T.C. received no rations for *four* days, and the "Sisters of Mercy" at the Right Wing L.T.C. none for *seven** days upon this system (save and except 9 loaves of bread after they had been drawn for) during which time they subsisted upon my own private Stores.

5. Having tried both systems I decidedly prefer that of Requisitions to Rations, for economy, simplicity & regularity – and I would beg the favor of a reply to inform me why the system victualling the Nurses is changed from what it continued to be, up to the day of Mrs. Bridgeman's departure, here.

At the same time I beg to repeat that I am willing to submit to the temporary inconvenience, if it can be of any advantage to the service – *especially if it be a means of clearing up accounts, so that Articles NOT drawn for the consumption of the Nurses, but drawn according to Medical Officers' Requisitions, for sick Officers, or Patients, be not charged to the account of Nurses' consumption.*†

I have the honor to be
Sir
Your obedt. servt.

B.L. Add. Ms. 39867, f. 115. (*Cal.* omitted).

In response to the inquiry instituted by Sir John Hall on receiving this letter a number of doctors, purveyors and clerks were all called on to testify that the nuns and nurses were not starved, and that in so far as rations or requisitions were not drawn for nurses it was because Miss Nightingale herself ordered it so.[21]

Miss Nightingale could have avoided this quarrel. She had anticipated trouble and brought her own supplies. In her letter to Herbert of 3rd April she admitted that her nurses had not starved. But in her view an important principle was at stake, as she was to explain to Dr Hall on 26th April, when she also asked that the subject now be dropped.

*This should be inquired into most carefully and minutely as I gave positive orders that all demands from Miss Nightingale, or the Superintendents, for the personal wants of the nurses should be immediately attended to. Subsequently – Dr. Taylor wrote to say it was Miss Nightingale's wish that they should be dieted like the orderlies. *J.H.*

†No submission is required on the part of Miss Nightingale in this matter and the only complication that has ever existed has been occasioned by the nurses drawing stores for the sick as well as the Med*l*. Officers. This has been fully pointed by me in writing to Miss Nightingale. *J. Hall.*

To Sir John Hall

General Hospital, Balaclava
26th April 1856

My dear Sir

I beg to acknowledge your letter of April 24, with its enclosures from Drs. Taylor, McArthur & Doherty – & I hasten to state that these gentlemen did everything which could be done by them (& a great deal more than I had any right to expect) for the comfort & convenience of the Nurses, even to drawing stores upon their own Requisition for the Nurses, in the absence of the promised Rations.

The rest of the case, it appears to me, remains where it was – viz. that the Rations did not come and the Requisitions did.

It is obviously not the duty of the Medical Officer to be running about ascertaining whether his Nurses have bread & meat. As well might I send in Requisitions to Sir John Hall.

It was obviously the regular course that I should go to the Purveyor about rationing the Nurses, which I did, the day previous to their going to the L.T.C. Hospitals, the day subsequent & many succeeding days.

It was obviously my duty not to acquiesce in the make-shifts so kindly resorted to by the Medical Officers, in default of the Rations – but to persevere in claiming the regular Diets upon which we had been placed.

Otherwise, the transaction would have been as irregular as if the Patients' Diets had stopped, & we had supplied them with bread & meat from our table.

Dr. Taylor was of the same opinion. I received a message, purporting to be from him, thro' the Sisters at Karanyi, to the effect that he did not approve of the system of the Sisters receiving stores in bulk or otherwise than upon their own Requisition – & that these stores were to be returned – in which I so fully concurred that I had expressed it in the previous day in the same terms to the Sisters.

My reason for this I have fully stated viz. that to be responsible for an expenditure, it is necessary to have cognizance of what it is.

The question was not at all as to the Sisters "starving", but as to their living upon Requisitions or upon Rations, being supposed to have the latter.

I see that Dr. Taylor has slightly misapprehended the transaction in some respects, the Sisters having repeated to me the statement made by me to the Purveyor. It is not, however, worth wasting with further explanation either your time, Dr. Taylor's or my own.

I have only to express my regret to & even to entreat the forgiveness of the three Medical Officers, whose time has been so unwarrantably occupied in both purveying for us & in answering for a failure in purveying, obviously not their business (& which they gave so much trouble to remedy) & tending, I fear, to depopularize the Nurses with them.

I wish the subject to be now dropped – only repeating that my whole reason for ever taking it up was that which I have already stated viz. that no ground should be left for any farther "Reports" as to extravagance of Nurses, repudiated, it is true, by the War Department, but which might be revived & founded upon a false idea that Rations, which never had come, had been drawn, besides Requisitions.

> I beg to remain
> dear Sir
> yours faithfully

B.L. Add. Ms. 39867, f. 139 (*Cal.* omitted).

While Sir John Hall was determined to behave rigidly correctly, while at the same yielding nothing beyond what was necessary to fulfil the terms of the General Orders, there can be little doubt that Fitzgerald, championing his chief against Miss Nightingale's pretensions, deliberately set out to be as obstructive as he could. His note to Sir John of 17th April amply substantiates Miss Nightingale's belief in his malice:

Private
My dear Sir John
It is opportune that Miss N— has given us no opportunity of refuting the charge of starving Nurses; – if Dr. Taylor – and the Officers under him will be sharp – they will fix any blame attaching to the transaction in the Commissariat, who I am informed, refused to issue to Nurses; – of course I have only hearsay – but it is with the Land Transport Authorities to adduce proofs; I wrote a sharp letter to the Hosp*ls*. pointing out the duty of the Commissariat to comply with any Requisition furnished from the Hospitals, for which the Officer signing solely became responsible.
Dr. Taylor will now taste the first fruits of his Nurse system.[22]

Miss Nightingale was not the only person to have found Fitzgerald difficult to deal with. Mother Bridgeman, after initial difficulties, had succeeded in winning his allegiance. But Dr Beatson had felt compelled to forbid him to "interfere" with the running of the hospital, and ordered the attendants not "to receive orders from Mr. Fitzgerald with regard to the internal arrangements of the Hospital."[23] In a more serious episode Dr Mouat actually had him arrested, and complained to Sir John Hall:

Mr. Fitzgerald acts in a double capacity – sometimes he issues as a purveyor at others he retires upon his independent position as Dy. Purveyor in Chief just as suits his caprice – or as he considers his dignity compromised . . .
This kind of independent authority . . . must be fraught with inconvenience & delay – more particularly with a man like Mr. Fitzgerald – who even presumes to question the validity or authority of a requisition because a word is spelt differently from the accepted mode – altho' I do not consider him a competent philologist to

decide such a point – much less to make impertinent comments thereon.

I think were I to refuse to comply with an order from you, the Adj*t*. Gen*l*. or chief of the Staff because either in the hurry of business – a signature had been omitted or a word spelt wrong – such conduct would only be viewed as Contumacious or disrespectful.

After securing Fitzgerald's apology to Dr Mouat, Sir John recommended that he be released and return to his duty.[24]

Whatever the truth behind this tangle of cross-purposes, failures of communication and doubtful motives, the affair caused Miss Nightingale to react with fury when Sidney Herbert's reproof of 6th March caught up with her in the thick of it all, at a time when she was physically and emotionally exhausted.

To Sidney Herbert

Crimea
3rd April 1856

Dear Mr. Herbert

I received your letter of March 6 yesterday.

It is written from Belgrave Square. I write from a Crimean Hut. The point of sight is different.

I arrived here March 24 with Nurses for two Land Transport Hospitals "required" by Dr. Hall in writing on March 10, but owing to the severe gales of wind, the Transport could not get up the Bosphorus, & our arrival was therefore delayed – tho' announced by return of Mail.

We have now been ten days without rations.

Lord Cardigan was surprised to find his horses die at the end of a fortnight because they were without rations & said that they "chose" to do it obstinate brutes!

The Inspector General & Purveyor wish to see whether women can live as long as horses without rations.

I thank God – my charge has felt neither cold nor hunger, & is in efficient working order – having cooked & administered in both Hospitals the whole of the Extras for 260 bad cases ever since the first day of their arrival.

I have, however, felt both. I do not wish to make a martyr of myself; within sight of the graves of the Crimean Army of last winter (too soon forgotten in England) it would be difficult to do so. I am glad to have had the experience. For cold & hunger wonderfully sharpen the wits. But I believe that it is difficult to those who never, by any possibility, can have imagined either, (except by the side of a good fire & a good dinner which they will have every day of their lives) to imagine what is the anxiety of being responsible for the lives & healths *and the efficiency* (for the sake of the lives & healths of those we are come to nurse) of those placed under one's charge when the means to feed & warm them have all to be obtained by irregular & private channels. During these ten days, I have fed &

warmed these women at my own private expense by my own private exertions. I have never been off my horse till 9 or 10 at night, except when it was too dark to walk him over these crags even with a Lantern when I have gone on foot. During the greater part of the day, I have been without food necessarily, except a little brandy & water (you see I am taking to drinking like my comrades of the Army). The snow is deep on the ground. But the object of my coming has been attained, & my women have neither starved nor suffered.

I might have written to the Commander of the Forces, who came to see me the day after my arrival. But this would only have marred our work by making a quarrel.

I might have accepted presents which were poured in upon us, – for all, Military, Medical, Clerical in the Land Transport are our sworn friends. But this would be against a rule which I have been obliged to make so strict that nothing but sheer necessity would induce me to break it.

I might have drawn upon the Extras for the Patients. But then the whole would have gone into the Account of *Nurses* Expenditure as their extravagance.

I believed it, on the whole, best for our work to do as I have done, notwithstanding the urgent pressure upon me from others to adopt one of these courses. But I do not think that that work can be said, pursued thus, to have been pursued in a "vehement or irritable spirit."

I received your letter at 10 o'clock p.m. on my return to our hut upon a pitch-dark snowy night after having been 15 hours on foot or on horse back & almost without food.

I confess it cost me a sleepless night thinking over within myself, Have I injured the work by showing "vehemence or irritation", by not bearing persecution, moral & physical, rather than not complain, except when the very existence of the work itself was perilled?

I thought & considered. And I determined I had not. I think I can prove my assertion.

About this matter of the rations, foreseen to a certain extent by me, so that I had brought up with me from Scutari, every article for cooking, furnishing, warming the huts, even stoves, & every article of food that would keep –

every formality not only of routine but of politeness had been observed by me – within 24 hours of my arrival, the rations had been settled by me in person (after having been "required" in writing from Scutari) with the P.M.O. of the Land Transport in the office of the Deputy Purveyor in Chief Fitzgerald – had received the approval of Inspector General of Hospitals – & by a curious coincidence of the Commander of the Forces from his calling upon me while in the Purveyor's office. Every form was observed there & then. Both the Purveyor's Clerks, both the Medical Officers in charge at the two Land Transport Hospitals were visited by me, distant some miles from

Balaclava & not together, in company with Dr. Taylor, the P.M.O. Every form was there strictly observed. The rations were to begin from the day before. Every day since, I have ridden some miles, or walked, in the severest weather, with driving storms of sleet & snow, to see the Purveyor in his office on these businesses. I have never brought him a yard out of his office on my business. I have never "prévaloir"d myself, even on my quality of woman, to avoid hardship or fatigue, or allow him to say that I had entailed either on him. Never, by word or look, can he have detected that I know how he had slandered us.

Why do I give you this long detail, you will ask, which can be of no use.

It is not because I ask you to do anything. It is merely because I wish to leave on record some instance of that which nobody in England will believe or can even imagine. But we in the Crimea know it. And we know, & knew at the time, *what* filled the Crimean graves last winter. K.C.B., I believe, now means Knight of the Crimean Burying Grounds.[25]

As I stood yesterday on the Heights of Balaclava, & saw our Ships in the Harbour, so gaily dressed with flags, while we fired the salute in honor of peace, (it was a beautiful sight), I said to myself, more Aireys, more Filders, more Cardigans, more Halls — we are in for them all now — & no hope of reform.

Believe me when I say that everything in the Army (in point of routine versus system) is just where it was eighteen months ago. The only difference is that we are now rolling in stores. But indeed we were so then — only most of them were at Varna.

"Nous n'avons rien oublié ni rien appris."

2. Those who say that there is a "Popish Plot" are quite mistaken. It is not a Popish plot, but a split of the R. Catholics against themselves.

Of all the Oriental mysteries which I have been made acquainted with since I have been in the East, this has been not the least curious.

The seculars are divided against the regulars. This we have often seen before but never so much as now.

But, as the Old Whig families are said always to have a Tory heir apparent, in order to be "in" both ways, so the R. Catholics have one set of priests & nuns *with* the Govt. & one *against* it.

Mrs. Bridgeman & the Jesuits are against, the secular priests & Bermondsey Nuns for.

Mrs. Bridgeman & her 11 Irish Nuns have been instructed to resign & go home & make themselves Martyrs, which they will do, I am afraid, on Saturday — tho' I have piped to her & done the Circe in vain.

The Revd. Mr. Duffy, Jesuit, has been instructed to refuse Confession & therefore Holy Communion to, or even to visit those Bermondsey Nuns, whom I brought up with me from Scutari to one of the Land Transport Hospitals, & he calls them, among other epithets, in a note to themselves, a "disgrace to their Church." For none can be so coarse as a R.C. priest. This note we have forwarded to Dr. Grant, Bp. of Southwark, for approval.

Cardinal Wiseman has recalled the Revd. Mr. Unsworth, Senior R.C. Chaplain here, who always took part against the Jesuits & Irish Nuns "under these circumstances".

On the other hand, the secular priests repudiate the Irish Nuns, & do the civil by the Gov*t*. & me & the Bermondsey Nuns with principle & interest – & even Father Cuffe, who used to call me "Herod", now licks my hand, as the Provost Marshal says, "like a good 'un".

Irish "Regulars" are little else than "Rebels" as has truly been said here.

Such are a few of the premises. You say that the English like to draw their own inferences. Here they have done it already. And here Deputy Purveyor in Chief Fitzgerald is supposed to be the tool of the Jesuits & the Irish Nuns.

The "Confidential Report" is not a secret to anyone here.

3. You say this is but one bud of the bed of roses upon which Secretaries of State are wont to lie. I have just seen enough of Gov*t*. to know what that bed must be. But, till Secretaries of State have known what it is to have the reputations of their wives & daughters slandered, for party purposes, till you have known what it is to be uncertain for many days where you should get food or warmth for those*beautiful children who are standing round your table, & to feel that grinding anxiety for the responsibility of the lives and healths of those under your charge, & to doubt whether you are not sacrificing them, in your turn, to considerations for the good of the work, I deny that you can cull one bud from my bed of roses, or even imagine its fragrance afar off. Had I told but half the truth in my answer to Mr. Fitzgerald, you would have said, What a fool she was not to make her complaint before!

But no one in England has yet *realized* the graves of Scutari or the Crimea – or their causes.

4. I deprecate most earnestly your judgment that "the highest proof of success is when a mission is carried thro' without producing attack" as being against all experience & all history from the sacred history down to the fable of the "Wolf & the lamb," which was the incarnation of a pretty wise experience too. I beseech you to re-consider your opinion. I am not a lamb – far from it. But I have been a lambkin in many instances & principally in one, & yet have not "avoided attack."

I know that yours is the principle of most government now, & that to steer clear of "attack" & to promote & praise both sides, if possible is its theory. But I do not see that it succeeds even in averting attack. A *"quarrel"* always, it is true, vulgarizes both sides. (Witness Sir J. Graham & Napier). But I don't see that the lamb could help the *attack*. If Joan of Arc had been said to have had a "quarrel" with the D. of Bedford, or the lamb with the wolf, it would have been a misapplication of the word.

*My poor nurses are not "beautiful" *Bien s'en faut*. But they are not less my charge.

247

I will give one "instance". In all the Hospitals of our Army which I have seen where women have not been, the Doctors go round so late* that the Diet Rolls cannot be made out in time for the men to have their dinners before 3 or 4, & their Extras before 5 or 6 o'clock. It was (*partly*) on this account that I have insisted so strenuously on our Extra Diet Kitchens. The Drs. do not like sending their Diet Rolls in to us late – & the men always get consequently their Extras at 12 & their dinners at 1 from our Kitchens – making the difference for a weakly man between waiting for his Beef Tea from 8 A.M. till 4 or 5 P.M. – & waiting till 12 or 1 P.M. – I have never, in one single instance, got in my Diet Rolls except as a "lamb", never reported a Medical Officer for being late, but I know the Medical Officers have opposed our Extra Diet Kitchens in many instances like "wolves", on this account, tho' no single case can be found against us of having given any thing but upon Diet Roll – to patients. Yet this is the ground alleged against us.

5. You may well say that Sir John McNeill's Report is the model of a Report. It is indeed – accurate, lucid, cool & conscientious. But had Sir J. McNeill made nothing but a Report, he would have done little. But he put his hand to the plough & did much out here. So did Col. Tulloch.

It still remains to be seen whether his *Report* will do *anything*. Hitherto nothing has been done but to promote those reported on – to make Ld. Panmure say "I am very sorry, but I did not know that these men had been promoted" – to make Ld. Hardinge[26] say, "I am very sorry. I did hear that the Army had suffered. But I did not know that their sufferings had been at all attributed to these men."

In 6 months, all these sufferings will be forgotten. And I *indeed* agree with you that, in the presence of that colossal calamity & of the national disgrace of promoting the author of it, the promotion of that petty offender, Mr. Fitzgerald, tho' in some respects, his offences are not petty, (for none dare offend him, because he can starve any Hospital in the Crimea, & leave, as he recently did, 130 typhus fever cases for 24 hours without wine,) but compared with our other disgraces, *his* promotion sinks into the shade – and I feel more shame than will ever crimson his face at having but mentioned it.

Oh! Lord Stratford – Oh! Kars.[27] And now, what do I want?

Not that you should do anything, not ten thousand times *not*, that you should alter your opinion about the Ho. of Commons, still less that you should alter your opinion of me – (though I own I am anxious that you should not prejudge a work because it has been "attacked" – anxious too to believe that I have not injured the work).

But all I wish is to leave some record of what will not be believed in the homes of London a twelve month hence – of what, tho' a trifling instance, is a true example of what ruined our Army.

*notwithstanding the Queen's Regulation

Believe me, dear Mr. Herbert, (and if I have used some strong expressions, let me say that there is no more comparison between Sir J. McNeill's case & mine than between the calm review of a historian of the causes of a war, & the officer in the heat of battle providing for his men's safety,)

believe me very truly yours

B.L. Add. Ms. 43393, f. 224 (*Cal.* F. 4. F14, 250).

When writing to the Rev. Mother Bermondsey on 10th April, however, Miss Nightingale gave little or no hint of her great difficulties and anxieties. She mentioned, in passing, much "Ration" and other business: otherwise the letter seemed imbued with the calm serenity that she always assumed in her correspondence with the Rev. Mother. Her greatest concern at the moment of writing was with the Rev. Mother's own health.

To Reverend Mother Bermondsey

Balaclava
10th April 1856

My dearest Revd. Mother,

Many, many thanks for your three letters – all of which I received last night. The mails are late & irregular.

I am afraid that I have written very hastily & not very perspicuously, a great fault in a Sup*t*. But I assure you that my letters have been the result of thought, not hasty but anxious thought.

The great distance of the hospitals from each other in the Crimea, & having to settle much "Ration" & other business with officials, converts her Holiness[28] into a tramp & makes her "rescripts" scrawls.

But first – about your dear health, which must be the most anxious thing to us at present.

I can easily understand & I am afraid cannot remove the reasons which would prevent your going to Malta. At the same time, I do earnestly hope that you will go, if possible. And I hope that you do not think that you would be allowed to go at the charges of your Community. General Storks will give you passages. And I enclose a Cheque for £100, which any house at Malta would cash. Dr. Trench, whom Sister Gonzaga [29] will remember at the Gen*l*. Hosp*l*. at Scutari, has *asked* to take charge of any of us going to or at Malta and he will meet you on board the vessel, & provide for you medically & comfortably – Dr. Cruikshank will know he is at Malta now, & will write to him before you go – that you may be comfortably put up on arriving. I hope that you may also know Catholics there.

Dear Revd. Mother, I hope that, whatever you determine upon, you will do no work at Scutari. A slight imprudence might have such consequences. I have begged my Aunt to let me know if you begin to work, or to do anything imprudent. And, if you do, you know I must come back. Your life is the most precious thing we have, both for the work's sake & for the Community, & to peril it for the sake of C Store or for any Store would break our hearts.

Mr. Wills will take C Store for the present.

The Linen Divisional Store Miss Morton will take, with such help as we have planned.

Sister Gonzaga will keep the Extra Diets till you go to Malta, if you go, or till you come to the Crimea. But that must not be yet – Balaclava would not suit you yet. Pray do not do the Extras yourself. Miss Morton will take them, when Sister Gonzaga leaves with you.

And all these arrangements will be understood to be but temporary, while you & I are away. And the bustle of moving 70,000 men makes the Hospitals uncertainly full or suddenly empty.

I cannot decide quite at present about another Nurse from Scutari – tho' I fear we shall have to make some changes. But we shall be truly thankful for the three Sisters, whenever they come. Mrs. Bridgeman and my Birds are not yet flown from Balaclava. So that I shall have the consolation, I hope, of not separating the Sisters at the L.T.C. Mrs. Roberts, Mrs. Logan & I shall go in with the three sisters from Scutari. You will direct which is to be "Revd. Mother."

The Sisters are well & cheerful at the L.T.C. & very busy. Sister M. Martha has a slight cold but nothing more. And as, at the other wing, Sister Stanislaus taxed me with saying that Mrs. Skinner "gives in", & that Mrs. Holmes "has an affection of the heart," she wishes to know which malady I think that Sister M. Martha has. They have never seemed to take their troubles to heart. And I believe Sister M. Helen & I are the most anxious ones.

On the 20th, the Commander in Chief expects to have his Orders – & I think we shall then be able to make some kind of plan – & to know whether it will be desirable to give more Sisters from Bermondsey the trouble of coming out. I only wished to prepare you for the possibility of its being asked, & misexpressed myself if I implied it as desirable to write off directly.

I saw however the Director General of the L.T.C.[30] yesterday, & his opinion was (but it is only an opinion) that we shall be 5 months moving out of the Crimea – & the L.T.C. Hospitals & the Gen*l*. Hosp*l*. at Balaclava will be kept up last of all. But all this will depend, of course, upon conditions of which we know nothing as yet. It may be that we shall be out of the Crimea before you & S. Gonzaga will have time to come to us.

Believe me
ever my dearest Revd. Mother's
grateful & affecte.

Convent of Our Lady of Mercy, Bermondsey; copy, Wellcome (*Cal.* B. 4. G2, 256).

Five days later Miss Nightingale wrote to reassure Rev. Mother of the safe arrival of three additional nuns[31] from Scutari, and to explain in great

Men dining in F corridor. Water-colour sketch by Anne Morton in spring 1856

The linen store. Water-colour sketch by Anne Morton in spring 1856

detail how and why she had placed the Sisters as she had. This consideration for Rev. Mother Bermondsey's anxiety for her nuns was in marked contrast to her virtual refusal to acknowledge the obligation Mother Bridgeman felt towards her charges.

To Reverend Mother Bermondsey

General Hospital
Balaclava
15th April 1856

My dearest Revd. Mother,

I had the comfort of receiving our Sisters quite well & safe on Sunday afternoon as they will tell you. And we have arranged thus – Sister Mary Joseph went yesterday to join Sister M. Helen at the L.T.C. Hospital. Sisters M. Stanislaus, M. de Chantal, and M. Anastasia stay here doing work. Sister M. Martha is, I am sorry to say, at present laid up here with feverish cold. As soon as she is able, she will join Sister M. Helen. I am not sorry that her illness (or rather unwellness) should be here, as we have greater facilities of nursing her. And the Dr. is such a clever one.

I am afraid that you would rather have mixed the two parties of Sisters, so that the recent ones should not be all together at one Hospital. I see the objection myself. But my reason was this. Everything we do at Karani is right – everything we do here is wrong. Sister Stanislaus is very brave & has already charge of the Extra Diets here which are very disorderly, & which you will manage so beautifully, if you come. Sister Anastasia is such a very steady quiet worker. She has seven sick Huts – & Sister de Chantal is commanding & courageous & not easily daunted. Of course whatever we do will be blamed. I do not mean that the recent Sisters would be less likely to go on with their duty steadily, with a single eye to God, although evil eyes are all around them. But it requires very good spirits to bear being always misconstrued without being a little depressed. And these old Sisters are very cheerful & used to be "abused"!

Mrs. Roberts & I, Mrs. Logan & Mrs. Skinner are also here. We sleep in one half a Hut & our sick Sister in the other half. The three other Sisters in the next hut. We have hardly had time to make any arrangements yet for ourselves.

I hope that you will not think of coming up here for three weeks at least. Thank God you are better! Perhaps it will do you good. But there will be time to talk of that.

Ever my dearest Revd. Mother's
grateful & affecte.

Convent of our Lady of Mercy, Bermondsey; copy, Wellcome (*Cal.* B. 4. G2, 258).

To Uncle Sam, two days later, Florence revived briefly the memory of the "ten days" without rations; and added a horrifying description of the state of the General Hospital and its patients when she moved in.

To Uncle Sam Smith

Balaclava, General Hospital
17th April 1856

Dear Uncle Sam

I enclose the 2nd half of the Treasury Bill, indorsed by me.

I am very sorry that you should have had so much trouble with it. The former Treasury Bills which I sent were indorsed by General Storks – & when I had leave to draw Treasury Bills on my own account, I said to the Commissariat Officer "I suppose I must indorse these". No he said, there is no occasion. I was sure he was wrong. But we are not allowed in the Army to know better than our Officers, be they Military, Medical or Commissariat. And therefore I can only hope that you have not had very much trouble extra, & that you will not think the worse of my habits of business.

Thank you very much for your letters. I have not time now to reply at length. Suffice it to say that, now, at the eleventh hour, peace concluded, flags flying, Army supposed to be next door to perfection, I have had a three week's bout in the Crimea worse than anything we have had since November/54.

On our first arrival here last month, we were ten days without rations by Mr. Fitzgerald's malice. When I moved in *here*, the day of Mrs. Bridgeman's departure, Sir John Hall gave the nurses' huts over my head to Purveyors' Clerks. I sat down before the door, it being then dusk, & said quietly that I should stay there till the keys were brought – in about two hours they were produced. Every day for the last week it has been a repetition of the same thing – a contest for the Stores for the Patients, for food, lodgings, "leave to toil" for ourselves.

Your pig sty is cleaner than our Quarters or than the wards of the Hospital, as left by Mrs. Bridgeman. The patients were grimed with dirt, infested with vermin, with bedsores like Lazarus, (Mrs. Bridgeman, I suppose, thought it holy). I have never seen but one similar scene to it. Mrs. Roberts & the Scutari Nuns whom I brought with me were horrified. After two days hard white washing, & cleaning – after three days washing & dressing the Patients, one of whom takes Mrs. Roberts 6 hours daily – being one mass of bed sores – Sir John Hall visited the Hospital and – wrote an angry letter, saying that he was "disgusted with the state of the Hospital" & "ordered it all to be put back into the admirable order it was in previously" — instructing the Principal Medical Officer of the Hospital, who shewed me the letter, "not to interfere with the Purveyor, Mr. Fitzgerald's, arrangements".

This is the man on whom the lives & healths of the Army in a great measure, depend (For he is clever & this is all temper).

ever yours faithfully & gratefully

B.L. Add. Ms. 45792, f. 28 (*Cal.* B. 4. G2, 259).

Two years later when Florence Nightingale's point of view was triumphantly embodied in the *Report of the Royal Commission on the sanitary state of the*

Army the Rev. Mother Bridgeman wrote to Sir John Hall, now in retirement, commenting on this case. Her description provides an interesting commentary on Florence Nightingale's account, and gives, besides, a rare and fascinating glimpse of the details of nursing in the Crimea.

The frost-bitten patient McDonald was not able to leave his bed from the time he entered hospital, a period of some months I think. It is not true that the bed sores on his back had remained undiscoverd . . .

For a considerable time after McDonald's admission his wounds were dressed twice a day. After he had become so diseased and so miserably irritable, Dr. Murray considered any advantage that might result from the second daily dressing should be more than counterbalanced by the irritation and torture that always resulted; so latterly he was dressed but once a day. The daily dressing used to be regularly done, generally under the superintendence of the Medical Officer.

Probably it is not necessary for me to tell you that it was not by any of us that McDonald's wounds were dressed.

While I was in Scutari under Miss Nightingale in January '55, an order was issued forbidding any nurse to dress wounds, as this was considered to belong entirely to the surgeons and their appointed dressers. From that time on we never opened or dressed any wound without the express permission of the surgeon in charge. The Medical Officers never deputed to us the charge of McDonald's dressings; therefore we never did attempt them . . . Drs. Huish and Murray together usually examined this poor sufferer's wounds, and it is our conviction that he received the kindest and most considerate care and attention. His every wish and even fancy used to be complied with if at all possible.

It is quite true that McDonald's *bed* had not been changed for a week (and this is one of the many cases in which a truth may be forced to the work of a falsehood). The Sister who nursed him says she believes it was nearly a fortnight before we left since his *bed* had been dressed, and that the intervals between the changes before that had often been longer, but the inference those unacquainted with nursing should naturally draw from this does not really follow.

Every nurse knows that there are means which prevent the necessity of frequent changes of the *beds* of helpless patients, which are used when those changes are productive of great suffering or exhaustion . . .

At length it was effected under Miss Nightingale's own superintendence. This was the last time, and was about ten or twelve days before we left Balaclava on 12 April.

I can well believe that between the doctor's visits on two successive days, a patient in poor McDonald's state might be neglected by the orderlies and get into a condition which could not bear description; but I did not know before that any nurse however clever, might put a patient through the ordeal described by Mrs. Roberts without the express consent of the surgeon in whose charge he was . . .

P.S. Do you know how long McDonald survived Mrs. Roberts' dressings? Clever indeed must she be if she could make him comfortable. I believe the Rev. Mr. Parker, perhaps Mr. Crosier too, must remember the case. Both were Church of England Chaplains and they seemed much pleased with the state of the hospital.[32]

Dr. Murray, in his evidence before the Royal Commission, also denied that McDonald suffered from any neglect, and asserted:

That we did not consider it advisable that he should be put to the amount of suffering caused by having his bed changed daily; and that in this case, as in all others requiring great attention, we found Mrs. Bridgeman and *her* Irish nurses quite equal to Miss Nightingale and *her* nurses, and much more willing to be guided by the wishes of the medical officer. That the charge of neglect is utterly false and unfounded.

He went on to condemn the evidence of the Nightingale party:

I may be permitted to express my astonishment that the Commissioners should have allowed such uncontradicted statements to go before the public, when an examination of Sir John Hall, Mr. Deputy-Purveyor-in-Chief Fitzgerald, and other officers connected with the hospital would have shown how much such statements were exaggerated and biassed.[33]

Somewhat strangely, Florence barely mentioned these trials in her letter to Parthe of 19th April; rather she ends on a note of quiet triumph.

To Parthenope

General Hospital, Balaclava
19th April 1856

My dearest – As I sit in my den, opposite the Surgery Door, watching the Extra Diets from my window, and the thick forest of masts over the Extra Diet Kitchen's felted & white washed roof in Balaclava Harbour, with a beautiful tuft of primroses on my table gathered for me by a man of the 39*th*, I think of thee on this thy birth-day & think how likely it is that the birth-day may soon come which will see both of us pursuing the work of God in another of His worlds, – some natural tears I drop, but there is nothing to me melancholy in the thought. I think of all the real love there has been between us which is eternal – & how curiously your aspirations for me have been realized, even to the roc's egg.

The last tug of war has been the worst, these last four weeks in the Crimea. But we have now *five** Hospitals under our care in this Crim Tartary in beautiful order. And if I could think that the tug of war would continue, that would be the best hearing for me, for that alone would bring reform.

ever yours faithfully
in war & in peace
in the active & the passive

*Castle Hospital   under Sister Bertha[34]
  Monastery   "   "   Miss Wear
  Two Land Transports   "   Mrs. Shaw Stewart
       "   Karanyi   "   Sister Helen R.C.
  General Hospital B'clava   "   me

Is it not curious that we should begin to be acknowledged now at the eleventh hour, so that now they cannot form a new or a miserable Hospital without sending for us, & extending what Mrs. Shaw Stewart calls my "sad but noble domain" or servitude, it matters not which, all at once so much. For this was before the General Order.

Claydon; copy, Wellcome (*Cal.* B. 4. G3, 261).

With her position at last consolidated and "7 Hospitals under my charge," as she wrote to Colonel Lefroy, she again had time to revert to questions of wider reform, this time the victualling and cooking for the military hospitals.

To Colonel Lefroy

> General Hospital
> Balaclava
> 22nd April 1856

My dear Sir

In reply to your kind letter of April 1 I have many things to say but no time to say them in.

I must, however, make time to say something about the fact which you state viz. that the average consumption of the main articles of diet in the Crimean Hospitals in the quarter ending 31 Dec. exceeds 3 lbs. per man per day.

I am very sorry that you did not examine me on this important point, because I think that there is perhaps no one now here, who could have given you more information – both because I am now the oldest inhabitant in the largest Hospitals in the world, because it is already 18 months since I established my first Extra Diet Kitchen, which system has been gradually extended to every one of the 7 Hospitals now under my charge & because diets are peculiarly the province of a Nurse.

I have now no Returns before me – nothing to refer to. But I should be most happy to make any cooking experiments, or supply any tables for the information of the War Department.

In explanation of the fact which excited your surprise, I should like to make 5 observations, which I would support by any evidence which may be of use to you.

1. In England, when bone, offal, the useless parts of meat, are removed, it loses about from 1/6 to 1/5 of its weight.

In the Crimea & Scutari, when the bone, offal & useless parts of the meat are removed, & the meat cooked, (owing to the small quantity of moisture in it & other causes which I cannot now stop to enumerate), the meat loses from 4/5 to 5/6 of its weight – so that your Patient, even were he ordered 3 lbs. Meat for his 3 lbs. solid food, might receive about ½ lb. This is the experience of all my kitchens & this the *main* cause of the fact which surprises you.

2. All acute cases & generally, all cases which, as a Nurse well knows, can seldom touch bread, are put upon Spoon Diet. Spoon Diet includes 8 oz. Bread. This does not appear much. And there are Convalescent Cases, who are put upon Spoon Diet for the sake of the Extras, for whom Extra Bread even is drawn. But, generally, Spoon Diet having been constructed for the sake of appending Extras to it, Spoon Diet Patients do not eat bread.

At the time of our great pressure at Scutari, I will calculate the Spoon Diets at 1000, all Dysenteric & Frost-bitten cases – & the average of their consumption of bread at 2 oz. which I consider to be an outside calculation. There were therefore 6000 oz. bread wasted daily, at a time that we were told the Purveyor could not take upon himself to incur any expence whatever for the Hospital & that all our stores were at Varna. This bread was given, when stale, to the Patients who could eat it, but more frequently to the Turks about the place, a whole population of whom we thus fed. It may have been a very good thing to feed the poor Turks, but it should not be set down as consumed by Patients.

Of all the features of the Hospitals of /54 most conspicuous, at the time of our greatest penury, was our waste.

The above things were obvious to the meanest capacity and our 1st Class Staff Surgeons are men of no mean capacity at all. But when a man is obliged to walk about his wards, looking not at his Patients, but at "Regulations for the Management of Army Hospitals, at home *& abroad*, & for the rendering of Hospital Accounts; with an Appendix of Forms etc.", the result is obvious.

Let no one suppose that I under-value that invaluable work. I went into Dr. Sutherland's hut the other day & found him reading "Troilus & Cressida". As, for 18 months, I was unaware that British literature embraced any other work than "Regulations for the Management etc. & for the rendering etc., also, instructions to etc. with an appendix etc." (& I can truly say that without that work, I should have ceased to read or to spell,) I can scarcely be said to undervalue it.

3. A Spoon Diet is generally put down for 1 pint Arrow Root A.M.

1   "   "   "   P.M.

which pint, whether of Arrow Root or of Sago, is constructed by the "Regulations" Book of 2 oz. of the same.

Now 1 oz. Arrow Root makes, by experiment, 1 pt. thick Arrow Root as daily exemplified in all my Kitchens, where I allow no more – 2 oz. Arrow Root in the *General* Kitchens make 1 pint thin Arrow Root – *so* thin that the men will not drink it. Part of this is attributable to certain conundrums which regard boiling water – but not all. Where that Arrow Root goes is a conundrum which has never yet been guessed by me.

In the same way, 2 oz. Rice are saved upon every 4 puddings, with us. As to Sugar, tapioca, barley, sago, etc. etc. from all these, there is the same proportionate saving. Each day in our Kitchens, the overplus is put up in a covered vessel. Savings returned into Purveyor's Stores end of month. Thus Diet Rolls are paramount & yet the Queen not robbed.

But is the Queen not robbed? We can prevent the excess of Arrow Root etc. being wasted. But we cannot prevent the Purveyor from issuing the last month's savings for the next month as a *fresh* issue. And little items of this kind will go far to swell out your "3 lbs."

We have tried to obviate this in 3 ways.

(1)   by drawing in bulk for the materials to answer Diet Rolls – this system the 1st Class Staff Surgeons prefer. But we were obliged to discontinue it for two reasons – one that we were ordered to draw *according to "Regulations" Book* by our supreme master – the other that, to punish us for not having done so, that which had been so drawn in bulk was set down to our own consumption.

(2)   We have followed the System above explained, of drawing the Quantity prescribed in "Regulations" Book & returning the surplus. But this is then charged as two issues for this month & the next. For the accounts must tally with the "Regulations" Book.

Certainly, this "Regulations" Book was written by a very clever man, but he was no cook.

(3)   a most laborious plan, but which I am now pursuing here. I make the 1st Class Staff Surgeon draw in bulk for my Extra Diet Kitchen. I throw all my own private stores into the same. And I account each night to the Purveyor for whatever I have thus drawn, out of the two above sources, to answer the Diet Roll.

(4)   A large amount of waste is incurred by the Extra Diets being ordered for the next day, as they are in some but not in all the Army Hospitals.

A patient dies, is discharged, or undergoes one of the manifold changes of acute disease which certainly alters his mode of treatment. But still his Extras *are to be drawn* – when once on the Diet Roll, or, even if not drawn, they are set down. At the rate at which we died & discharged, the Extras thus drawn but not eaten must have gone far to swell your "3 lbs."

(5)   Waste there must essentially be in every sick-room. The Patient tastes his chicken-broth to-day, to-morrow he takes his pint. But the waste in a Military Hospital can scarcely be calculated. And here it is that *we* might be so useful, where permitted. *A* ought to have a table-spoonful of Beef Tea or Arrow Root & Wine every half hour. But his mess of two pints or perhaps the *whole* of his Extras is put down at his bed-head *at once* – & the whole is consequently wasted or stolen.

I do not make any comment or suggestions upon the above five heads, which it must be left to Medical Officers to do. But I think they will throw some light upon your curious fact, which, as you say, is staggering.

At the Castle Hospital, you say there were 70 bottles of malt liquor per day to each 100 diets. But this is hardly 1 pint per diet. Those bottles holding hardly 1½ pts. (one of those bottles is the allowance per diem to a woman). The men prefer their Malt Liquor to their wine & it is better for them.

One thing more; – I believe, if the Spoon Diets were allowed 4 oz. Bread & 1/4 oz. Butter with it, that actually more bread would go down the man's throat than with his 8 oz. This, however, is a point for Medical Officers & not for me to decide. But no one ever saw acute disease eating dry bread yet – at least, of the kinds we have had here.

Now, if we subtract

6 oz bread	from 8 oz.
2 oz. Arrow Root	from 4 oz.
12 oz. Mutton	from 16 oz.
20 oz.	28 oz.

it is a large subtraction, being what the man does not eat or what the cooking takes away.

"Nineteenthly" – The Diets & Medicines are prescribed, not by the heads of the profession who have no time to do what they are there for, being wholly taken up by Returns, but by the youngest & most inexperienced members of the profession. The head of the most important Hospital in the world told me himself that he did not know his way about his own Hospital.

I infer from this that the Extras are often heterogeneous, excessive & capricious. I could give instances of a composition of Extras which a trusty old Nurse (not a "Gamp") would not incur the risk of administering.

But, generally, I repeat that it maybe deduced from the above facts that, though 3 lbs. may bave been upon the Diet Rolls, ½ lb. was more nearly what actually went down a man's throat – & that the fault did not lie in the Doctors.

I have much more to say, & I would willingly take the trouble to furnish information & make experiments to prove what I say. I do not know whether I have hit upon the main points of what has struck you as unaccountable. I should be glad to answer any questions I am able.

C.J. Fox said, "No, don't read me history. For that I *know* is false."

I have learnt to say, No, don't shew me Returns. For those I know (are *not* false, but) give a false impression.

Believe me to be dear Sir
Yours faithfully

If it should be said, Yes, but supposing it be true what you say about Fresh Meat losing weight, there remain the Preserved Meats to account for – I would answer that it has often happened to us to find a 3 lb. tin of Preserved Meat to contain exactly 1½ lbs in weight, & to make up the difference, so as to answer the Diet Roll from our own Stores. But this would, of course, only be done in our Kitchens. And I mention it only to shew how deceptive returns may be. And many a Surgeon I have known reprimanded for extravagance in Extras, who has chosen to do his patients justice in spite of it, or who, horror of horrors! has drawn the difference privately out of our private stores. But this would bring him into trouble.

I have lately been shewn some returns, placing the daily expence of each Patient at the Civil Hospitals, Renkioi & Smyrna, (including Doctoring etc.) at 4/- & a fraction – that of each Patient at some of our Military Hospitals here at 1/-. Regimental Hospitals, if the stoppage were placed at /9, as self-supporting. Is this so?

Allow me to observe that, in re. "Troilus & Cressida", I was not reflecting on Dr. Sutherland. He had been 7 hours on horseback about the Camp that day, & he turned up "Troilus & Cressida" for a very curious purpose, viz. to find the passage in which Thersites mentions boils as being common at the siege of Troy, our own men suffering very much from the same affection. For Shakespeare, as an acute observer, had no doubt met with the allusion in some book he had read.

I was only reflecting on the power of reading surviving a Crimean imbroglio. But Dr. Sutherland has not had 18 months of it as I have.

N.B. I have had a second & even a third Edition of Mr. Fitzgerald & his "Confidential" proceedings since I have been up here this time. But sad experience makes me "up to" these things now. You do not do me justice.

Wellcome (*Cal.* B. 4. G4, 264).

Rats figured largely in everybody's consciousness in the Crimea.

To Parthenope

Crimea
22nd April 1856

Would not you like to see me hunting rats like a terrier-dog? Me!
Scene in a Crimean Hut
Time midnight
Dramatis Personae –
Sick Nun in fever perfectly deaf
me the only other occupant of the hut
except
rat sitting on rafter over sick nun's head
& rats scrambling about.
Enter me, with a lantern in one hand & a broom-stick in the other (in the Crimea, terrier dogs hunt with lanterns in one paw & broom-sticks)

me, commonly called "Pope" by the Nuns, makes ye furious Balaclava charge. i.e. the light cavalry come on & I am the Russian gun.

Light cavalry ensconces itself among my beloved boots & squeak – Desperate Papal aggression.

Broom-stick descends – enemy dead – "Pope" executes savage war dance in triumph, to the unspeakable terror of Nun (& of himself)

Slain cast out of hut unburied.

Fan[35] is a fool to me.

If there is anything I "abaw", it is a Rooshan & a rat.

Claydon; copy, Wellcome (*Cal.* B. 4. G4, 265).

To Reverend Mother Bermondsey

General Hospital
Balaclava
29th April 1856

My dearest Revd. Mother

Your going home is the greatest blow I have had yet.

But God's blessing & my love & gratitude go with you, as you well know.

You know well too that I shall do everything I can for the Sisters, whom you have left me. But it will not be like you. Your wishes will be our law. And I shall try & remain in the Crimea for their sakes as long as we any of us are there.

I do not presume to express praise or gratitude to you, Revd. Mother, because it would look as if I thought you had done the work not unto God but unto me. You were far above me in fitness for the General Superintendency, both in worldly talent of administration, & far more in the spiritual qualifications which God values in a Superior. My being placed over you in our unenviable reign of the East was my misfortune & not my fault.

I will ask you to forgive me for everything or anything which I may unintentionally have done which can ever have given you pain, remembering only that I have always felt what I have just expressed – & that it has given me more pain to reign over you than to you to serve under me.

I have now only to say that I trust that you will not withdraw any of the Sisters now here, till the work of the Hospital ceases to require their presence, & that I may be authorized to be the judge of this. Unless the health of any of them should make her return desirable, in which case I will faithfully inform you.

I will care for them as if they were my own children. But that you know, now it is a sacred trust from you.

Sister M. Martha is, thank God, quite convalescent.

Dearest Revd. Mother, what you have done for the work no one can ever say. But God rewards you for it with himself.

If I thought that your valuable health would be restored by a return home, I should not regret it. But I fear that, unless you give up work for a time, which I do not well see how you can at home, your return to Bermondsey will only be the signal for greater calls upon your strength.

However, it matters little, provided we spend our lives to God, whether like our Blessed Lord's, they are concluded in three & thirty years, or whether they are prolonged to old age.

My love & gratitude will be yours, dearest Revd. Mother, wherever you go. I do not presume to give you any other tribute but my tears. And, as I shall soon want a "character" from you, as my respected S. Gonzaga would say, I am not going to offer you a "character."

But I should be glad that the Bishop of Southwark should know & Dr. Manning, (altho' my "recommendation" is not likely to be of value to you but the contrary,) that you were valued here as you deserved & that the gratitude of the Army is yours.

Pray give my love to S. Gonzaga & thanks for her letter.

Will you thank the Bishop of Southwark with my respectful remembrances for his very kind letter to me?

Will you ask one of the Sisters at home, I dare say S. Gonzaga will do so, to write to me about your health.

And believe me ever, whether I return to see you again in this world or not,

ever my dearest Revd. Mother's
(gratefully, lovingly, overflowingly)

Convent of our Lady of Mercy, Bermondsey; copy, Wellcome (*Cal.* B. 4. G5, 268).

Notes

1 A copy of the "notorious" General Order is preserved in Sir J. Hall's papers, box 13 FCO7/28, R.A.M.C. Historical Museum, Aldershot.

2 B.L. Add. Ms. 39867, f. 85.

3 Dr George Taylor (1808–67), P.M.O. Land Transport Corps. When he died of Mauritius fever in 1867 F.N. exerted herself to try to get help for his widow from the Patriotic Fund in memory of his work organising the L.T.C. hospitals. (F.N. to Captain Fishbourne, B.L. Add. Ms. 45800, f. 229; F.N. to Lefroy, Wellcome.)

4 See Mrs. Shaw Stewart's letter to F.N., p. 203.

5 (Sir) Frederick Peel (1823–1906), second son of Sir Robert Peel; in 1855, as Under-Secretary for War, he was the responsible Minister in the Commons. In the course of the debate on the report of McNeill and Tulloch into the supplies in the Crimea, Peel justified the appointment of the Board of General Officers, set up on 28th February 1856 to enquire into that report, and paid tribute to the improvements effected in the Medical Department in the Crimea by Sir John Hall (*Hansard*, 3rd series, 1856, vol. 140, 1613).

6 Squeers was the villainous headmaster of Dotheboys Hall in *The Life and Adventures of Nicholas Nickleby*, by Charles Dickens, 1838–39.

7   Sir John Hall to F.N., 26th March 1856, B.L. Add. Ms. 39867, f. 100v.

8   Hall papers, box 14, FCO9/9, R.A.M.C. Historical Museum, Aldershot.

9   Mitra, p. 478.

10   Sir J. Hall to F.N., B.L. Add. Ms. 39867, f. 103v.

11   A. Smith to Sir J. Hall, 27th April 1856, Hall papers, box 11, FCO2/45, R.A.M.C. Historical Museum, Aldershot.

12   Fitzgerald to Hall, 3rd April 1856, B.L. Add. Ms. 39867, f. 107.

13   Hall papers, box 13, FCO7/30, R.A.M.C. Historical Museum, Aldershot.

14   Dr George Stewart Beatson, who as P.M.O. at Koulali had championed the nuns to Dr Hall for their efficient nursing and religious tolerance (p.119 n.28). B.L. Add. Ms. 39867, f. 65.

15   B.L. Add. Ms. 39867, f.112v.

16   Sir J. Hall to F.N., B.L. Add. Ms. 39867, f. 100v.

17   F.N. to Sir J. Hall, 27th March 1856, B.L. Add. Ms. 39867, f. 101.

18   Dr Taylor to Sir J. Hall, 28th March 1856, Hall papers, box 13, FCO7/27, R.A.M.C. Historical Museum, Aldershot.

19   Sir J. Hall to David Fitzgerald, 29th March 1856, Hall papers, box 13, FCO7/27, R.A.M.C. Historical Museum, Aldershot. In view of Mrs Shaw Stewart's complaint to F.N. in January this must have been a reasonable provision.

20   David Fitzgerald to Sir J. Hall, 29th March 1856, Hall papers, box 13, FCO7/29, R.A.M.C. Historical Museum, Aldershot.

21   The evidence gathered from all who were concerned in the matter is preserved among Sir John Hall's papers in the B.L. Add. Ms. 39867, f. 122 *et seq.*

22   David Fitzgerald to Sir J. Hall, 17th April 1856, B.L. Add. Ms. 39867, f. 117.

23   B.L. Add. Ms. 39867, ff. 142–6.

24   Hall papers, box 13, FCO7/44, 46, R.A.M.C. Historical Museum, Aldershot.

25   F.N. was not the only one to pour scorn on the decorations in this way. George Lawson, a more light-hearted observer than Miss Nightingale, wrote home derisively about an earlier batch of decorations: "It is expected that our Commissary-General, Mr. Filder will – like all the other heads of departments – be made a K.C.B. Does this mean Knight of the Carrion Bullock, or Killer of Corrupt Beef?" (V. Bonham Carter, ed., *George Lawson*, p. 159)

26   Henry Hardinge, first Viscount Hardinge (1785–1856), Commander in Chief 1852–56; created field-marshal 1855.

27   A fortress in north-eastern Anatolia defended by a Turkish force under the English General Fenwick Williams in 1855. It fell to the Russians in November 1855 after a longe siege.

28   As the result of an outburst by an evangelical bigot who wrote of the absurdity of "Catholic Nuns transferring their allegiance from the Pope of Rome to a Protestant Lady," Sister Gonzaga, one of the Bermondsey nuns, addressed F.N. as "Your Holiness" F.N. in turn christened Sister Gonzaga "My Cardinal." (Cook, I. p. 249.)

29   Georgina Barrie, Sister Gonzaga, of the Convent of the Sisters of Mercy, Bermondsey.

30   Colonel (Sir) William Montagu Scott McMurdo (1819–94), appointed Commandant of the newly formed Land Transport Corps, 1855; he provided F.N. with a baggage cart for her private use. F.N. found in him a kindred spirit. It is

related how on one occasion, when Sir Charles Trevelyan, Secretary to the Treasury, wrote on one of his requisitions, "Col. McMurdo must limit his expenditure," McMurdo replied, "When Sir Charles Trevelyan limits the war, I will limit my expenditure." (*Dictionary of National Diography.*)

31 Sister Mary Joseph, Sister M. Helen and Sister M. Martha were new arrivals in the East, presumably those that F.N. had requested in 1855 and had been expecting for some weeks at the beginning of 1856. Sisters Stanislaus, de Chantal and Anastasia had come out in the first party of five with Rev. Mother and Sister Gonzaga. In her final report, No. IV, on nurses and ladies returning 26th June 1856 F.N. wrote of Sisters Stanislaus, de Chantal and Anastasia, "Their faithfulness, their spirit, energy, true discernment of the right in many difficult, trying & vexed questions, their judgment, devotion, zeal and accuracy, – their cheerful resignation to inevitable opposition & enmity, have made them among our most valuable allies . . . " (B.L. Add. Ms. 43402, f. 22.)

32 Mother Bridgeman to Sir J. Hall, 15th April 1858. Bolster, pp. 263–8. In her evidence to the Royal Commission F.N. mentioned that this patient "suffering from frost-bite . . . subsequently died." (*Report of the Royal Commission . . . on the Sanitary Condition of the Army. . . .*London, 1858, vol. 2, p. 379, q. 10,020 on the state of Balaclava on 11th April 1856.)

33 Bolster, p. 269.

34 Sister Bertha Turnbull, of Devonport Sisters of Mercy, "came out in October 1854 with me – has served the whole campaign – chiefly in the General Hospital Scutari & latterly in the Castle Hospital, Balaclava, as Superintendent. All that I have said of Mrs. Stewart with regard to moral qualities relates also to this lady. She is not a woman of such commanding abilities as the former. Nor have I placed her in so exposed a situation. But she has never given me one moment's uneasiness as to fear of her not taking exactly the right course. And I consider her, after Mrs. S. Stewart & the Revd. Mother of Bermondsey, the most valuable person I have as Superintendent. I cannot estimate too highly the advantage which the faithfulness of these two to the cause has been to us – their total superiority to the praise of men – their utter disdain of flirtations, spiritual or otherwise – their entire obedience to the law of God. Both are, besides excellent Nurses, so good that their great powers of nursing interfere, perhaps, a little, as frequently happens, with their duties as Superintendents."

35 Probably Frances Bonham Carter, a cousin, who was generally called Fan or Fan-Fan.

8
Winding up

The war had ended on 30th March with the signature of the Treaty of Paris. But the event passed unnoticed by Miss Nightingale, involved in her final battle with Sir John Hall and Mr Fitzgerald. Peace made little difference in the daily lives of those encamped on the heights above Balaclava or labouring in the hospitals, for hostilities had effectively ended with the fall of Sebastopol the previous September. There was nothing left for Miss Nightingale to do beyond organise the orderly run-down of the hospitals under her control.

On 10th May she wrote to Sir Benjamin Hawes suggesting that the nurses come home at the same rate as the troops rather than in one mass.[1] Miss Nightingale herself naturally refused to leave before the last of her helpers.

By the beginning of May she felt so exhausted by illness and overwork that, imagining that she might be dying, she wrote to General Storks acknowledging her debt to him and asking him to carry out some last requests:

As you are of all those in office, whether at home or abroad, the officer who has given the most steady and consistent support to the work entrusted to me by Her Majesty's Government, I venture to appeal to you to continue that support after my death, and to carry out as far as possible my last requests.

She paid tribute to Mrs Shaw Stewart's services by expressing an "earnest desire" that that lady should be appointed to succeed to the post of Superintendent of the Nursing Establishment in the East.[2]

As for the future, she protested herself unable to make any plans at that stage, and, in spite of her urge to reform, the fate of the McNeill-Tulloch report made her reluctant to pursue her mission. She wrote vaguely of retreating into some foreign hospital as a nurse, divorcing herself from responsibility and anxiety.

Probably to Parthenope

General Hospital Balaclava
10th May 1856

I so seldom see the Newspapers & for the last two months I have not even seen the outside of one – I have regretted this, because I wished to read the Chelsea Inquiry.[3] But I have taken care to keep myself au courant of it.

Tell Colonel Tulloch that if I could I would have come home merely for the pleasure of hearing his evidence. We have not even a Cassandra here. And soon we shall be a Troy. Tell him that so true is all his evidence, so desperately true, that if tomorrow we were set down at Batoum, we should have the whole scene of 1854 all over again. Some say this is a reason why we should have peace. I say it is a reason why we should have war.

Tell Colonel Tulloch that I have the deepest sympathy with him. And we look to him to maintain our cause. For there is none, no, not one, to do it here.

To me it is a melancholy sign of England's decay that a report, such as Colonel Tulloch's & Sir John McNeill's, a model report, as it was acknowledged by all, should have failed in accomplishing the only object of those two noble & honest men.

If they can do nothing, who can?

Our case is desperate.

I am so badgered & bullied by the great rat, the Inspector-General, & the little rat who lives in the corner of this yard, the Deputy Purveyor in Chief, – two men whose impunity & promotion has only done less mischief because their crimes were less apparent – that I can well sympathize with Colonel Tulloch.

But he will see that the world will do him justice – for his efforts for the truth & justice of our cause.

Pray tell the Dean of Hereford that, if the Mr. Taylor he enquires about, is Dr. George Taylor Principal Medical Officer of the Land Transport Corps – he is my present master & a very admirable exception to the general run of my masters. He is strict but not at all stricter than I like – upright, honest, independent, with the good of his men at heart, for which he has labored without praise & without reward. He will never be promoted for the melancholy joke that promotion is in proportion to demerit is here an axiom or a truism. He is a man of very considerable talent. And his Hospitals, late the worst, are now the best managed in the Crimea. He is indefatigable, efficient, able. But he serves a master, who non-plusses every effort. So do I. But . . . .

Incomplete. Claydon; copy, Wellcome (*Cal.* B. 4. G6, 274).

Copy of letter home, possibly to the Bracebridges

General Hospital
Balaclava
30th May 1856

I have no intention of bringing home the nurses otherwise than as the Hospitals go home – gradually. I have sent twleve home already, the least efficient of course first. We have now only

23 Crimea
17 Scutari
_____

40 including

washerwomen & shall soon be fewer. I shall of course remain to the last nurse. We have only 17 Regiments off yet. It is said we shall be out of this by middle August, out of Scutari by end ditto. Of course we send home sick as fast as we can. But of course also the Regiments, as they move, empty the sick they cannot move upon the General Hospital here & Fever & Cholera you cannot move. We have some of the former, not yet of the latter. But we shall.

I do not think it would do to sell any of the Free Gifts. At least I should shrink from doing so. What I incline to would be to write to the Commandants of our now over crowded depots in Malta, Corfu & Gibraltar where in consequence of the *hutting*, the over crowding & the heat there is certain to be much sickness, & from our strengthening our posts there so much one would surmise war ultimately, & deposit with them proportional share of all that is left, which, except wine & shirts, does not amount to much. Rev*d*. Mother's departure without my seeing her has multiplied all my difficulties as there is not one at Scutari now who has been there since the beginning or can tell what is what, & it is impossible for me to return yet to Scutari. The Crimean Fund stores were of course unavoidably mixed with our own. Tell me if you see any objection to any of these things.

As for me I have no plans. If I live to return, what I should like to do, after a short visit at home, would be to go to some foreign Hospital where my name has never been heard of & discharging myself of all responsibility, anxiety, writing & administration, work there as a nurse for a year. Every other position seems to me impossible. At home I should go distraught with admiring friends & detracting enemies, with answering attacks like poor Col. Tulloch – at a foreign watering place I should go mad with inaction. My health is too much broken for a position of responsibility & power. With the story I have to tell I never would enter the world again, not on account of the sickness & suffering, but of the corruption & incapacity I have to tell of. My last two months (most dreadful of all) experience would make me wish to live to fight the battle of the Medical Officers against their Inspector General, disgusting and disgraceful as it is, but the fate of Sir J.

McNeill's report, which report I could never equal in its completeness, makes me feel such work hopeless. Were my Grandmother or Aunt [4] alive I would go to them. But how deep the meaning of those words "Foxes have holes & birds of the air have nests, but the Son of man hath not where to lay *his* head."

I say nothing about yourselves for you tell me nothing but God bless you.

I shall buy a revolver & shoot the first person who asks me questions in private, (excepting the Queen, Lord Panmure & Sir B. Hawes). In public I shall decline answering all questions excepting in a report as to what I have done with Private Fund & Free Gifts, i.e. as to accounts. Depend upon it the "tug of war" is to come.May I *not* be there to see!

Claydon; copy, Wellcome (*Cal*. B. 4 G8, 284).

Relatives and friends now began to bombard Miss Nightingale with requests that she find trustworthy servants from among the nurses and troops she knew. On this occasion she was unable to oblige, as she explained, but for many years she was to act as a sort of unofficial labour exchange, helping to provide secure and relatively well paid positions for nurses and retired soldiers.

Now that the pressure of work was to some extent eased and her position secure, Miss Nightingale once more began to indulge in the wide-ranging political and philosophical reflections of her youth. In this letter she displays all the influences of her liberal education and upbringing, and the self-assured self-righteousness of Victorian imperialism, which were to inspire her work in the future.

To Parthenope

General Hospital
Balaclava
2nd June 1856

My dearest
1. All my invalided sons are gone home & it would be only out of these that could be found a man that would do for the Marseilles purpose. And alas! of those gone home it is impossible for me to remember names. I could mention names of some still out here – but who being still in the Service would not, of course, leave it for such a position.

But amongst the multitude of discharged men in England, there must be some who would do.

General Sir Howard Douglas or Lt. General Sir W. Herries[5] would either of them be the man to ask.
2. *Mrs.* Beste, alias Sister Mary Martha, a girl of 23, is now with me here. She has been at death's door with Typhus Fever. Do you remember a

scene with a Rat which I pourtrayed to you in the night? That happened when I was sitting up with *her*. I love her the most of all the Sisters. She is a gentle, anxious, depressed, single-hearted, single-eyed conscientious girl, not energetic, but a worker & no talker – I am very fond of her. And she is honest & true. She is very interesting, almost too patient & diffident. And she has been rescued from Death's door. She is heavy & stupid – trustworthy & noble.

3. I know nothing of the Honb*le*. Mr. Hardinge's prologue.

4. Dr. Manning writes to me "I need not say that the justification of the employment of the Sisters of Mercy under you in the Papers was written by me!" As I observe that no one has ever realized the 8000 graves at Scutari, so I observe that every one pictures me with a cup of tea at my elbow reading the Public Prints, especially those parts which concern ourselves. As I have not seen a paper for 10 weeks, as I have *never* read any thing in them but what pertained to Sir J. McNeill's Commission, not from contempt (for I think it an inspiring thing to be writing, not to a party as the Record, the Standard, the Daily News, the Guardian do, but to the world as the Times does – & if I had not such a misgiving about the persons, I could almost wish to be a newspaper writer myself) not from contempt therefore but from sheer lack of time day or night have I never read the papers.

I should therefore, as I have always entreated that any *piece* of a paper which it is important for me to read should be cut out & sent to me (with the name of the paper whence it comes), so I should be glad to know *what* Dr. Manning has said & *where* – & *when*.

With regard to him, I neither trust him nor distrust him. But as the Roman Church has never been accused of incapacity & as the whole of Mrs. Bridgeman's conduct evidences either a want of capacity or of faith on the part of her rulers, let each man draw his own conclusion.

Rev*d*. Mother Moore & Rev*d*. Mother Bridgeman told me directly opposite stories – I have never had occasion to doubt the former (in a long experience).[6]

I have written no explanation to Dr. Manning & shall not. The thing is spoiled & can't be unspoiled. But who suffers? Not I – not the work – but the R.C. Church in whom there is now a direct split. She is quarrelling within herself – & publicly, which is not her wont. All the priests here have taken sides. And one has been recalled. Those priests who hated me are now my firm friends.

Depend upon it, there never was an age *where the principles of abstract justice were so surely & immediately the "best policy"*, nor *where they have been so disregarded* – & the disregard surely & immediately punished.

For 5. Look at the whole political history of these last 3 years. Who has been the gainer? France. What has she advocated? The principle of *abstract justice*. This has never been done before – Louis Napoleon is the deepest politician of the world. He advocates the principle of justice as the most successful policy.

England, Sardinia, Sweden, all these nations have sympathy with abstract justice – all have sided with France & gained more or less.

Austria, *America*, &, of course, most of all, Russia have *no* sympathy with abstract justice. See what a pickle they are in.

Russia will never forgive. I judge of this more by their undervaluing everything we have done than by their suffering. It appears certain that she has been drained of every man she can afford. It is thought that the estimate of 500,000 loss is not at all too large. She was losing 3000 men per day at the time of the bombardment. I have seen Sevastopol. It reminds me of Egypt. The ruins of the Dock Yard, of the white Barracks are like those of Kalabsheh or of Thebes. In their colossal desolation I can compare them to nothing else. And the town is like three towns. And there is not one stone left upon another. Now don't give in to the weak wishy-washy sentiment which is here talked about poor Sevastopol, poor Russia. What was Sevastopol there for? For aggression – for aggressive fanaticism. Not for the purposes of defence. I can feel for the poor wretches who have suffered & died. But what did they die for? To make Russia the tyrant of the world. I should like to have seen the Crimea held by us as the outpost of civilization – the Russians driven beyond the Caucasus – & the Caspian a sea of British trade – this is all I felt when I saw Sevastopol.

Now see how all that the Russians have done is directed against us. The neutralizing the Black Sea, the point about the Caspian is all against England. England they will never forgive. And their whole policy now will be to lower us.

"The Battle of Inkerman! oh nothing at all – a mere childs' play."

I have had many Russians come to see me.

"What compensation are England & France going to make to Russia for coming into the Crimea?" one officer asked.

They are incurably stupid about trade. It never occurs to them that one nation cannot enrich itself by trade without its benefiting other nations. Dr. Sutherland told me that, in some discussion which he had one day with a Russian of great political eminence about covering Russia with rail-roads, & suspending all military conquest till this was done (I forget the origin of the conversation but) the point was that it had never struck this Russian that England would make money of every pound thus made by Russia.

6.   I think we shall be out of this much sooner than we expected. Sir W. Codrington said this day fortnight – "The Guards won't go till the middle of August". Admiral Fremantle told me yesterday – "The Guards will go on Wednesday". The Agamemnon & St. Jean d'Acre are unloading their guns at Constante. & are to take them home.

Lothian & the Sappers & Miners go by the Cleopatra on Wednesday. I will send you by him a bunch of flowers or rather withered sticks picked on Inkermann by me.

Men of war are coming out from England to take home 8000 – from the

Mediterranean 23,000 – in fact the whole of the Mediterranean fleet is coming. And we have transports enough for the rest. We have about 41,000 men left here. All the Mediterranean regiments but two are gone. What is left is all for England. Sir Houston Stewart says we shall all be gone by middle of July from here.

What I surmise (but am not certain) from this sudden change is this – Sir W. Codrington was excessively irritated at the indifference at home about us.

He said Now our services are no longer wanted, we shall be left to die of Cholera & Fever here. The French lost in one camp of Cholera 40 in one night. But of course *they* kept this a dead secret. We had a threatening, not fatal. And Sir W. Codrington telegraphed it home. Lord Panmure was frightened lest there should be a Commission of Enquiry upon *him* – a Sir J. McNeill upon the War Department – & the fleet comes out to take us home. I am sorry. I had much rather run the risk of Cholera & Fever here than leave Austria to work her wicked will in Italy.[7]

Pazienza.

But all is forgotten. We are beginning to think that we were too hard upon Crimean mismanagement.

We are beginning to pity Russia.

There is no formal ending but the letter appears to be complete. Claydon; copy, Wellcome (*Cal.* B. 4. G10, 289).

Her depression lifted, and by 9th June she was once again writing with her old briskness and acerbity to Colonel Lefroy. Since early in life Miss Nightingale had been deeply interested in matters statistical. Cook described her as a "passionate statistician."[8] This interest developed during the Crimean War with her estimation of the worthlessness of such records of mortality and sickness as were kept in the army hospitals during the campaign. She described with scorn the anomalies and inexactitudes of the present system – or no system.

In the years immediately after her return home she was to devote a great deal of time to improving the methods of record-keeping both in the army and in civil hospitals. This letter to Colonel Lefroy also foreshadows the work she was to do to improve the position of the army doctors through the reform of the Army Medical Department.

The letter appears to have been written over twelve days, for the end is dated 21st June 1856. During the intervening period Miss Nightingale was extremely busy writing home about the despatch of other nurses, writing to the ambassador about the Sultan's expression of gratitude to the nurses, writing characters for the remaining nurses — all the business involved in the closing down of the nursing establishment.

To Colonel Lefroy

General Hospital
Balaclava
9th June 1856

My dear Sir

In reply to your letter of May 10, which has only just reached me, & particularly to that part about the Land Transport Corps, where you say "we are much puzzled to account for the excessive mortality of the L.T.C." I would suggest that there is some mistake in their Statistics.

The Medical Statistics of the L.T.C. are in a state of great confusion, so that it is hardly possible to obtain correct results. I have seen the weekly states for 21 weeks which give an average strength of about 8000. The total No. of deaths 242. Mortality to average strength 3 per cent for 21 weeks.

The uncertainty exists in our extraordinary method (or no-method) of keeping Statistics. The average strength in our Returns sometimes includes, sometimes excludes natives. Now the Native Strength is about 3000.

Taking, however, all the sources of uncertainty into account, Dr. Sutherland estimates the mortality in that Corps at not more than 7.2 per cent pr. ann.

Even this is excessive. But quite to be accounted for. The L.T.C. were exposed this last winter to all the influences to which our Army was exposed the winter before – bad organization – severe labor – improper & uncooked food – no means for cleanliess – long exposure & fasting.

Even then, had they been recruited from country carters, accustomed to exposure in all weathers, they could have stood it. But they were chiefly discarded gentlemen's servants, trades-people & townspeople. At least one half never ought to have come out, were unfit for any work under any circumstances.

Our object being to keep the Army in magnificent condition for the supposed coming campaign, the L.T.C. did all their work. They got up at 5 A.M., watered the mules, went down to Balaclava without breakfasting, had no means of drying themselves, no means of cooking their food etc. etc. Now that they are organized and in Battalions, their mortality is not much greater than that of the rest of the Army.

Sir W. Eyre's "fool's parade" cost 40 men in Hospital. If this was the result of one Crimean snow-storm, the poor L.T.C.'s repeated snow-storm might well do what we have seen.

The soldiers among the L.T.C. did not lose above the average mortality of the Army.

2. I was struck in going over the French Divisional Ambulance of the Corps de Réserve yesterday with the Mèdecin en Chef at what you say & what we all have remarked about the French.

While the Typhus cases were all under canvass – while the bedding, bed-steads, absence of flooring, diets, cleanliness, proportion of Medical

Officers to Patients were all infinitely inferior to ours, their Medical Statistics should make us envious. How they keep any is a physical problem. Given one Surgeon to 300 wounded, which the Médecin en Chef told me was his own share during the siege, how does he find time to keep the "*Cahiers*" he does? Yet these Cahiers present the complete history of each case – the dieting, medical treatment, medical obsevations of each day of each Patient.

In your Report of Renkioi which you were kind enough to send me & which I read with the greatest interest, you will observe that the defect of its system is that this daily view of the Patient's dieting cannot be kept on record. I know that Dr. Parkes lamented this. It was the same at Smyrna – the same, to a lesser degree, at Scutari. But during the pressure there, it was unavoidable.

I mean that, while encouraging, in acute cases, as much as possible, every facility for the Surgeon to obtain on Requisition at a moment's notice from the Extra Diet Kitchen the articles of Diet suddenly wanted, which otherwise he would have had to wait for till next day at the General Kitchens, it was a constant battle with me to make the Surgeon enter these next day against the Patient's name on his Diet Roll as for yesteday so as to shew what the Patient's Diet has been – otherwise the history of his case is manifestly incomplete.

N.B. I am aware that, owing to the neglect of this Military Hospital Rule, much of these *casual* Diets, (enormous at the time of the great pressure at Scutari) has been set down in Purveyor's Accounts, as part of "*Nurses'* Consumption."

P.S. I have been more careful to enforce, more convinced of the necessity of, military Hospital discipline & accuracy than the Doctors, (especially the Junior Doctors,) themselves.

3. Our best Military Hospital is the Monastery Hospital at St. George's, Crimea, as to organization, cleanliness etc. etc. etc. – our best Administrator without any comparison is 1st Cl. S.S. Dr. Jameson[9] at that Hospital. Our worst Military Hospital is this.

N.B. Dr. Jameson has never been promoted, because it was convenient to lay the blame of the non-transmission of the Varna Stores to Scutari upon him, without whom we should never have had them at all.

& 2. because he told Mr. Stafford at Abydos that we had no Port Wine there.

Considering Dr. Jameson as our best Administrator, I shewed him your Report, & we talked it over together. I asked him to put down some of the details of his administration (the proof of the pudding etc.[10] the proverb is somewhat musty) which I now enclose and in the necessity of most of which I concur. I will ask you to return it to me, because I have had no time to take a copy. And there may come a time, I fear it is not now, when it may be useful.

4.   Touching the promotion of Medical Officers. The manifest injustice of most of the latter promotions will, I trust, upset the system. But what is to be put in its place?

One injustice is easily "constaté" – that of giving all the honors to Crimean Medical Officers, in preference to those at Scutari, on the plan of the greater risk to life in the Crimea & of the Scutari Medical Officers having gone to "enjoy themselves in four-post beds," as I have heard Dep. Inspector-Gen*l*. Mouat express himself.

The fact would appear to be exactly the reverse. The figures given to me are

Died at	Scutari	20
	Koulali	3
	Smyrna	1
		24

	Crimea	20
	Bulgaria	3
	Sick Ship	1
		24

But, while the figures belonging to the Bosphorus Command are official, those of the Crimea are not. And therefore require verifying.

N.B.   Three of the Medical Officers who died at Scutari certainly came from the Crimea – others MAY have contracted illness in the Crimea. A very large proportion however had never been there. So that the number of deaths, supposed to be nearly equal – while the actual number of Medical Officers at Scutari was always *much* below the numbers in the Crimea – proves that the proportion of deaths, – in other words, the risk to life, – was greater to the *Medical* Officers at Scutari then in the Crimea.

The total No. of Medical Officers invalided during this Campaign in the Bosphorus Command is 50. Of these, half had been in the Crimea.

5.   I agree with you, the fate of Sir John McNeil's Report has struck us all with despair.

A few more of those who have done the most mischief will be rewarded. And then the Army, which has deserved so well of us, will sink back into its former condition. And no one any more will talk, even, of Reform.

For the Medical Officers, however, something might be done. Altho' the irresponsibility of opposition is always unsafe, & an alliance with Mr. Stafford an un-"holy alliance", I wish that he had been urged to keep his Committee[11] open till the Medical Officers at present here can come home & give evidence. But I am told that this will be purposely prevented by their being ordered elsewhere.

There are many now here who would abide by their evidence, however little the Military Officers have, alas! done so by theirs. Two of these I could but will not name who have given opposite evidence at Chelsea from that which they have been heard to say here. We were astounded.

Of the Medical Officers now here, whose evidence would be valuable to Mr. Stafford & who would speak the truth, there are

Dr. Alexander	Dy. Ins. Genl.
" R. Jameson	S.S. 1st Cl.
" Beatson	"
" Matthew	"
Mr. Jackson	S.S. 2nd Cl.
Dr. Holton	"
Dr. Jephson	1st Drag. Gds.

& I have no doubt many others.

I do not profess to feel any respect for the Military Medical Profession, any more than for any other race of slaves, of whom they have all the vices & all the virtues, but a strong compassion & a burning desire to see them righted.

"I know them too well to complain because I do not find in them veracity, fidelity, consistency, disinterestedness." They have been reduced to this state by dependence upon the caprice of an Inspector Genl., a Director Genl. for promotion (not always the caprice but even the trick) supported by the "Confidential Report" System which has been carried to its utmost perfection by the present Inspector Genl., which perfection consists in employing some other person, generally the Deputy Purveyor in Chief, to give evidence concerning matters of which he is in no wise legitimately cognisant, and *to take the evidence of Orderlies against their Medical Officer in Charge.*

In the last two months at this Hospital alone, two Medical Officers have been superseded upon evidence collected in the above manner, unknown to them.

Since June/55, there have been but three Medical Officers here with sufficient independence to resist this system. All three have been superseded.

What can be expected from this training but what actually happens?

An unfortunate 1st C[lass] Staff Surgeon, in charge here during 8 months, one of those who was found most easy & submissive to work this system, was brought in here two days ago to the very Hospital he had contributed to ruin, in a fit of Delirium tremens, & cut his throat this morning with his own Scalpel.

If Inspectors-General & Deputy Purveyors in Chief could take a lesson, one would think the death of this wretched man might convey one.

But how can you expect a better race under such circumstances?

Unlike Sidney Smith, I would I had no "Pennsylvanian Bonds".[12] I am sorry that the Inspector General has so injured me that it prevents me from taking up the quarrel of the Medical Officers, for fear it might be considered my own.

In France, the promotion of Medical Officers depends upon Seniority.

In Sardinia, upon the "Examen" & "Concurrence". (The three *first* of the lower Grade and *one* designated by the Conseil, go in for the Examen for the next "Grade".)

I enclose the principle of Promotion which, it is said, would generally *satisfy* our Medical Department – in the justice of which I need not say I do *not* concur. It is also drawn up by Dr. Jameson.

> Believe me, dear Sir
> most faithfully yours

Wellcome (*Cal*. B. 4. G11, 293).

At last, at the end of June, she was able to announce her imminent departure from the Crimea.

To Aunt Mai Smith

> General Hospital
> Balaclava
> 27th June 1856

Dearest

On Monday or Tuesday I, with all the Crimean woman-kind, leave the Crimea per "Ottawa" with all the Patients. Eleven go on to England – of my "monde" I, &, I believe, Mrs. Roberts, land at Scutari. I earnestly wish that Miss Morton may take advantage of this "Ottawa" (which is placed at my disposal) to go on to England in her. I shall never be able to get her so good a passage again. And she will also look after the Nurses – while at Scutari I feel that her work is done – though I can never be too thankful to her for having staid with you. She was perfectly right & you were wrong. You could not have staid alone.

I will beg Miss Morton, however, in consequence of that sentence in her letter to me which says that "there are great deficiencies in the linen of the Hospital & Mr. Robertson wishes to see" me "about them" – although it appears to me impossible that those deficiencies can exist in the *Issuing* Stores, where every month we took stock – yet I am going to land the two Nuns at Scutari, who were in the Issuing Stores, in order that they may give evidence to Mr. Robertson – and I have caused the vessel to stop a whole day at Scutari for this purpose. I will therefore beg Miss Morton to give Mr. Robertson all the information in her power before I come, to be ready to give me information during the single day the vessel will tarry at Scutari, which will be Wednesday, Thursday or Friday, & to be present when Mr. Robertson examines the Sisters.

Should he not be satisfied, I shall even detain the Sisters for another Ship.

My own conviction is that there was irregularity in all Accounts *but ours*. And these "great deficiencies" I am not at all surprised to hear of. Every house of every Greek in Scutari is full of stolen goods.

Please thank Miss Morton very much for her letter. I have written the characters of all the women to Lady Cranworth, & to the ladies who recommend them. I seldom or never give a written character to the person herself. Mrs. Woodward's was an unmitigatedly good character.

Ever yours

Claydon; copy, Wellcome (*Cal.* B. 4. G13, 302).

Back at Scutari, Miss Nightingale found herself still being harassed by Sir John Hall in the matter of her requisitions, as she complained to Colonel Lefroy. And for the second time she found the opportunity to lecture him on the unsatisfactory state of medical statistics and classification of disease in army hospitals.

To Lieutenant Colonel Lefroy

Scutari
Barrack Hospital
7th July 1856

My dear Sir,

My probably last letter shall thank you for having been a, I might indeed say *the*, most material assistance to my work – which I shall ever remember with gratitude – and, altho' "La reconnaissance n'est qu'un vif sentiment des bienfaits futures" in general, it is not so in my case, for I am now going to trouble you for the last time, & hope on that score to receive your forgiveness.

Sir John Hall has, in my absence in the Crimea, written to Dr. Linton[13] here to desire the Purveyor-in-Chief to send him an Abstract of all Requisitions signed with my name, since Nov./54 which had accordingly been done without my knowledge, before I returned here two days ago.

These Requisitions are for Scutari & embrace all that I drew from Public Stores for our Extra Diet Kitchens, as well as for the Nurses' own consumption.

This will appear from the Abstracts printed in the Blue Book of the Cumming-Maxwell Commission, which gives the average of the Issues from my Extra Diet Kitchens and sorts the sources whence the materials were supplied, whether from Purveyor (upon whom I drew by my own Requisition, according to a principle laid down by the War Office & the Inspector General of Hospitals in the Bosphorus, but too long here to insert, and recognised even in the Crimea by Sir John Hall till about six months ago,) or from Private Stores.[14]

Bref, *the whole* of these Requisitions appears in Sir John Hall's Abstract as having been for our own private consumption.[15]

The fact is almost too ridiculous to make any comment upon – as unless the women could eat 6 lbs Beef each daily, the Abstract disproves itself. The consumption of the women of meat has always been under 1 lb. daily. For one Extra Diet Kitchen alone, on the other hand, I drew 80 lbs. Meat daily. The great economy effected for Government by drawing thus in bulk is obvious & well known to all housekeepers.

Again, I have never drawn one oz. Arrow Root for the Nurses, nor one oz. Wine or Brandy – as I have already stated in another place.

I shall endeavor, before I leave this, to settle all these matters with the Purveyor-in-Chief – so that I shall be ready when I come home to answer any question which may arise. But I think it wise, under the circumstances, to place myself in the attitude of an accused person, and to lodge my statement [16] with one of those men of honor who, alas! are not so plentiful as I once imagined them to be. But that was before I had been initiated into ye Crimean Mysteries.

2. The absence of Statistics (Medical) of which you complain, is unavoidable in consequence of the Rules, chiefly obtained from the Ancient Britons, which prevail in our parts.

e.g. the bed-tickets at the head of each Patient might as well consist of three, Febris c.c., Diarrhoea, Dysenteria & be hung up promiscuously. For if Diarrhoea puts on Fever in a Military Hospital, Diarrhoea has to be discharged and Fever admitted, thus standing for *two* Patients. A Regimental Surgeon may appear by his books, as if he had admitted 60 Patients per month, whereas he may only have admitted 20.

The Director-General would then say, "something is wrong". But he would not look & see what was wrong. And the Surgeon, not the System would suffer. Surgeons therefore are compelled to let any Patient bear the name of any disease ad libitum, rather than go through the discharging & re-admitting process which "looks so bad". But all Medical Statistics are thereby rendered impossible.

Again, they are compelled to name the disease within a certain nomenclature, also inherited from the Picts, & which does not contain the names even of some diseases, unknown at the times when Diagnosis was more imperfect than it is now.

Again, no history of case is transmitted with Patient, when he is transferred from one Hospital to another. His own Statement has to be taken, if indeed he be capable of making a statement as hundreds in the winter of /54 were not.

I dare say you know all these things usque ad nauseam. But Hospitals cannot have been your profession as they have been mine.

3. Many of the best Medical Officers will agree with Dr. Linton that one Ward Surgeon to 30 Patients only is *not* too much, due regard being had to

the Patient, in attention to his case, to the Public, in attention to economy, to Science, in attention to Medical Statistics & history. Many will agree that one Senior to 350 Patients only is not at all too much.

And that for every 600 Patients a separate Hospital Establishment is desirable.

4. I cannot agree with you in "taking the General Hospital at Scutari as the most favourable specimen of our Military Hospitals, the building having been originally designed for this use." Surely there are things of as much importance as a "building" to the good administration of a Hospital.

I could say much more on all these subjects. But cui bono?

Believe me ever
most faithfully yours

Wellcome (*Cal.* B. 5. A2, 311).

Early in July Florence announced her own imminent return home with an advance gift of strange and "barbaric" gifts:

I cannot remember whether I told you that, by the kindness of Capt. Champion of the "Melbourne", I send you home a wild puppy, found in a hole here in the Krim with eleven brothers & sisters. I tried in vain to tame him. The only time he was beaten, for doing something very naughty, he was very quiet at the time, but never would speak again to the person who did it.

His name is Roosh – supposed to be an abbreviation of "Rooshan". His mama is about as big as a calf. There are not 6 dogs of his species gone home, so he is supposed to be valuable.

Claydon; copy, Wellcome.

Perhaps her original travel arrangements for the puppy broke down, or maybe she was referring to some different "spoils of war," but on 14th July Miss Nightingale again announced the despatch of a "Rooshan" trophy – and again, while paying tribute to the courtesy and kindness of a few friends, expressed a sense of aloneness.

To her family

[14th July 1856]

My dearest people

I sent home, by the Revd. Mr. Hort, on board the Calcutta, a *"Rooshan"* trophy for you, & 2 prs. Bracelets in a small box, of which Lothian is to have the refusal. I sent for them to Sinope on purpose, by medium of my faithful friend, Colonel McMurdo, Director General of the L.T.C. without whom I do not think I should be alive.

Pray, if you see Mr. Hort, make much of him. He is a good man, Hibernicè.

General Codrington has been courteous, Gen*l*. Windham more than courteous, kind, Lord Rokeby & Gen*l*. Barnard, who brought Lord Gough to see me, talk to me as to an old soldier – & brother in the field. But Gen*l*. Storks & Col. McMurdo have been & will remain my only friends out here.

ever yours

Claydon; copy, Wellcome.

Still she refused to say when she would herself be coming home – she dreaded the possible fuss and publicity.

To *her family*

[Scutari, 17th July 1856]

My dearest people

I cannot yet fix the day for coming home. It depends upon many things, not dependable upon myself.

I am just working as hard as I can – to get home —

All I want is to get home quietly, without any body knowing it. I shall take out my Passport under the name of Smith.

Lord Lyons has offered me passage to any port I like.

Aunt Mai & Co. gone over to Stamboul to the Bazar.

Ever yours

Claydon; copy, Wellcome.

One of the last letters she wrote from the East, just before leaving for home, was to her dear friend Sister Gonzaga of Bermondsey, her "Cardinal".

To *Sister Gonzaga*

Scutari, Barrack Hospl.
23rd July 1856

Dear S. Gonzaga

Again I return to my Sisters my dearest Revd. Mother's letters but this time I had a letter from her all to myself.

You do not give me a good account of her. But do not write again – for I shall soon be home now.

I shall not stop in London at all, but go to Bermondsey to call upon Revd. Mother & then sneak quietly out of the way.

And this reminds me to ask you to look out, if Revd. Mother will allow it, any Requisitions or Lists which she may have left belonging to this place, also her Inventory of the wine expended as I shall have to add up & furnish

Abstracts of all these things. All her papers concerning this place will be necessary.

She kept all her Books so beautifully that I trust this will cost her no trouble at all. And I almost expected to find that she had left these documents in the hands of my aunt for me.

Perhaps you will have them ready for me when I come – as I shall come to see dear Revd. Mother, not on business but on pleasure – & shall have but a flying taste of her both for her sake & my own.

> dear Cardinal Gonzaga this comes with best love from your
>
> poor old Pope

The last of our Invalids go home today.

Convent of Our Lady of Mercy, Bermondsey; copy, Wellcome.

Miss Nightingale left the Crimea within a day or so of writing this letter and was as good as her word. The first call she made on arrival in England was to the Bermondsey convent, early in the morning. She walked in on her family, unannounced, on 7th August.

The family was inundated with congratulations on the safe return of the prodigal daughter, and tributes to her work poured in. But for the moment what she needed above all was complete rest and quiet. Parthe described her state to Mrs Herbert. Florence, she wrote:

looks well in the face & seems well for a few hours in the morning, then she sinks down quite wearied'out for the rest of the day – we are most anxious to give her the breathing time which alone can restore her to a chance of work for the future. We see how little she feels equal to anything of the kind at present. She feels *quite worn out at heart* & absolute quiet is all that she desires . . .

We cannot but feel very uneasy about the extreme exhaustion which she shews.[17]

But it was not in Florence Nightingale's nature to be quiet for longer than absolutely necessary for the continuation of her work. Nor could she for a moment contemplate a resumption of the dawdling life of the fashionable lady from which she had fought so hard to escape. Besides, there was a new spirit abroad in the attitude towards the place of women in society, as evidenced by Caroline Bathurst's letter to Parthe:

I grow more & more silent about her – because deeper & deeper becomes my consciousness, of the *revolution* she is working, in English Society. . .

There is a deep & wide stir in the hearts of Women themselves.

Florence has explained to many, the cause of the sense of unsatisfied existence they have had – & in what direction to look for satisfaction – viz. in the fulfilment of some service; some real, active service of love to their fellow beings. And men's hearts & eyes are preparing to recognize something more in the nature of woman than has hitherto been supposed to belong to it.

A movement has been begun which *will* henceforth work . . . I believe the movement is of God – & that the *true* & the good in it will prevail. Florence's *whole*

Florence Nightingale shortly after her return to England in 1856. The photograph on which the sketch (frontispiece) was based

influence will have been thrown exclusively into the scale of "grace & truth". What a veiled & silent wonder she has always been – manifesting her womanhood in deeds, not in words, by the fulfilment of duties, not by the assertion of rights . . .[18]

Notes

1   F.N. to Sir Benjamin Hawes, 10th May 1856, copy in Sam Smith's? hand (in note of same date F.N. asked Uncle Sam to deliver it himself), Nightingale papers, Claydon.

2   Cook, I, p. 294.

3   As a result of the clamour following the publication of McNeill and Tulloch's *Report of the Commission of Inquiry into the Supplies of the British Army in the Crimea* in January 1856, Panmure stated in the House of Lords on 27th February "that any representation which might be made by officers who felt themselves aggrieved by the Report of Sir John McNeill and Col. Tulloch would be presented to Parliament." Accordingly a Board of General Officers was appointed "to inquire into Statements contained in the Report of Sir John McNeill and Col. Tulloch . . ." This was popularly known as the Chelsea Board, which sat through the spring. *The Times*, which had printed the original report almost verbatim during February, championed the cause of McNeill and Tulloch and poured scorn on the Chelsea Board, which found that the true cause of the Crimean disaster was the failure of the Treasury to send out a particular consignment of pressed hay. (Cook, I, p. 336–7; for list of papers relating to the McNeill–Tulloch affair see *Calendar*, Appendix II, fiche 37, A8–9.)

4   Mrs William Shore and Miss Elizabeth Evans, who died in 1853 and 1852 respectively, shortly before F.N. went to Harley Street.

5   Sir William Lewis Herries (1785–1857), Commissioner of the Chelsea Hospital.

6   If F.N. was here referring to accounts of their contracts of service given by the two Mothers Superior, neither was necessarily prevaricating. They went out under different conditions. Bolster, p. 17–21.

7   F.N.'s sympathy with the cause of Italian liberalism had been aroused when she visited Italy with her parents in 1837–38 and met some of the Italian refugees from Austrian tyranny (Cook, I, p. 17) and was reinforced during her visit to Rome with the Bracebridges during the winter of 1847–48 (Cook, I, pp. 74–8). She would have sympathised with Cavour's hope that Sardinia might have benefited from his alliance with the French and English in the Crimean War. But in the negotiations of the Congress of Paris which marked its conclusion all he got was expressions of sympathy, and the notice of the existence of the Italian problem.

8   Cook, I, pp. 16, 129

9   ? Thomas Ross Jameson (d. 1886), Deputy Inspector General, 1858.

10   The proof of the pudding is in the eating.

11   The Roebuck Committee on the Army before Sebastopol, of which Stafford was secretary.

12   Sydney Smith was glad that he had Pennsylvania bonds, as they gave him the right to protest when Pennsylvania threatened to repudiate its debts. In 1843 he sent a petition to Congress, which caused some excitement and a great deal of

correspondence both in England and in America. (*Memoir of the Rev. S. Smith*, by Lady Holland, 1855.)

13   Dr (Sir) William Linton (1801–80), Deputy Inspector General of Hospitals of First Divison of the Army in the Crimea and one of the senior medical officers at Scutari from 1855. Linton had been commissioned by Dr Smith to report on the climate and diseases of the country in 1854 preparatory to making the necessary medical provision for the army. His "Report on the climate and diseases of Rumelia" was printed as appendix II in *Medical and Surgical History of the British Army which served in Turkey and the Crimea during the War against Russia in the Years 1854–55–56*, 2 vols, London, 1858.

14   Table showing "Average daily issue of extra diets supplied from F. Nightingale's kitchens to the Extra Diet Rolls of the Medical Officers, Barrack Hospital, Scutari, from 13th January to 13 February, p. 41," *Report upon the State of the Hospitals of the British Army in the Crimea and Scutari*, 1855, p. 41.

15   It is interesting to compare F.N.'s indignation at this confusion of patients' requisitions with her attitude to a similar show of over-consumption on the part of the nuns which she had noticed with amazed derision.

16   On her return from the Crimea F.N. prepared *Statements exhibiting the Voluntary Contributions received by Miss Nightingale for the Use of the British War Hospitals in the East, with the Mode of their Distribution in 1854, 1855, 1856*, London, 1857. Drawn up with the help of Mr Bracebridge, the *Statements* provided a comprehensive and meticulous survey of the funds and goods she had received for the hospitals in the East, and how they had been expended and distributed. (*Biobibliography*, No. 49, p. 49.)

17   Parthe to Lizzie Herbert [August 1856], Nightingale papers, Claydon; copy, Wellcome.

18   Caroline Bathurst to Parthe, *c.* 16th July 1856, Nightingale papers, Claydon; copy, Wellcome.

Epilogue: "I shall never forget"

Florence could not rest. Apart from her own unquiet spirit, old friends and allies looked to her to lead the campaign for reform. Sir James Clark invited her to visit his home at Birk Hall, Ballater at a time when the Queen would be staying at Balmoral, near by. Miss Nightingale at once wrote to Colonel Lefroy asking advice as to what she should say to the Queen and expressing some doubt as to her own usefulness; her popularity was a double-edged weapon, as she was the first to appreciate:

Now, should I not cut myself off from all chance of ever obtaining employment in the Military Hospitals by suggesting the necessity of any great reform to my Magnates three *now*? It is certain that I should, if any of the Army *Medical* Magnates were to have a scent of it.

Would it not be better for me to ask directly & humbly for a Female Nursing Department in the Army Hospitals, which I have little doubt the Queen would grant, without making myself more obnoxious than I am, – or should I state boldly the whole case at first?

Should you say that I had better keep myself to the objects pointed out by the Nightingale Fund, I should like to be allowed to say before you the reasons which convince me that, with the buz-fuz about my name at present, which is against every condition of success, I had better have nothing to do with *that* for some time.

If I could not, therefore, gain access to the Army Hospitals, I should take some small, remote & poor Hospital for some years where I might indirectly but *not nominally* pursue my object of training women . . . If I could find a mouth-piece, not obnoxious to the same hostility which the Army Surgeons naturally feel towards me . . . I would gladly give every suggestion that has occurred to me to be worked up & promulgated for the benefit of the Service.[1]

The reformers needed her popularity, her prestige and her social position if they were to counter the conservative forces of rank and privilege represented by the embattled Horse Guards. Lefroy, as one of her most ardent admirers, immediately wrote back, with urgent persuasiveness:

In some form or other we have almost a right to ask at your hands an account of the trials you have gone through, the difficulties you have encountered, and the evils you have observed – not only because no other person ever was or can be in such a position to give it, but because, permit me to say, no one else is so gifted . . .'[2]

In the same letter he put forward detailed plans for the reorganisation of the Army Medical Department, and suggested that Miss Nightingale should press for "a Commission to enquire into the existing Regulations for Hospital Administration."

Armed with these suggestions and good advice from other friends, Miss Nightingale accepted Dr Clark's invitation and made the journey to Birk Hall. And so began two years' work as hard and exhausting and frustrating as anything she had known in the Crimea.

She found the Queen and Prince Albert interested, knowledgeable and sympathetic. But the man with the power to carry through the reforms was the Secretary for War, Lord Panmure, and of him Mr Herbert warned that "tho' he has plenty of shrewd sense, there is a *vis inertiae* in his resistance which is very difficult to overcome."[3] Miss Nightingale was to appreciate this insight during the coming months, during which she spent much time and energy in the exhausting and frustrating work of "bullying the Bison."

For the moment, however, her enthusiasm animated the "terrible" Secretary of War and he was cajoled into requesting her to put her experiences into a formal report. He also promised to set up a Royal Commission. She revelled in once more having practical work to do, and in a letter to her family wrote, "For the next three or four months I shall have business (imposed upon me by Panmure) which will require hard work & time spent in London & elsewhere to see men & Institutions whom & which I must see to get up my Précis, demanded of me by Pan."[4]

The précis "demanded" by Lord Panmure took the form of a long, detailed account of her Crimean experiences, and recommendations for the reorganisation of army hospitals and general welfare based on those experiences. It culminated in the printed work *Notes on matters affecting the health, efficiency and hospital administration of the British Army, founded chiefly upon the experience of the late war* (1858), which formed the basis of her own evidence submitted to the Royal Commission, and incorporated much of the material from the report of the Royal Commission.

Back in London, Miss Nightingale established herself at 30 Old Burlington Street and set to work with her usual vigour, drawing up lists of commissioners, drafting instructions for the commission, consulting all who could give useful evidence in the interests of the reformers. She was in constant daily communication with the small circle of friends and advisers who formed her "Cabinet"; Sidney Herbert, Dr Sutherland, Colonel Lefroy, Dr William Farr and the Secretary, Dr Graham Balfour. Sir John McNeill in Edinburgh acted as consultant and adviser.

By the middle of November the reformers were ready to put before Lord

Panmure concrete proposals for the composition of the Royal Commission and draft instructions. But another six months were to pass before Panmure could be "bullied" – or rather blackmailed by the threat of the publication of Miss Nightingale's own *Notes* – into signing the warrant for the appointment of the Royal Commission.

A long letter to Lady Canning written on 23rd November 1856 described Florence's past campaign, her present occupation and her future work. It demonstrates clearly how the proposals of the Précis arose directly out of her own personal experiences in the Crimean War and how the reforms proposed had in many instances been practically anticipated during its final months.

To Lady Canning

30 Old Burlington St.,
London
23rd November 1856

Dear Lady Canning

I have just received your very kind letter "finished Oct. 7 at Barrackpore". You have been too kind & efficient a Mistress to me & mine for me not to think it an "official" duty to give you some account of my stewardship, & answer your letter step by step.

1.   *This* seems to me like a dream & not my past "campaign". It seems to me like a dream to see the women driving about in little bonnets & big petticoats & hear them saying that "poor Lord Raglan", (that most chivalrous & noble old man in his disregard of mere public opinion), "died of the 'Times'"[5] – to see the men playing the game of party politics over the graves of our brave dead, & trying to prevent us from learning the terrible lesson which our colossal calamity should have taught us. Oh my poor men, who died so patiently – I feel I have been such a bad mother to you, coming home & leaving you in your Crimean graves, – unless truth to your cause can help to teach the lesson which your deaths were meant to teach us.

2.   The public has been, on the whole, very considerate of me. Two or three of my friends have made very great mistakes & been unable to understand that publicity must, by injuring my cause, be painful & worse to me. And puffing always injures any real work, were it only by collecting round it elements of frivolity, vanity & jealousy. On the whole too, the War Dep*t*. has been very kind to me & forgiven me my popularity as well as it was able – tho' it was very angry with a speech of Sir John McNeill's at Edinburgh[6] which was made contrary to my earnest and written re-monstrance.

3.   The Hospitals of the East were, at the end, quite perfect, as also the Sanitary arrangements. I conceive that this year, the Barrack Hospital at Scutari was the finest in the world. Also, the deaths in the second week of January 1855 were 578 per 1000 in the Army – (& this was not our highest

mortality, which was in the end of that month). The deaths in the corresponding week of January 1856 were 17 per 1000. The deaths from Epidemics were reduced from 70 per cent of those from all causes to 45 per cent. And the sickness from Epidemics from 60–80 per cent to 16 per cent. This, of course, is attributable to the excellent Sanitary arrangements in the Army, introduced by the Sanitary Commission[7] – as well as to those in the Hospitals. The frightful mortality in the Barrack Hospital at Scutari diminished in like manner. During 54–55, that Hospital was literally living over a cess-pool – & the Military Medical Officers ascribed the unmanageable outbreaks of Cholera which took place up to November/55 to a Cemetery 3/4 mile off!!

To give you some idea of the way in which H.M.'s Ministers are informed of the health of H.M.'s troops the only authorized returns of Cholera (of course Ministers may have had private returns) sent home were (& are) of the Patients who are in Hospital from Cholera on *Saturdays* (Cholera running its course in 3 or 4 hours) & the Patients who are admitted the other six days in the week, dead & buried, – of them there is no other record than in the Death Returns & not always there. The excess of burials over recorded deaths was 4000.

4. I am sure that you will be pleased to hear that, of your "friends", as you kindly call them, Nurses Logan, Sullivan, Cator, Jane Evans, Miss Tattersall, Woodward (from Koulali) Montague, Orton, Maloney etc. turned out "all right". Miss Morton so good – & many others honestly anxious to do their duty. I do not mention the virtues of those who were before your reign, as they will be less interesting to you. But I cannot help just recording the gratitude we owe to Miss Shaw Stewart, to the "Revd. Mother" of the R.C. "Sisters of Mercy" at Bermondsey, to Sisters Bertha & Margaret of the Anglican "Sisters of Mercy" of Devonport & to the immortal Mrs. Roberts.

5. I have not had time to read the Koulali[8] & Smyrna books.[9] But even had I, I would not. For women who had had the happiness of serving God & the honor of serving their country in Her War-Hospitals to make a book about it is to me quite enough, whether that book were prompted by their own vanity or by silly or astute advisers. The Koulali authoress, Miss Fanny Taylor, has now joined the R. Catholic Church, which indeed she had done privately before she went out.

With regard to what you say about the necessity of Chiefs at home having the cause of dismissal always sent them, it is so true, both theoretically & practically, that I only wish it had been more strictly enforced. But, on one occasion, that of Miss Salisbury, a woman proved to be profligate, intemperate & dishonest, the War Dept. did not act upon the character sent home by the Commandant as well as by myself.

6. I am very much obliged to India for their zeal in our cause. I am pleased to hear it, because, ignorant as it is, it is upon a right principle. One

is sick of the cant about Women's Rights. If women will but shew what their duties are first, public opinion will acknowledge these fast enough. I dislike almost all that has been *written* on the subject, Mrs. Jameson[10] especially. Let the "real lady" as you call her, be as much professional, as little dilettante as possible – let her shew that charity must be done, like everything else, in a business-like manner, to be of any use, (a thing I found it more difficult to make my ladies understand than anything) – and all that is good will follow – provided, of course, that the real love of God & mankind is there. And, *with this*, I conceive that we have even an advantage over the R. Catholics. (A vow implies a fear of failure) just as the really sober man is undoubtedly better off than the man who has taken the Temperance pledge. Besides this, R. Catholics, even the best, are essentially incapacitated (from their inherent Manichaean-ism)[11] from doing the best kind of good. They are to console the suffering which evils have produced. They are not to remove the causes of those evils. As a curious instance of this, I will mention that I tried to persuade a great ally of mine, the Superioress of the Sardinian "Sisters" at Balaclava, Countess Cordero, [12] (one of the most remarkable women it has ever been my good fortune to know,) to join with me in a strong protest against a certain Canteen, up to which we used respectively to see our respective Patients – in Hospital slippers & clothing – stealing past the (conniving) sentry – out of the Hospital Huts. The protest was to have been addressed to our respective Chiefs of the Staff & would have been easily attended to. But I never could persuade her that it was any use to take any Preventive Measures against drunkenness or any thing else. I have seen this even among the excellent French "Sisters" at Paris.

You will be glad to hear that Miss Shaw Stewart[13] is hard at work improving herself at Guy's Hospital, where she is training as Nurse. I envy her. For I have much more harassing work to do.

7.   I am sorry to hear your account of Indian (middle-class) women. But I really think that it might be read aloud here to great advantage, for "Indian" substituting "English".

India is a wonderful field for you. There is very much that we might imitate, with much advantage, out of the Indian Army, & what you say of the Sepoys reminds me of it.

I saw hardly anything of the Turks, as you may suppose. And what little I did see made me think that poor Turkey's days are numbered. But men, far better informed than I am, say that she is making steady progress onwards. The merest sight of Turkey impresses one, of course, with the immense superiority in civilization which Constantinople has attained over her provinces. The Turkish Contingent was the best thing we did. And I regretted much its being disbanded. They, the soldiers, were getting so attached to us.

How Tropical colouring must call out your artistic feelings. We had small time to look at colouring but even I feel the change to this London sky deaden all my artistic perceptions.

8.   You will wonder what is the grievance with us when everything was so perfect about the Army when it left. The fact is we have not made one step towards a system which will prevent the recurrence of such a disaster. If we were set down at Batoum tomorrow, we should have all /54 over again. I have never heard any sensible man doubt this who was with our Army in the East. We are no nearer having the next Army live on fresh meat at 1½d. per lb. instead of die on salt meat at 8d. per lb. We are no nearer having the next War-Hospitals drained & ventilated – the next Land & Sea Transport well organized than if we had not died & lived respectively in the years of Disgrace /54 & of Grace /56. Because the system does not exist to compel it. Nothing has been done but a violent expenditure & the relaxation of all rules & all logical scheme of Government. And the very luxury & expence of /56 was bad for our cause. Because it gave the supporters of the old system (or no-system) the right to say, Look what these innovators do.

Lord Panmure is going to give us a Royal Commission of Inquiry into all that concerns the health of the Army at home & abroad. And I have been commanded by the Queen & by him to write a Précis for the Government. I do not feel very sanguine as to the result of either. But I shall "*eat*" straight through. Of all those in Office whom I have had to do with since I came home, you will, perhaps, perhaps not, be surprised to hear that I have found the Queen, Lord Palmerston & Mr. Herbert the most free from the Office Taint. These are really, (after their different fashions), not officially, interested. I have had much to do with two Taints lately, the Scorbutic & the Office Taint. And the latter is the worse.

The points in my Précis will be to try to shew

1.   that the Army must be taught to "do for" themselves – kill their own cattle, bake their own bread, hut, drain, shoe-make, tailor etc. etc. But in this the Camp at Aldershot is, if possible, behind that in the Crimea. Everything is done for it by civil contract. (Its clothing only is going to be given to it to do). You will hardly believe that, in the Crimea, even when we had fresh meat, we buried one fifth part of it & that the most nutritious. Our Naval Brigade & the French dug up our ox heads & made soup of them – & I dug up the feet & made jelly of them.

2.   that the Commissariat must be put upon the same footing as your East Indian Commissariat which has, I believe, never broken down except during the first Burmese War,[14] which was not its fault, instead of which our Commissariat is made, with other arrangements, to destroy an Army.

3.   that the Quarter-Master General's stores must be periodically repor-ted, as to what they contain, to the General Officers of Divisions. You are probably well aware that, while our men were lying in one wet blanket & one muddy great-coat, – wet & muddy because they had been 20 hours out of the 24 in the trenches, – while they were dying of Scorbutic Dysentery upon salt meat, rum & biscuits, our stores at Balaclava were full of rice, lime juice, great-coats, coatees, rugs & even blankets.

4.   that, in time of war, the Transport must be under military control. For, while stores were daily arriving at Balaclava, & every man in the front would gladly have given 1/- to have his blanket carried up to him, & every man in the Transport Service could have carried up 10 blankets, we positively never thought either of using or of paying the seamen on board the Transports to carry up stores to the front.

5.   that a Sanitary Officer must be attached to every Quarter Master Gen*l*.'s Office – to advise upon matters relating to encampment, diet, clothing, hutting, sick transport. Even after our great distress was over, it was found that the 79th, altho' down at Balaclava, was in such a state from Fever that, if matters went on thus, the whole Regiment would pass thro' Hospital 4½ times in 6 months. After the usual recalcitration from Commanding Officers as to "Military Position" etc., it was found that by moving the lines 20 yards, which did not alter the military position in the least, the troops were saved from Fever. The boards of the huts were found positively covered with green algine matter. But now a Medical Officer, if he analyses the water & finds it unfit for human health, & remonstrates in writing, may be placed under arrest. Military health, as was written 57 years ago, is sacrificed in an enormous proportion to ignorance.

I have 11 other points which relate

1.   to the Government of General Hospitals, which, being in the hands of eight Departments, the Officers of which are appointed by different authorities, ensures delay, irresponsibility & inefficiency. A requisition to mend a broken pane of glass must pass thro' six Departments.

2.   the Sanitary Element in Hospitals

3.   the Army Medical Department, – its rate of pay, – education, – system of promotion, – confusion of its administrative & professional functions, – absolute necessity of a *Practical* Army Medical School at home, – impossibility of its producing, as at present constituted, a good nursery of good surgical science.

4.   the necessity of a Hospital being complete in itself & furnishing a Hospital kit for each man. We positively had no power of inventing any scheme, (when the men were ordered to leave their knap-sacks on board ship when we landed at Old Fort, which knap-sacks they never recovered), of clothing these men when they came into Hospital with nothing on but an old pair of trowsers & a dirty blanket – nor of feeding them, because it was a Queen's Warrant that they ought to bring their Spoons with them into Hospital

5.   Cooking & Dieting of the Army

6.   Washing

7.   Canteens

8.   Soldiers' Wives

9.   Nursing by male & female

10.   Uniformity of Stoppages, the non-uniformity of which engenders a want of confidence in the men, (and justly), as to the accuracy of the balance of pay they receive, there being one Stoppage of 3½d for the field, another for on

board ship, another for wounds in Hospital, another for sickness in Hospital. I have had so much to do with the little money-deposits of the men that I know how badly this works on their moral confidence, without any proportionate saving to Gov*t*.

11.   Engineering of Hospitals

12.   Mode of keeping Statistics

That good little Sardinia has adopted our civil mode of keeping these at the Registrar-General's Office, while we are not allowed to have any sickness in the Army but what they had in Charles II's time. And I could make you laugh at one classification which seems made to deceive & bamboozle Gov*t*. as to the causes of our disease. Just as the system of the Army Medical Department seems made to prevent it from rising to the level of the Medical Science of the day.

I think, if you could see our *real* Statistics, you would think that I have been moderate in my Statements. In eight regiments in the front, of which the 46th actually lost more than its average strength from disease alone, we lost 73 per cent in seven months from disease alone. I am not aware that we can show any instance in our history of a similar disaster except in the Burmese War in /26. At Walcheren, [15] which is called the "ill-fated" expedition, we lost 10¼ per cent in 6 months from disease, – in the Peninsula 12 per cent in a year from disease.

Contrasting this 73 per cent with the loss in our Naval Brigade, which was scarcely 3¼ per cent from disease, & among our Officers which was 3¾ per cent from disease, shewing that there was no fault in the climate – & with the loss, more fearful than ours, from disease among the French this year, – when they began to do *on purpose* what we did from stupidity, – namely, ill-feed, ill-clothe, ill-shelter the troops, shewing that it was not only over-work in the trenches which killed us, – I think we arrive at a pretty just conclusion.

The question is, shall we have any Reform? The queen has been most earnestly interested – so is Prince Albert. But I fear they have taken the wrong sense as to the Crimean Commission. They do not see how, if all the men, therein blamed, were so excellent, what must the system be which killed from disease alone 50 per cent of all our infantry *in the front* in 7 months – & 39 per cent, taking *all* the Infantry & Cavalry together.

You will wonder at the din & bustle of our English business in your Indian life, &, may I say so?, I think you a little prefer the former in your approbation. I wonder more at the way we have here of making out of the most critical subjects conversation only. I think the proof of this is the degree to which, in England, the newspapers influence people's opinion or rather talk. It is said that the speeches may be counted, which, in the House of Commons, have commanded a vote. (That is because an M.P. has an opinion about his vote). And it is impossible to believe that, if any one has a definite opinion upon any subject, the Article of a newspaper gentleman, who has to get up his opinion before 4 o'clock, could alter it. Yet how many people read & talk newspaper – shewing, I am afraid, both how little definite opinion there is, even upon important subjects, & how much these are made mere grinding-organs to grind a talk of.

However, one could not be too thankful for one's own free press when one saw the disastrous consequences to the French this spring of having none.

Lord Panmure has given me six months' work (but no wages or *character*). After that, I go to the nursing business again.

Believe me, dear Lady Canning,
sincerely & gratefully yours

Leeds Record Office HAR/Ld C 177/23 (*Cal*. B. 5. B10, 378).

Throughout December and January Miss Nightingale slaved at preparing her Précis – visiting and inspecting hospitals and barracks; interviewing doctors and chaplains; preparing statistics of sickness and mortality for the army during the Crimean War, and at home and abroad. In addition an endless correspondence on trivial matters connected with her Crimean days continued to demand attention.

She consulted Bracebridge on the preparation of her *Statements exhibiting the voluntary contributions received by Miss Nightingale for the use of the British War Hospitals in the East, with the mode of their distribution in 1854, 1855, 1856,* which was published in 1857. On 21st December she wrote to Lady Cranworth on the subject of the female nurses whom Lord Panmure planned to install at the Woolwich Artillery Hospital; on 1st January she wrote to Lord Panmure about the Sultan's gift, and suggested that unappropriated money be distributed among the Sisters of Mercy of the Bermondsey Convent and the Devonport Sisters of Mercy; on 6th January she sent a cheque for £60 to Rev. Mother Bermondsey with the proviso that it was to be at Rev. Mother's sole disposal; on 8th January she requested Dr Bowman to see a woman who might require a cataract operation – Miss Nightingale herself would pay the necessary subscription for in-patient treatment.

And on 8th January she wrote to Dr William Farr, a new ally, about the mortality statistics of London hospitals; this was the first letter in a long correspondence spanning twenty years. Dr Farr shared her passion for statistics and advised her on the preparation of tables and diagrams for that section of the report of the Royal Commission which was reproduced as the pamphlet *Mortality of the British Army, at Home, at Home, and Abroad, and during the Russian War, as compared with the Mortality of the Civil Population in England,* (1858).

On13th January she reported to Parthe that she had met Sir John Liddell, Director General of the Naval Medical Department, to discuss the introduction of female nursing into naval hospitals. On 22nd January she again reminded Lord Panmure that she awaited his decision on the report by Dr Sutherland and herself on the vast new military hospital being built at Netley, near Southampton, and on her Précis, and on the progress of the plans to introduce female nursing in army hospitals.

She was being worn out by her ceaseless work and felt thoroughly depressed by the apparent lack of progress. In a letter to Dr Sutherland, or maybe to Dr Pincoffs – it is not clear which – she expressed her disillusionment:

> I have thought well on what you told me, & have come to the same conclusion as you, viz. that the War Office people mean to do nothing about anything . . . What am I to do? No one can feel for the Army as I do. These people, who talk to us, have all fed their children on the fat of the land, & dressed them in velvet & silk, while we have been far away. I have had to see my children dressed in a dirty blanket & an old pair of Regimental trousers, & to see them fed on raw salt meat & rum & biscuit – and nine thousand of my children are lying from causes, which might have been prevented, in their forgotten graves. But I can never forget. And mothers have begged round the country before me for their children. People must have seen that long, long dreadful winter to know what it was.
>
> I have been home six months today. And Lord Panmure has amused himself with our suffering.
>
> And it is twenty years today since I devoted myself to the Spirit of Good – And He knows whether I have amused myself with His work or not.
>
> I am ready now to do anything for my poor men which is practical. But if there is nothing, which I can do, I shall not give my experience to the Queen & Government, merely to shut myself out from making use of it for good, if they mean to make use of it for nothing.[16]

Three days later she wrote to Sidney Herbert, threatening that "three months from this day I publish my experience of the Crimea campaign, and my suggestions for improvement, unless there has been a fair and tangible pledge by that time for reform."[17]

The Précis was ready for publication by the end of March, and she submitted it to Sir John McNeill, who had given a great deal of help and advice during its preparation, for his "candid criticism." But she remained pessimistic.

> I have little hope of Reform. What is politically fun to our Masters is death to us. The disgraceful state of our Chatham Hospitals, which I have been visiting lately, is only one more symptom of a system which, in the Crimea, put to death 16,000 men, the finest experiment modern history has seen upon a large scale – viz. as to what given number may be put to death at will by the sole agency of bad food and bad air.[18]

Not until 5th May 1857, six weary and frustrating months after Panmure had reluctantly agreed to appoint a commission to inquire into the sanitary condition of the army, was the warrant instructing the commission signed.

Sidney Herbert, as chairman, drafted the two volumes of the report himself, helped and supported by Dr Sutherland and Miss Nightingale in constant daily communication. Between them these three organised the examination of the witnesses, sifted the masses of evidence and tabulated the statistics.

Florence Nightingale's own evidence, presented in the form of answers to written questions, was based on the material collected for the *Notes*. The tables of disease and mortality which appeared as the pamphlet *Mortality of the British Army* appeared in appendix LXXII of the *Report*.

The work was completed and the *Report* ready for the printers after only three months. Sidney Herbert, who had laboured ceaselessly in spite of his own deteriorating health, acknowledged his debt to Miss Nightingale. "I never intend to tell you how much I owe you for all your help during the last three months, for I should never be able to make you understand how helpless my ignorance would have been among the medical Philistines. God bless you!"[19]

Florence had now come to the end of her strength. On 11th August she collapsed and was so ill that her family feared she might be dying. However, she rallied, and when she was well enough to travel she went to Malvern, where she stayed for a month. Towards the end of the year she was to some extent recovered and back at work. But she had discovered the advantages of isolation. She determined to cut herself off from the demands of family and friends in order to conserve her energies for the work ahead. She erected an impregnable barrier against the exigent demands of her mother and sister in particular.

In the event Miss Nightingale lived to a ripe old age. She quickly learned that not only her physical strength but also her power and prestige were conserved and enhanced by reclusiveness. It became her life long practice, pursued long after the need had passed, to keep to her room and refuse to see more than one person at a time, and then only if she felt her visitor could contribute to her "work."

She throve on work. In January 1858 the *Report of the Commissioners appointed to inquire into the regulations affecting the sanitary condition of the army, the organization of military hospitals, and the treatment of the sick and wounded; with evidence and appendix*, was published, and she organised the publicity from her sick bed. During the next three years she worked as hard as ever to set in motion the four sub-commissions she and Sidney Herbert had together extracted from Lord Panmure to carry out the proposals of the report. But Sidney Herbert's health was failing. He was created Lord Herbert of Lea in 1860 to relieve him of the necessity of appearing in the House of Commons. However, he was not one to spare himself, and Miss Nightingale drove him mercilessly, fearing that without him the reforms would be lost. By the time of his death in 1861 a measure of success had been achieved: a permanent Barrack and Hospital Improvement

Commission had been set up; the new Army Medical Warrant reorganised the Army Medical Department on an independent footing, with the army doctors gaining in prestige and pay; the Army Medical School had been set up at Fort Pitt; the Statistical Department was established – a fitting monument to a unique partnership based in friendship and community of spirit.

Whatever field she was to labour in in the future it was the past from which Florence Nightingale drew her inspiration. The source of her strength was in her identification with the dead: she dedicated her life in atonement for their needless sacrifice. "I stand at the Altar of the murdered men and while I live I fight their cause."

Notes

1 F.N. to Colonel J. H. Lefroy, 24th August 1856, Wellcome.

2 Colonel J. H. Lefroy to F.N., 28th August 1856, B.L. Add. Ms. 43397, f. 244.

3 Cook, I, p. 325.

4 F.N. to her family, 13th October 1856, Claydon.

5 Lord Raglan was a shy man, averse to publicity. He laid himself open to Russell's vituperative pen when he rebuffed and ignored him in the Crimea. For an account of Raglan's relations with the press, and with Russell in particular, see Hibbert, p. 219.

6 Sir John McNeill's "Appreciation of Miss Nightingale and her work at Scutari," *Daily News*, 3rd November 1856, p. 3, col. d.

7 Other factors contributed to this improvement: better weather, new supplies of warm clothing, better food, the ending of trench duty after the fall of Sebastopol.

8 Frances Margaret Taylor, *Eastern Hospitals and English Nurses – the Narrative of Twelve Months' Experience in the Hospitals of Koulali and Scutari, by a Lady Volunteer*, London, 1856.

9 *Ismeer or Smyrna and its British Hospitals*, by a Lady, London, 1855.

10 Anna Brownell Jameson (1794–1860), writer, particulary concerned with the question of women's position and rights.

11 A religious system founded in the third century A.D. according to which Satan (Evil) is co-eternal with God (Good). It is useless therefore to attempt to combat evil.

12 F.N. was to refer to Sister Cordero as 'one of my dearest friends.' According to Peter Pincoffs, "The Sardinian Sisters of Mercy experienced much kindness at her hands when put to great straits in consequence of the destruction of the ship 'Croesus' by fire."(*Experiences of a Civilian in Eastern Military Hospitals . . .*

13 Although usually referred to as *Mrs* Shaw Stewart by F.N., she was not married and was frequently referred to as "Miss" by others. F.N. seems to have used "Miss" to people who knew the lady in private life.

14 In May 1824 a force of 11,000 officers and men of the Indian Army occupied Rangoon without transport or supplies of fresh food on the assumption that the local population would provide boats and provisions. During the ensuing five

months the salt pork, rice and biscuit which was all the expedition had with it went bad. More than 3,100 of the 3,500 British troops died before the end of the campaign and of these nineteen out of twenty died of disease. (Sir Llewellyn Woodward, *The Age of Reform, 1815–1870,* Oxford, 1962.)

15   In 1809 a British army of 30,000 men was sent to Walcheren, an island off Antwerp, to prevent French movement in and out of the port. Of the British garrison half died of malaria, the remainder were evacuated at the end of the war. F.N. included a study of the medical statistics of the expedition in the *Notes on Matters affecting the Health* . . . *of the British Army,* 1858, pp. 547–56.

16   F.N. to ? Dr John Sutherland, 9th February 1857, B.L. Add. Ms. 45796, f. 139.

17   F.N. to S.H., 12th February 1857 (Stanmore, II, p. 123.)

18   F.N. to Sir John McNeill, 28th March 1857, G.L.R.O. HI/ST/NC.3/SU 76.

19   Cook, I, p. 312.

Appendix

Copy
Confidential Report on the Nursing System, since its introduction to the
Crimea on the 23rd January 1855 [24th December 1855]

The Mother Eldress, Miss Emma Langston, and 7 Nurses, disembarked at
Balaclava on the 23rd January 1855; among the Nurses were two Ladies –
unpaid, – Mrs. Shaw Stewart and Miss Clough:

1.2   Arrangement was in its infancy, and no fixed appointments appeared to have
been assigned to the Nurses, each attending at pleasure through the Wards.

2.3   After some few weeks, the Mother Eldress became unwell, and the
Supertendence devolved on Mrs. Stuart [sic] and Miss Clough, alternately;
insubordination and discontent were manifested about this time among some
of the Nurses, and continued; about this time, also, a Nurse, Mrs. Gibson,
became affected with Drunkenness while attending a Sick Officer, and the
circumstances attending the Crime were such as to render her removal
imperative.

Miss Langston left, and the superintendance was adjudged to Mrs. Stewart,
discontent prevailed; and Miss Clough, the only remaining Lady beside Mrs.
Stewart, relinquished her allegiance to the old system of control, and parted in
disgust, or discontent; this step on her part was viewed as desertion, and
communication with her by the other Nurses was discountenanced from the
time she joined the Hospital of the Highland Division on the Heights to the time
of her illness.

There was then a question as to her right to draw Articles from the Public
Stores, which occasioned a reference to Dr. Anderson, then the Principal
Medical Officer of Balaclava:

Dr. Anderson consulted with Mrs. Stewart and hesitated to approve of a
Requisition for Articles for Miss Clough, although submitted through the
Surgeon 42nd Regiment:

An application was made on that subject to the Inspector General of
Hospitals on the 24th March 1855 and he decided that Miss Clough's

Requisition should be recognised if approved of by the Principal Medical Officer of the Highland Division present.

After this separation some freedom was observed between Mrs. Whitehead and the Orderlies, and a Mrs. Disney was thought to be occasionally under the apparent influence of drink.

3.   Much insubordination existed; some time afterwards Mrs. Stewart was superseded as Superintendant, and replaced by Miss Weare; whether from disinclination to serve under another, or by pre-arrangement with Miss Nightingale, soon after the arrival of Miss Weare, Mrs. Stewart left and went to the Castle Hospital, accompanied by a Mrs. Noble.

4.   By a letter dated, 5th July 1855, reporting confidentially to the Purveyor in Chief, the following passage occurs; —

"I can only judge of the efficiency of the class from mere rumors, and judge of its difficulties and working, by the number of removals, which I presume were not intended as rewards – four or five from this Hospital, but as I was not called on to enquire the cause, and had no control whatever given me with regard to them, and any interference of mine would be considered impertinent, as I on a few occasions felt, I cannot state the reasons."

Mrs. Disney was one of the removals alluded to:

At that date there were,

One Superintendant and

Six paid Nurses at Balacalava; – and

One Superintendant, and

5 paid Nurses at the Castle Hospital, –

besides Miss Clough at the Highland Hospitals:

Of these five were sent Home – not I presume as rewards, –

Mrs. Davies

   "   Sandhouse

   "   Lawfield

   "   Noble

   "   Tuffill

5.   Without describing faults or assigning Crimes – four from this Hospital were removed for insubordinate, violent or irregular conduct; and scandal ascribed faults to two dismissed from the Castle Hospital, which subsequently led to explanations between Miss Weare, Miss Nightingale, and Dr. Jephson, 1st Dragoon Guards.

Other Nurses subsequently arrived, and among them a Mrs. Brookes to this Hospital, who was sent away for some irregularity, another was so violent to the Superintedant, Miss Weare, that she had to send for the Commandant, Colonel Harding at a late hour of the night, apprehensive for her life, by the threats used by one Nurse; she was removed.

6.   The Changes at the Castle Hospital and conduct of the Nurses, were remote from my observation and I cannot describe them.

Miss Weare the then Superintendant here, often complained of the misconduct, or insubordinate demeanour of the Nurses, and in one letter of the 3rd August 1855, she says of them, –

"Mrs. Davy is quite an opposite character, sickly and weak minded to say the *best* – the others with the exception of one, have been persons quite unfitted for their position here, either from one reason or another, but none have shewn themselves more unfit than the last arrival, whose manners are low and violent in the extreme."

Miss Weare was finally left with a Lame Nurse, – on the Sick List, and the Extras Cook – the best of the paid Nurses.

The efficiency of the Nursing system depends much on numbers; a sufficient attendance should be secured for each Ward, and the wants of every Patient should be tended to; in extreme and delicate conditions of disease the Nurses are most desirable; but in this Service intelligence and punctuality should characterise the Nurses; jealousies may pain the Patients of the same Ward, if one Nurse is hurried from Ward to Ward, and can only spare a moment by the bedside of a selected case; this is not a mere hypothesis or sentiment.

Miss Weare earned more of praise for attention, care and tenderness in her visits to the Sardinian Officers under treatment, than all else of the Nurses of her time together; yet, from the paucity of her Nurse Assistants, an evil, far more than the good her individual exertions achieved, rankled in the jealousies of Patients in the same Wards, that witnessed her unwearied devotions to the Foreigner; open murmurs spoke the flame of dissatisfaction in the soldier Patients, as they saw her pass their beds towards the Sardinian Officers; and her merits, and the opinion she was creating in favor of English sympathies with her favorite Patients, were nearly, if not altogether effaced, by one open – insubordinate act of one of the Nurses; this woman – in the same Ward with the Sardinian Officers, was called on to assist Miss Weare in attending a Sardinian General or Colonel, – She refused – and loudly protested against the partiality that would neglect the English soldier for the Foreigner; the Sardinian understood the rebuke, and expressed his disgust, and soon after left the Hospital.

Miss Weare was openly reproved by a Patient for this partiality, in another Ward of the Hospital, and the circumstance was brought to the notice of the Inspector General of Hospitals.

On another occasion, a Nurse, Mrs. Drake, reported to Miss Weare the repeated taunts expressed towards her by Patients on the same subject, and the matter was reported to Dr. Hadley.

Though it is to be regretted that the Sick Soldier was wanting in high feeling and courteous preference for the foreigner, jealousy in them must be excused; the mind, struck down by disease, becomes an easy prey to the more degenerate feelings, and neglect is their most bitter incentive: There could have been no neglect, and no ill-feeling resulting from neglect, had there been a sufficient number of Nurses; it were far better to have none than an inadequate number; their absence would never have been complained of – but their presence – devoted to preferences – pained the neglected.

The word "neglected" is not intended to imply want of necessary attention on the part of Orderlies, but rather an absence of those delicate services, which a woman of feeling and propriety can bestow, and the calm soothing of a mild commiseration for the sufferers pangs.

The efficiency therefore of the Nursing system depends largely on numbers appropriate to the extent of Sickness to be attended.

An element of discord, detracting much from the extended utility and beneficial operation of the system, exists in the undue interference of Superintendants with general arrangement and economy of Hospitals, bringing them into collision with Medical Officers and Purveyors, in this Hospital such interference has led to a Court of Investigation and other untoward results; it should be the duty of a Superintendant to obey the Instructions of the Hospital Authorities, and not to criticise or contravene them; the Superintendant should limit her control to a vigilance over the actions and conduct of her subordinates; further – the Superintendants should be exclusively under the orders of the Principal Medical Officer of the Army or his subordinate local Representatives.

The existence of a supreme superintendant is incompatible with local controls, actions, obedience, and co-operation; the Local Lady Superintendant, considering herself not a subordinate of local Hospital Authorities, but of the superior Lady Superintendant, and this has predisposed to warranted meddling and unpleasant feeling.

The question of expense should therefore be regarded, not collectively, but individually, – as the larger the number – the greater the benefits bestowed, provided there is harmony, and unanimity, and obedience among all.

The superiority of an ordered system is beautifully illustrated in the "Sisters of Mercy", – one mind appears to move all; – and their intelligence, delicacy, and conscientiousness, invest them with a halo of confidence extreme [sic]; the Medical Officer can safely consign his most critical case to their hands; – stimulants or opiates – ordered every five minutes, will be faithfully administered, though the five minute labor were repeated uninterruptedly for a week.

The number of the Sisters, without being large, is sufficient to secure for every patient needing it, their share of attention; a calm resigned contentedness sits the features of all – and the soft cares[s] of the female and the Lady breathes placidity throughout.

Lady Nurses – of the disposition and experience of Miss Stewart and Miss Weare, will be equally useful as the Sisters, if the pride, and will, and

301

independence of Action of former years could be silenced, and humble obedience connect and maintain an amicable union between large numbers; experience shows the preponderance of the former conditions, and the transitory nature of negative and contradictory obligations – of subordination and obedience.

On pages 13, 14, & 15 are given the Tables of Expenses of the Nursing Establishments and Miss Nightingale's Superintendants at the General Hospitals at Balaklava, and the Castle, during the month of June; selected – because during that period the Establishments were most effective; and the system of drawing settled.

In the absence of Authentic records, and assuming numbers from the detail in my letter of the 3rd July,

The Castle Hospital is rated at 6 Nurses.

The General Hospital at Balaklava at 7.

One month's expense of the Sisters of Mercy is contrasted, – the prices being arbitrarily fixed as in June – for equality.

P.R.O. WO 43/963. Pages 13–15 have been omitted, as they add nothing to the description of the nursing. F.N. deals with the disputed figures in her letter to Lefroy (p. 198)

Copy

Supplementary Confidential Report on the Nurse system, submitted in explanation of a Memorandum of the Inspector General of Hospitals, Dr. Hall, received this day 1st Jany. – 4th Jany. 1856.

The Tables pages 9–13, Confidential Report of 24th December 1855, were compiled from the Requisitions of June, for the Nurses of the Hired Class, because in that month they were most numerous, and approached the standard of competency intended, before sickness, or misconduct was contemplated to diminish their strength.

The Sisters of Mercy arrived here on the 10*th* October, and as Miss Weare was then resident here, from feelings of delicacy Requisitions for articles required for the Sisters were signed by her, and generally comprised the wants of Miss Weare, Mrs. Davis, and Mrs. Whitehead; and as one month of the system of the former Nurses was seleced as a metre of expense, the same period was adopted for the Sisters, and comprised the Requisitions for their own use, rendered by them to the date of the Report, therefore no anterior period could be available for concomitant comparison.

The nurse system at Balaklava was on suspension or abeyance for some months before the arrival of the Sisters, and its condition under such circumstances was unsuited as an indication of contrast, or status of relative merits or demerits; Miss Weare was Superintendant and subordinates in her own person, Mrs. Whitehead having been confined to bed, and unfit for duty for months, and Mrs. Davis during her whole stay an Extra Cook.

The month of June was further preferred as a period of which I had the most satisfatory information, taken from my letter of the 3rd July. The nurses mentioned in that letter I assumed, to have been in employment during the preceding month, as I remember no recent antecedent arrivals.

The system of supreme control given to Miss Nightingale, and ˙the reflected or modified system of independence and control assumed by her deputed superintendants or representatives excluded all interference in their arrangements. I was neither informed of arrivals, or departures, of paid or unpaid nurses, or Requisitions intended for Extras of Patients, or Nurses, or both conjoined; and I am therefore unable to offer any precise distinctions. I was left to observation alone – indirect or confidential, and inferences from both: in my Report of 24 December I distinguished statements made from such sources as "assumed". I imparted as I received under the conviction of having recorded the most accurate information I could have acquired under the circumstances. I cannot, therefore, with any efforts determine the articles drawn for nurses exclusively, and those for which Patients had been partially supplied; I can offer no more discriminating Tables than those of my Report.

At the urgency of Miss Weare, and with your approval, I applied to the Purveyor at Smyrna to know if two nurses could be spared from that station, for service under Miss Weare at the Monastery.

Miss Nightingale was not consulted, as from communications exhibited to me, and which she addressed to Miss Weare, she had resolved the suspension, removal, or extinction of her Nurses from the Hospital, and directed Miss Weare to leave; Miss Weare thought otherwise, – that her services were necessary in the Crimea, and formally accepted her dismissal from adherence to the old control; I thenceforward viewed Miss Weir [*sic*] in the same relative position to Miss Nightingale as Miss Clough previously to her indisposition.

The supreme or any control of Miss Nightingale over Miss Weare was objected to by the latter, and this repugnance to Miss Nightingale's control, supervision, or interference, is more strongly protested by Miss Weare's successors – the Superioress of Sisters of Mercy and Sisters.

Rejection of such control has become a principle in them; they exist, they declare, as Nurses free from interference; and cease as Nurses the moment Miss Nightingale's supremacy is decided to rule or influence them.

This antagonism or repulsion of official feeling has been explained by Mrs. Bridgeman to the authorities; she offered her services and those of her Sisters to Miss Nightingale on arrival in the East and they were declined, excepting 5, who were provisionally engaged with the power of withdrawing when they pleased. Mrs. Bridgeman subsequently became attached to the Hospital at Coolalee, over which Lady Stratford de Redcliffe exercised sole control, and from there Mrs. Bridgeman transferred her services to the sick of the Crimea under the immediate and undivided direction of the Principle Medical Officer of the Army.

(signed) David Fitzgerald
Purveyor to the Forces

P.R.O. WO/43 963, f. 296.

Bibliography

Barnsley, R. E., "'Teeth and Tails' in the Crimea," *Medical History*, 7, 75–9, 1963.

Bentley, Nicholas (ed.), *Russell's Despatches from the Crimea*, Panther History, 1970.

Bishop, W. J., and Goldie, S., *A Biobibliography of Florence Nightingale*, London, 1962.

Blackwood, Lady Alicia, *A Narrative of Personal Experiences and Impressions . . . on the Bosphorous throughout the Crimean War*, London, 1881.

Bolster, Evelyn, *The Sisters of Mercy in the Crimean War*, Cork, 1964.

Bonham Carter, Victor (ed.), *George Lawson, Surgeon in the Crimea*, London, 1968.

Cook, Sir E. T., *The Life of Florence Nightingale*, London, 1914.

Cope, Sir Zachary, *Florence Nightingale and the Doctors*, London, 1958.

Goldie, S., *A Calendar of the Letters of Florence Nightingale*, London, 1983.

Government publications: *Reports of Commissions*, etc.

Report upon the State of the Hospitals of the British Army in the Crimea and Scutari, together with an appendix, London, 1855. *Parliamentary Papers, 1854–1855, 33.*

Report of the Commission of inquiry into the Supplies of the British Army in the Crimea, with the Evidence annexed. London, 1856. *Parliamentary Papers, 1856, 20.*

Report on the Pathology of the Diseases in the Army in the East, London, 1856. *Parliamentary papers, 1857, Sess. 2, 18.*

Report to the Right Hon. Lord Panmure, G.C.B. etc. Minister at War, of the Proceedings of the Sanitary Commission despatched to the Seat of War in the East 1855–56, London, 1857, *Parliamentary Papers, 1857, 9.*

Army in the East, Copy of a Report . . . relative to the Sanitary Condition of the Army in the East, furnished . . . by Dr. Henry Mapleton in June 1857. Parliamentary Papers, 1857–8, 37, p. 105.

Medical and Surgical History of the British Army which served in Turkey and the Crimea during the War against Russia in the Years 1854–55–56, in 2 vols. London, 1858. *Parliamentary Papers, 1857–58, 38.*

Reports of the Select Committee on the Army before Sebastopol. Parliamentary Papers 1854–55, 63.

Hansard, *Parliamentary Debates*, 3rd series, vol. 136.

Bibliography

Kinglake, A. W., *The Invasion of the Crimea*, 6th edn, vol. VII, Edinburgh and London, 1883.

Kirby, P. R., *Sir Andrew Smith*, Cape Town and Amsterdam, 1865.

Lady, A., *Ismeer or Smyrna and its British Hospital*, London, 1855.

Lane Poole, S., *The Life of the Right Hon. Stratford Canning, Viscount Stratford de Redcliffe*, London, 1888.

Mitra, S. M., *The Life and Letters of Sir John Hall, M.D., K.C.B., F.R.C.S.*, London 1911.

Nightingale, Florence, *Biobibliography of F . . . N . . .*, see W. J. Bishop and S. Goldie.

— *A Calendar of the Lettes of F . . . N . . .* compiled by S. Goldie.

— Evidence and Appendix LXXII in *Report of the Commissioners appointed to Inquire into the Regulations affecting the Sanitary Condition of the Army, the Organization of Military Hospitals, and the Treatment of the Sick and Wounded, with evidence and appendix*. London, 1858, *Parliamentary Papers*, Reports of Commissions, 1857–8, xviii (*Biobibliography*, No. 51, p. 53).

— *Notes on Matters affecting the Health, Efficiency and Hospital Administration of the British Army*, London, 1858 (*Biobibliography*, No. 50, p. 50).

— *Mortality of the British Army, at Home, at Home and Abroad, and during the Russian War, as compared with the Mortality of the Civil Population in England*, London, 1858, (*Biobibliography*, No. 52, p. 54).

— *Statements exhibiting the Voluntary Contributions received by Miss Nightingale for the Use of the British War Hospitals in the East, with the Mode of their Distribution in 1854, 1855, 1856*, London, 1857, (*Biobibliography*, No. 49, p. 49).

— *Subsidiary Notes as to the Introduction of Female Nursing into Military Hospitals in Peace and in War*, London, 1858 (*Biobibliography*, No. 3, p. 14).

Nightingale, Parthenope, *Life and Death of Athena, an Owlet from the Parthenon*, privately printed, 1855.

Osborne, Sidney Godolphin, *Scutari and its Hospitals*, London, 1855.

Pincoffs, Peter, *Experiences of a Civilian in Eastern Military Hospitals, with Observations on the English, French and other Departments*, London, 1857.

Seymer, Lucy, *Florence Nightingale's Nurses: the Nightingale Training School, 1860–1960*, London, 1960.

Shepherd, J., "The civil hospitals in the Crimea (1855–56)," *Proceedings of the Royal Society of Medicine*, 1966, 59, 199–204.

Smith, F. B., *Florence Nightingale: Reputation and Power*, London, 1982.

Soyer, Alexis, *Soyer's Culinary Campaign*, London, 1857.

Stanmore, Lord, *Sidney Herbert, Lord Herbert of Lea; a Memoir*, London, 1906.

Taylor, Frances Margaret, *Eastern Hospitals and English Nurses – a Narrative of Twelve Months' Experience in the Hospitals of Koulali and Scutari*, by a Lady Volunteer, London, 1856.

Woodham Smith, Cecil, *Florence Nightingale, 1820–1910*, London, 1950.

Manuscripts

Greig, D., Letters from Scutari and the Crimea, R.A.M.C. Historical Museum, Aldershot.

Loy Smith, Sgt Major, Diary. Royal Hussar Museum, Winchester.

Index

Abdul Mejid, Sultan, 15

Aberdeen, Lord, 16, 87

Abydos General Hospital, 71, 98

Accounts, nurses', 241, 242; trouble with F.N.'s, 253

Airey, General Sir Richard, QMG, letter to, **163–164**; 165, 166, 177, 187 note 21, 208, 222, 224, 226, 246

Albert, Prince, 286, 292

Alexander, Dr. Thomas, Deputy Inspector General, 275

Allobroges, 109, 143; *see also* Soldiers' wives

Alma, battle of, 1, 17, 18, 71

Anastasia, Sister M., of Bermondsey, 252

Anderson, Mrs., nurse, 112, 153

Anderson, Dr., PMO General Hospital, Balaclava, 129, 148 note 5, 194, 196, 199

Anderson, Sir Charles, 195

Anderson, Miss Emily, Superintendent, General Hospital Scutari, 98, 122 note 43, 195

Antonio, 144

Army, ordered to abandon kits, 71; reform of officering necessary, 85; in same state as eighteen months previously, 246; F.N.'s proposals for reform, 290–2; sickness and mortality statistics during the Crimean War, 293

Army Hospitals, female nurses never previously admitted, 23; necessity of strict discipline in, 45, 50, 51, 273; proposals for reform of administration of, 62, 63, 69, 70, 72–6, 77–80, 85, 86, 291, 292; cooking for sick in, 71, 77, 78, 85, 86, 248, 256; F.N.'s determination to reform, 87; position of females in hs. in the East, 114, 115,

128; agreement with nurses in, 152; nurses not to be admitted without F.N.'s consent, 161; usage in, 237; diet in, in the Crimea, 257; cooking and victualling in, 256–60; waste in, 257; statistics in, 271, 277, 278; classification of disease in, 277, 278; staffing of, 279; reform doubtful, 285, 290; F.N. could request female nursing department in, 285; mortality in the East, 287, 288; nursing by male and female in, 291; proposals for reform of washing in, 291; sanitary element in, 291; proposals for administrative reform of, 291, 292; sanitary engineering in, 292; statistics in, 292; introduction of female nurses, 294; *see also* Crimean hospitals, Koulali, Scutari

Army Medical Department, 5–8; F.N.'s battle with, 3; breakdown of administrative function of, 18; relationship of Superintendent of nursing and medical authorities, 26; F.N.'s scheme for improving training of medical officers, 70; F.N.'s determination to reform, 87, 96, 291, 267, 268, 271, 275, 285; promotion of Medical Officers, 276; Lefroy's proposals for reform, 285; against Science, 292; reorganisation of, 296; *see also* Hall, Dr. John; Smith, Dr. Andrew

Army medical school, F.N. proposes establishment at Scutari, 96, 97; founded at Fort Pitt, 296

Army welfare, F.N.'s measures for; remitting money home, 127, 143; provides material for Reading Rooms, 144, 164, 168; provides books, games, stationery, etc., 209, 210; soldiers' wives, 47, 175, 291; description

*General references to Koulali may be interchangeable with those to the Barrack Hospital, the main hospital at Koulali.

†General references to Scutari may be interchangeable with those to the Barrack Hospital, F.N.'s headquarters.